The Lost Promise of Civil Rights

The Lost Promise of Civil Rights

◆ ◆ ◆

Risa L. Goluboff

HARVARD UNIVERSITY PRESS

Cambridge, Massachusetts

London, England

2007

For my parents,
for everything

Copyright © 2007 by the President and Fellows of Harvard College
All rights reserved
Printed in the United States of America

Cataloging-in-Publication Data available from the Library of Congress

ISBN-13: 978-0-674-02465-6 (alk. paper)
ISBN-10: 0-674-02465-6 (alk. paper)

Contents

Abbreviations Used in the Text

AAA	United States Department of Agriculture, Agricultural Adjustment Administration (1932–1942), or United States Department of Agriculture, Agricultural Adjustment Agency (1942–1945)
ABA	American Bar Association
ACLU	American Civil Liberties Union
AFL	American Federation of Labor
ALI	American Law Institute
BAE	United States Department of Agriculture, Bureau of Agricultural Economics
CIO	Congress of Industrial Organizations
CLU	United States Department of Justice, Civil Liberties Unit
CRS	United States Department of Justice, Civil Rights Section
DOJ	United States Department of Justice
FBI	United States Department of Justice, Federal Bureau of Investigation
FEPC	Fair Employment Practice Committee; also known as President's Committee on Fair Employment Practice
FLSA	Fair Labor Standards Act
Garland Fund	American Fund for Public Service
ICC	Interstate Commerce Commission
ILA	International Longshoremen's Association
ILD	International Labor Defense
Inc. Fund	NAACP Legal Defense and Educational Fund, Inc.

Lawyers Guild	National Lawyers Guild
NAACP	National Association for the Advancement of Colored People
NBA	National Bar Association
NFLU	National Farm Labor Union
NIRA	National Industrial Recovery Act
NLRA	National Labor Relations Act
NLRB	National Labor Relations Board
OSG	United States Department of Justice, Office of the Solicitor General
PWA	Public Works Administration
RLA	Railway Labor Act
SCAD	New York State Commission Against Discrimination
SG's office	United States Department of Justice, Office of the Solicitor General
STFU	Southern Tenant Farmers' Union
Taft-Hartley	Labor Management Relations Act
UAW	United Auto Workers
UMW	United Mine Workers
USDA	United States Department of Agriculture
USES	United States Employment Service
VA	Veterans Administration
Wagner Act	National Labor Relations Act
WDL	Workers' Defense League
WLB	National War Labor Board
WPA	Works Progress Administration

Introduction

LETTERS CAME to the United States Department of Justice (DOJ) and the central office of the National Association for the Advancement of Colored People (NAACP) from across the nation. They came from the North and the South, rural areas and urban ones. Each reported the violation of constitutional rights. Each begged, asked, or demanded that lawyers take action. Telegrams, phone calls, and personal visits to Federal Bureau of Investigation (FBI) field offices and NAACP branch secretaries reinforced the urgency of the pleas.

One whole series of complaints—postmarked Memphis, Birmingham, Mobile, and a small south Florida town called Clewiston—described the situation of hundreds of young African American men who had traveled from cities across the South to work for the United States Sugar Corporation during World War II. The men described flyers produced by the United States Employment Service (USES), a federal agency that linked unemployed workers with available work. The flyers enticed "colored farm workers" to "enjoy the Florida sunshine during the winter months." Workers would cut cane for high wages of between $3 and $8 per day. Transportation to Florida was free, as was rent. Food would be provided on the journey there, but workers would have to pay for their board at the sugar plantations.[1]

As workers and their concerned relatives later told FBI agents and Justice Department lawyers, the journey to Florida did not go as expected. After long train and bus rides with little food, young men arrived at the sugar camps to learn that the "free" transportation cost between $6 and $20. That debt to the company increased with the required purchase of necessary implements: board, blanket, identification badge, sharpening file, cane knife. At the surprisingly paltry salary of $1.80 per day, earning enough to pay such debts would take some time. Company supervisors warned the workers not to leave without paying their debts. "[I]f you do you'll be put in jail and kept there until we come after you. That [is] if we don't kill you. You're liable to be found in one of those lakes." Guards would not allow letters in or out, "locked the hands up at night," carried blackjacks and pistols, and even killed men for asking for their wages or trying to leave.[2]

Conditions at what some workers described as "slave camps" were so bad that many tried to escape despite the threats. The men complained about long days of brutal work pervaded by fear and punctuated by violence. Sleeping facilities were so "filthy" that some preferred sleeping around an outdoor campfire. Meals of "cabbage and beans out of a bucket" that "aint fitting to eat" added to the sense that workers were "being treated like dog[s]." Even so, escaping without money, maps, or knowledge of the landscape was not easy. Canals surrounded several camps, and "men with sticks would hang out" by the bridges that connected the camps with the rest of Florida. All apparent avenues of escape held peril: one superintendent warned "that we would be shot if we tried to catch a ride on the sugar train and that we would be arrested for hitch-hiking if we tried to get away on the highway." Making enough money for a bus or train ticket was almost impossible. And the men had heard that sugar officials not only had convinced the bus company to refuse tickets to the farmworkers but also monitored the railroad station to ensure that no one left by train.[3]

Against the odds, some of the men did manage to escape. Swimming canals, hiding in cane fields, finding assistance from locals, and receiving money from home, migrants trickled back to the cities from which they had come. Rumors about the horrors of the plantations had preceded them home. Relatives and friends—and ultimately the workers themselves—called upon the FBI and the Civil Rights Section (CRS) of the Justice Department to stop the "virtual slavery" in Florida's sugar camps.[4]

Around the same time the Florida workers contacted the federal government for legal help, hundreds of other African American workers telegrammed, wrote, and called upon lawyers in the NAACP.

These workers too traveled long distances for jobs USES recommended. They too were outraged by the treatment they received. According to the Employment Service, the Kaiser Shipbuilding Company in Portland, Oregon, like other shipyards on the West Coast, desperately needed skilled or trainable workers to work as machinists, welders, burners, pipe fitters, and the like. Hundreds of black workers had boarded trains in New York City in response to Kaiser's call.

Just as the sugar workers had found, the recruiters' rosy picture began to fade even before the workers had reached their destination. On board the train, Kaiser representatives assigned the black workers positions as general laborers, whereas they upgraded some of the white men to skilled jobs. Upon arrival, the black recruits learned that the company was not their only, or even their primary, problem. The International Brotherhood of Boilermakers, a union affiliated with the American Federation of Labor, had recently established closed-shop agreements with Kaiser and other West Coast shipyards. These agreements required the companies to hire only union members. If the new African American workers wanted skilled work in the shipyards, they would have to join segregated locals of the boilermakers' union. But those locals deprived African Americans of virtually all of the rights of union membership. As a brief for the black workers later put it, "The only matter in which there is entire equality, without discrimination, is with reference to dues. *The dues are equal.*"[5]

Some African American workers joined the segregated locals in order to keep the jobs for which they had traveled across the country. Justifying his membership, one worker explained that "of course the babies have got to eat." Skilled work had never been readily available to black workers, and if union membership, even segregated union membership, opened doors, then some were willing to pay the price. Others refused to join, either because they objected to the segregated auxiliaries on principle or because they saw no point in joining auxiliaries that provided no benefits and no power. Many lost their jobs. Black shipyard workers up and down the West Coast organized in opposition to exclusionary and discriminatory boilermakers' unions. And like the sugar workers, they turned to lawyers for help.[6]

As civil rights lawyers took on these and other black workers as clients, the legal practices they created played a critical role in challenging Jim Crow in the 1940s. But they have played a negligible role in subsequent understandings of constitutional law and history. Although scholars of African American and labor history have recently unearthed a labor-based civil rights movement during the decade, their attention to African American workers has largely failed to penetrate legal histories of civil rights.[7]

In part, this is a consequence of the way *Brown v. Board of Education* has captured our cultural, legal, and constitutional imaginations since it was decided in 1954. When the Supreme Court declared segregation in public primary and secondary education unconstitutional, it achieved a great milestone for racial progress in the United States. In the half-century since *Brown*, scholars have unsurprisingly lavished attention on the case as the pivotal moment in the creation of modern civil rights doctrine. Focusing on *Brown*, conventional histories of civil rights law long viewed the 1940s as a period of relative stasis, important only for its contributions to the development of the *Brown* litigation. Although these narratives are slowly being replaced by a new understanding of the importance of the 1940s to civil rights, *Brown* remains central to both the dominant historical narrative and the reigning legal canon.[8]

That centrality continues to obscure an important point: *Brown* represented only one possible form of modern civil rights doctrine. When NAACP lawyers succeeded in *Brown*, they realized a major victory over Jim Crow. They also largely eclipsed the other legal experiments in civil rights lawyers undertook in the 1940s. Although the Supreme Court's opinion did not fix in stone every detail of civil rights law, *Brown* served as a crystallizing moment that channeled legal energy toward some kinds of cases and legal theories rather than others. Because of *Brown*, psychologically damaged schoolchildren and the state-segregated school became the icons of Jim Crow. It was out of these particular and poignant materials that complainants, lawyers, and judges constructed subsequent civil rights doctrine. In the wake of *Brown*, that doctrine has primarily addressed questions of racial classification (as well as classifications on the basis of other personal characteristics like national origin and gender), focused on the stigmatic harm of such governmental classifications, and relied upon the equal protection clause of the Constitution's Fourteenth Amendment.

This book, by contrast, takes as its subject the varieties of civil rights complaints and legal practice in the era before *Brown*. The 1940s and early 1950s were not a relatively uneventful interlude between the New Deal's creation of the modern bureaucratic state and the Supreme Court's fulfillment in *Brown* of a long-immanent promise to protect the rights of racial minorities. Rather, during that decade and a half, the world of civil rights was conceptually, doctrinally, and constitutionally up for grabs. Those years were a signal period of ferment, in which the boundaries of the bureaucratic state, the form of individual rights, and the relationship between them were still unclear. Contemporaries saw how deeply uncertain were the contours of civil rights, their foundational constitutional texts, and the extent of public and private responsibility for their vindication. The political and social fundamentals of late-twentieth-century American liberalism remained deeply uncertain as the New Deal made way first for World War II and then for the Cold War.

In this era of instability and upheaval, civil rights law barely resembled the field as we now know it. In particular, both laypeople and legal professionals included not only the rights with which we associate the term today but also collective labor rights to governmentally provided economic security and affirmative rights to material and economic equality. Contemporaries saw an explicit connection between discrimination and economics, rights and reform, individual entitlement and government obligation. Lawyers who took the cases of black workers treated as civil rights issues labor-based and economic harms as well as racial ones, and they placed responsibility for rights protection within government as well as in opposition to it. Their constitutional imaginations were also more heterodox: they turned for constitutional authority to the antislavery imperative of the Thirteenth Amendment and the due process as well as the equal protection clause of the Fourteenth Amendment.

Taking the complaints of black workers as my starting point, I explore the construction of civil rights in the era before *Brown*. At heart, this book is a legal history, though one in which social history is inextricable. Legal change does not begin with the doctrines courts create or even the rhetorical strategies lawyers employ. It begins with the injuries individuals experience. When those individuals complain to lawyers, they invoke the machinery of the law on their behalf. (I thus leave the words of the complaints intact and unadulterated.) Understanding law creation as beginning with complaints illuminates the human, institutional, and doctrinal mechanisms of legal change. The process begins with the claims individuals assert. It continues with the choices of lawyers to recognize some lay claims and not others. It crystallizes with how lawyers manipulate, translate, and transform those claims through the legal process. And it culminates in the validation of some legal strategies over others.

In part, then, this book is a study of how social phenomena become legal problems, who sees them as such, and how they change once within legal channels. I reconstruct legal practice—rather than judicial doctrine—in order to illuminate both the world of civil rights possibilities in the 1940s and the extent of their later transformation. In particular, I explore the potential of black workers' claims to spur the creation of new civil rights doctrines, their eventual disappearance as a force for legal change, and the consequences of that disappearance for constitutional law today.[9]

From the standpoint of civil rights lawyers, the complaints of African American workers represented the emblematic civil rights claims of the 1940s. Throughout the decade, lawyers with a commitment to challenging Jim Crow pursued cases unrelated to labor. They challenged police brutality, lynching, and voting discrimination as well as segregation in education, transportation, and housing. But both the nature of the workers' claims and the larger political and intellectual currents that shaped the lawyers' responses to them made those claims central to developing legal practices and understandings of civil rights.

The claims of the workers who sought legal advice about the Florida cane fields and the West Coast shipyards differed from one another in many respects—they occurred in agriculture and industry, involved near slavery and modern forms of discrimination, reflected a lack of personal autonomy and opportunities for concerted protest—but they all traced their roots to the racial slavery as old as the colonies. For many southern whites, the abolition of slavery following the Civil War had spawned two related problems: a race problem and a labor problem. How, they asked themselves, would they prevent the newly freed African Americans from contaminating the white race and debasing white politics? And how would they find a replacement for the cheap labor black slaves had previously provided and on which the southern economy was largely based?

The answer to both questions was the complex of laws and customs that arose in the late nineteenth century and eventually came to be called Jim Crow. When southern states managed through both violence and legal chicanery to nullify the vote blacks had so recently won, they made it possible to inscribe Jim Crow into legal and political structures for generations. When railroads decided to segregate their railroad cars and local school boards decided to allocate fewer tax dollars to black schools than to white ones, they helped create Jim Crow. When white planters preferred black to white farmhands and tenants because they could get more work out of black workers for less pay, they drew on and reinforced Jim Crow. When unions excluded black workers and companies refused to hire them, they perpetuated Jim Crow. When the Ku Klux Klan, often with the acquiescence of law enforcement officers, lynched black men and women, they enforced Jim Crow. Jim Crow existed because every day, in ways momentous and quotidian, governments, private institutions, and millions of individuals made decisions about hiring, firing, consuming, recreating, governing, educating, and serving that kept blacks out, down, and under.[10]

Outside the South, African Americans could usually vote, and social isolation and terror were less ubiquitous. But Jim Crow as a system of economic exploitation, if not complete segregation and political exclusion, was very much in evidence across the country during the first half of the twentieth century. For black workers trying to make a living, Jim Crow North and South meant job announcements addressed specifically to white or "colored" workers. It meant that whole swaths of industry, whole sectors of the workplace were off limits. It meant inadequate schooling, inaccessible labor unions, and unavailable government benefits. Black workers usually performed the worst work for the lowest pay. They could not eat in lunchrooms or use bathrooms on site. They worked in segregated gangs and were forced to join segregated unions or found themselves excluded from unions altogether. They had limited, and usually segregated, access to tolerable housing and other services.

By the time World War II began, Jim Crow as a system of both racial oppression and economic exploitation was well entrenched. The "virtual slavery" practiced on the sugar plantations of south Florida and the employment and union discrimination the black boilermakers

faced on the West Coast were both products of the systematic and usually legal discrimination, segregation, disfranchisement, and coercion
of African Americans in Jim Crow America. When black workers
brought these injuries to civil rights lawyers, they implicitly challenged
the very crux of Jim Crow.

Civil rights lawyers' positive responses to the workers' complaints reflected a political, intellectual, and legal climate that was increasingly
hospitable to precisely such rights claims. Although all periods of history can be understood as indeterminate and contingent to some extent, the simultaneous revolutions in American legal, social, economic, and political life made the decade of the 1940s particularly so.
Prior to that time, there was neither substantial space in constitutional
doctrine for civil rights lawyers to construct frameworks that would
break down Jim Crow nor much political will or institutional capacity
to do so. By the time the Florida sugar workers contacted the Department of Justice and the West Coast boilermakers telegrammed the
NAACP, the time was ripe for exactly the legal challenges the workers
sought.

Before the late 1930s, federal civil rights litigation held out little
promise for African Americans. In the late nineteenth century, the
Supreme Court had largely undermined the power of the Civil War
amendments to protect African Americans. It read narrowly the Thirteenth Amendment's prohibition on involuntary servitude, the Fourteenth Amendment's promise of due process of law and equal protection of the laws for African Americans, and the Fifteenth Amendment's
protection of their right to vote. In two cases in particular, the Court
gutted the Fourteenth Amendment's equal protection clause. In the
1883 *Civil Rights Cases,* the Court concluded that the amendment protected against rights violations only committed by governments, not
those committed by private actors. In the 1896 case of *Plessy v. Ferguson,*
it upheld state-mandated racial segregation as constitutional.[11]

Between the turn of the twentieth century and the 1930s, the Court
had instead protected a very different set of individual rights under
the due process clause of the Fifth and Fourteenth Amendments—the
right to make and enforce contracts, the right to property, and the
right to pursue one's livelihood and obtain the fruits of one's labor.
Those rights came to be associated with the 1905 case of *Lochner v. New
York,* which struck down a state law that prohibited bakers from

working more than ten hours per day. In the first third of the twentieth century, courts frequently viewed these due process rights as under-mining the constitutionality of progressive social and economic regu-lation. African Americans' enjoyment of contract and property rights had been central to Reconstruction-era ideas of civil rights, but during the *Lochner* era the Court largely divorced due process rights from those of African Americans. Although the Court's protection of such rights sometimes redounded to the benefit of black workers in the first decades of the twentieth century, more frequently they redounded to the benefit of corporations at the expense of both black and white workers.[12]

By the Depression decade of the 1930s, the Court began to de-throne the right to contract and uphold New Deal and other legislative interference in the economy against constitutional challenges. The en-suing expansion of federal power and denigration of *Lochner* rights created what was widely perceived as a revolution in constitutional law. It was not apparent at the time how completely courts would eschew contractual rights or what, if anything, would replace *Lochner.* Legal professionals disagreed about what civil rights were, where in the Con-stitution courts could find authority to protect them, who exactly should provide that protection, and how they should do so.[13]

Nevertheless, with *Lochner* displaced, one particular type of rights did seem poised to serve as a replacement in the late 1930s. The polit-ical concerns of the Depression made workers' collective rights to or-ganize into unions, bargain, and strike appear paramount. These rights were also a crucial component of the larger set of rights to eco-nomic security—to minimum subsistence, unemployment insurance, old-age assistance, housing, and education—that the New Deal aspired to provide. No single doctrinal approach to civil rights was yet en-trenched, but the collective rights of workers appeared the most likely to replace the *Lochner*ian right to contract within dominant legal dis-course.

When World War II brought black protest to the fore, the civil rights issues with the most political traction became those that combined claims to racial equality with still-robust claims of labor and economic rights. In particular, the attempts of black workers to build on the labor and economic rights of the New Deal represented the most po-litically promising civil rights issues of the 1940s.

Within the context of both black workers' experience of Jim Crow and changing understandings of civil rights, then, the central civil rights dilemma of the era before *Brown* was whether and how civil rights lawyers would integrate the various strands of labor rights that survived the 1930s into civil rights practices largely focused on African Americans. In practical terms, this translated into the question of whether and how civil rights lawyers would take the cases of the black workers who sought their counsel. The answer to that question depended on the lawyers' own institutional, political, and doctrinal constraints and opportunities as much as on the contents of the complaints themselves. As clients interacted with their lawyers, their experience of Jim Crow had the potential to shape the lawyers' own understandings of the law and its possibilities.

In this book, I focus on how lawyers in two institutions responded to the complaints of black workers: those in the Department of Justice's Civil Rights Section and those in the legal department of the NAACP. Although a number of other public and private agencies devoted themselves either partially or exclusively to the problems of African Americans, these other organizations did not see themselves as essentially and fundamentally constructing a new legal and constitutional framework for American civil rights in the 1940s. The lawyers in both the CRS and the NAACP understood their professional projects and institutional roles in precisely that way. They were self-described civil rights lawyers at a time when civil rights was a marginal and unformed field of law. They took the challenge to Jim Crow seriously, and they hoped to play instrumental roles in the construction of modern legal doctrine.

Much as they shared, the lawyers in the two institutions were situated quite differently. One group of lawyers was white and one largely African American, one public and one private, one electorally accountable and one increasingly membership driven. The CRS lawyers worked in the first federal agency in American history whose mission it was to offer legal protection for civil rights. Finding federal jurisdiction for such protection was not easy, but the very difficulty of the task spurred the lawyers to look to the complaints of black agricultural workers for insights. Those complaints offered the lawyers creative ways of balancing an initial mandate of protecting the rights of labor with the World War II imperative of responding to the rights claims of African Americans. In doing so, however, the lawyers had to contend with the politics of the Department of Justice, the Roosevelt administration, and the southerners in the Democratic Party.

For their part, the NAACP lawyers worked for an organization that took as its original mission the destruction of Jim Crow. But even into the 1940s, the association remained open to a number of understandings of that mission. In choosing among them, the NAACP lawyers too took seriously the complaints of black workers. Because of the lawyers' relatively elite social and economic status, however, their experience of Jim Crow differed from that of their clients. Those differences shaped the nature and extent of the legal assistance they would offer black workers, as did the institutional context in which they worked. The lawyers had to answer to the higher-ups in the NAACP as well as to the association's white funders and black members. They had to navigate between attacks on the association as Communist and attacks that it was too bourgeois.

Consequently, the CRS and the NAACP lawyers approached the complaints of black workers—and the larger project of formulating and establishing new civil rights doctrine—in very different ways. The lawyers' disparate strategies, and the implications of those strategies for the civil rights that eventually emerged, suggest an implicit confrontation between (at least) two contending views. On the one hand, the CRS lawyers understood civil rights in part through the lens of labor rights. They built the foundations of some of their cases on the claims of workers like those in the Florida cane fields, and they made the Thirteenth Amendment's prohibition on involuntary servitude central to their practice. The involuntary servitude cases the CRS lawyers pursued on behalf of black agricultural workers, and the understandings of civil rights those cases suggested, neither monopolized the section's legal practice nor offered up a single, linear plan for a new civil rights doctrine. Nonetheless, the CRS used the Thirteenth Amendment to extend to some of the most destitute black workers affirmative New Deal protections for personal security, labor rights, and rights to minimal economic security. In part because the CRS took seriously the complaints of African American agricultural workers, its civil rights practice accepted an affirmative responsibility to challenge economic exploitation as well as racial discrimination.[14]

The NAACP lawyers' more complicated relationship with the black workers who would be their clients led their civil rights practice in a different direction. For much of its history, the NAACP had not seen itself as deeply concerned either institutionally or programmatically with the economic fortunes of black workers. The exigencies of the Depression and World War II finally convinced the NAACP and its lawyers to view black workers as institutionally, politically, and doctrinally promising clients. As the NAACP lawyers experimented with due process as well as equal protection frameworks in their wartime legal practice, their cases on behalf of black workers challenged both the public and the private, the stigmatic and the material harms of Jim Crow. Nevertheless, in the years after World War II ended, so too did the NAACP lawyers' pursuit of complaints like those of the West Coast shipyard workers. By 1950, when the NAACP's legal team embarked on the direct attack on segregation that would eventually lead to victory in *Brown*, it largely rejected the possibility that workers' complaints would shape its litigation agenda. The lawyers eschewed labor cases, the due process clause, private defendants, and material inequality in favor of a frontal attack on state-mandated educational segregation. They eventually came to regard as the essence of Jim Crow the stigma of governmental classifications, not the material inequality black workers experienced as a result of the interdependent public and private Jim Crow complex.

As a result of the NAACP's overwhelming success in the courts— NAACP lawyer Thurgood Marshall alone won twenty-nine cases before the Supreme Court—*Brown* and its progeny succeeded in establishing the NAACP's legal strategy as American constitutional law. The influence of black workers on the NAACP's earlier, labor-related cases and the Civil Rights Section's Thirteenth Amendment practice disappeared from view. That disappearance was in large part a function of the power of *Brown* itself. Once the Court decided *Brown*, the case, the image of Jim Crow it projected, and the civil rights doctrine it initiated captured, and thereby limited, the legal imagination. The Court's validation of the NAACP's litigation choices made the kinds of arguments the NAACP had constructed on the road to *Brown* more culturally available to future lawyers than the arguments the lawyers had discarded.[15]

By emphasizing the historically situated choices of lawyers more than the decisions of courts, this book aims to recreate the interwoven legal, political, and institutional cultures that informed the lawyers' decisions. How the lawyers in the CRS and the NAACP came to practice civil rights law in precisely the manner they did cannot be reduced to any single cause. Clients had the potential to shape legal strategies. But that potential was realized only insofar as those clients' complaints complemented the legal culture the lawyers inhabited, the larger political culture they imbibed, and the material realities they faced. To complicate matters further, the relationship between those influences was constantly in motion. Thus, the contours of legal doctrine alone—the doctrine the lawyers learned as students, the opportunities and constraints they saw in the Supreme Court's fluctuating decisions—are not enough to explain their choices or describe the process of historical change. By the same token, the social and institutional circumstances of the lawyers cannot wholly account for their litigation strategies. The forces at play in lawyers' construction of their civil rights practices in the 1940s instead reveal both less legal autonomy than doctrinal determinism would imply and more than economic or social determinism would allow.

In excavating the multiplicity of civil rights complaints and practices of the 1940s, *The Lost Promise of Civil Rights* reveals how much of Jim Crow the victory of *Brown* left unchallenged. My goal, however, is not to identify a particular lost alternative. Rather, it is to highlight the consequences of lawyers' strategic litigation choices about which cases to pursue and which to avoid, which harms to emphasize and which to ignore, which constituencies to address and which to disregard.

The legal and political upheaval of the 1940s—during both World War II and the Cold War that followed—offered several possibilities for a new civil rights. That upheaval also required lawyers to make critical doctrinal and strategic decisions. What aspects of Jim Crow should they target first—the poverty in which the worst-off black workers lived, the material inequality of the private market, the psychological stigma of state racial classifications? What would be the terms on which their clients sought equality, and how would the lawyers define racial progress so that their clients' harms would be remedied?

Reconstructing the CRS's Thirteenth Amendment practice and the NAACP's labor-related cases in the 1940s shows how important these questions were—and how contingent the answers—in the decade and a half before *Brown*. During the 1940s, lawyers built on their clients' experiences of Jim Crow to challenge the idea of state action as well as state-sanctioned segregation itself. They fought for economic advancement within segregated workplaces even as they lodged principled objections to segregation. They relied on substantive right-to-work arguments rooted in due process as much as, if not more than, equal protection arguments about formal nondiscrimination. And they used the Thirteenth Amendment as well as the Fourteenth as constitutional authority. The civil rights doctrine we have today, the doctrine born in education cases and culminating in an anticlassification rule, was not inevitable. It was the product of the explicit and implicit judgments of historically situated actors and institutions—of lawyers who decided which clients to take on and how to create legal claims out of their complaints.

Reconstructing the civil rights practices of the 1940s also reveals how partial the NAACP's Supreme Court successes were. The cases that the NAACP eventually took to the Supreme Court in the 1950s and beyond sometimes involved poor and working-class African Americans. And sometimes they concerned material inequality as well as formal discrimination. In the end, however, the NAACP's lawyers did not allow the claims of working African Americans as working African Americans to influence their legal strategies. Had they done so, they might have seen that providing legal redress for black workers required an attack on more than state-mandated segregation. It required as well an attack on the private economic orderings that were equally a part of Jim Crow America. Answering the entirety of black workers' complaints meant not only establishing a norm of racial nondiscrimination but also shoring up the rights to work, to join a union, to participate in the labor market, to minimal subsistence.

As black workers and their complaints receded from both the NAACP's legal practice and *Brown*'s notion of civil rights, the distillation of racial classification as a harm in itself came to be expressed in terms of psychological injury. Once the NAACP had obtained its victories in the education realm, Thurgood Marshall began to think about how "to extend that doctrine to other areas," including labor. But the antidiscrimination paradigm had already begun to take hold of the legal imagination. It was a paradigm with little space for the kinds of claims African American workers and their lawyers in the NAACP and the CRS had made on their behalf a decade earlier. In opening the way for the attack on Jim Crow as formal, government-enforced segregation, *Brown* short-circuited lawyers' efforts in other realms. Whether an alternative strategy would have produced a different outcome is impossible to know. But the problems of African American workers disappeared from the most influential civil rights practice at a pivotal moment in civil rights history, and our civil rights doctrine has largely failed to address the kind of material inequality black workers endured.[16]

The Lost Promise of Civil Rights thus explores the implications of the cases that lawyers brought based on the workers' complaints, and the implications of the cases they did not. It suggests that by uncovering historical alternatives to the civil rights law we know as our own, we can broaden our imagination about the possibilities for addressing the remnants of Jim Crow still facing the nation today.

ONE

❖ ❖ ❖

Transition, Uncertainty, and the Conditions for a New Civil Rights

> In any growing and vital social organism rights are
> not static and for that reason can never be bound by
> the limitations of minute definition.
>
> Francis Biddle, *The World's Best Hope,* 1948

IN THE INAUGURAL ISSUE of its *Bill of Rights Review* in 1940, the American Bar Association's Bill of Rights Committee expressed its conviction "that a distinct field of law—that of civil rights—is emerging." From the standpoint of lawyers looking forward from that moment, the contours of the new field were largely unknown. In the late 1930s and early 1940s, the Supreme Court systematically dismantled the dominant doctrinal framework that had governed the relationship between individuals and the state for two generations. The *Lochner* era was over. Individual rights to contract and property no longer reigned supreme. The old constitutional order was unsettled, but no obvious and immediate replacement for the certainties of the past was forthcoming.[1]

In fact, a concrete replacement did not begin to surface until the Supreme Court's 1954 decision in *Brown v. Board of Education.* Only after *Brown* would the contours of current civil rights doctrine become clear. They were not apparent much before it. It was not obvious during the 1940s, for example, that the rights of racial minorities would come to dominate legal and popular conceptions of civil rights. It was not clear, in particular, that the formal legal rights of such minorities would overshadow rights to economic equality. And it was not evident that courts would protect those rights largely by scrutinizing government action under the equal protection clause of the Fourteenth Amendment.

Indeed, between the end of the *Lochner* era and the *Brown* decision, massive social, economic, and political transformations deepened and exacerbated the doctrinal uncertainties the New Deal revolution had unleashed. As the nation moved rapidly from a decade of depression to total mobilization for World War II to the continuous mobilization of the Cold War, lawyers trained in the old paradigm tried to make sense of the emerging field of civil rights. It was not easy, as lawyers could not take for granted even the most basic characteristics of that emerging field throughout the period between the end of the *Lochner* era and the *Brown* decision.

Lawyers looking forward could, however, identify four trends that have largely disappeared from view since *Brown*. First, the most likely immediate replacement for the individual contract rights the Supreme Court had previously protected seemed to be new collective labor and economic rights. Such rights constituted a key part of the New Deal's aspirations for economic security in the 1930s. Second, labor and economic rights remained robust even as the domestic and international dimensions of World War II brought African American civil rights into greater national political relief. Indeed, black civil rights activists during the war tried to harness for black workers the labor and economic rights white workers had already begun to enjoy. Third, when the Cold War again changed the political context for the legal understanding of new civil rights, the labor and economic rights that had gained prominence during the Depression and World War II—for both white and black workers—remained prominent and viable. Finally, even as rights to racial equality became more salient, there was no automatic or instant doctrinal clarity about their constitutional form. Even at the beginning of the 1950s, both the kinds of rights courts would protect and the constitutional framework they would use to protect them remained deeply uncertain.

For the forty years prior to World War II, the Supreme Court had a distinct idea about the kinds of individual rights it would protect from government incursion. After the Civil War, the northern-dominated Reconstruction Congress passed the Thirteenth, Fourteenth, and Fifteenth Amendments to the Constitution. The amendments respectively ended slavery, made African Americans citizens and assured Americans due process of law and equal protection of the law, and protected black citizens' right to vote. In the decades after Reconstruction ended in the mid-1870s, however, the Supreme Court eviscerated the power of all three amendments to protect the rights of African Americans. Instead, it gave sanction to the legal segregation and discrimination that was spreading throughout the country.

As an initial matter, many African Americans, Reconstruction congressmen, and jurists had thought the Thirteenth Amendment would be broad in scope. It would not only end slavery but affirmatively establish freedom, equality, and the right of the freed slaves to "the fruits of their labor." One supporter of the amendment saw it as standing on as broad a base as the Declaration of Independence. He declared that the amendment's effect would be not only the end of slavery but also "a practical application of that self-evident truth, 'that all men are created equal; that they are endowed by their Creator with certain unalienable rights; that among these are life, liberty and the pursuit of happiness.'" Another announced that the amendment was "designed . . . to accomplish . . . the abolition of slavery in the United States, and the political and social elevation of Negroes to all the rights of white men."[2]

In the 1870s, however, the Supreme Court began to narrow the amendment's scope. In particular, the Court refused to apply the Thirteenth Amendment to either labor exploitation or racial discrimination that did not closely approximate slavery. In the *Slaughter-House Cases* in 1873, the Court rebuffed the claim of a group of white butchers under the amendment. The butchers had argued that a state law prohibiting them from slaughtering animals except in a single state-licensed slaughterhouse in New Orleans had placed them in unconstitutional involuntary servitude. The monopoly prohibited them from enjoying the fruits of their own labor. The Court recognized that the amendment's prohibition of "involuntary servitude" went beyond slavery itself, but it nonetheless emphasized that "the obvious purpose was to forbid all shades and conditions of *African slavery*." The Court was accordingly unwilling to read the Thirteenth Amendment as offering robust protection for the rights of all workers to their livelihoods.[3]

Somewhat ironically, federal courts took the broader message of *Slaughter-House* to be that they had limited authority to protect even the rights of African Americans. Ten years later, in the *Civil Rights*

Cases, the Court reinforced that lesson. It read the Thirteenth Amendment as silent on a broad range of racial harms inflicted on African Americans that did not constitute slavery itself. In an opinion by Justice Joseph P. Bradley, the Court struck down portions of the Civil Rights Act of 1875 that prohibited racial discrimination in places of public accommodation and on common carriers. Bradley saw little connection between slavery and such discrimination. "It would be running the slavery argument into the ground to make it apply to every act of discrimination which a person may see fit to make." Where *Slaughter-House* rejected the possibility that the Thirteenth Amendment would protect the free labor of all workers, the *Civil Rights Cases* restricted its racial equality potential by disaggregating slavery and discrimination.[4]

In the 1906 case of *Hodges v. United States,* the Supreme Court took the final step in the evisceration of the Thirteenth Amendment. It refused to apply the amendment even where white workers intentionally tried to curtail the free labor of black workers. In *Hodges,* the federal government criminally prosecuted a white mob that had forced black lumber workers to leave their jobs at a lumber mill in White Hall, Arkansas, because the whites opposed their employment. Prior to *Hodges,* federal protection of black workers in such circumstances had not seemed particularly controversial. Even Justice Bradley, author of the majority opinion in the *Civil Rights Cases,* had previously deemed such protection within the Thirteenth Amendment's ambit. If whites joined together to deny an African American an opportunity to work as a farmer because of his race, he had previously written, "it cannot be doubted [the] case [would be] within the power of [C]ongress to remedy and redress" under the Thirteenth Amendment.[5]

The Court in *Hodges,* however, took a far narrower view. "The meaning [of the Thirteenth Amendment] is as clear as language can make it. The things denounced are slavery and involuntary servitude, and Congress is given power to enforce that denunciation. All understand by these terms a condition of enforced compulsory service of one to another." The lesson of *Hodges,* in combination with *Slaughter-House* and the *Civil Rights Cases,* was clear: only where slavery, or something closely approximating it, existed would the Thirteenth Amendment offer constitutional protection.[6]

The Fourteenth Amendment underwent a similar process of doctrinal distillation and diminution. The *Civil Rights Cases'* invalidation of the public accommodations provisions of the Civil Rights Act of 1875 again played a prominent part. The Court made clear that just as the Thirteenth Amendment did not prohibit discrimination generally, discrimination perpetrated by *private parties* was beyond the reach of the Fourteenth Amendment. Justice Bradley declared that it was "State action of a particular character that is prohibited. Individual invasion of individual rights is not the subject-matter of the amendment." The Court objected that "civil rights . . . cannot be impaired by the wrongful acts of individuals, unsupported by State authority." Such private acts were "simply a private wrong, or a crime," or nothing at all.[7]

In 1896 in *Plessy v. Ferguson,* the Supreme Court further truncated the power of the Fourteenth Amendment. Louisiana had passed a statute requiring its railroads to "provide equal but separate accommodations" for whites and African Americans. Homer Plessy was seven-eighths white, and when he attempted to ride in a whites-only railroad car in New Orleans, he was arrested. The *Plessy* Court upheld the statute, thereby validating the constitutionality of legislatively mandated segregation. *Plessy* came eventually to stand for the proposition that segregation statutes of all kinds were constitutional so long as the separate conditions were (formally) equal.[8]

The Fifteenth Amendment, which had promised black Americans that they would not be denied the right to vote because of race, met a similar fate. In cases in 1876, the Court made it difficult for African Americans to vindicate their voting rights without proving they had been discriminated against specifically because of their race. Avoiding race-based exclusions, southern states instead disfranchised African Americans through various other means around the turn of the century. They used poll taxes, literacy tests, and plain old intimidation. The Court provided little relief. In *Giles v. Harris* in 1903, the Court recognized the intent and efficacy of such techniques in Alabama but refused to require the registration of African American voters. If "the conspiracy and the intent exist" to prevent African Americans from voting, the Court explained weakly, ordering the state to register African Americans to vote was unlikely to have any effect.[9]

Meanwhile, as the Supreme Court read the Reconstruction amendments narrowly in cases concerning the rights of African Americans, it expanded other constitutional protections under the Fourteenth Amendment. Most significantly, it broadened the meaning of the due process clause of the Fourteenth Amendment and the similar clause restraining the federal government in the Fifth Amendment. The clauses prohibited the state or national government from "depriv[ing] any person of life, liberty, or property, without due process of law." The Court read the clauses as protecting civil rights to economic autonomy that had roots in the free labor ideology of the Civil War era. These "substantive due process" rights—as legal professionals would eventually dub them—included the right to make and enforce contracts, the right to property, and the right to pursue one's livelihood and obtain the fruits of one's labor. Courts often saw these rights as constraining progressive social and economic regulation like the maximum hours law invalidated in *Lochner v. New York*. The Court determined that these kinds of regulations trenched on the rights of both employers and employees to make contracts as they saw fit.[10]

To be sure, the Court occasionally vindicated other kinds of individual rights during the *Lochner* era—in early free speech, procedural due process, and voting cases, as well as in cases concerning parental decisions about raising their children. But the judicial vindication of the rights of contract and property dwarfed such decisions. Out of 604 cases involving the Fourteenth Amendment before 1911, twenty-eight affected the rights of African Americans, and in twenty-two of those, African Americans lost. As C. W. Collins stated in 1912, "It is not the negro but accumulated and organized capital, which now looks to the Fourteenth Amendment for protection from State activity." That conclusion was bolstered by the Court's determination in *Santa Clara County v. Southern Pacific Railroad Company* that corporations would be treated as persons under the Fourteenth Amendment and would receive its protections.[11]

The Court itself described the transformation in *Buchanan v. Warley* in 1917. Striking down a residential segregation ordinance in Louisville, Kentucky, the Court reflected, "While a principal purpose of the [Fourteenth] Amendment was to protect persons of color, the broad language was deemed sufficient to protect all persons, white or black, against discriminatory legislation by the States. This is now the settled law." The Court recognized that in "many of the cases since arising the question of color has not been involved and the cases have been decided upon alleged violations of civil or property rights irre-spective of the race or color of the complainant." The trend continued for the next several decades.[12]

In the late 1930s and early 1940s, however, established constitutional thought underwent dramatic change. In response to the Depression, Congress passed economic legislation that trenched on the *Lochner* rights to contract and property that the Supreme Court had seemed committed to protecting. Beginning in 1934, that commitment began to wane. The Supreme Court dismantled the doctrines underpinning and structuring *Lochner*-era jurisprudence when it validated New Deal legis-lation like the National Labor Relations Act (NLRA), the Fair Labor Standards Act (FLSA), and the Social Security Act and when it ex-panded Congress's power under the Commerce Clause. In 1939, polit-ical scientist Robert Cushman described Justice James C. McReynolds, one of the minority of justices who still adhered to *Lochner*-era prece-dents, as "stand[ing] like the boy on the burning deck amidst what obvi-ously appears to him to be the imminent destruction of the old constitu-tional system."[13]

In fact, *Lochner* reasoning would survive in various forms in state courts for several decades. But the end of *Lochner*'s hegemony destabi-lized established understandings of civil rights and in broad strokes transformed crucial balances of governmental power. The Supreme Court previously had viewed government as an umpire distantly over-seeing private contractual relations in which it was occasionally forced to intervene. That perspective made it difficult to recognize rights vio-lations that occurred as a result of structural social and economic in-equalities. The New Deal Court, by contrast, sanctioned a far more ro-bust role for the federal government as protector and provider. The constitutional revolution shifted power from the courts to the execu-tive and legislative branches and "unshackled" both state and federal authority. It created space for the federal executive and legislative branches to use the power, bureaucratic prowess, and substantial man-power with which the New Deal and World War II had endowed them.[14]

To civil rights lawyers, the demise of the right to contract—and the changes in the relationships between governments, individuals, and private industry wrought by that demise—undermined the legal cate-gories that had formed a bedrock of their professional training and doctrinal understandings. But the precise ways in which the doctrinal terrain had shifted, and the consequences of the shift, lacked the kind of clarity with which we might endow them today. To most commentators, only one thing was clear: the future would be different from the past. Many observers saw the post-*Lochner* "period of acute social change" as destroying the old order. One loyal member of the Republican Party tried to adapt to the changed circumstances of American politics during the war: "We cannot go back to a past which countenanced a widely-exploited labor, a greatly depressed agriculture, an irresponsible Wall Street; to a past which knew no old-age pensions, no unemployment insurance, no maximum hours and minimum wages."[15]

The future of individual rights was less apparent. Legal doctrine provided no definitive answer. The Court revealed its own uncertainty in fractured opinions and frequent overrulings of precedent. Between 1937 and 1946, the Court overruled twenty-seven decisions by name and modified or qualified a number of others. Practitioners and scholars recognized that "the exact meaning of the general terms in which [civil rights statutes] are couched was not clear." Special assistant to the attorney general Frederick Bernays Wiener described civil rights and civil liberties in 1947 as "terms that actually beg the question they purport to answer." When President Harry S. Truman's Committee on Civil Rights published its final report that same year, its authoritative statement on civil rights put an optimistic gloss on these uncertainties. The committee was "convinced that the term 'civil rights' . . . has with great wisdom been used flexibly in American history." "The phrase, 'civil rights,'" it posited, "is an abbreviation for a whole complex of relationships among individuals and among groups."[16]

As the decade came to a close, the contours of a new civil rights still remained fuzzy. In 1948, political scientist Robert Cushman included under the heading "civil liberties" a number of categories of cases arising between 1937 and 1947: those involving First Amendment rights, rights against race discrimination, rights against private parties, and wartime conflicts between civil liberty and military power. In 1950, the best one commentator could say was that "constitutional law [was] attaining at least a state of superficial repose."[17]

Even treatise and casebook writers, who generally tried to assimilate and make sense out of doctrine, were at a loss. Authors of general constitutional law casebooks recognized that "substantial changes [had] taken place in the field of constitutional law," but they still largely retained substantive due process as a major organizing principle. Substantive due process was discredited, perhaps, but with no obvious replacement, it remained substantively and structurally important. The foreword to the only casebook on political and civil rights in the United States in existence in 1952 explicitly recognized these uncertainties. "Perhaps the best thing that can be said about the law in this field is that it is unsettled," it observed. "If ever there was a branch of law that was 'developing,' this is it."[18]

Indeed, the very terminology lawyers in the 1940s inherited was clumsy and imprecise, riddled with multiple and unresolved meanings. During the *Lochner* era, the kinds of individual rights the courts would protect were quite clear, but the language judges, legal scholars, and lawyers used never was. "Civil rights," "civil liberties," and "liberty" itself contained both distinctive and overlapping meanings. On the one hand, those trained in the law used the term "civil rights" in "a narrow . . . technical sense" to refer to "constitutional discussion concerning the legal rights of free Negroes in the years before and immediately following the Civil War." This definition of "civil rights" stood in contrast to that of "civil liberties." The latter "connote[d] the freedom of the individual with respect to personal action, the possession and use of property, religious belief and worship and the expression of opinion." During the 1920s and 1930s, when speech claims often sparked controversy in labor-management conflicts, lawyers and activists associated civil liberties with the First Amendment and with the collective rights of labor more generally. Alternately, "liberty" referred, at least some of the time, to the *Lochner* Court's interpretation of the due process clause of the Fourteenth Amendment. It could include rights "to be free in the enjoyment of all [of a man's] faculties in all lawful ways; to live and work where he will; to earn his livelihood by any lawful calling; to pursue any livelihood or avocation; and for that purpose to enter into all contracts which may be proper, necessary, and essential to carrying out the purposes mentioned above."[19]

On the other hand, legal professionals also used terms like "civil rights" and "civil liberties" generically and interchangeably. Writing in 1943, political scientist Cushman discussed segregation in an article entitled "Some Constitutional Problems of Civil Liberty." He inherited that usage from the ambiguities of the *Lochner*-era terminology. During the *Lochner* era, civil rights and civil liberties had referred to the then-sacred rights of contract, and First Amendment rights, and racial equality rights. One 1917 treatise thus defined "civil rights" as "those rights which appertain to a person by virtue of his citizenship in a state or community"; "those rights which the municipal law will enforce at the instance of private individuals"; and "certain rights secured to all citizens of the United States by the thirteenth and fourteenth amendments of the federal constitution." As to the final category, the treatise included "the rights of property, marriage, protection by the laws, freedom of contracts, [and] trial by jury," in contrast to political, natural, or social rights. The same treatise included in its definition of "civil liberty" "the right of every person living under our government to acquire and dispose of property by lawful means and for lawful purposes, and to pursue any lawful business, trade, or calling."[20]

Once the Supreme Court withdrew its protection for the bedrock rights of the *Lochner* era, the clumsiness of the professional terminology of civil rights became more pronounced. So long as the kinds of rights the Court would protect had been clear, the fact that legal professionals lacked a precise vocabulary with which to discuss them was not deeply problematic. But the imprecise *Lochner*-era terminology left commentators at a great loss when conceptual clarity dissipated as well. In 1942, the Colorado Supreme Court, for example, hesitated even to label a First Amendment case. It described the case as yet another in a series "involving a conflict between liberty and authority, a conflict that is sometimes labeled 'civil rights v. the police power' or 'liberty of the individual v. the general welfare.'" As late as 1947, the *Boston Globe* used the now odd-sounding phrase "civil liberties rights" when referring to Thirteenth Amendment rights. The language of rights and liberties, like the substance of legal doctrine, was fundamentally unclear.[21]

As Court watchers and lawyers tried to make sense of the destruction of the old constitutional order, some glimpsed what they thought was a new order emerging from the ruins. Eminent Supreme Court scholar Edward Corwin, for example, observed that "the social teachings of the New Deal" had led the Court "practically to dismiss the conception of 'freedom of contract' as a definition of 'liberty' and to substitute for it a special concern for 'the rights of labor.' " Corwin thought the right of the individual laborer to contract had given way to the collective rights of labor to organize, bargain, and strike.[22]

The evidence for such a belief was considerable. Throughout the *Lochner* era, laborers, unions, and progressive reformers had challenged the Supreme Court's protection of contract and property rights with alternative conceptions of labor rights. Until the 1930s, the claims of workers and unions had largely fallen on deaf, indifferent, or hostile judicial ears. Strikes led largely to injunctions, arrests, and violent reprisals. Courts struck down state and federal statutes mandating minimum wages or maximum hours. They rebuffed attempts to protect labor rights under federal civil rights statutes. The Supreme Court prohibited state laws outlawing yellow-dog contracts (contracts in which employees agreed as a condition of their employment that they would not join a union). Without legal protections, as one labor supporter put it, "All that the employees had was a right to try to organize if they could get away with it."[23]

The position of organized labor changed dramatically over the course of the 1930s. The new Congress of Industrial Organizations (CIO) challenged the dominance of the more craft-oriented American Federation of Labor (AFL). The CIO offered a sweeping vision of industrial unionism and industrial democracy. With the Depression raising the stakes and unions attempting to organize ever more workers, battles between increasingly powerful unions and desperate employers grew more pitched and more violent. Like industrial workers, agricultural workers joined unions in unprecedented numbers. As union membership swelled during the decade, the rights of labor took on greater importance for greater numbers of Americans.

As the membership of the CIO and the AFL grew, unions became formidable political actors and key components of the Democratic Party's electoral base. But labor rights were critical to national politics during the 1930s for other reasons as well. They were programmatically critical to the New Deal's larger economic and political agenda— what Franklin D. Roosevelt called in a 1932 campaign speech the creation of a new "economic constitutional order." Reinventing American liberalism for the modern era, Roosevelt made "economic security" part of the 1936 Democratic Party platform and a central catchphrase of Depression-era politics. The national government would henceforth pursue policies to ensure a standard of living above the subsistence level. The "liberal movement of the present," Roosevelt's Solicitor General Robert Jackson declared in 1938, "is concerning itself more with economic rights and privileges than with political rights and privileges." In his description of the new economic bill of rights, Jackson included "the ending of the oppression of starvation wages and sweatshop hours, the right of the willing to work, the right to a living when work is not available, [and] the right to some shelter from the cruelties of impoverished age."[24]

In order to vindicate the economic constitutional order's "right to work" and "right to live," workers would need the protection of unions. Unionization facilitated the achievement of decent work at decent pay; it was a prerequisite for the economic well-being of workers throughout the nation. Thus, Jackson also included "collective bargaining for labor [and] the right to work free from industrial espionage" in his description of the economic bill of rights.[25]

Throughout the 1930s, labor rights—the rights of workers to organize, bargain collectively, and strike—ultimately took center stage in discussions of and predictions about new rights frameworks. As one journalist wrote in 1936, "The crucial struggle for civil liberty today is among tenant farmers and industrial workers, fighting for economic emancipation and security." The American Civil Liberties Union (ACLU) agreed that labor rights were the central struggle involving civil rights during the decade. "However important or significant may be the struggle for the political rights of fifteen million Negroes; however important or significant the defense of religious liberties; of academic freedom; of freedom from censorship of the press, radio, or motion pictures, these are on the whole trifling in national effect compared with the fight for the rights of labor to organize."[26]

During the 1930s, then, the rights of organized labor seemed in some ways, and to many observers, more pressing than the rights of racial minorities. In fact, all three branches of the federal government backed the rights claims of industrial workers and unions in various ways during the decade. The president, Congress, and the Supreme Court each appeared to take labor's side in what *Fortune Magazine* called in 1937 "the irrepressible conflict of the twentieth century." Congress and the president first sanctioned the rights of labor in the 1932 Norris-LaGuardia Act. The act restricted the power of courts to issue injunctions against labor unions involved in labor disputes. It emphasized that the worker should "have full freedom of association, self-organization, and designation of representatives of his own choosing, to negotiate the terms and conditions of his employment, and that he shall be free from the interference, restraint, or coercion of employers of labor, or their agents in . . . [his] self-organization or in other concerted activities for the purpose of collective bargaining or other mutual aid or protection." Without organization, "[a]ctual liberty of contract" would elude workers in their bargaining with more powerful employers. Congress thus used the Court's own protected category of contract rights to justify a new kind of labor rights.[27]

Early New Deal economic regulation went further toward vindicating the rights of labor, though the Supreme Court ultimately invalidated much of it. Most prominently, section 7(a) of the 1933 National Industrial Recovery Act (NIRA) prohibited employers from discriminating against union workers or requiring membership in company-dominated unions. The section not only reiterated the importance of organization but also unequivocally declared that "employees shall have the right to organize and bargain collectively through representatives of their own choosing, and shall be free from the interference, restraint, or coercion of employers of labor." Senator Robert F. Wagner of New York, long an ally of labor, described "the right to bargain collectively, guaranteed to labor by section 7(a) of the Recovery Act, [as] a veritable charter of freedom of contract; without it there would be slavery by contract." President Roosevelt himself said when he signed the NIRA into law, "Workers . . . are here given a new charter of rights long sought and hitherto denied."[28]

When the Supreme Court struck down the NIRA in 1935, Congress passed the National Labor Relations Act (NLRA, also called the Wagner Act for its sponsor). That act explicitly gave workers in interstate commerce the federally protected right to organize into unions and bargain collectively. In addition to facilitating a surge in union membership—which grew from 3.7 million to almost 10.5 million between 1935 and 1941—the NLRA solidified legal validation for new labor rights. Promoting the bill, Representative Terry McGovern Carpenter of Nebraska stated that the "worker's right to form labor unions and to bargain collectively is as much his right as his right to participate through delegated representatives in the making of laws which regulate his civic conduct. Both are inherent rights." Senator Wagner described "[t]he spirit and purpose of the law" as the creation of "a free and dignified workingman who has the economic strength to bargain collectively with a free and dignified employer in accordance with the methods of democracy. . . . The imposition of legal restrictions upon the right to strike . . . would merely deprive the worker of his inalienable right to protest against the substitution of . . . [an] authoritarian state" for a democratic one.[29]

Which workers were entitled to these new rights was not always clear during the 1930s. On the one hand, the NLRA did not guarantee labor rights to all workers equally. Like many of the New Deal's economic protections, it excluded agricultural and domestic workers. Many of those workers were African American, so their exclusion marked a concession to southern white congressmen. The image of the worker entitled to such rights was largely that of a white man supporting his wife and children. The work in which such rights would be protected was, by legislative fiat, industrial work.[30]

On the other hand, other congressional action suggested a broader expanse for labor rights. The hearings of the La Follette Civil Liberties Committee, chaired by progressive Wisconsin Senator Robert La Follette, Jr., were telling in two ways. First, the "civil liberties" with which the committee concerned itself primarily referred to the collective rights of labor. Second, the Committee aimed to protect all workers— from industrial workers in NLRA-covered unions to black and white farmworkers across the nation. For at least some in the federal government in the 1930s, then, workers entitled to rights included those in both industry and agriculture.[31]

When the Supreme Court upheld the Wagner Act in *NLRB v. Jones & Laughlin Steel Corp.* in 1937, it appeared to bolster labor's rights even further. The Court described as "a fundamental right" "the right of employees to self-organization and to select representatives of their own choosing for collective bargaining or other mutual protection without restraint or coercion by their employer." It recognized the structural inequalities of the labor market, reasoning that unions "were organized out of the necessities of the situation; that a single employee was helpless in dealing with an employer; that he was dependent ordinarily on his daily wage for the maintenance of himself and family." And it stressed that "if the employer refused to pay him the wages that he thought fair, he was nevertheless unable to leave the employ and resist arbitrary and unfair treatment; that union was essential to give laborers opportunity to deal on an equality with their employer."[32]

The Court's language seemed both to vindicate the federal government's authority to regulate the national economy and to constitute a revolution in rights. The *Newsweek* caption under a photograph of sit-down strikers at General Motors accompanying an article on *Jones & Laughlin* read, "Sit-downers looked out at a future of court-given rights." Robert Morss Lovett, a "G.M. stockholder," saw what he called "industrial liberties . . . on the way to becoming legally recognized." Chairman J. Warren Madden of the NLRB stressed that the "most significant result" of the Wagner Act was "that it has created a new and important civil liberty and has given new vitality to the old civil liberties." And Roger Baldwin of the ACLU saw the act as "a turning point not only in the history of labor but in the history of constitutional rights." To these and other observers, federal legislation and judicial approval had not only created a regulatory apparatus; they had not merely created statutory rights; they had created new "civil liberties."[33]

The Court's apparent solicitude for labor's rights could be seen not only in its decisions upholding New Deal legislation but also in the development of First Amendment jurisprudence later in the decade. "[F]ree association and self-organization are simply the result of the exercise of the fundamental rights of free speech and assembly," Senator La Follette summarized in 1942. "The most spectacular violations of civil liberty . . . proved upon investigation to have their roots in economic conflicts of interest." The ACLU's Roger Baldwin "viewed the free-speech issue as . . . inseparable from the rights of workers to organize and bargain collectively."[34]

The Supreme Court seemed both to draw on and to help constitute the increased prominence of labor's rights by going out of its way to emphasize these rights in First Amendment cases. In several cases in the late 1930s, the Court expressed its willingness to legitimate labor organizing, as well as organizing around other New Deal economic rights. It carefully distinguished those activities from what in the past would have been seen as the undifferentiated and wholly subversive activities of the Communist Party. In the view of political scientist and Republican C. Gordon Post in 1941, "What was once subversive [was] subversive no more." The Court emphasized the "lawful[ness]" of a meeting in which the Communist Party organized protests about "illegal raids on workers' halls and homes," local jail conditions, police shootings of strikers, and strike-breaking and red-baiting by the steamship and stevedoring companies. The Court characterized as "more or less harmless" attempts by an African American Communist to address unemployment relief and appeal to "the white and negro unemployed to organize and represent the need for further county aid." And it viewed the closed shop as essential to "the right to strive to earn [a] living." "Earning a living," the Court stated in a case allowing unions to publicize labor disputes, "is dependent upon securing work; and securing work is dependent upon public favor. To win the patronage of the public [the union and the employer] each may strive by legal means." The Court distinguished between the potentially criminal (advocating revolution) and the actually lawful (protesting violations of workers' rights and seeking to organize the unemployed). These distinctions suggested that the Court was willing to recognize, and instantiate, the legitimacy of labor's rights.[35]

Indeed, at times, the Court explicitly justified First Amendment protection precisely because the speakers addressed labor rights. For example, when a black improvement organization arranged a "Don't Buy Where You Can't Work" campaign in Washington, D.C., the grocery store it picketed requested an injunction. In rejecting the company's request in *New Negro Alliance v. Sanitary Grocery Co.*, in 1938, the Court did not hold that the First Amendment constitutionally protected peaceful picketing. Rather, the Court held that courts could not enjoin the New Negro Alliance because the protest of the company's lack of black clerks occurred in the course of a labor dispute. The Norris-LaGuardia Act restricted injunctions in "labor disputes," and the Court made it clear that such disputes were not limited to those in which "the disputants stand in the proximate relation of employer and employee." The Court found that the "desire for fair and equitable conditions of employment on the part of persons of any race, color, or persuasion . . . is quite as important to those concerned as fairness and equity in terms and conditions of employment can be to trade or craft unions or any form of labor organization or association." In fact, the Court allowed that such discrimination "may reasonably be deemed more unfair and less excusable" than anti-union discrimination. Nonetheless, the black picketers only won their case by convincing the Court that theirs was a labor dispute, owed the statutory protections Congress had put in place for laborers. As African Americans complaining about race discrimination, they had only the rights they could borrow from labor.[36]

In *Hague v. CIO,* the Court also chose a narrow, labor-related analysis rather than a general First Amendment principle for its decision. Individual workers, unions, and the ACLU brought suit against the mayor of Jersey City, New Jersey, for violating their civil rights when they tried to organize workers there. The Supreme Court found for the unions. Again, the Court avoided adopting a general First Amendment principle. Instead, it decided the case on the ground that the "freedom to disseminate information concerning the provisions of the National Labor Relations Act, to assemble peaceably for the discussion of the Act, and of the opportunities and advantages offered by it, is a privilege or immunity of a citizen of the United States secured against state abridgment by Section 1 of the Fourteenth Amendment." To decide otherwise, the Court argued, would be to reduce "[c]itizenship of the United States [to] little better than a name." Justice Harlan Fisk Stone disagreed, charging the Court with unnecessarily creating "novel constitutional doctrine" when it could have relied on the First Amendment. Perhaps the Court's doctrinal choice lay in the perception that a more specific ruling based on labor rights was less of a departure, less controversial, than a broader First Amendment ruling.[37]

Even when the Court began moving toward a general First Amendment right to picket peacefully, it continued to emphasize the importance of picketing in labor disputes. "In the circumstances of our times," Justice Frank Murphy opined in *Thornhill v. Alabama* in 1940, "[f]ree discussion concerning the conditions in industry and the causes of labor disputes [is] indispensable to the effective and intelligent use of the processes of popular government to shape the destiny of modern industrial society." In 1950, a legal scholar described *Thornhill* as "the high water mark in the constitutional rights of labor." Supreme Court watcher C. Herman Pritchett wrote sometime later, "The Roosevelt Court's concern for the protection of labor and for the maintenance of civil liberties generally tended to re-enforce each other, as when labor's right to picket [was] assimilated into the larger problem of freedom of speech." Fellow Court watcher Edward Corwin even went so far as to say that the Court had treated freedom of speech "as an adjunct of the 'rights of labor.'"[38]

In light of New Deal legislation and judicial opinions, a number of Court watchers and commentators believed that a new regime of collective labor rights had indeed replaced the old *Lochnerian* one. Corporate lawyer Grenville Clark, writing in the *Bill of Rights Review* in 1941, did not approve of what he saw as the Court's new support for labor rights. He described as a "perversion . . . of sound doctrines of civil liberty" the assertion that "[t]he right to strike [is] a conclusive argument against even the most moderate and reasonable regulatory provisions." He conceded, as he apparently felt he had to, "that the right to choose one's occupation and to quit work for any reason or no reason is a traditional American privilege of great importance and not to be lightly curtailed." But, he countered, "[I]t is to be hoped that some recent claims which seem to forget that the principle of relativity operates in the field of labor relations as in others, will be moderated." Writing in the same pages, prominent Chicago lawyer William B. Hale took an even more critical stance toward what he saw as the new "policy of the United States." "In the earlier decisions, the law [of liberty of contract] was applied to members of labor unions as well as to employers." But things had changed. In the current policy, he complained, "employers are restrained from entering into agreements to fix prices or to create monopolies which constitute unreasonable restraints of trade and may not organize themselves in any way which will produce these results." By contrast, "[l]abor unions are not so restrained but may take any peaceful action in order to increase their numbers, extend their organization through any industry or throughout all industries, even though the effect of such organization or the acts done in connection with it shall restrain commerce and thus affect competition."[39]

From the perspective of 1941, Corwin thought the Court had "contrived to compensate itself to an important extent for [its] seeming surrender of power" in the New Deal revolution. That compensation took the form of "setting [itself] up as a sort of superlegislature in the interest of organized labor." Corwin compared decisions from forty years earlier in which "the right of employers to the unrestricted use of their economic superiority in bargaining with employees, or those seeking employment, . . . appears as the very essence of 'liberty,' " with recent decisions in which "it is the opposed right of employees, or those seeking employment, to use their organizing strength which furnishes the term its special importance."[40]

As the 1930s came to an end, lawyers, judges, and scholars agreed (whatever their opinion on the matter) that new forms of labor rights were replacing the older *Lochner*ian regime. The rights of labor to organize, bargain, and strike, not the rights of the isolated individual to contract, now seemed paramount.

Just as legal observers began to get a handle on the new labor rights, World War II unsettled the political landscape once again. In the context of wartime economic mobilization, striking unions and workers became highly unpopular. Most unions agreed to a no-strike pledge for the duration of the war, though many workers engaged in unauthorized strikes. Low voter turnout, a flagging war effort, and popular resentment of federal regulation of the economy led to record gains for conservatives in the 1942 election. Congress then reined in the power of organized labor both on the shop floor and in the political arena. Congress imposed, among other things, a cooling-off period before unions could strike, criminal penalties for strike leaders under certain circumstances, and prohibitions on political contributions made by unions during the war.[41]

Not every twist and turn of wartime politics resulted in losses for the unions, however. The same economic necessity that made striking problematic continued to give workers some leverage. That leverage translated into legislative and administrative support for greater union security and limited but substantial wage increases. The result was a significant increase in union membership during the war (to 14.8 million), along with considerable improvements in the standard of living of unionized workers. And despite the political adversity they sometimes faced, the unions, and especially their rank-and-file members, continued to speak of labor rights.[42]

Moreover, the economic developments of the war kept economic rights politically salient. Liberal economists dominated some important New Deal and wartime federal agencies, most notably the National Resources Planning Board, and they continued to champion economic rights. So too did scholarly work in economics, law, politics, and philosophy. The speeches of the president himself figured most prominently in keeping labor and economic rights in the foreground of rights talk. In 1941, Roosevelt announced that the Four Freedoms essential for human flourishing included freedom from "want" and "fear" as well as the more traditional American freedoms of speech and worship. In 1944, he repeatedly publicized what he called an "Economic Bill of Rights" and a "Second Bill of Rights." These included the right to a job at an adequate wage, decent housing, medical care, and education, as well as security from the ravages of sickness, old age, accident, and unemployment. Roosevelt's support for these rights drew sustenance from and paralleled the related embrace of economic rights in other nations and in nascent international law.[43]

Particularly significant to legal scholars and lawyers attempting to sort out the possibilities for new civil rights were the signals the elite legal academics of the American Law Institute (ALI) broadcast. The ALI convened an international committee to write up the "Essential Statement of Human Rights." The final product emphasized that economic rights were a necessary part of any modern state. "Everyone has the right to work," the ALI announced, under reasonable conditions and, if necessary, at a job guaranteed by the state. The United Nations, established in 1945, basically agreed. Its charter pledged to promote "higher standards of living, full employment, and conditions of economic and social progress and development."[44]

These arguments maintained their cultural salience and political viability throughout the war. The 1944 election was not a resounding victory for Democrats, but they did regain some of the ground they had lost in 1942. When VJ Day finally arrived on August 15, 1945, the GI Bill made real for returning veterans many of the aspirations of the Second Bill of Rights. Moreover, "the right to work" seemed poised for American legislative enactment if not constitutional embrace. The Full Employment Bill of 1945 took as its starting point that "[a]ll Americans . . . have the right to useful, remunerative, regular, and full-time employment," and it obliged the federal government to vindicate that right.[45]

Just as World War II brought the full employment understanding of the "right to work" into national politics, so too it made prominent another meaning of "the right to work": what one Fair Employment Practice Committee (FEPC) bill described as "the right to work and to seek work without discrimination because of race, creed, color, national origin, or ancestry." For decades, organizations like the NAACP and the National Urban League had pursued African American rights in the courts, in electoral politics, and in negotiations with private businesses, unions, and other organizations. Prior to the 1940s, they saw little success in court. Of the few victories they managed, most occurred in cases in which *Lochner*ian rights to property or contract were also at stake.[46]

African Americans also wielded little political clout nationally before the war. More than three-quarters lived in the South before 1940, where they were almost completely disfranchised. Although the Great Migration of the World War I era brought more African Americans to northern cities where they could vote, they still lacked significant political power. And even when the New Deal offered African Americans federal assistance unprecedented in the twentieth century, many of its economic protections excluded most black workers, and almost all federal programs discriminated against African Americans. During the 1930s, white liberals often treated the rights of African Americans as subsidiary to, and basically addressed by, labor and economic rights. This approach fit relatively comfortably within a Democratic Party whose success rested in some measure on the support of white southerners.[47]

With the onset of World War II, all of that changed. The war's domestic and international dimensions gave black civil rights greater salience both in mainstream political discourse and among legal professionals. The mobilizing economy once again drew African Americans out of the South into northern and western regions where they could vote. As they turned increasingly to the Democratic Party, their political support became critical to its success. Bolstering their protests with reference to the war, African Americans engaged in what the *Pittsburgh Courier* dubbed a "Double V" campaign for victory against fascism at home and abroad. In unions, the military, organizations like the NAACP, and outspoken black newspapers, African Americans protested American segregation, discrimination, and inequality. Even those who lacked such organizational support protested on a more individual level—on streetcars in the South, in relationships with employers, and by calling on the federal government to vindicate their rights.[48]

The most prominent black civil rights issue during the war—"the right to work . . . without discrimination" in war industries and labor unions—capitalized on the labor and economic rights that were also prominent. In fact, contemporaries used a wide variety of phrases to describe the problems black workers faced in industry: "the right to work without discrimination," "economic discrimination," "racial-economic discrimination," and the denial of "economic equality . . . because of . . . color." These phrases all drew on the prominence of labor and economic rights and used that prominence for the benefit of black workers.[49]

Embracing these new rights was not without its problems and potential downsides for African Americans. Mostly white unions were historically hostile to African American membership, and black leaders, workers, and lawyers alike had long debated whether and on what terms African American workers should pursue union membership. Some saw alliances with industry as more promising than those with white workers. Others turned cautiously but optimistically to cross-race, class-based strategies for economic change in Popular Front organizations and amenable unions.[50]

The possibility that greater union power under the NLRA would harm black workers heightened these conflicts in the mid-1930s. African American leaders sought a provision in the NLRA that prohibited protected unions from discriminating on the basis of race. Senate shepherds of the bill rejected the proposal, worried that it would doom the NLRA's passage altogether. Even without the provision, many African Americans embraced the bill, labor rights, and unions themselves. They saw potential benefits in the growing power of organized labor, the rising prominence of labor rights, and the increased opportunities in the war economy for black workers. National support for workers could, African American workers and leaders realized, redound to the benefit of black workers as well as white ones.[51]

Indeed, both the most visible African American protests and the most significant federal initiatives on race during the war not coincidentally overlapped with the labor and economic rights that were also prominent. The black protest activity of the era was not simply a generic precondition for the racial change that was to come. Rather, it frequently involved African American workers attempting to harness the rights white workers had already begun enjoying in the 1930s. Unions in every region became particularly fertile sites for African American activism. Much of that activism concerned the right to work without discrimination and under adequate conditions. At the national level, it was A. Philip Randolph and his all-black union, the

Brotherhood of Sleeping Car Porters, who initiated the generally acknowledged preeminent racial protest during the early 1940s. Unless
the federal government eliminated discrimination in government contracts, war industries, and the military, Randolph—along with other
African American leaders—threatened to march on Washington with
100,000 African Americans by his side. President Roosevelt successfully
appeased Randolph and forestalled the march by issuing an executive
order creating the FEPC. Roosevelt made nondiscrimination in employment federal policy, and he charged the committee with investigating and publicizing race discrimination in war production. Many
were dissatisfied with Roosevelt's failure to desegregate the military
and with the weakness of the FEPC's enforcement mechanisms.
Others, like the black *Amsterdam News,* declared the order "epochal to
say the least. . . . If President Lincoln's proclamation was designed to
end physical slavery, it would seem that the recent order of President
Roosevelt is designed to end, or at least curb, economic slavery."[52]

The federal government took additional, though equally equivocal,
actions to protect the rights of African American laborers during the
war. The War Labor Board required the elimination of wage differentials based on race. The NLRB sanctioned unions for some, though
not all, racial discrimination and exclusion. And the United States Employment Service (USES) made halting progress toward nondiscrimination in its role as liaison between would-be workers and potential
employers. FDR himself, often hesitant to alienate his southern party
members by supporting black civil rights, even took to clarifying in his
key 1944 speeches that the Second Bill of Rights should apply to all,
"regardless of station, race, or creed."[53]

The prominence of labor and economic rights for all workers and
specifically for African American workers continued even as the political context changed yet again with the end of World War II. As part of
the Cold War with the Soviet Union that followed, President Truman
expounded the Truman Doctrine and the Marshall Plan, committed
the United States to non-Communist NATO, and involved the nation
in the Korean War in the late 1940s and early 1950s. Domestic repression grew along with the Cold War. The House Un-American Activities
Committee (HUAC) investigated possibly subversive activities, and
Senator Joseph McCarthy initiated his own witch-hunts. Unwilling to

allow Republicans to monopolize political traction from the specter of domestic Communism, Truman instituted his own loyalty program for the federal government.[54]

These international and domestic developments led to an intense contestation over the contours of the rights that had come to prominence during the Depression and World War II. On the one hand, claims about the government's responsibility for individual or collective economic well-being and racial reform could be, and often were, vulnerable to attack as Communist or socialist. Such attacks combined with an increase in conservative power nationally to defeat many pro-labor and pro-African American legislative initiatives. The watered-down Employment Act that passed in 1946 traded "full" for "maximum employment," placed no requirement on the federal government to ensure even the lower standard, and eliminated mention of any right to employment. In addition to the failed Full Employment Act, both unions and the goals of workers were weakened by the failure of the fight for a permanent FEPC, the success of conservatives in limiting the reach of the Fair Labor Standards Act in the Portal-to-Portal Act, and the passage of the Administrative Procedure Act.[55]

Moreover, "the right to work" took on a new and quite incompatible meaning after Republicans gained control of Congress in the 1946 elections. A coalition of Republicans and southern Democrats passed the antilabor Taft-Hartley amendments to the NLRA. Taft-Hartley was perhaps most famous and vilified for its restrictions on strikes and boycotts and its provisions excluding Communist-led unions from NLRA protections. The purges of those who refused to sign the required loyalty oath meant the loss of the most left-leaning union members and led to greater bureaucratization of union functions. Also problematic for unions was a provision that allowed for state open-shop laws. As state after state, especially in the already hard to organize South, prohibited the closed shop, the security unions had enjoyed during the war began to dissipate. Organized labor's opponents described this trend as vindicating a "right to work" very different from the right to work at a decent job provided by the government or the right to work without race discrimination. They sought and frequently obtained a right to work more directly reminiscent of the *Lochner* era: the individual right to work without joining a union.[56]

Even legislative attacks on unions and the intensifying Cold War did not, however, completely vitiate either union power or the prominence of collective labor and economic rights. Union density continued to increase throughout the 1940s and the early 1950s to a height of over 30 percent of the non-farm labor force. It was not until the very end of the 1940s that the Supreme Court began pulling back on its association of labor rights with free speech rights. Even as late as 1948, commentators continued to see labor and free speech rights as fundamentally linked.[57]

As for economic rights, FDR's Four Freedoms and his Economic Bill of Rights continued to mark the writings of economic planners, economists, political scientists, philosophers, politicians, and anti-Communist liberal organizations like the Americans for Democratic Action. Economic rights also flourished in influential international discourse. The 1948 United Nations Universal Declaration of Human Rights, for example, drew on the ALI's Essential Statement of Human Rights to elaborate upon the economic rights the United Nations Charter had already embraced.[58]

Indeed, postwar economic rights gained some traction from the Cold War even as domestic anti-Communism narrowed acceptable political and economic discourse. When President Truman introduced his Fair Deal in 1949, it had all the hallmarks of the economic rights that had begun in the New Deal and carried through World War II. The Fair Deal proposed to raise the American standard of living; to provide medical care, housing, and education; and to reinvigorate the rights of labor by repealing the Taft-Hartley Act. Truman explicitly framed these labor and economic rights for the Cold War era, declaring that "[o]ur domestic programs are the foundation of our foreign policy." The United States' simultaneous fulfillment of both traditional American political rights and newly minted economic rights could actually serve as a weapon in the Cold War. It would demonstrate American superiority in all realms over the Soviet Union. That Truman's proposals ultimately failed attests to the power of Republicans and southern Democrats during the Cold War. But Truman's continued support of labor and economic rights attests as much to the considerable position such rights claims continued to hold in mainstream political discourse.[59]

Moreover, legislative defeats for the new rights were hardly absolute. When Truman succeeded in expanding Social Security in 1950 to include some agricultural and domestic workers, few southern Democrats or conservative Republicans opposed him. And it was under Republican President Dwight Eisenhower that Congress in 1954 finally included most agricultural and domestic workers (except the least regularly employed) for Social Security coverage. Social Security—the embodiment of some of the New Deal's most basic economic rights—was no longer a partisan program or a marginal aspiration. It was a fact of American life. "Should any political party attempt to abolish social security," Eisenhower thought, "you would not hear of that party again in our political history."[60]

Much as conservatives tried, the Cold War and domestic conservatism also failed to inter the rights of African Americans in the postwar period. The chilling Cold War had a paradoxical effect on the possibilities for racial change. Although domestic anti-Communism narrowed racial discourse just as it narrowed labor and economic discourse, the Cold War simultaneously created a political imperative to address racial inequality. As the United States competed with the Soviet Union for the loyalty of the developing world, domestic racial concerns became a flashpoint for international propaganda. Progress on the American treatment of African Americans offered a way to deflect Soviet criticism and prevent Communist defections in decolonized nations in Asia and Africa.[61]

Domestic political concerns reinforced international incentives for government officials to pay attention to the rights of African Americans. As World War II ended, a rash of lynchings, particularly of returning black veterans, kept African Americans in a heightened state of vigilance for their rights. Empowered by their experiences in the military, in unions, and in cities, black individuals and civil rights groups grew more vocal and organized. Support of this energized black electorate grew more important to the Democratic Party as its sectional cleavages widened. The party could no longer count on the support of white southerners. Rather than find a majority through some northern and some southern support, the party relied more heavily on northern states in which African Americans increasingly held the electoral balance. The 1948 Democratic platform emphasized black civil rights to such an extent that the party's southern wing walked out of the presidential nominating convention, created its own party, and fielded its own candidate.

Once again, the racial questions that dominated national discussion after the war concerned the working lives and economic status of African Americans. In part, this stemmed from new economic realities. Both the return of white veterans to jobs newly held by black workers and the economic dislocations that accompanied peacetime reconversion meant that the gains black workers accrued during the war were fragile. In part, however, it stemmed from the fact that such issues drew sustenance from a still-robust rhetoric of economic rights.[62]

As a result, throughout the late 1940s and early 1950s, economic discrimination remained a key civil rights issue in national politics. The landmark 1947 report of the President's Committee on Civil Rights reflected the continued importance of economic discrimination. It quoted African American sociologist Charles S. Johnson as declaring that "the biggest single forward surge of Negroes into the main stream of American life in the past ten years has been their movement into the ranks of organized labor." The first topic discussed under the heading "the right to equality of opportunity" was not education, as one might have expected from the vantage point of 1954, but "the right to employment." It was telling that the report discussed that right in far more detail than any other issue—spending nearly twice as much space on it as on education, housing, or health care.[63]

Moreover, permanent FEPCs remained a key legislative goal of African Americans. Between 1945 and 1955, twelve states and additional localities passed FEP bills. Every year during this period, senators and congressmen submitted bills for a permanent FEPC. Although southern congressional power frustrated the passage of such bills, the Democratic Party included a permanent FEPC as a major component of its far-reaching 1948 civil rights platform. That same year, by executive order, Truman both desegregated the military and renewed executive commitment to nondiscrimination in federal employment. In 1951, he extended the prohibition on employment discrimination to federal contractors. In 1953, even Eisenhower, a reluctant supporter of African American civil rights, followed the by then decade-long precedent of taking executive action to eliminate discrimination in government contracting. Eisenhower endowed his compliance committee with weight by placing Vice President Richard Nixon, who then had a progressive record on race, at its head.[64]

Into the 1950s, economists and social scientists concerned with economic discrimination argued that "fair employment" could not succeed without "full employment." "Full employment and a feeling of security on the part of America's workers are necessary conditions for the successful functioning of FEPC laws," historian and civil rights scholar Louis Ruchames wrote in 1953. Without full employment, fair employment efforts were "doomed to failure." The rights of African Americans still seemed, to a considerable extent, bound closely together with the rights of workers of all races.[65]

Uncertainties in the legal doctrine of civil rights in the 1940s underscored the complex interaction of economic and racial rights. When *Lochner* lost its hold, no single new approach to civil rights cases involving race took its place in Supreme Court doctrine. During the 1940s and early 1950s, the Supreme Court vindicated black civil rights in a smattering of cases. The cases concerned various aspects of economic, social, and political life in Jim Crow America: peonage, union discrimination, police brutality, voting rights, graduate education, and interstate transportation. And they involved a variety of constitutional and statutory provisions: the Thirteenth Amendment, the equal protection clause of the Fourteenth Amendment, the due process clause of the Fifth Amendment, the Peonage Act of 1867, the Civil Rights Act of 1866, the Interstate Commerce Act of 1887, and the Railway Labor Act of 1926.[66]

If the Supreme Court appeared to be moving in any particular direction in its race cases, it was toward expanding the Fourteenth Amendment's equal protection clause to apply to private actors. Private actors generally had not been vulnerable to Fourteenth Amendment challenges since the *Civil Rights Cases* limited the Fourteenth Amendment to state action in 1883. Yet during the 1940s, in both the race context and beyond, the Court suggested that the Constitution could redress rights violations perpetrated by private individuals as well as the state itself. In *Smith v. Allwright*, for example, the Court struck down the white primary by finding that Texas's essentially privatized primary process could be attributed to the state itself. When the privilege of private party membership "is also the essential qualification for voting in a primary to select nominees for a general election," the Court concluded, "the State makes the action of the party the action of the State." Beyond the race context, in *Marsh v. Alabama*, the

Court treated a privately owned company town as a state actor for First Amendment purposes. By 1948, in the case of *Shelley v. Kraemer,* the Department of Justice suggested in its brief that whether the Fourteenth Amendment only applied to state action remained an open question. Without answering that question conclusively, the Supreme Court in *Shelley* found state action in the judicial enforcement of an entirely private agreement between private parties that limited the sale of certain property to whites only. Scholars and civil rights lawyers like Osmond K. Fraenkel concluded that "[t]here are possibilities . . . that the rights guaranteed by the 14th Amendment may be extended over areas previously considered wholly private."[67]

Less obvious during the 1940s was whether the Court would treat race as a unique doctrinal category unto itself, and if so, what kind of solicitude it would provide the rights of African Americans. Even before the war began, the Court seemed to suggest a possible new paradigm in *United States v. Carolene Products Co.* In its 1938 opinion, the Court reviewed the constitutionality of a federal statute penalizing the shipment of filled milk in interstate or foreign commerce. Speaking for the Court, Justice Stone upheld the act in a routine application of the Court's post-*Lochner* presumption that rational economic regulation was constitutional. Congress was well within its power when it frowned on the shipment of milk in which the butterfat was removed and replaced with cheaper and less nutritious coconut oil. Such legislation was no longer vulnerable to constitutional challenges that might have succeeded during the *Lochner* era. The Court would no longer closely scrutinize federal regulation of the economy.[68]

Where Justice Stone broke new ground was in suggesting greater judicial scrutiny for other kinds of governmental action. He floated the idea in what would become, in another justice's words some forty years later, "the most celebrated footnote in constitutional law." In footnote four of the opinion, Justice Stone explored the possibility that although economic regulation would no longer receive the kind of scrutiny it had in the *Lochner* era, some types of government action might warrant heightened judicial scrutiny. Justice Stone suggested that the Court might more strictly review laws under three different conditions: where a specific constitutional prohibition existed, where political processes were inhibited, or where "discrete and insular minorities" were affected. Heightened scrutiny under these circumstances would likely lead to the constitutional invalidation of state and federal actions.[69]

In the years after *Brown v. Board of Education,* legal scholars and jurists re-created a historical pedigree for *Brown* that began with footnote four. The footnote, they argued, offered an immediate replacement to the *Lochner*-era understanding of the Court's role in protecting individual rights. Rather than protect contract and property rights, scholars re-called, the Court had decided in *Carolene Products* in 1938 that it would protect the rights of minorities, especially racial minorities. *Brown* was merely the culmination of a well-settled constitutional framework for individual rights created as the *Lochner* era ended.[70]

Throughout the 1940s, however, any new constitutional paradigm embodied in the footnote remained just a suggestion. *Carolene Products'* footnote four did not actually govern either Supreme Court or lower court decisions on race, and it did not capture the attention of legal academics. Lawyers thinking about civil rights in the 1940s did not see *Carolene Products* as an established new paradigm and did not see their role as bringing cases within that paradigm.

Had the Supreme Court quickly applied this new standard to the race context, it might have provided some certainty in civil rights cases concerning racial minorities. But even when clear opportunities to apply *Carolene Products* in the race context arose, the Court did not embrace them for some time. A few months after the Court decided *Carolene Products,* it passed up its first opportunity to apply footnote four. In *Missouri ex rel. Gaines v. Canada,* the Court found unconstitutional Missouri's failure to provide a state law school for black residents as it did for white residents. Despite that ruling, the Court neither cited *Carolene Products* nor applied its reasoning.[71]

In the 1944 case of *Korematsu v. United States,* the Court came closer to, but again shied away from, applying footnote four explicitly. The Court upheld the decision of the United States Army (as authorized by executive order) to exclude Americans of Japanese ancestry from certain geographic areas that the Army deemed vulnerable in light of the war with Japan. In what has become iconic language, the Court stated that "all legal restrictions which curtail the civil rights of a single racial group are immediately suspect" and that "courts must subject them to the most rigid scrutiny." These statements echoed the Court's opinion from the year before in *Hirabayashi v. United States,* which described "[d]istinctions between citizens solely because of their ancestry" as "odious" even as it upheld a curfew for Japanese Americans. And they implicitly recalled footnote four's presumption that the Court would not allow state-enacted racial classifications—regulations that single out groups based on their race—except under unusual circumstances.[72]

Yet in neither *Hirabayashi* nor *Korematsu* did the Court embrace the obvious opportunity to invoke footnote four explicitly. Although the Court indicated in *Korematsu* that it would scrutinize more strictly any government activity that singled out racial minorities, it did not actually cite *Carolene Products*. And even if the reasoning of *Korematsu* and *Carolene Products*—that some kind of stricter scrutiny might be appropriate for race cases—was cut from the same cloth, *Korematsu* upheld the racially discriminatory regulation at issue.

Had the Court linked *Carolene Products* and *Korematsu* in 1944, it might have established a determinative civil rights framework centered on race. That still would have left the contours of civil rights doctrine uncertain between 1938 and 1944, but it would have clarified the doctrine for the rest of the decade. The Court would have subjected state racial classifications but not nonracial government regulation to rigorous judicial review. Had that been the case, then the days of *Plessy v. Ferguson* would have been over. In *Plessy*, the Court had allowed segregation as a reasonable exercise of governmental power. If the Court had adopted a strict standard of review for racial classifications, it would likely have doomed *Plessy* as a precedent.

But throughout the 1940s, the Court mostly ignored footnote four, and it certainly did not link *Carolene Products* and *Korematsu*. During a decade in which African Americans gained increasing political support, the courts provided no settled framework for the judicial protection of their rights. Louis Lusky, Justice Stone's law clerk when *Carolene Products* was written, had it right. "The Footnote was being offered," he later wrote, "not as a settled theorem of government or Court-approved standard of judicial review, but as a starting point for debate—in the spirit of inquiry, the spirit of the Enlightenment. . . . [I]t did not purport to *decide* anything; it merely made some suggestions for future consideration."[73]

That future consideration did not arrive for some time. Neither *Carolene Products* nor *Korematsu* played a significant role in judicial or scholarly discussions of the civil rights of racial minorities in the 1940s. No court addressed *Carolene Products'* footnote four in connection with racial inequality and discrimination until 1947. Even then, the one lower court to cite it did not understand the Supreme Court to have clearly differentiated between economic and racial regulation or to have established greater scrutiny for the latter set of cases. In *Takahashi v. Fish and Game Commission,* the California Supreme Court divided on the constitutionality of a state statute limiting those eligible for commercial fishing licenses to citizens and aliens eligible for United States citizenship. This meant that Japanese aliens, who were not so eligible at the time, were denied fishing licenses. In response to Takahashi's equal protection challenge, the court read *Carolene Products* as limiting the general presumption of constitutionality only "where the legislation attempts to restrict fundamental liberties." Concluding that commercial fishing was not such a fundamental liberty, the classification needed only be reasonable. According to the court, it was not only reasonable but "logical and fair." Significantly, the dissent applied the same standard of reasonableness but came to a different conclusion: It found "no conceivable basis for discrimination between different classes of aliens."[74]

Korematsu's relative absence from judicial opinions—and its confused meaning where it did appear—is similarly striking. Even when courts began to invoke *Korematsu* and *Hirabayashi* in race cases later in the decade, they were uncertain of the opinions' meaning. Some judges seemed to take as a lesson the opposite of what we today think *Korematsu* and *Hirabayashi* meant. They cited *Hirabayashi* for the proposition that "where factors relevant to the attainment of legitimate legislative policies are shown, their use as a basis for distinction is not to be condemned." Others thought that *Hirabayashi* prohibited only "arbitrary and groundless distinctions between citizens." Only once, and only at the end of the decade, did a court use a "compelling justification" standard explicitly on behalf of a minority group.[75]

Indeed, the Supreme Court itself was equivocal in the few cases at the end of the decade in which it cited *Korematsu* or *Hirabayashi*. The only case in which the Supreme Court seemed to see *Hirabayashi* as having created a higher standard was *Oyama v. California* in 1948. There the Court considered the effects on Japanese American citizens of California's ban on land ownership by aliens ineligible for naturalization.

The Court struck down the law. Nonetheless, the case reflected considerable confusion about the governing doctrinal rules. In his concurrence, Justice Murphy, perhaps the staunchest supporter of the rights of Japanese Americans on the Court at the time, vacillated between "rigid scrutiny" and a "rational basis" review in which "those factors which reflect racial animosity" were "render[ed] irrational." Thus, Murphy would likely have struck down much discriminatory legislation not because he would have reviewed it more stringently than ordinary economic legislation. He would have done so because it would have failed even to pass the generally applicable standard of reasonableness.[76]

Not only did courts in the 1940s fail to embrace *Carolene Products, Korematsu,* and *Hirabayashi,* but so did scholars. Three new journals largely committed to civil rights began publication at the beginning of the war: the *Bill of Rights Review,* published by the Civil Rights Committee of the conservative American Bar Association; the left-leaning *Lawyers Guild Review;* and the *National Bar Journal,* the journal of the all-black National Bar Association. None of these journals mentioned *Carolene Products* at all during the war. In fact, *Carolene Products* appeared only twice in any article in a major law review. *Korematsu* and *Hirabayashi* received some attention during the mid-1940s, but most articles concerned the specific outcomes of the cases, not any new legal standard they might have created.[77]

A case note discussing 1938's *Missouri ex rel. Gaines v. Canada* is telling. The author saw the Court's invalidation of Missouri's racially unequal provision of higher education as still clearly within both *Plessy*'s reasonableness standard and the old undifferentiated equal protection clause. He described the equal protection clause as "vitiat[ing] what is done only when it is without any reasonable basis in point of fact." The author then cited an economic regulation case, showing that the author saw no need to differentiate between economic and racial regulation cases. Under the reasonableness standard, segregation continued to pass muster. An article on racial discrimination in jury service in 1939 similarly described "[c]apricious and arbitrary exclusion of certain classes" as the Fourteenth Amendment's prohibition and "reasonable and legitimate" as its governing standard.[78]

A few articles in the late 1940s began to make more substantial use of *Carolene Products* and *Korematsu* in discussing the rights of national and racial minorities. These referred mostly to the rights of Japanese citizens and noncitizens, not to the rights of African Americans, racial minorities, or noncitizens generally. Only a few scattered law review articles in the late 1940s began to apply *Carolene Products* and *Korematsu* to cases involving black rights. But these articles demonstrated that the cases began their real rise to prominence in race cases only after civil rights lawyers had begun to see some success on other grounds. The fame of the footnote derived less from its role as a resource for civil rights lawyers during the 1940s and more from its character as a by-product of their successes using other resources.[79]

For lawyers working on civil rights cases in the 1940s, it did not appear that *Carolene Products* had wholesale replaced *Lochner*. It did not seem that their work was simply to bring cases under a new legal standard. Race cases, and commentary about them, continued to discuss "unconstitutional," "unreasonable," and "irrational" discrimination. These cases indicated that *Plessy* still reigned, that economic and racial regulation had not been doctrinally disaggregated, and that *Carolene Products, Hirabayashi,* and *Korematsu* were not yet seen to have inaugurated the new legal doctrine they would eventually represent. Indeed, in 1949, a pair of respected legal scholars explicitly discussed how the standard of review for equal protection challenges to racial regulation was in considerable flux. Equal protection doctrine prohibiting discriminatory legislation "is variously phrased." "[W]here the clause is held to govern," they concluded, "its application is halting, indecisive, and unpredictable."[80]

Throughout the 1940s, then, the Supreme Court's approach to race cases remained unclear. Indeed, the legal revolution that the New Deal had wrought had not come to a settled place in constitutional law. The Court had not decided whether the collective rights of laborers would find distinctive constitutional protection, whether the demise of *Lochner* would lead to the demise of *Plessy*, whether economic regulation and racial classifications would receive different constitutional treatment, or whether equal protection would serve as the center of civil rights.

More broadly, both labor and economic rights and the rights of African Americans remained politically salient to American conceptions of individual rights. For lawyers practicing at such a time, the ultimate role that race, labor, and economic rights would play in modern civil rights conceptions, and their possible relationships, remained uncertain. Would additional political upheavals continue to highlight racial, labor, and economic rights, and if so, in what way? Would the national will to address race discrimination fade with the war and a reassertion of southern Democratic power? Or would the rights of African Americans come to define the legal meaning of civil rights? To civil rights lawyers in such a time of change, the answers to these questions were unknown and unknowable.

All these questions would have to be decided in the context of both the politics of the day and the concrete cases civil rights lawyers ultimately decided to bring to court. The legal strategies lawyers would pursue depended on who complained to them, and what they complained about—the complainants' identities, the harms they suffered, and the kinds of rights those harms implied. Those strategies also depended on the institutional location of different lawyers—whether they worked for the government or a private association—and on the lawyers' attendant goals, political constraints, financial resources, and personal proclivities. And finally, those strategies depended on what lawyers understood was, or was becoming, or was still, governing constitutional law.

How civil rights lawyers responded to the doctrinal opportunities and limitations they faced within a rapidly changing legal and political climate fills the remainder of this book. In re-creating the process by which these lawyers undertook the work of civil rights in the 1940s, I begin with those at the beginning of the law-creation process—the complainants themselves.

TWO

◆ ◆ ◆

Claiming Rights in the Agricultural South

> We live's in a free house such as it is, but you can't
> live in the free house with nothing to eat one half of
> the time and no shoes and cloth to wear in the
> winter.
>
> Robert Hammond, letter to the NAACP, 1947

IN NOVEMBER 1943, A man signing his name Col. Elton D. Wright VI wrote the Department of Justice. "I am only asking for my rights the above named men violated the citizens rights bill of the constitution of the U.S.A. by compelling me to work for them at low wage unfair and inhuman treatment, threatenad me with death." Throughout the 1940s, rural African Americans sought similar help from the Department of Justice's Civil Rights Section in Washington, D.C., and the NAACP's national office in New York City. Letters came from cotton pickers and sugarcane choppers, from workers at turpentine stills and lumber yards. Poor, isolated blacks across the South wrote about powerful landlords and conspiratorial government officials. They described trying unsuccessfully to protect their property and their persons. They expressed the desire to move and the frustrations of not being able to make a living. They used terms like "slavery," "involuntary servitude," and "peonage" to portray their experiences. They charged "violat[ions] under the Federal Civil Rights statute and under the Thirteenth Amendment to the Constitution."[1]

Some letters came directly from workers themselves. Others came from organizations and individuals assisting the workers. Whereas some writers emphasized need and helplessness, others used the language of legal rights. Some set forth their grievances in barely literate prose. Others filed affidavits with private lawyers or told their stories to investigators from the Federal Bureau of Investigation (FBI) who transcribed them into formal legal complaints.[2]

51

However rhetorically shaped, the complaints reveal the continuing power of the system of racial subordination and economic exploitation that had dominated the rural South since the late nineteenth century. To be sure, many African Americans had left the region since then. Indeed, during the 1940s alone, almost 1 million left for better prospects in booming war industries and the armed forces. But the wartime transformation of American economic and political life had a paradoxical effect on southern agriculture. On the one hand, it opened up new economic opportunities and fostered a greater sense of political empowerment among African Americans. On the other hand, it made white planters all the more determined to maintain control over increasingly assertive black workers. The result was that for the 29 percent of African Americans who stayed in the rural South as late as 1950, much remained the same seventy-five years after the end of chattel slavery.[3]

The appeals of those left behind are important both for what they reveal about the world of Jim Crow in the rural South of the 1940s and for what they reveal about the claims being made by those who would resist it. Each complaint on its own provides only a starting point for this unveiling. Each marks a single intervention into the Jim Crow system, framed and limited by the writer's own experiences. Taken together, however, the complaints illustrate how the system of southern agriculture in the 1940s depended upon both public and private power and both racial and economic domination. The complaints show in particular how white planters and employers used three interrelated types of power to maintain dominance: private economic and physical force; state and local laws that had their roots in the postbellum era; and federal, state, and local laws enacted in response to the Depression and World War II. The complaints thus expose Jim Crow in the rural South as a fully integrated, public and private, racial and economic caste system.

What the complaints reveal about the civil rights possibilities for challenging that structure is equally important. To read the words of the workers themselves is to understand not only the nature of the harms they suffered but also the nature of the rights they wanted vindicated. Like the system that produced their complaints, the rights African American farmworkers sought were both racial and economic. The complaints of African American agricultural workers thus implicated the two most prominent understandings of civil rights at the time.

Ever since the end of slavery, powerful white planters had used every available means—political, economic, legal, violent—to control the black workers the Thirteenth Amendment had forced them to free from slavery. They disfranchised African Americans and excluded them from juries. They created an agricultural system that often kept black farmworkers indebted and immobile. When all else failed, whites terrorized African Americans with lynchings, outright servitude, and other forms of violence.

To some extent, white control over black agricultural labor loosened during the first half of the twentieth century. The Great Migration during and after World War I began the process. In the 1920s, blacks left for more propitious economic prospects and more favorable political, social, and cultural lives elsewhere. For very different economic reasons, the Depression continued the exodus: African Americans were pushed off plantations by a combination of unprofitable crops, New Deal agricultural policies, and farm mechanization. With less opportunity for any work other than seasonal wage labor, many black farmworkers were less attached to the land and the region. They sought work elsewhere.[4]

World War II transformed national economic opportunities for black workers even more dramatically. Booming wartime industry and the tighter American labor market it fostered offered many African Americans opportunities for more lucrative, more independent, less back-breaking work. Black men and women who may never have earned anything but scrip good in the company store could earn cash wages outside rural areas. Women also found themselves occasionally able to get by without working, living instead on the dependent checks they received from relatives in the military. Not only did new destinations attract African Americans, but higher wages meant more mobility. African Americans could buy cars and more readily move when better work beckoned. White farmers complained to federal officials in the Department of Agriculture's Bureau of Agricultural Economics (BAE) that they were "losing the best workers to the airports and to the Army and to the labor battalions." One Florida farmer told a federal official, "[W]e have the dreg labor here, the sorriest labor there is."[5]

The national demand for wartime labor even redounded to the benefit of some black workers who remained in the rural South. Some managed to avoid debt to planters because of higher crop prices and higher wages. Others controlled their time. They worked fewer hours for more money. This concerned white planters. "The problem," one planter complained, was "that the Negroes are getting from five to ten times as much money as they used to for farm work here and it has ruined them." Said another white farmer, "We have had a system of two Negroes for one job and now we have got ten jobs for one Negro." Workers could now dictate when, how long, and for how much they would work. "[T]hey will work two or three days a week—just long enough to get the money that they want to spend and then they quit," another farmer grumbled. "The Negroes go to the field and look at the beans and if they think that they are not ready to pick they just walk off and say that they will be back in a day or two and there is nothing you can do about it." Yet another complained, "Five days a week is the most that we can depend on for getting them (any workers here) to work; working on Saturday for these Negroes is a thing of the past."[6]

As these comments suggest, blacks were asserting their autonomy with unprecedented boldness. This newfound independence challenged planters' sense of order and stiffened their resolve to resist change. Planters blamed some of the African American workers' assertiveness on their uprootedness. "You can take a good Negro and make a migrant out of him and he will be as sorry as can be," one farmer complained. "[T]hey lose the association of white people that know them and they get to where they don't care."[7]

Uprootedness was hardly the only problem. White landlords and farmowners complained that the "perfect harmony" they had previously shared with African American workers was "under attack by the New Deal, assisted by the President's wife, the FSA [Farm Security Administration], and the CIO [Congress of Industrial Organizations]." They also blamed the socialist-led Southern Tenant Farmers' Union (STFU) and "[a]ll the Negro papers up north . . . running articles written by Jews playing up incidents of where Negroes are beat up, playing up the mistreatment of Negroes." Such articles were "getting these Negroes stirred up here." One BAE investigator saw a variety of "forces disrupting old relationships." Among these were "Negro movements" increasing "race consciousness" and "strong demands for equal rights";

"[i]ncreasing federal activity in the South"; union officials and "liberals" condemning discrimination; "war aims" stated "broadly as freedom, equal rights and equal opportunities for all peoples"; and the increasing number of northerners in the South, especially northern African American soldiers. As a home supervisor for the FSA recognized, "The farmers used to drive [the negroes] and they have got to get that out of their minds. . . . Things are changing, and they are going to have to change their mind about labor."[8]

But many white farmers were not ready for change. Rather than pay higher wages, landowners tried to find new sources of free or cheap labor. They persuaded the federal government to contract with Mexico and countries in the Caribbean to import workers. They used Axis prisoners of war. And they capitalized on the Department of Agriculture's campaign to encourage people from all walks of life—schoolchildren, city dwellers, the elderly—to do their patriotic part by performing farm labor.[9]

Most importantly, white planters resisted the new assertions of African American independence. Convinced that higher wages and better working conditions would not solve their problems, farmers ignored those regular market mechanisms in favor of force and coercion. They would simply make African Americans work. "Negroes have got to be bossed," one planter commented, "and you can't boss them when they make that kind of money and when they can get another job anywhere they want it." As political scientist Howard Devon Hamilton mused in 1951, "[S]omehow the natural laws of economics do not work . . . in the cotton belt." One FSA home supervisor clearly supported planters' efforts. "We have plenty of labor here but they will not work—why not make them work?" she asked. "The southern darkie stops working when he gets the money that he wants—they are just born that way. They should be made to work; put them in uniform just like the soldier and put them to work."[10]

Taking note of such attitudes, observers across the political spectrum commented on the deep continuities throughout southern history of freely exploiting black labor. According to at least one planter, the laws and customs of the twentieth-century South enabled the white landlord to "treat [his Negroes] like some planters did in 1850." The Workers' Defense League (WDL) reported how "intimidation and often violence are used to keep sharecroppers and day laborers in virtual slavery despite a Supreme Court ruling of long standing that it is contrary to the Thirteenth Amendment to exact forced labor because of actual or alleged debt." The WDL saw such peonage as existing "in many sections of the Deep South." William Henry Huff, an African American lawyer and vociferous opponent of involuntary servitude, called the situation to the attention of President Franklin Roosevelt. "I think you know by now that the Negro people of this country are looking to you for a new emancipation," Huff wrote. He wanted the president to abolish "for all time to come" "that new form of slavery known as peonage, which entered the back door as the Proclamation of immortal Lincoln drove chattel slavery out of the front door." At least some in the Roosevelt administration saw Huff's point. "[T]o a very large extent," thought Civil Rights Section attorney Eleanor Bontecou, "the Southern Negroes . . . were being treated in many cases as if there had never been a Reconstruction. They lived in fear just as they had many years ago."[11]

Indeed, the main change World War II wrought in southern agriculture was to make planters increasingly desperate to prevent change. The all-white Georgia Baptist Convention went so far as to conclude that "[t]here are more Negroes held by these debt slavers than there were actually owned as slaves before the Civil War between the states." Although that was certainly an exaggeration, the group was not alone in thinking that the problem was getting worse rather than better. Leslie Perry of the NAACP connected the "growing antagonism against the Negroes" to planters' worries about wages and labor availability. One federal government employee came up with a memorable phrase to capture his impressions of planters' efforts in 1941: "[t]he back-to-peonage campaign."[12]

That same year, Willie May Washington of Hattiesburg, Mississippi, begged the NAACP to help her aunt and uncle and their children. They were being held, she wrote, by "some old white farmer out from Maco Miss . . . oh thay are under slavery please Do some thing for them . . . we are afraid to go at there." Washington's letter offers a glimpse of the extent to which the "back-to-peonage campaign" was a product of the seemingly limitless private power of white planters and employers. Some seventy-five years after the Thirteenth Amendment outlawed "slavery and involuntary servitude," an "old white farmer" could simply hold a black family "under slavery."[13]

Complaints like Washington's are only comprehensible as a product of the basic political and economic structures of the agricultural South. Despite the Thirteenth Amendment, southern whites had recaptured, sometimes swiftly and sometimes incrementally, political and economic power over those they had once enslaved. As one observer commented in 1936, "Slavery was too integral a part of the social life of the South and too vital to the interests of certain classes to be suddenly eliminated by a mere constitutional amendment." Rather, the amendment made "necessary the finding of new ways of perpetuating the Negro's enslavement."[14]

Toward that end, whites established control over the legal system and political structures of the late-nineteenth-century South. This control allowed whites to dominate government at all levels into the 1940s. It also gave whites extensive private power by largely immunizing them from public oversight. Most black southerners, and especially rural southerners, could not vote, let alone hold public office. Despite favorable long-standing constitutional precedent, they could not sit on juries. Southern legislatures deemed even reading about elections or voting inappropriate for African Americans, and they required textbooks for Jim Crow schools to omit references to such topics.[15]

At every level and branch of governance, black agricultural workers were unrepresented. Whites with economic power over black farmworkers dominated the local boards and committees that implemented and administered various New Deal programs in agriculture, as well as wartime draft, wage, and price boards. African Americans did not serve as judges or police officers. In fact, those officials often perpetrated violence against African Americans rather than protected them from it. At the very least, white government officials, white police, and white juries acquiesced in racial violence committed by private white citizens. The President's Committee on Civil Rights observed in 1947 that "[t]he almost complete immunity from punishment enjoyed by lynchers is merely a striking form of the broad and general immunity from punishment enjoyed by whites in many communities for less extreme offenses against Negroes." Indeed, black southerners might not have directed their protests to lawyers outside the South if they had not been completely unrepresented in government and politics within the region.[16]

Such political powerlessness made possible, and was made possible by, an economic structure aimed at keeping black agricultural workers propertyless, dependent, and obedient. White planters desired cheap and docile labor whereas black farmworkers wanted financial and phys-

ical independence. The tenancy system that developed in the late nineteenth century facilitated white economic exploitation of black farmworkers while simultaneously making black land ownership a distant
possibility. As tenant farmers and more frequently sharecroppers, many
African Americans lived on the land of a (usually white) landowner.
They paid the landlord either with money made from the crop (as for
cash tenant farmers) or with a share of the crop (as was the case for
other types of tenants and sharecroppers). Those who could not even
afford such arrangements, or preferred mobility to potential advance-

African American sharecropper and wife, Mississippi, 1937. They have no
tools, stock, equipment, or garden. (Farm Security Administration, Office
of War Information Photograph Collection, Library of Congress.)

ment, worked as wage laborers. They had no stake in the land they tilled and even less hope of eventually owning their own land.[17]

Planters tried to ensure that both renters—tenant farmers or share-croppers—and wage laborers lived within a closed economic universe. They wanted black farmworkers to spend what little money they had in plantation commissaries or in stores that took advantage of their lack of mobility, choice, and contact with the outside world. Planters made every effort to keep both tenants and wage workers in debt. Most renters of any type rarely had the cash necessary to buy the seeds, fertilizer, storage space, or tools they would need for the coming season. They had to rely on their landlords (or other local white landowners or merchants) to "furnish" some or all of these things. The rates at which they repaid the loans after harvest were usually exorbitant and nonnegotiable. Sharecroppers were often so far into debt by harvest time that their share of the crop could not even cover the prior season's debt, let alone provide enough capital to forego debt for the coming season. Debt prevented renters from gaining financial independence and land ownership, and it undermined for wage workers and tenants alike physical independence and the ability to choose their work. Although the Supreme Court had repeatedly outlawed such peonage—whereby employers forced workers to work out their debts—the practice persisted into the 1940s.[18]

Indeed, many of the complaints of black farmworkers reveal the extent to which white planters and employers succeeded in creating a political and economic structure that often obviated any need for them to turn to formal legal structures. When black farmers beat the odds and raised a profitable crop, for example, landlords simply avoided paying them. The general custom of negotiating only oral, not written, contracts helped. Frank Welch, the head of the Department of Agricultural Economics at Mississippi State University and the author of a comprehensive study on southern agriculture published in 1943, concluded that "nearly all agreements are oral." This made laborers vulnerable to "arbitrary and unfair treatment." Landlords also refused to allow sharecroppers to examine the landlords' records. This prevented sharecroppers from effectively contesting alleged and often fraudulent debts. Even with written contracts and transparent account books, how would black renters, many of whom were illiterate, have challenged their meaning?[19]

Whereas some sharecroppers complained that their landlords co-erced or swindled them into giving up profits from their crops, others complained about outright theft. In 1944, an NAACP branch member wrote up the complaint of a widow whose landlord had taken her crops because of her late husband's alleged debts. "[T]he case of Mrs. Bass is a deserving case and is typical of the many cases in North Carolina and the South where the tenant, by devious means is robbed of his work under the pretense of the law." The following year, black farmer Charley Bright wrote Walter White of the NAACP about his own problems. Bright described how after he had planted and harvested a cotton crop, his landlord had taken the crop and refused to give Bright his share of the proceeds. "I have a case her," he told the association's executive secretary. "I have been robe out of my Livin and rights."[20]

The NAACP and DOJ papers are filled with letters describing similar situations. One family had refused to borrow fertilizer and seed from their landlord. When he ordered them to vacate the farm so he could take their crops, they concluded that the landlord "resented their fore-sight in managing without his credit, and used this method to cheat them out of their entire earnings." Likewise, Willie Dixon complained about having been run off the farm he had worked before harvest time. He told the attorney general, "It is a common thing for negroes to be done just as I have been done. . . . In fact bad white men make much of their money by taking crops from poor negroes after the work has been done."[21]

How far would a landlord go to harvest his crops for less than market wages? For some particularly independent and unlucky ten-ants, violence and even death could result if they asserted their prop-erty rights. When Wyatt Trueblood refused to give his syrup over to the Bryant brothers, for example, they shot him in the head and then beat him with an iron bar. It was not the first time one of their sharecrop-pers lost his life protecting his livelihood. For others, the death of the planter after a violent confrontation could lead to years in prison, exe-cution, or a lynching. Such violence reveals the extent to which African American financial success and property ownership threat-ened the very fundamentals of Jim Crow.[22]

Luckier black farmers lost only their livelihoods. Like Charley Bright, Valco Harris complained the landlord took his crops, declined to show him cotton gin receipts, and refused to pay him for the crops. Harris, his pregnant wife and four children, and three other families wanted to know, "Is it any laws to fource Mr. George Chambers to give me my account and settle with me." Some black tenants on Albert Sydney Johnson's farm in Arkansas (a farm that generated many complaints during the war) chose to forego the settlement of their crops altogether in exchange for escaping Johnson and making a clean start elsewhere. Other families on the same farm agreed to pay Johnson what they allegedly owed him and forego the settlement of their crops in order to get his "permission" to move.[23]

Many landlords threatened eviction along with confiscating crops. Lettie Franklin reported that the farmer on whose land she worked had taken her crop, refused to furnish her or give her barn space, and wanted to throw her out of her house. Others actually found themselves where Franklin only feared she would end up. Tinnie Mary Rodgers wrote, "I am a woman and is out of a home and is asking you for help I had a crop but the man draw a gun on me and I am afreaid to go back. . . . He told me if I come back he wourd kill me so please come see about me I ant got know home nothing to were are eat."[24]

Unlike Rodgers, who lost her crop and her home at the same time, many rural African Americans complained more of whites forcing them to stay on a particular farm than forcing them to leave. Crop loss, indebtedness, and eviction left tenant farmers and sharecroppers poor. But as long as they could move freely, they remained at least somewhat able to exert market power. Because they at least had some property worth taking, these victims of property crimes were not the worst-off African Americans.

Wage workers were often in considerably more dire straits. Compared to renters, they were simultaneously more mobile and more vulnerable to planter control. Although wage workers frequently expressed complaints sharecroppers and tenant farmers shared, the focus of their complaints differed. Wage workers emphasized how white landlords and employers limited where they could work, whom they could work for, and when and under what conditions they could move.

The dual role of employer and landlord that enabled Rodgers's landlord to take both her crop and her home frequently led to the opposite problem: it enhanced whites' ability to enforce isolation and immobility. Landlords worked to impede all channels of information

from the outside world. One field worker for the BAE noted this practice: "Some farm area Negro day laborers are told not to have radios in
house for fear of their hearing some law forbidding such low wages
and long hours. [Planters] try as much as possible—with the coopera-
tion of the county official—to hold to a minimum the out-county news
received in the county." As one peonage complainant put it in 1937,
"All or nearly all my mail is tampered with opened before I get it. So
you can see all important things from the outside world that comes
that way is know to my master before I get it."[25]

Other complaints showed the way in which the planter's frequent
dual role as employer and landlord endowed him with considerably
more power to coerce labor than he would have had in either role
alone. Teenaged Walter "Pete" Tarver was living with his family on the
property of one brickyard owner but working for another when his
landlord approached him. When Tarver told the landlord that he was
working at another brickyard, the landlord "told [him] to quit and to
be at his place the next morning." "I didn't know what he would do if I
didn't go," Tarver later told the FBI, "but I thought I had better go like
he said." Stetson and Kay Kennedy, southern human rights activists
who investigated peonage in the early 1950s, summed up the problem:
"In some cases employers have threatened eviction even when the
worker sought alternative employment on idle days. In other words,
job and housing are a 'package' proposition." Once the worker accepts housing, he "also accepts whatever work is available and at the
same time, the employer's wage rate, whether or not it remains as
promised. On such a package proposition, the workers' [sic] ability to
choose his work and to bargain on wages is materially limited."[26]

Another consequence of living on an employer's premises was that a
landlord could commandeer the workers' personal property. A
common theme among the complaints was that landlords and employers would theoretically allow farmworkers to leave but bar them
from taking any of their furniture or other property. Henry Morgan
McDonald expressed the urgency of obtaining his belongings to a
judge in Texas: "I am ask for your all please for healp so I can get my
thing a way from they place. . . . Please healp me. thir is peoples will
take me on they place but they will not let me get my thaing out of they
house. they said I ouit them $50. and they work me every day and no
pay." Fate Stewart, another worker, was even accused of burglarizing

the house in which he had formerly lived and in which his furniture remained. When Essie Lee Rice received permission to leave Albert Sydney Johnson's farm, he gave her a note stating that she could leave and take her belongings with her. Nonetheless, when her new employer brought her back with a truck and the note, Johnson sent her away empty-handed.[27]

Control over transportation proved especially problematic for farmworkers. Sometimes workers objected that they were unable to leave a particular employer because he had confiscated their cars and trucks. In one instance, when an employer "lured" a group of workers from Louisiana into Mississippi with a promise of lucrative work, one of the workers owned a truck and used it to drive the others to the new job. Once there, "the truck was taken to the [owner's] house. Log chains were put on the wheels and securely fastened there with locks." The employer literally prevented the men from leaving by sequestering their transportation.[28]

In some parts of the South, planters also prevailed upon railroad companies to stop black workers from leaving. As a result, many African Americans found it impossible to buy railroad or bus tickets out of the region. They frequently had to buy successive tickets with short hops in order to escape local employers and law enforcement.[29]

Whereas some workers protested that landlords made them stay by refusing to hand over the workers' property or transportation, others complained that landlords made them stay by claiming that the workers first needed to work out debts to their employers. Renters often accrued debts as a result of employers' manipulative loan and accounting practices. Sometimes the figures were so artificially high as to be ludicrous. At a time when more than a third of rural African American families made less than $500 per year, Albert Sydney Johnson claimed William Reddick had accrued a debt of $600 in a single year and that Corrie Duckett owed almost $300 for a six-month period. "We could never 'get even' in the money we owed Mr. Johnson," complained Felix Williams. Without getting even, the landlords argued, the workers were bound to remain and pay the debts through more work.[30]

Wage workers ended up in debt for different reasons, but they too complained of peonage. They usually accrued debts as a result of exorbitant prices for travel, food, or shelter that their wages were unable to cover. This was a major problem for the African American men who traveled to Florida to work in the sugar cane fields during the war. The $1.80 they made per day could not possibly cover what the company charged for transportation to the cane fields, the cane knives and sharpening files, the identification badges, and the food and board.[31]

Despite the illegality of peonage, employers made little effort to hide the practice. One employer wrote the sister of a man he was holding, "[Your brother] is in my debt. He owes me $75.00. He cannot leave this island until I receive my money." Workers reported that on the Florida sugar plantations, camp superintendents "threatened to kill us if we left before our transportation had been paid."[32]

Such violence pervaded many involuntary servitude complaints during the war. One case received considerable attention nationwide because of its scale and brutality. W. T. Cunningham of Oglethorpe County, Georgia, was said to have "work[ed] colored people for as much as 10 and 17 years without paying them and whipping them to insensibility with pistols and other deadly weapons when they at-tempt[ed] to escape from his peonage plantation." The situation was not unique. One worker described threats of death from an employer angered that he had left. "He have come up here and got me and my Brother and Cosern and Beat us up and we left againe and he coming up her roning us all over town." On one Mississippi plantation, a land-lord "beat [a man] to death with ax handles" for protesting the meager pay he had received for two weeks' work. Other workers complained of being beaten with cat-o'-nine-tails and hoses and of being shackled to their beds to prevent escape. For some, the immobility that accompa-nied such treatment was so severe that they perceived themselves to "belong" to their employers. What one letter writer described as a landlord's "plantation Negroes" were, she said, "under rigid control."[33]

Other complaints about peonage, slavery, and involuntary servitude focused on living and working conditions rather than violence and economic coercion. Some letters in this category, as in others, con-cerned rural agricultural and nonagricultural workers. Additional complaints, however, especially in the later 1940s, came from female domestic workers and their defenders. African American neighbor Mattie Lomax learned about Polly Johnson's situation in King George's County, Virginia, when Johnson approached Lomax's brother Daniel for help. Johnson wanted Daniel to take her from her employers' home so that she could escape. Fearing kidnapping charges, he agreed instead to meet her on the road. Mattie subsequently wrote the NAACP: "[S]ome white folks raised [her] as a slave without the knowledge of her age and no schooling and her hands look like they have been cracked open with corns and callouses from hard labor." Johnson told Lomax "that she has been whipped with lashes and treated real cruel and slept in a chicken house and rain on her bed." Johnson was "not allow[ed] . . . to have any playmates . . . was never sent to school nor allowed to visit anyone, nor to attend church." She did not receive regular pay, and she was forced to do "men's work." In Lomax's opinion, "the way the girl acts, she has been treated even worse than she can explain." Although Johnson regularly went to the grocery store for her employers, she felt she could not leave them.[34]

Witnesses described in similar terms the "actual slavery" in which

Daniel Lomax, Mattie Lomax, Polly Johnson, and an NAACP attorney. (Library of Congress.)

Elizabeth Coker lived, working long hours at inappropriately hard labor for little or no pay. Her employers forced her to sleep in a chicken coop without a bathroom and denied her education, church, or visitors. At the end of thirteen years of service to her employers, she "had no clothes, no shoes, and but seventy cents in money." As she put it, "In all the time I was in the Franklin home I never enjoyed any privileges of a free person."[35]

Clifton Barber raised a good crop in 1940, but he did not see the proceeds. Instead, Barber's landlord swindled him out of much of what he thought he deserved. Barber moved away in protest, and he was promptly arrested. Barber's story is instructive: when private efforts at finding and keeping cheap labor failed, white planters knew they could turn to the law for help. Both the legal system as a whole and the specific laws it enforced buttressed the power of individual white planters rather than provide redress for African Americans. Whites had a racial monopoly on jobs as police officers and sheriffs; only they served on juries and in county governments. The racial caste system and the highly stratified economic system worked together to prevent rural blacks from exercising the kind of freedom over their lives and livelihoods most Americans took for granted.[36]

Moreover, many specific southern laws existed precisely to shore up the power of white planters and employers. The roots of many of the laws went all the way back to the post–Civil War Black Codes. Though their overtly racial character had been eliminated by the 1860s, their purpose never changed. Some laws helped ensure that black renters would fail to see any profit from their crops. Crop lien laws gave priority to landlords, and many gave second priority to others, like merchants, who lent supplies to tenants. As a result, financial losses fell disproportionately on tenants. Meanwhile, sharecroppers often had no legal rights to the crops they raised. Combined with white efforts to keep prices for supplies high and farmworkers isolated from other options, these laws enabled landlords to yoke African American renters to white plantations and to harvesting them at minimal cost to the landlord. Such heavily biased legal rules and their pervasively discriminatory implementation succeeded in making "[t]he so-called agricultural ladder . . . largely nonexistent." African American tenants and croppers who hoped eventually to farm their own land were usually disappointed.[37]

Other laws curtailed black economic opportunity by controlling the freedom of both renters and wage workers to move and to find information about jobs. Prohibitions on hitchhiking, for example, made moving from place to place especially hard for poor southerners. Emigrant-agent licensing laws made learning about new job opportunities equally difficult. Such laws required labor recruiters to pay often exorbitant amounts for the right to recruit labor in southern states. Some states, like Virginia, required agents soliciting on behalf of employers outside the state to pay $5,000 per year for each county or city in which they operated. Alabama went even further, requiring the same amount not only for counties in which an agent operated, but also those through which he transported workers.[38]

African American farmworkers hated so-called anti-enticement laws in particular. These laws originated in the Reconstruction era and remained on the books into the 1940s. Any time a planter hired a farmhand who had a contract with another planter, the new employer could be prosecuted for enticing away the farmhand. Some planters used advertisements to ensure that other planters knew who not to hire. The Yanceyville, North Carolina, *Caswell Messenger* ran an advertisement that warned, "NOTICE: I forbid anyone to hire or harbor Norman Miles, colored, during the year 1939.—A. P. Dobbs, Route 1, Yanceyville." A neighbor explained the efficacy of such notices: "Few landlords will risk incurring the wrath of some good Christian, Democratic freeholder by hiring his hand after he has warned us not to. As long as folks don't know the statute is unconstitutional it can be made to serve its intended purpose." The political calculation was easy: "The Caswell legislator who would try to take that law off the books would lose many votes."[39]

As the notice indicates, anti-enticement laws led many landlords and employers to believe that they had rights to the continued service of their black workers. Wrote an employer whose employee was picked up by another and taken away, "I feel and my friends say I have been treated wrong. I hate to report my neighbor (supposed to be) but the only recourse I have is the law." In another case, one Mr. Conner had a sheriff arrest a former employee in the presence of his new employer. When the new employer asked the sheriff if he had a warrant for the arrest, the sheriff replied simply, "Don't monkey with Mr. Conner's hands."[40]

In fact, peonage complaints frequently resulted from disputes be-tween two employers over a single employee and his debts. It was "cus-tomary in these parts," T. J. Lord told the FBI, "that when a negro leaves and goes to a new employer for the new one to pay the old one what the negro owed him." Lord candidly informed the FBI that he had personally prohibited a former employee from taking his belong-ings until the new employer paid the employee's debt to Lord. As late as 1953, a U.S. attorney in Mississippi worried about presenting a pe-onage case to a jury because he "would have to overcome in the minds of a jury a custom that has prevailed for quite a long time in this area that a landlord in contracting with a moving farm tenant is expected to pay the tenant's indebtedness to his former landlord." The custom "appear[ed] to be on the wane," but it was nonetheless still pow-erful.[41]

African Americans, in turn, saw themselves caught in a bind be-tween anti-enticement laws and employers who would not release a worker until the new employer agreed to pay the worker's debts. A farmworker could not leave a particular landlord until he had paid his debts. He usually had no money to pay the debts, so he had to find a new employer to pay the debts for him. He would then owe the new employer what he had owed the old one. Once the new employer agreed to hire a farmworker who already had a contract with another planter, however, that new employer became vulnerable to the anti-enticement laws. In one case, several black workers stated that "they were in no way indebted to [their employer] but that the only way they could get away from [his] farm was by having a white man come after them," pay their alleged debts, and employ them. Stetson and Kay Kennedy asked a turpentine worker in 1952 if "there are some [em-ployers] who . . . won't let you go even if you find a man to pay your debt at the commissary." The worker answered in the affirmative: "That's right, sir: if you're a good worker, some of them don't want you to leave." Willie Furg Will made the point well in describing how his employer refused to accept payment for an alleged debt: "He stated that he didn't want my money, but that he wanted me to work."[42]

Into the 1940s, most southern states also made it a crime for a la-borer to borrow money from an employer and leave the employment before finishing the contract term and paying the debt. These laws were often separate from generally applicable fraud laws, and they often presumed criminal intent. The Arkansas law even specified that a laborer who left his employment before fulfilling his contract would be penalized not only with paying his debts but also with the loss of any wages or portion of the crop that the employer would have owed him. Tom Clark, as assistant attorney general, described these laws as "a perfect instrument for terrorization by the threat of prosecution." Even after the Supreme Court struck down such laws for the second time in the mid-1940s, state and local officials either defiantly or ignorantly continued to make use of them. Arkansas recodified its law until at least 1947, several years after the Supreme Court's decisions. Florida refused to take its law off the books until 1951.[43]

Workers also protested that vagrancy laws performed a similar function. They gave governments the legal authority to threaten or actually require individuals, usually black individuals, to work. In Virginia, for example, the vagrancy law punished not only those who did not work but those who "refuse[d] to work for the usual and common wages given to other laborers in like work." Tennessee passed a vagrancy law in 1875, recodified in 1938, that made it "a misdemeanor for any person having no apparent means of subsistence to neglect to apply himself to some honest calling" and to stroll "through the country without any visible means of support." Arkansas's law allowed prosecution of those "not actively seeking some honest employment."[44]

The local officials who enforced these laws usually targeted African Americans. Such discriminatory enforcement spawned frequent complaints. In one case, an employer rounded up several employees to harvest his crop with the help of local law enforcement. He admitted "giving the Negro victims the alternative of working for [him] or being arrested for vagrancy." The police officer described the process as "ordinary procedure." He stated, "I have never forced anyone to work although I have assisted in hiring negroes for the city of Homestead and for various farmers both before and since I have been on the police force." Another local employer said "that it was customary and was the habit for a large number of Negroes to loaf on the streets and decline to work, and that the police would round them up every now and then and tell them they would have to go to work or leave town, and things like that." In such cases, the threat of arrest was sufficient to compel work, and the police rarely carried out the arrests.[45]

African American workers also lodged grievances about other criminal laws used to make them work. In one common procedure called criminal surety, an employer would have an employee arrested and convicted of some petty offense. The employer would pay the employee's fine and then require the worker to work off the debt in his employ. Although the Supreme Court had struck down the criminal surety system in 1914, this practice persisted for decades without the explicit sanction of state law. One writer described "a conspiracy between a few white men and the court in order that they might work the negro. The judge thinks it is good politics and I guess it is, for he has been in office for 35 years[,] and there has been a lot of this kind of work done in this district." Employers were often willing to pay "big fines for negroes in getting them from jail," which left them with "quite a bit of money tied up in this help." At times, no private employer was involved, as law enforcement officials abused their positions to obtain black workers for their own financial gain.[46]

Arthur Shores, a black attorney and prominent member of the NAACP in Birmingham, Alabama, described another scenario. Employers commonly jailed African Americans on "trump[ed] up charges." The jailers "then let them out without finally settling their cases, and if they leave these farming districts, have them returned on the pretext that they are either fugitives or probation violators." One merchant who helped a parolee procure a job found out the power of such schemes a little too late. He had thought that "changing jobs is not considered a felony anywhere in America," so he took the threat of rearrest lightly. "[B]ut sure enough a deputy Sheriff came and returned Pope to Parchman [Prison], and there he is now."[47]

Milton Konvitz, assistant NAACP counsel, recognized the paradox of parole-related cases in which there were not even debts or fines to discharge. In such cases, the convict received a life sentence. He was then paroled "on condition of his working on a farm. The involuntary servitude comes in only with respect to the absence of a choice of employment, and also with the fact that the parole, conditioned as it was, gave him only the appearance of freedom but certainly not the reality."[48]

The justifications for arrest in these various schemes ran the gamut from the ludicrous—arresting an illiterate worker for forgery—to the simply unbelievable. Frequently, mere absence from work was enough to lead to arrest, even without any intent or attempt to leave the employment altogether. Walter "Pete" Tarver, the young man who felt compelled to work for his landlord's brickyard, informed his land-lord/employer that he would not be at work one day so that he could register for the draft. The employer "laughed and said that if I didn't come to work on Monday he would send a policeman after me." When Tarver did not go to work Monday, he was indeed arrested. Tarver's employer told him he now owed $25, part of which was promptly de-ducted from Tarver's pay. Tarver explained that when he asked why he was arrested, his employer replied that he had already warned Tarver that "the police would get me if I didn't come to work."[49]

Poor job performance could lead to the same result. A local attorney wrote the FBI about a lumber company in Florida that employed "old men in the logging and stacking of lumber. When one of the em-ployees finds he cannot hold up at the work and wishes to be relieved, he is immediately put in jail, at the request of the Lumber Co."[50]

Where minors were involved, complaints identified yet another way employers utilized local law: to bind out African American children to white planters in a process reminiscent of practices that prevailed during slavery and Reconstruction. In one case, the local ordinary bound out a boy to an employer under an "indigent orphan statute" without complying with the law's advertisement requirement and in an ex parte proceeding. According to a local attorney, "it had not been the first time, nor the last time, the Ordinary of Jasper County had made such orders at the request of various people." The ordinary him-self agreed that "there are several other cases in his county where indi-viduals are bound out under the above Statute."[51]

Even as planters used vagrancy, hitchhiking, enticement, contract labor, and other long-established laws to control black workers, World War II itself augmented the legal powers of southern whites. Many lo-calities used the war to justify arresting even more blacks and forcing them to work. For example, numerous municipalities passed, and many others enforced informally, so-called work or fight laws, in which "police officers . . . form[ed] a 'Gestapo' to force local Negroes to the cotton fields." The NAACP had "information [in 1943] that large farmers and county police officials, in an effort to stop Negro farm workers from leaving the area for more lucrative employment in in-dustrial centers, have resorted to placing them under arrest on spu-rious charges and when unable to pay fines requiring that they work on local plantations." The FBI found that under a " 'work or fight' program" in Broward County, Florida, the sheriff had arrested "many Negroes who were in fact regularly employed." The sheriff justified the practice in light of difficulties "during the past winter season getting negro labor to harvest their crops." He knew "that there were plenty of negro workers in the area, but that they were independent and refused to work more than a few days each wee[k]." The sheriff reiterated that "his policy of directing negroes to work or go to jail for vagrancy arose out of the above condition and reaffirmed that he felt it his patriotic duty in war-time to require that negroes work on the ground that our men fighting overseas were given no days off."[52]

The sheriff of Mobile, Alabama, also arrested those known to have jobs. When the judge of the county inferior court dismissed the sheriff's vagrancy charges, describing them as peonage-like, the sheriff replied that he would simply arraign future individuals for vagrancy in the Mobile city courts or before a justice of the peace. If whites could not rely on one governmental body, they would find others to perform the function white planters and their law enforcement allies expected of them.[53]

Indeed, federal law obliged employer preferences almost as much as most local officials did. Long before the war, southern landlords had figured out how to use New Deal programs to their advantage. Some of these programs had promised to benefit tenants. Complaints revealed that they often did not. The Agricultural Adjustment Act offered subsidies to farmers who reduced their crop production. By law, it required planters to share these payments with their tenants. Instead, some landlords culled their renters, hired them back as wage workers, and kept the subsidies for themselves. Others retained their renters but took the latter's subsidy checks as their own. Sharecropper Felix Tate reported that when he asked his landlord for his "part of the rental check [the landlord] said that I could get it the best way I could." At other times, the tactics were (slightly) more subtle. Lulu White of the Houston NAACP branch informed the NAACP's national legal department that in her area merchants had applied government checks "to the accounts of the farmers without their consent." This action transformed potentially independence-producing government funds into further black dependence and white profit. Complaints like those from Tate and White usually fell on deaf ears. White planters were well represented in, and tenants largely absent from, the federal agencies and local committees that oversaw such subsidy programs.[54]

Wartime regulations offered new opportunities for planter manipulation. One planter boasted that "he had been able to control the practice of truckers hauling pickers to the plantation paying highest rates by virtue of being a member of the local [Office of Price Administration] rationing board . . . and denying gasoline to truckers who failed to follow orders." In other cases, employers kept employees' wartime ration books. If employees left or tried to leave the job, the employers withheld the ration books from them.[55]

Employers also limited black job opportunities by controlling draft status. In one case, a young man left Dublin, Georgia, for a new job in Tallahassee, Florida. He was about to be inducted, and his new employer in Florida applied to the local draft board in Dublin to have him classified as a farmer. That would have allowed him to continue working on the Florida farm. The board said no. Subsequently, his former employer in Dublin was able to reclassify him, provided he returned to Dublin to work for the employer. A member of the local draft board defended his actions without really explaining them. He acknowledged that "it does appear I favored [the local employer] over [the worker's] employer in Florida." He nonetheless claimed, "Our board does not, as a rule, show any preference to a local farmer over an employer in another county or state." The chairman of the draft board equivocated similarly. On the one hand, he maintained that he "always tr[ied] to help the farmers in any section and [had] given deferments to many farmers in Florida and elsewhere." He did acknowledge his local prejudices, however. "Labor recruiters, particularly from Florida and Pennsylvania have come in this section at night and taken many negro laborers off the farms. . . . [I]f a man will agree to come back from out of the county or the State and work on the farm, he can be classified as a farmer."[56]

One local Agricultural Adjustment Agency (AAA) agent in Mississippi even acknowledged that when sharecroppers left the area to take up defense work, the draft board would move them to the top of the list. He also admitted to "gross favoritism" in allowing good sharecroppers to remain on the farms. "Draft boards are made up of planters—and they naturally take care of keeping their own croppers." Those croppers, in turn, did "not feel free to leave the farm of the operator who requested their deferment."[57]

Federal wartime legislation also provided more direct aid to landowners. A 1943 federal law created the Emergency Farm Labor

Supply Program, which simultaneously promised and withheld complete freedom of movement for agricultural workers. On the one hand, the law gave the federal imprimatur to increased mobility by organizing a program to transport Mississippi Delta farmworkers to other regions where higher-paying jobs were available. On the other hand, the law prohibited the spending of federal funds on transporting workers who did not have a release signed by the county farm agent. County farm agents, like those who served on local draft boards and AAA committees, were usually powerful whites. Funds for migration, then, were only available when it suited the white employers of black workers.[58]

Planters also used the Emergency Price Control Act of 1942 to control black workers. The act delegated authority to regulate the wages of agricultural workers to the secretary of agriculture, Clinton P. Anderson. That authority included imposing wage ceilings that ensured that farmers would have a steady supply of cheap labor. With no competition for wages, workers would be able to mobilize little market power. In exercising this authority, the secretary had to follow certain procedures—holding public hearings, giving public notice, and imposing a wage ceiling only where "a [representative] majority of the producers of the commodity" requested it. In 1945, the secretary held referenda in Mississippi, Arkansas, and Missouri and set ceilings on cotton for the former two states.[59]

Complaints about the ceilings immediately reached the NAACP from H. L. Mitchell of the Southern Tenant Farmers' Union and from Alfred Baker Lewis, the secretary-treasurer of the National Sharecroppers' Fund and a member of the NAACP Board of Directors. Mitchell and Lewis were outraged. Wartime and reconversion wage ceilings were generally meant to curb inflation by preventing wages from rising so quickly that they would affect the economy generally. But it was "an absurdity," Mitchell argued, "for the Secretary of Agriculture to impose a ceiling on wages of cotton pickers or any other agricultural labor in the cotton South since they enjoy the lowest wages of any workers in the nation."[60]

Farmworkers and their advocates did not think inflation was the target. The target was instead the mobility of African American day laborers, sharecroppers, and tenant farmers. As Leslie Perry of the Washington Office wrote to Secretary of Agriculture Anderson, the "farm lobby" had succeeded in using "the power of your Agency . . . to freeze the wages of this class of agricultural laborer at levels patently substandard. . . . [N]othing in the national economy or the economy of the cotton industry . . . would justify the drastic action that has been taken." The "action runs counter to the entire national wage policy" to enact minimum, not maximum wages. According to the National Farm Labor Union, planters "wanted a wage ceiling set so that Negro sharecroppers would not be tempted to move into town where they could earn more money as wage hands on nearby farms working 100 days a year in the chopping and picking seasons." The main goal of the agriculture ceilings was "to keep producers from pirating employees by offers of higher wages when workers are scarce in a given area." So long as the market determined price, laborers could move freely from one place to another in response to higher wages. The planters hoped to stem their freedom.[61]

Department of Agriculture officials essentially agreed with the landowners. W. C. Holley, the chief of the department's program division, described how prior to the wage ceilings the "supply situation" was "characterized by spiraling wage rates, pirating of workers by employers, high labor turnover and excessive loss of working time by employees going from place to place seeking the highest wage rate frequently on the basis of mere rumor." He was pleased that the institution of the ceilings yielded a "more stable" situation, in which "pirating was minimized; wages tended to become uniform[;] [w]orkers settled down to perform the specific task; and all together more food and fibre was harvested and workers were afforded the opportunity of earning more total wages." Holley thus conceded that the department was using the wage ceilings not to curb inflation—their intended use—but to restrict mobility.[62]

Just as the wage ceiling curtailed the market power of black agricultural workers, its approval by referendum represented and perpetuated their political powerlessness. An atmosphere of intimidation, Mitchell pointed out, pervaded both the local hearings on whether a ceiling was necessary and the voting itself. At the Mississippi hearings, not a single cotton picker testified, and "in Arkansas, those who represented the point of view of labor were subjected to insult and intimidation." The voting proved problematic in a number of ways. In more than one county in Arkansas, "a group of small farm owners, tenants, and sharecroppers . . . having [been] notified of the time and place to cast their ballots, waited throughout the day and no one appeared to conduct the referendum." And the lack of secret ballots intimidated those who did vote. Public voting enabled landlords and employers with control over sharecroppers' livelihoods, their homes, and even, as the cases above indicated, their lives to coerce their workers into voting in favor of the referendum.[63]

Moreover, the referenda literally defined some African American farmworkers out of the polity. They limited voting rights on the ceilings to "producers" and defined the term to exclude the wage workers who were directly affected. Mitchell claimed that the referenda were unconstitutional and illegal because "[c]otton pickers whose wages were to be set, were not permitted to participate in the voting." Leslie Perry likewise concluded that a law that excluded farmworkers was "not only . . . undemocratic in that it does not give the workman a real voice in determining what he shall earn, but we think that it invades basic rights guaranteed to him by our Constitution." Left almost voiceless in the political process, farmworkers found that even the ability to vote with their feet—and move to new jobs in response to higher wages—lost its efficacy when planters imposed low, uniform wages.[64]

The racial underpinnings of the political economy described in these complaints was obvious to planters, African Americans, and observers alike. Although white tenant farmers and sharecroppers certainly fell victim to some of the same practices African Americans confronted in the 1940s, they were on the whole better off than black farmworkers. Moreover, they were definitionally exempt from some of the abuses black farmworkers faced. Whites were part of the polity, they served on juries, they shared a racial identity with those in power, and they were not subject to lynchings or racial terror. Broward County, Florida, provides just one small example of the racial tenor of legal coercion to work: of 162 arrests made for vagrancy between June 1943 and August 1944, only seven were of whites.[65]

Indeed, white planters and landlords explicitly stated that they treated black and white workers differently. One North Carolina planter explained in 1939 why he preferred black workers: "A white tenant has his notions of running a farm and is less amenable to suggestions. I can say . . . 'Go hitch up the horse' when I want a horse hitched . . . to a negro . . . and I can't to a white man." Similarly, when black farmer Ned Cobb recommended a white family to a landlord who had asked him if he knew anyone looking for land, the white landlord, according to Cobb, responded, "Aw, hell . . . I don't want no damn white man on my place." Cobb interpreted the response, "He gets a nigger, that's his glory. He can do that nigger just like he wants to and that nigger better not say nothing against his rulins."[66]

Planters similarly distinguished between white and African American women. A Mississippi AAA agent told a BAE interviewer that he was angry about "loafing" black women who were refusing work because of the income they received from family members in the military. The interviewer asked whether it was true that more white women refrained from working than black. "Yes," replied the AAA agent, "but [you] can't do anything about that—many of them never picked cotton and you can't force white women to work."[67]

Agricultural economist Frank Welch described in 1943 how "many plantation operators . . . regarded cotton, Negroes, and mules as a 'natural combination.'" He summed up simply: Landowners preferred "docile, low-status" sharecroppers—code words for African Americans—under "detailed management involving social and economic supervision."[68]

None of these attitudes were lost on African Americans. They saw the world as one in which white planters ruled, and the white planters especially ruled black farmworkers. One youth interviewed by the BAE complained that "[t]he white people won't let you buy land any more. They want it all for themselves so they can make a great big farm and get rid of the poor colored farmers." Another stated, "Colored farmers can barely make a living by doing twice as much as the white farmers because the buyers won't give them the same prices they give white farmers." Whites had tremendous control not only over land and markets but also over other jobs: "Negroes will only get the jobs the white people allot to them, with a few exceptions." "The white folks ain't gonna let us get any better jobs." Whites "don't want the colored people to get too much education because they are afraid they will want to leave, then they won't have anybody to work for nothing for them any more."[69]

The comments of both white landlords and black farmworkers reflect the particular combination of racial subordination and economic exploitation that made the political economy of the rural South unique. "The economy of the South," wrote political scientist Howard

Devon Hamilton in 1951, "is a hierarchy of exploitation in which each class and group exploits the one beneath it, and in which the Negroes are on the bottom." Observers often connected racial and economic oppression explicitly. Frank Welch stated unequivocally, "It . . . cannot be too strongly emphasized that the plantation tenancy system has racial and political as well as economic implications. It is the partially

Peonage cartoon, 1940s. (General Research and Reference Division, Schomburg Center for Research in Black Culture, The New York Public Library, Astor, Lenox and Tilden Foundations.)

accepted solution to a race problem that has existed since the Civil War." One undated cartoon from the 1940s showed an African American farmer plowing a field with a mule, as a whip held by a white hand is about to strike his back. The heading read, "Slavery in the United States, Peonage," and at the bottom of the picture were the words "Racial Economic Bondage."[70]

That Jim Crow operated in the agricultural South as a way both to keep African Americans subordinate and to keep labor cheap was apparent to those who advocated on behalf of the farmworkers. "To an appreciable extent," Stetson and Kay Kennedy observed, "the mere fact of whiteness provides protection" from the worst abuses of the plantation system. Black lawyer William Henry Huff described people in peonage as "under the bottom rail. They are, indeed, defenseless; no one wishes to bother with them because, first, they have absolutely no money, and second, they are at best a debased, ignorant and servile crew." But Huff worried that "if we sit idly by and allow the overlords to enslave all who are of their type, ere long the same bell will toll for us in some manner." He told the NAACP that he was on board with "equal pay for teachers" and "all the other necessary reforms." But, he insisted, "we want none of them at the expense [of] liberty for the peons, the people farthest down." He saw an anti-peonage crusade not as separate from or contrasted to other kinds of racial injustice but rather as "a companion fight to the nation-wide struggle to pass the anti-Poll-tax and anti-Lynching bills and the fight of John L. Lewis to lead the way toward smashing the wage differential."[71]

Alfred Baker Lewis saw the wage ceiling fight in similar terms. He asserted that the "situation is a rotten one from every point of view both racial and economic." He repeatedly emphasized "that this is the sort of case on economic, legal, and racial grounds we ought to support in every way we can." Lewis explained why he felt "rather strongly about the matter": "[T]hose who suffer from the imposition of wage ceilings are on the lowest rung of our economic ladder and are also among those most completely denied political, economic, or social rights of all of our citizens." The interconnectedness of racial and economic injury made the agricultural cases urgent, significant, and unique.[72]

For black agricultural workers in the 1940s South, racial barriers were only one part of a full-blown white assault. Their complaints depict a world of white economic domination and black economic dependence; of white political power and black disfranchisement; of the ubiquitous potential for legally unrestrained white violence and the almost certain swift retribution against black violence, real or imagined. African American farmworker Robert Hammond articulated it this way: "The negroes here most of them is afreaid of the white people here and all of them is afreaid to go to the court house to vote, now take thing's to a consideration, we live's in a free house such as it is, but you can't live in the free house with nothing to eat one half of the time and no shoes and cloth to wear in the winter."[73]

Hammond's complaint was one of many that found their way to civil rights lawyers in the 1940s. These complaints called for legal intervention into the rural South's particular form of Jim Crow. As such, each letter provided two distinct but related resources for lawyers. First, the letters reminded distant professionals that despite the signs of racial progress they saw around them in Washington, D.C., or New York City, the combined racial and economic subordination of African Americans in the rural South continued to represent a massive target for any challenge to Jim Crow.

Second, the complaints embodied concrete litigation opportunities for lawyers setting forth deliberately and self-consciously to fashion a new, legally enforceable civil rights in the 1940s. The farmworkers complained about combined racial and economic subordination. These grievances mirrored the uncertainties in the future of civil rights doctrine—the relative centrality of racial and economic claims, the long-standing prominence of workers' rights, and the newer prominence of African Americans' rights. Whether their complaints actually would lead to new civil rights doctrine depended on the ability and willingness of lawyers to see legal possibilities for attacking the "Racial Economic Bondage" workers like Hammond described.

THREE

❖ ❖ ❖

Claiming Rights in the Industrial Economy

Colored people as well as white . . . have to make a living.

Letter from "A group of nurses who want justice"
to the NAACP, November 14, 1947

IN 1941, JOHN ALLEN was living in Chicago, looking for work as an engineer. He and several white engineers applied to an Indiana firm with national defense contracts. The white engineers received positions, went to Indiana, and began work. Allen too received a telegram informing him of an open position. Allen and his wife "were so sure of [John] having a job with said company" that they traveled to Indiana and found housing before he reported for work. When Allen showed up with the telegram, the company stenographer "looked like she had seen an apparition from 'West of death.'" "[S]he could not speak instantly." She summoned the chief engineer of the firm, who was "frank" with Allen: "[T]he company," he said, "has not given me the authority to employ Negro engineers." Allen and his wife returned to Chicago, and Allen wired an acceptance to the position to create a paper trail. Hearing nothing, he wired again indicating that the firm had broken its contract. The firm took umbrage at "the attitude expressed in [Allen's] second telegram" and concluded that it was "therefore not interested" in hiring him. Allen wrote to the NAACP, testified about his injuries in an affidavit, and sought assistance pursuing a remedy.[1]

Allen's complaint typified the experiences of many black industrial workers who sought economic advancement during World War II. When the war interrupted the Depression with a literal retooling of the machinery of industry, the resulting industrial mobilization offered new economic opportunities to African Americans outside the

81

rural South. The experiences of black workers within and those outside Southern agriculture thus diverged even more dramatically than
they had in the past.

Complaint letters from the rural South were often written by others
for illiterate, uneducated men and women. Or they were written in the
workers' own hand, with poor spelling and worse grammar. Allen was
an engineer, literate and savvy enough to wire telegrams, create paper
trails, and gather documents into a comprehensive affidavit. The
farmers sought subsistence and survival. Allen sought a high-paying
job consonant with his skill level. The agricultural workers' letters were
threaded through with violence and terror. Allen's gave the sense of
righteous frustration. Agricultural workers often feared for their lives
in writing for outside help. Rarely did an industrial worker have such a
fear, as evidenced by the prevalence of notarized complaints. The
public act of seeking out a registered officer to validate a complaint
could be dangerous and deadly in the rural South. When industrial
workers occasionally preferred anonymity or confidentiality, it
stemmed from the fear of losing one's job more than one's life.[2]

The farmers sought freedom of movement. Allen chose his own
housing and moved freely from state to state. Although industrial
workers sometimes required clearances to move from defense jobs,
they had far more mobility than agricultural workers. Allen enjoyed
greater personal freedom, the legal ability and practical capacity to
vote, housing separate and independent from his employers, and the
autonomy to join black protest organizations and labor unions.
African Americans outside the South could largely speak their minds.
Rural blacks experienced constant surveillance, pervasive legal and extralegal threats of violence, and economic dependence on a small
group of powerful local whites.[3]

Nevertheless, for both groups of workers, the war seemed to
promise more than it would deliver. The beginning of the 1940s did
not magically transform a depression into a boom. Even after the nation began to mobilize economically in response to the war in Europe,
black industrial workers did not benefit proportionally. From April to
October 1940, white unemployment dropped from 17.7 percent to 13
percent, but it remained constant at 22 percent for African Americans.
Despite ubiquitous propaganda about the need for workers in national
defense industries, African Americans found that they could not "buy

a job." They pointed out the irony of race discrimination in a war for democracy and against fascism, in an economy with no room for waste. In the spring of 1942, a majority of African Americans described themselves as either the same or worse off than they had been before the start of the war. One writer expressed a common sentiment when he signed his name, "Want to help in Defence but can't."[4]

Once the armed services started siphoning off available workers in 1942, black workers found greater opportunities. They made inroads in jobs, companies, industries, and cities that had previously shut them out. The average African American working in a city increased his earnings from $400 to $1,000 per year over the course of the war. The number of unemployed African Americans dropped from 937,562 in 1940 to 151,000 in 1944.[5]

Throughout the decade, however, black industrial workers continued to face pervasive obstacles to economic advancement. When the war ended, reconversion threatened and in many cases reversed their gains. The very industries in which black workers had made the greatest advances—shipbuilding, aircraft manufacturing, ordinance, and munitions—suffered the greatest job losses. And when the economic emergency that had led some reluctant employers to overlook their prejudices had subsided, so too did the tolerance for black workers.[6]

Moreover, throughout the 1940s, the law provided erratic and largely ineffective legal protection. At the beginning of the war, only Massachusetts, New York, and Illinois had even limited nondiscrimination laws, mostly in public utilities. All but a handful of federal agencies allowed discrimination. In 1940, the civil service stopped requiring applicants to provide photographs, and Congress prohibited discrimination in classified civilian federal jobs. A lack of enforcement mechanisms made these new prohibitions largely ineffectual, however. Federal laws did not require private employers to hire applicants regardless of their race. Even the creation of the Fair Employment Practice Committee (FEPC) in 1941 and the passage of state fair employment laws after New York paved the way in 1945 had modest effect. Legal protection against discrimination throughout the 1940s was grossly inadequate to the task.[7]

In the face of stunted economic opportunities and few obvious legal options, many black industrial workers, like their agricultural counterparts, wrote to the NAACP for help. Most of the complaints came from workers seeking skilled and high-paying work, usually in defense industries. When governmental channels became available, black workers used those as well.

Like the complaints of farmworkers, industrial workers' appeals are important both for what they reveal about Jim Crow and for what they reveal about the claims of those who contested it. Read as a whole, the industrial complaints offer a window into the world of work-related racial inequality across the nation in the 1940s. The complaints show how, for all their differences, black agricultural and industrial workers had much in common. To be sure, the workers shared a racial status and all that came with it—segregation, discrimination, marginality. Moreover, the livelihoods of both groups of workers were to some considerable extent in the hands of whites who insisted on racial and economic subordination. For those still in the rural South, planters, draft boards, and local sheriffs dominated. For those like Allen, indifferent middle managers, stereotyping secretaries, and whites unaccustomed to African Americans who asserted themselves were in control. Agricultural workers complained that they could not maintain dominion over their property or person; industrial workers complained that they could not gain access to economic opportunity.

Like their agricultural counterparts, black industrial workers depicted Jim Crow as a product of both public and private power, both racial and economic subordination. From defense training programs to government employment services, from private employers to white trade unions, African American industrial workers complained that their right to work, and to work at their full capacity, was stymied, frustrated, and downright quashed. The operation of Jim Crow in every aspect of the national economy simultaneously maintained racial stratification and curtailed economic opportunities.

Read as documentation of the possibilities for challenging industrial Jim Crow in the 1940s, the workers' letters are equally instructive. Like the farmworkers, black industrial workers sought economic and racial redress against both government actors and private individuals, associations, unions, and companies. The particular form Jim Crow took and the particular grievances of the workers differed for agricultural and industrial workers. Still, the industrial workers' complaints in their own way implicated the two most prominent understandings of civil rights at the time—race and economics. Indeed, although race pervaded the complaints, black workers were overwhelmingly preoccupied with the economic consequences of racial discrimination. The problem was not discrimination in the abstract, but discrimination that interfered with making a living. The concerns of these black workers were conceptually embedded in the economic conditions of the United States and the economic status of African Americans within it.

In July 1942, Bessie Armstrong went to the recently federalized Ohio employment office in Cincinnati to answer an advertisement "for women to do war work, no experience necessary." She "was some what stung" when she learned that "they were not hiring colored women." She was especially surprised because "the ad did not specify colored or white." When she asked why the ad did not mention race, the official told her that it was not permitted to do so. She found it more than frustrating to think "that each and every day our boys are going to the front and yet the Negro women in supposedly Northern cities are not allowed to work in defense jobs which require no experience."[8]

Such confrontations with the federal government's halfhearted nondiscrimination policies and frequently discriminatory practices were commonplace in the 1940s. That discrimination took a number of economically debilitating forms. Three kinds of federal discrimination in particular populate the complaints African Americans lodged with the NAACP during the decade: complaints like Armstrong's about the United States Employment Service (USES), those about training programs for defense work, and those about the federal government's own hiring practices. In each instance, the complaints emphasized both the racial basis of the discrimination and the severe economic consequences it visited on black workers.[9]

Prior to 1942, regional offices of USES acted as liaisons between hiring employers and would-be workers. After the administration of President Franklin Roosevelt federalized those offices, USES stated its general opposition to race discrimination. However, the central administration encouraged its branches, especially in the South, to accommodate racial discrimination. Wartime instructions to local offices stated that USES policy was "to make all referrals without regard to race, color, creed, or national origin except when an employer's order

includes these specifications which the employer is not willing to eliminate." Moreover, even if the employer included no racial specifica-
tion, "but community custom or past hiring practices of the employer"
suggested racial restrictions, interviewers were supposed to inquire
proactively about such restrictions.[10]

As a result, the employment offices remained regional in many of
their policies and practices. USES officials frequently asked employers
about their racial preferences. And they referred very few African
Americans to jobs in war industries, defense-training courses, or youth
work defense projects. In keeping with the racially segmented labor
market, USES maintained segregated offices in the South. Black offices were often located in a worse part of town than white offices, did
not receive placement orders promptly, and referred unskilled and domestic labor, whereas white offices filled orders for skilled labor. Even
outside the South, physically integrated USES offices used a segregated referral system. They often referred African Americans only to
unskilled or domestic jobs that paid far less than the jobs the black
workers sought.[11]

It is difficult to separate out where the prejudices of private employers left off and the independent policies and attitudes of USES
and its officials began. The sense that USES could not eliminate private discrimination began at the top. Although the chief of USES saw
race discrimination as "an undesirable social and economic practice,"
he did not think USES could do anything to end it. That sense filtered
through the immense bureaucracy. One federal employment official
fielded a complaint from Arthur St. Cyr about hiring discrimination at
General Motors. The official said that "though he did not agree with
the said Plant's attitude in said matter . . . the Plant Officials were
within their rights, and . . . nothing could be done about it."[12]

A similar dynamic—of public ambivalence combined with presumed private hostility—plagued black efforts to take advantage of
federal job-training programs during the war. When the federal government began providing funds to train skilled workers in 1940, black
economist and administration official Robert Weaver and the Labor
Division of the National Defense Advisory Commission took on the
task of assisting African Americans into defense training and jobs.
They faced an uphill battle. The National Defense Training Act prohibited discrimination in training programs, but it allowed for segre-

gation. The administrative agencies in charge of the funds had little capacity to implement the nondiscrimination requirement, and they were neither enthusiastic nor aggressive about enforcing it.[13]

Moreover, states determined how to use their allocations of federal training money. So in the first two years of training for defense industries, African Americans never made up more than 6 percent of trainees. In June 1940, out of 175,000 trainees, only 4,600 were African American. By July 1942, blacks amounted to 7 percent of trainees in the South and Washington, D.C., even though they made up 22 percent of the population of those areas. Some states had no courses for African Americans; others had one or two. In Knoxville, Tennessee, white trainees could choose from nine classes in drafting, machine shop practice, welding, and sheet metal. African Americans could take two in "auto servicing." "These supposed defense classes," bemoaned Weaver, "actually were no more than training in polishing cars, filling gasoline tanks and the like. They were to be located on a parking lot."[14]

Even when classes were integrated, opportunities for African Americans were severely limited. Ella Hamilton was rejected for sheet metal training at Grumman because the program admitted only two African Americans per class. Training officials were not always forthright with applicants; instead, they limited African American opportunities through obfuscation and indirection. Ferdinand M. Barry went to Pensacola, Florida, for sheet metal training in response to a call for workers from "the Government over the radio & through the press." Once there, however, he was "put to doing odd jobs." He hoped the NAACP could help him "get the training that I have a right to."[15]

Like USES's rationale that referrals for skilled jobs were futile so long as employers refused to hire African Americans, many in charge of training programs refused to admit African Americans because they assumed that blacks would have difficulty finding jobs that utilized their training. "The taxpayers' money," explained the Alabama supervisor of trade and industrial education, "should not be wasted on training persons for occupations which they could not expect to pursue." John Joseph Woods spent 400 hours learning the skills of aircraft riveting. He then heard that the Brewster Aeronautical Company for which he had been trained would only hire local African Americans. This came as no surprise to the principal of the school Wood had attended. Wood described how the principal said that "he didn't know how he had 'missed me,' that he had talked to the other Negro students privately, explaining the situation and the difficulty in securing employment, and persuaded some of them to withdraw."[16]

The problem with trained black workers was twofold. First, training African Americans for skilled positions prepared them to take jobs away from potential white applicants. Second, it might place them in positions of power over white workers without comparable training. Gloster Current, the secretary of the Detroit branch of the NAACP, accompanied a woman to a plant to advocate on her behalf. According to Current, the man in charge of the plant described the incident as follows: "A short while ago a black nigger by the name of Gloster Current brought a colored girl all dolled up out here demanding that she be sent to the training school." The man at the plant declared that "he would not be dictated to by a 'nigger' nor would he put a 'nigger' over white girl as inspector." Training black workers, government officials concluded, would only lead to further rejection and disappointment for African Americans and a waste of federal resources.[17]

When government agencies were the employers themselves, they also had mixed records on hiring African Americans for appropriate positions. A few New Deal agencies, like the Works Progress Administration (WPA), prohibited discrimination in local public works job assignments and wage rates. And the Public Works Administration (PWA) under Harold Ickes's directorship went beyond its congressional mandate to set contract quotas. The U.S. Housing Authority and the Federal Works Agency later followed Ickes's precedent. But for the most part, federal agencies before and during the war practiced pervasive racial discrimination.[18]

The Veterans Administration (VA) in New York City, for example, provoked widespread protest from African American women. The women complained to the NAACP in 1945 that they had not been promoted since the VA had hired them almost a year before but the VA had promoted more recently hired "white girls." In addition, their manager discriminated against them in job assignments, discipline, and other on-the-job matters. The black woman who had most vocally protested the discrimination had been fired. On March 25, Ernestine Welch, one of the black women who worked at the VA, described how "the bombshell exploded" there in terms of its "Jim Crow tendencies."

The VA transferred several black and white employees to a particular office and relegated the black employees to menial tasks they refused to perform. "[A] disturbance occurred which required police interference," Welch reported. "It is to the progress of our war effort and the betterment of a true democratic way of life," Welch proposed, "that such conditions be abolished."[19]

Some discrimination at the Veterans Administration masked itself in bureaucratic garb. Grace Morton found a temporary job as an X-ray technician in the New York Regional Office. She asked why she, the only African American technician, had still not been made permanent when more recently hired whites had been. She received a number of different excuses. First, she was told her papers had been lost; then she was told that a shortage of clerks meant that they were unable to change her status. When the head of the department intervened on her behalf, "one excuse or another [was] given as the reason for me not receiving my status."[20]

Other workers complained about similar bureaucratic mazes with no apparent successful routes. Complaints about the civil service were legion. Lela P. Leverette applied for numerous jobs after she qualified as a typist and stenographer in the civil service examination. Time after time, she received inquiries about her availability. Each inquiry led nowhere. Sometimes she would show up for an interview and learn that the proper interviewer was not available. She was told she would be contacted. But the further contacts never came. Some African Americans who did receive civil service interviews did so because hiring officials had not realized initially that the qualified applicants were African American. Annie E. Powell was convinced of racial discrimination after an interview at the Detroit Tank Arsenal. The interviewer had been "obviously very shocked to see that he had to interview a Negro, or that a Negro had even qualified for a position."[21]

Even after P. M. Sunday met with civil service interviewers in Jacksonville, Florida, they still did not realize the light-skinned man was African American. He was only rejected when his interviewers learned he had attended historically black Fisk University. One sympathetic interviewer suggested he register for a position in "the western or northern sections of the country," where he might have more luck. Meanwhile, the civil service commission told him that in-state applicants had preference and he was unlikely to procure an out-of-state position. Shortly thereafter he was told an in-state position he had applied for was still vacant but would be filled by someone from out of state. For Sunday, as for so many black workers during the war, the federal government proved at best indifferent and at worst downright hostile to the search for adequate work.[22]

Black workers expected fair treatment not just from the government itself during World War II. They also wanted fairness from private industry. Private discrimination seemed as racially and economically problematic as public discrimination. When a Ford plant discriminated in hiring, the president of the Detroit branch of the NAACP not only thought Ford had "no right," but also that it had contributed to the "breakdown of the democratic process of hiring." Especially in the months immediately following President Roosevelt's creation of the FEPC in June 1941, African American industrial workers called upon the NAACP to redress discrimination in the defense-related private labor market.[23]

In part, the sense of entitlement against private employers reflected broader changes in the legal regulation of all employment relationships. After the 1935 National Labor Relations Act (NLRA), even private businesses had to cease discriminating against union members. That meant that employers no longer enjoyed an unfettered prerogative to hire whom they liked. The creation of the FEPC seemed to suggest that race, too, was an impermissible factor for employers to consider. Especially where companies received millions of dollars in contracts from the federal government, black workers thought private employers should be bound not to discriminate. Although workers' expectations varied with particular industries and firms—word went out about which plants were "sure" and which were "anti-Negro"—the war generally contributed to the sense that even privately run businesses had a patriotic duty to hire without regard to race. African Americans expected to find opportunities for economic advancement in the private as well as the public sector.[24]

Many business owners and managers saw the issue differently. The federal officials who refused to refer black USES applicants to skilled work or training courses were not entirely wrong in thinking that many private employers were reluctant about and even hostile to hiring African Americans. Indeed, 51 percent of respondents to a USES questionnaire sent to hundreds of businessmen with large defense contracts in early 1942 said they would not and did not employ African Americans. Only around one-quarter of respondents would employ them without reservation.[25]

The volume of letters complaining about overt discrimination in the private labor market reflects those statistics. Some prospective employers were frank about their policies of not hiring African Americans, as John Allen's prospective employer was in Indiana. According to Samuel Whitney, the employment officials at a construction company in Alexandria, Louisiana, were quite honest. "They told me that they believed I was a qualified electrician, and that they didn't have the least idea that I couldn't perform my duties." They explained that there was only a single "reason they couldn't hire me as an electrical worker, and that was because I was not white. I asked them what did color have to do with it. They told me that it was a shame to say so, but they just wasn't allowed to hire colored electrical workers." Across the country, black workers had similar encounters, as managers explained their policies of not hiring African Americans.[26]

African American women faced even greater rejection. According to one Kaiser shipyards personnel manager, black women were "not adapted to the work in the shipyards" because they "do not seem to want to take instructions. They don't seem to want to be trained. They don't seem to have the ability to work from past experience." A female personnel manager agreed that African American women were not "as well adapted" to work in the shipyards as white women, but her reasoning was different: "their size" prevented them from doing the "climbing and . . . walking around and getting into difficult places and positions."[27]

Judging by the numbers of African American women in many plants and industries, the attitudes of the shipyard personnel were common. One Ford plant with approximately 27,000 employees and 3,000 women, for example, did not employ a single black woman. Beulah Newton demanded to know why private employers hired white women and black men but not black women: "I wont to no why what is wrong with the Negress that they will hire Negro mans but not woman. They don't want to hire a Col. woman but our col. boys are fightin so why col. woman cant get job lake the white woman."[28]

Those employers who were reluctant to acknowledge their policies of discrimination tried to hide behind bureaucracies or personnel managers. African Americans complained about the need for forms, the need to see this manager instead of that supervisor, and the unending, unbearable wait that never resulted in a job for blacks while whites lined up behind somehow ended up ahead. Elizabeth Scott's story reflects the frustrations of facing evasion and dishonesty. The guard at one company

African American woman worker at the Richmond Shipyard No. 1 of the Kaiser Company, 1943. (Farm Security Administration, Office of War Information Photograph Collection, Library of Congress.)

she approached turned her away because the employment office was allegedly closed for payday. Her "suspicion [was] aroused" when she saw a white woman waiting in the office. She called and learned that the office was indeed open. The guard again gave her a hard time, but she did see an employment official, who told her she needed a birth certificate. But others, white and black, who the company had hired before her had not needed one. The same was true for four years of high school education. She knew the plant had hired African Americans before, but she heard "rumors that the white were finding fault saying too many coloured were hired and not enough white." "I thought," she wrote, "when a Defense Plant advertised for workers and could use them, they were to be placed, white or coloured. First come, first served." She believed "there must be some way of correcting such partiality" not only for her own benefit but for other "coloured employee[s] [who] may stumble into the same difficulty as I have."[29]

African American job-seekers seemed always to be waiting. The workers returned day after day to employers who told them there were currently no openings but there might be in the future. Others waited for word at home from employers who told them they would let them know when to report. Black workers stood in lines, filled out forms to fill out more forms, took buses and trains, called, and wrote. Whichever way and however often they approached prospective employers, whites got the jobs while blacks got the runaround.[30]

Just as federal employers and other officials hid their hiring discrimination behind the preferences of others, so too did private employers. They claimed that they themselves were not prejudiced but that white employees would refuse to work with the black applicants. When P. M. Sunday was refused a civil service position in Jacksonville, Florida, he asked the interviewer why. According to Sunday, the interviewer said "he personally was not prejudiced to my working with him, but that I had to work along beside other men who would be." The director of personnel at Bethlehem Shipbuilding on Staten Island, New York, also invoked the prejudice of his employees when he refused to hire African American welders. He "frankly admitted, that altho they employed colored workers in other capacities in the plant, that they had not hired any welders because there were many Southern men in that Dep't. and they just did not fit in with them." White workers, especially those from the South, would not accept black coworkers, these employers said regretfully. Like USES officials and federal training administrators, such employers clucked their tongues, wrung their hands, and concluded that nothing could be done.[31]

Frequently, these excuses only thinly veiled the attitudes of employers and managers themselves. When Edmond Van Osten applied for sheet metal work, a company official told him "that the white workers would not like to work with colored workers." The official then offered Van Osten a job as a porter, an unskilled, poorly paid position. When Van Osten pushed the matter a few days later, the official "stated that he would not hire any more colored workers, that he was through with hiring them."[32]

Even when companies hired African American men and women, they reserved the good jobs for whites. Companies denied black workers professional, clerical, and skilled jobs. Instead they offered them unskilled laborers' or domestics' jobs that entailed lower pay and worse conditions. Company officials did not hesitate to say so. Before Esterline Davis could tell a clerk who had asked her what position she was applying for in Oakland, California, in 1942 (a clerical one), the clerk answered her own question: "janitress." When Thomas Allen Trayler applied for a job as a welder at the Budd Wheel Company, the employment manager turned him down. He stated "that they did not hire Negroes in that department but they did hire Negroes in the foundry." Several other plants refused to hire Trayler as a welder but again offered him work in the hot and dangerous foundry. Joseph Gordon stated the problem simply when he wrote to the NAACP that he was hired as a janitor in St. Louis, Missouri, "a position that seems to be in conformity with the company's present policy of reserving such work solely for Colored Americans." "Surely," wrote one dissatisfied worker, "Negroes can work at better occupations than they get here, there are hundreds of jobs Negroes should have here and could get if the right kind of action was taken."[33]

Even as employers hired black workers as janitors or unskilled laborers, the workers found that "[m]uch of the work assigned the janitors is not really janitorial work." Employers hired African Americans as unskilled workers, paid them the meager salaries of such jobs, and worked them as skilled laborers. They were called "janitors" because, Joseph Gordon stated, "janitors are paid fifty cents an hour" whereas "white Americans are paid an average of 70 cents an hour." A "carpenter pusher" in Florida who worked with "a white man over me," complained that responsibility rested on him "while earning a wage of 40c. per hour. He do not know what to do on the job. I have to instruct him and see that everything is righted. I do not see then why I can't be made to receive the same wage or at least ¾ of his earning."[34]

Indignation grew when African Americans found themselves demoted after training white replacements. "I was the only one on the job who could [run a bulldozer and carrierall driver], which is classed skilled labor," William D. Radford wrote to the NAACP. Radford's supervisor asked him "to brake in three white men to do that line of work, so I complied and after I had trained them . . . they were employed to do that work, and I was offered a job flunking around the camp." The new job paid $.90 an hour, whereas Radford's old job had paid $1.65 an hour. He refused the demotion and quit. Reddick Strickland had also been demoted to a lower-paying job at the Newport News Drydock & Shipbuilding Company. "It seems to be the policy of late," wrote his local NAACP branch secretary on his behalf, "to put young whites in the Helper jobs previously held by Negroes and let them get the bonus while the Negroes do practically the same work and the so-called white helpers mostly stand around and draw the extra pay and do little work."[35]

Many workplaces were racially segmented and segregated. African American workers usually performed menial, hard, and low-wage jobs whereas whites performed skilled and higher-wage jobs. Those African Americans lucky enough to find jobs complained about such segregation, though not with as much frequency as they did about finding adequate work. Black workers found it particularly difficult to procure work in integrated settings when the interracial work crossed gender lines. One African American shipyard worker was denied the opportunity to work in the sheet metal shop. Because there were "white girls working there," African American men could not. Another incident in the shipyards reflected the same attitude. When Joyce Ray Washington, an African American woman who had been tacking for a white man, was switched to tack for a black fitter, she asked why. The white leadman replied, "It's because I don't like the idea of white women tacking for colored men and colored women tacking for white men."[36]

As previously white workforces gained black workers, companies increased segregation in the incidents of working life. One worker complained that his company had "approved and placed a tag on one of the wash room doors reading 'for colored only.' . . . The next step in such discriminatory acts is rumored to be a separate shower and locker room and a separate period for us to eat lunch" in a new company cafeteria. When employment came with housing, such workplace segregation proved even more consequential. It could mean the difference between a job and no job. Thomas Harrison, a sandhog working tunnel construction, was refused employment because white workers did not want to bunk with black workers. It was Harrison's understanding that the company "was unable to employ Negroes because they could not live in the bunkhouse." William Brinson learned the same thing when his foreman told him "there was no use in my going up to [the job] unless I had money I wanted to throw away, that there was no place for colored fellows to stay and that they would not allow colored fellows to stay in the bunk house." William Radford moved around Alaska looking for work where he would not face discrimination. At one stop, Radford wrote, "I was told I could work there but could not live in the camps with the white men. Well to live out in town the expense was to great." So he moved on again.[37]

Even as many employers hid their own prejudices behind claims that white workers resisted black advancement and integrated workplaces, the excuse itself had more than a kernel of truth to it. At times, white workers and employers both obstructed African Americans' ability to find work, and it was hard to know where to place the blame. This was the case in the West Coast shipyards. The workers could not always figure out where discrimination by the union ended and discrimination by the employers began.[38]

At other times, however, employers were sincerely willing to hire African Americans, and white workers refused to work with them. Sometimes white hostility took the form of harassment and brutality. At other times, it took the form of unorganized but mass violence. When the Alabama Dry Dock and Shipbuilding Company attempted to upgrade twelve African American welders in compliance with the FEPC, 20,000 white workers went on a rampage. They walked off the job and rioted for four days. Black workers also suffered "hate strikes" by rank-and-file white workers in violation of union policies across the country.[39]

Most frequently, African Americans complained about the systematic way that formal union rules established exclusion, segregation, and discrimination. When the federal government conferred the authority of exclusive representation on unions under the NLRA, it gave tremendous power to white organized labor. It also undermined their status as purely private associations. Since unions now drew power from the government regulation that protected them, they appeared in some sense to have taken on the mantle of the government itself. As a result, when unions curtailed the economic opportunities of black workers, they exercised governmental authority under the guise of their own private power.[40]

The extent to which unions shut out black workers varied considerably. Not infrequently, mostly white unions used federal authority to abuse, denigrate, and exclude black workers. African Americans faced constitutional or ritualistic exclusion in eighteen international unions, most of which were independent unions and American Federation of Labor (AFL) affiliates. Other unions, like the International Longshoremen's Association (ILA), included black workers but in their own segregated locals. Some black workers joined all-black unions like A. Philip Randolph's Brotherhood of Sleeping Car Porters, whereas others joined unions that aimed for integration. This was especially true after 1940, when the Congress of Industrial Organizations (CIO) and the AFL agreed to attempt to eliminate discrimination in defense work. Even in integrated unions, however, the majority ruled, and black workers seldom constituted a majority that could represent its own interests. Black workers were thus dependent on white unions to represent them. The unions frequently disappointed.[41]

The exclusion of African Americans from unions became even more devastating to black employment prospects when unions obtained closed-shop agreements with employers. These agreements prohibited employers from hiring nonunion workers. Defense contractors in Portland, Oregon, "committed in writing their willingness to use Negroes in any and all plant operations," according to a local affiliate of the National Urban League. But they had also entered into closed-shop agreements with discriminatory boilermakers' unions. The contractors thus felt themselves unable to hire African Americans as skilled laborers in the shipyards. The unions claimed "that most of the available supply of Negro labor . . . could be absorbed as janitors," and so hiring them as boilermakers would be unnecessary. A janitor made $.77 per hour to the boilermaker's $1.25.[42]

Even where no closed-shop contract existed per se, USES agreements with employers could function in the same way. African American painters excluded from a white union local in Kansas City faced just such a situation. "By virtue of an agreement of the U.S. Public Service Employment Office here with construction contractors," wrote Thomas A. Webster on behalf of the painters, orders for skilled workers were sent directly to the unions. "[T]he union registers are exhausted before other workers registered with the U.S. Employment Service are considered. As you can see," he emphasized, "this practice operates against the interest of Negro workers who are not union members."[43]

Where unions did accept African Americans, they often discriminated against them in referrals, held them back from being upgraded, and failed to protect them when employers discriminated against them. Two African American women pressers who had been unemployed for more than five years could be found in their union office "sitting on the bench every morning waiting for a days work." They felt they were "not given [their] rights." They were paying the same dues as employed white workers but were rarely given work. If they complained to the union, they were "put on a blacklist."[44]

In September 1941, a group of African American auto workers in Detroit sent the NAACP a series of affidavits concerning the United Automobile Workers' (UAW) treatment of their complaints of employment discrimination. Eddie Kemp complained to the union about the failure of Dodge to promote him. He testified that his union local told him, "The white employees will not work with the colored employees; this would slow up production." Another complaint elicited the following response: "[T]o a certain extent our progress in attaining promotions may be limited by certain racial prejudices of some of our white brothers." Although apologetic for not being able to help, a union official told James Phelps, "Local unions have autonomous rights which can not be violated by the International Union." He cautioned, "Age-old prejudice can not be entirely eliminated over night, by legislation or establish[ing] by-laws, but must come through the relatively slow process of liberal and progressive education of our membership."[45]

Black longshoremen in New York City who were dues-paying members of the ILA also felt that for years they "had been knocked around." By 1940, "the conditions [were] getting harder to bear" than a few years earlier. And "still we the Negroes have to pay the same union dues as the white longshoremen have to pay." The problem in general, wrote Alphonso Morris, was that "[t]he Negroes are not Recognize by the Union as a union man should be Recognize." More specifically, Morris complained that segregated white gangs intent on having "all hands white" on particular piers were edging out segregated black gangs. "The union are the only one to blame for all the discrimination," Morris alleged. Things were even worse in New Jersey, where those "Negroes [who took] the chances of trying to find work . . . are taking a chance of getting beat to death or been chase to the Ferry Boat Station." Morris concluded: "[A]nd so it goes over the whole waterfront." Adolphis Braithwaite echoed Morris's complaints. Braithwaite found "it very hard to obtain work because the Negroe's are being discriminated, the union still expect us to pay up our dues."[46]

When African Americans were useful to white unions, as when their votes were needed to gain recognition, white workers sometimes treated them well. But such welcomes were often short-lived. A vague sense of foreboding filled the African American members of a newly formed union at the Crocker-Wheeler electrical company in East Orange, New Jersey, in 1941. "Apparently, they were accepted [into the union] in the haste to form a local," the NAACP's Roy Wilkins observed. "As soon as the union was recognized, the Negro workers began to notice a distinct change in the attitude of the other workers." The union made clear that it did "not favor any further promotion in the shop, and, in fact, is on the verge of asking for their demotion."[47]

The African American workers who wrote to the NAACP did so out of anger, frustration, and desperation. They did so in times of rejection and crisis. Yet despite the discrimination they described, African Americans did make economic gains during World War II. By the end of the war, black men and women had entered industry in unprecedented numbers. In government employment, African Americans made noteworthy, though still geographically spotty, gains. In 1938, African Americans constituted 8.4 percent of federal employees, 90 percent of whom were in custodial work. By 1944, African Americans constituted 19.2 percent of federal employees, of whom 40 percent were in custodial work. Between early 1942 and late 1944, African Americans working for private defense-related firms rose from 3 percent to more than 8 percent. The number of African Americans performing skilled or semiskilled labor or acting as foremen doubled. Black incomes rose, and black unemployment fell. And even though they were often hired only after available black men and white women, black women in particular benefited from openings in industrial employment. Sixty percent of the 1 million African Americans added to the industrial labor force during the war were women.[48]

As the complaints of the workers reflect, however, new opportunities were still limited. As the war ended, African Americans held fewer than 2 percent of clerical and sales jobs and 5 percent of professional, proprietary, and managerial jobs. The average income of African American families remained only half of the income of white families. As Robert Weaver lamented in 1946, "Even in a period of national emergency and economic need, the color line gave way slowly and only after great resistance."[49]

By the end of the war, African Americans had obtained some new tools for combating discrimination in the form of state and local antidiscrimination laws. But they had also acquired additional problems. Even before the Allied victory, African Americans anticipated job losses and demotions like those they had experienced at the end of the First World War. When in 1944 the Senate passed a reconversion statute that made the states responsible for unemployment insurance after the war, the situation looked bleak. The *Norfolk Journal and Guide*, a black newspaper, lamented that the states would cheat "the Negro out of his equitable share of benefits . . . and grasp such an opportunity . . . to further depress the living standards of colored civilians and returned veterans during the postwar period." As African Americans came home after fighting for democracy, the *Journal and Guide* predicted, they would be "forced . . . into actual or virtual serfdom."[50]

Serfdom did not ensue, but many states did take the opportunity to downgrade black labor. Some states refused unemployment insurance unless black workers interviewed for jobs that often paid far less than wartime defense work. In the South, moreover, blacks found themselves forced to agree to accept available general labor and service jobs or forego unemployment insurance. This was an effective bureaucratic way to reverse the progress of black workers who had managed to obtain skilled and semiskilled jobs during the war.[51]

Changes in the postwar labor market itself also led to setbacks. As white veterans came home from the war, they expected their jobs back. The slowing economy could not always support both the new workers and the old. Because white workers usually had greater seniority than black workers, and especially black women, African Americans lost their jobs. The problem with resolving such cases was that, as Marian Wynn Perry of the NAACP put it in 1945, "the discrimination occurred in the years when they were not hired, and does not appear as such in the layoff." "In the typical pattern," Perry wrote, "Negroes, of course, were among the last to be hired, and therefore constitute a larger proportion of the provisional employees than whites."[52]

African Americans were particularly vulnerable because they had made the greatest gains in defense industries most likely to experience job losses after the war. The explosion of African American workers was particularly large in shipbuilding and aircraft manufacturing, for example. With 90 percent of African American war workers employed in those industries, ordnance, and munitions, the cancellation of wartime contracts was devastating. At the Alabama Dry Dock and Shipbuilding Company, the end of the war meant a labor-force reduction from 30,000 to 3,000. By December 1945, four months after Allied victory, 450,000 African Americans had lost their manufacturing jobs.[53]

Reconversion aside, the same problems African Americans faced during the war plagued them after the war as well. Some postwar job losses resulted more directly from discrimination than from reconversion. Rothana Serrano heard her supervisor tell the woman who had hired Serrano, "I don't like colored people and I am going to get them all out of my department." Shortly thereafter the supervisor fired Serrano. When a white foreman fired Walter Tannis after the war, the foreman vowed, according to Tannis, "I will hire no Negroes in my gang and I am trying to get rid of what I have now." When Tannis's union protected him, he returned to work. The foreman told him to "leave the job at once" or he "would be carried out on a stretcher." Tannis left, and he later filed a complaint with New York's State Commission Against Discrimination. According to a "group of nurses who want justice," the "most popular remark" of a white supervisor at a Bronx hospital was, "[T]he war is over now. We are going to get all of these Dam Niggers out of here."[54]

Discrimination affected new hiring as well. African Americans continued to complain that prospective employers told them that they "do not hire colored people." Black workers like Lloyd Joseph still got the sense that those in charge of hiring wanted "to confine as many Negroes as possible to the lowest paid jobs." Max Jacobs "charge[d] that it is the policy of [Vick Chemical Company] to employ Negroes only in certain departments and to refuse Negroes opportunities for employment in other departments." The evidence he marshaled was convincing: out of 300 employees, only eleven were African Americans. They all worked in the stock room, mail room, or mimeograph room. After Jacobs sought training for advancement, the company discharged him on what he was convinced was "a pretext of insubordination."[55]

Those who spent the war years acquiring education and knowledge that they could not use were particularly bitter about limited job opportunities. Andrew Gancy had gained two years of experience as a mechanic during the war and an additional year of training afterward under the G.I. Bill. Still he received the runaround when he sought work as a mechanic's helper in the civil service after the war. Shirley May Codrington blamed a perceived rise in "[j]uvenile delinquency" on the inability of young people to get jobs after the war. "The younger generation are graduating from various High . . . Schools and are not being given the chance to practice the trade which they have spent four years to learn. . . . These youngsters are not born criminals . . . but are victims of discriminatory practices." She complained as well about the inability to find appropriate work. "Young Negroes have educated themselves in the professional and clerical field; why should they be forced to do domestic work with a high school diploma? Is that why I spent the best years of my life in school to become a scrubwoman or a baby sitter? God Forbid!"[56]

Just after World War II ended, black economist Robert Weaver discussed the problems of African Americans in industry in the context of hundreds of years of racial and economic inequality: "Negroes . . . were brought here expressly and involuntarily to furnish cheap labor." Although slavery itself had "long been abolished," Weaver wrote, "[i]n the place of slavery we have substituted a color occupational system. That system perpetuates the concept of the Negro as an inferior being and establishes institutions to assure his inferior status. It serves to conceal the basic nature of economic problems and covers them with color situations." It might appear that an aircraft factory in Los Angeles or a jeep production line in Detroit existed in an entirely

different universe from the agricultural South and the problems of peonage, lynching, and political and economic powerlessness blacks endured there. Yet Weaver suggested that the economic problems about
which African American industrial workers complained nationwide
were still another legacy of American slavery.[57]

Indeed, both expert commentators and the black industrial workers
who wrote to the NAACP sensed the legacy of southern slavery pursuing them across the nation. Certainly, "[t]he most violent and in-
temperate statements" about fair employment, Weaver noted, "em-
anated from the South, where the color-caste system was most firmly
intrenched." But observers like historian and civil rights scholar Louis
Ruchames believed that the South "differed from other regions only in
degree." He quoted the FEPC as concluding that even "[t]he East . . .
tended to relegate Negroes to the so-called H jobs—hot, heavy and
hard." Although slavery had disappeared much earlier in the North
than the South, segregation, discrimination, and inequality had long
persisted throughout the nation.[58]

African American complainants nonetheless often blamed a mobile
white South for their troubles. With the nation—both white and
black—on the move for war work, regional differences in racial attitudes could not be pinned to their places of origin. William Radford,
who had a hard time finding suitable work in Alaska, had been told
"that Alaska is now over run with Southern people, mostly from Texas
Alabama & Tenn." "[O]ld timers" told him that "there had never been
any discrimination in the interior of Alaska until now."[59]

Even when the personnel in question were not literally southerners,
African Americans identified racial discrimination with the South and
egalitarianism with the North. Thus, when Bessie Armstrong complained about her inability to get war work in Cincinnati, she wrote
that "Negro women in supposedly Northern cities are not allowed to
work in defense jobs." And when John Grantham complained about
the Sun Shipbuilding and Dry Dock Company in Chester, Pennsylvania, he described the company executives as "mostly all Southerners
from the state of Delaware and southern Pennsylvania who are opposed to Negro unity and racial equality."[60]

Like the racialized southern labor market that often served as the
workers' point of reference, black industrial workers understood their
problems as both racial and economic. It was rare for African Amer-

ican workers to disassociate their problems from either the racial context in which they occurred or the economic sources and consequences that made them so fundamentally important. Some of the
complaints emphasized the indignity of race discrimination, others its
economic consequences, and still others the economic conditions of
work almost without regard to race. For the most part, however,
African Americans did not pigeonhole their complaints as solely about
either race discrimination or labor conditions. Even when the industrial complaints invoked clear discrimination on the basis of race, the
racial issues frequently remained intertwined with the economic ones.
What was at stake in most of these cases but the rate of pay, the hours
of work, the conditions of the job? And when they emphasized economic issues, race was never far from the fore. Even those who barely
mentioned race in their letters and made no explicit claims of race
discrimination frequently wrote on behalf of "colored workers" to the
NAACP. Their complaints depicted a racialized political economy
somewhat different from that of the agricultural South but one that
nonetheless intertwined racial and economic oppression.

Most of the letters black industrial workers sent the NAACP made
explicit reference both to racial discrimination and to economic hardship. An anonymous writer wrote to Walter White, the head of the
NAACP, that "Negroes are being unfairly treated" at a project in West
Palm Beach, Florida. Some workers were trying to unionize, and the
fee to join the union was $10—"[a] sum a poor person can hardly raise
of course. All that is to keep them out. If we don't get some help from
some kind of organization the laboring class of people will be out of
work. Please consider our plight." The exact relationship between the
"Negroes" who were being unfairly treated and the "laboring class of
people" who could not afford union dues was not clear, but in the
writer's mind they overlapped considerably, if not totally.[61]

Similarly, a group of stewards on dredge boats of the Memphis District of the United States Engineering Department complained about
overtime work without pay, about the injustice of paying for room and
board even during leaves, and about inadequate wages. William R.
Henderson, Jr., the Memphis agent of the National Maritime Union,
tried to get the NAACP and other "labor, liberal, and Negro organizations" involved in the case. He suggested that race played a greater
role than the workers themselves had indicated. "This is clearly a case

of Negro discrimination," he wrote to John P. Davis of the National Negro Congress. "Nearly all of the discharged employees to date have been Negroes." Both the stewards and Henderson himself described the goals of the stewards as "revis[ed] . . . wage scales" and "improved working conditions." But the fact that most of the stewards were African American, and that most of those fired were also African American, made this a case of race discrimination in his mind, or at least in his pleas for the involvement of black civil rights organizations.[62]

The most common melding of racial discrimination and economic hardship was also the most obvious: because of racial discrimination, the complainant was unable to support him- or herself. When Josephine Geary encountered a "manager who has willfully refuse to hire me because of my race and color" in Clearfield, Pennsylvania, in 1946, she "beg[ged] the N.A.A.C.P. to take over my case and see that I get fair treatments, and get a job to earn a honesty living for myself and one child." She had a "case," she needed "justice," and that justice entailed providing for herself and her child. When Melba Sunday reported civil-service discrimination against her husband to the NAACP, she wrote, "We are poor. We have two small children to support. Therefore we have no funds to start a court proceeding and thus, I am begging you and the NAACP to help us."[63]

When discrimination took the form of segregation, the economic impact of segregation garnered far more complaints to the NAACP than the principle of segregation itself. For some African Americans, especially those active in the NAACP, the essence of the harm of segregated unions was segregation per se. For others, the problem was both segregation and discrimination. Thus, shipyard worker Robert Rhone stated his opposition to a segregated boilermakers' auxiliary in the Northwest because "they didn't have any powers in the auxiliary, and I just felt that I didn't like segregation." He lost his job "[r]ather than join an auxiliary of this type." When asked what the precise problem was with the unions, Rhone failed to distinguish between segregation and discrimination. He was aggrieved that the auxiliaries "didn't have any power whatsoever, they didn't have any officers, that it was Jim Crow—that was enough for me right there."[64]

Still others faulted the auxiliaries for creating barriers to economic advancement, not because they constituted segregation per se. William

Johnson had joined the boilermakers' auxiliary union in order to get skilled work. He was unhappy with his membership because it was "discriminatory," because he did not "get the same benefits as members in the parent union." Lee Anderson said, "I wasn't joining no dirty discriminatory setup like that order there where I had no rights at all." These men did not care so much about being in the same local as white shipyard workers. They cared about the material benefits of membership: the pension plan, grievance committees, representation, and most of all, referrals to work. The creation of auxiliary unions for black boilermakers was, according to their formal FEPC complaint, "a willful and wrongful scheme . . . to limit and restrict the employment of Negro workmen and to deprive Negro workmen of economic security, equal participation in collective bargaining, and the several rights, privileges and benefits which are incidents of membership" in the union.[65]

The boilermakers' views were hardly idiosyncratic among those who wrote to the NAACP. John Grantham, an NAACP branch president and employee of the Sun Ship and Dry Dock Company in Chester, Pennsylvania, complained about "a so-called all colored yard" at Sun Ship. His long letter to Walter White illustrates the complex interaction between the desire for work and the desire for integration. Grantham criticized Sun Ship for convincing the media that it had set up one shipyard completely under black supervision. Grantham knew "that there are a great deal of Negroes and whites who really think that this segregated yard . . . is of vast importance to the welfare of the Negro people." African Americans were not actually in charge, though. Only after stating at length that the problem with Sun Ship's segregated yard was that it was not entirely segregated did Grantham display any objection to segregation on a principled basis. "Of course," he continued, "I am opposed to fact or action of establishing a separate yard for Negroes." He returned, nonetheless, to his central point, "[B]ut I do think it would be better for the Sun Ship to either turn one way or the other. . . . I don't feel that it should be falsely stated that this yard is operated by Negroes when the Negro does not hold any key positions in the yard. I would rather it be a mixed yard but if the Sun Ship continues to practice such unfair practices it will soon lead to a very destructive situation."[66]

The complaints of New York City longshoremen were less equivocal about the economic benefits of segregation. They protested that although some piers had historically been worked by black gangs and some by white gangs, white workers had of late begun colonizing the black gangs' piers. The one black gang that was allowed to function as a concession worked with only eleven men, as opposed to the usual twenty-one. Moreover, as new piers were built to which neither group could lay historical claim, whites would argue that "Negroes have never work[ed] on this pier before." Of course they had not, the black union delegate responded, because it was "a brand new pier and neither white or negro longshoremen have work[ed] on the pier yet." What every black longshoreman wanted, wrote Alphonso Morris, was "a chance to make fair living for his family." The essence of Adolphus Braithwaite's complaint, like that of Morris's, was economic: "I am the father of three children and I have to work to keep my family together, condition are very good on the pier there are plenty of work the men are working day and night, but I find it very hard to obtain work because the Negroe's are being discriminated." Again, the goal was work, not integrated work. When Braithwaite asked the union for work on a particular pier, a union official told him "that the boys in the neighborhood do not want negroes to work on [that pier] and he will see to it that negroes do not work on" it. "Sir," Braithwaite pleaded, "we do not ask for 100 per cent only give us 1 full gang on each pier."[67]

For some African American workers, then, economic opportunity meant the end of segregation. For others, it meant a willingness to accept segregation (at least in the short term) in exchange for economic survival and advancement. Although race runs through these complaints, the central goal of these letter writers was simply work. They wanted the right to a job commensurate with their abilities. They saw union organization and governmental protection as keys to achieving that goal. What many complainants wanted most, then, was a combination of what the *Lochner* era had promised workers (the right to pursue a calling, a livelihood chosen by the worker) and what the New Deal had promised them (economic security and union organization).[68]

African American leaders and intellectuals also recognized that the inequality black workers faced had both economic and racial roots. In 1944, Rayford Whittingham Logan, a Howard University history professor and the driving force behind the Committee on Participation of Negroes in the National Defense Program, edited a controversial volume called *What the Negro Wants*. The title implied a single "Negro," with a single vantage point and a single set of desires. Indeed, the entries in the book—written by university presidents, trade union organizers, and intellectuals—all desired full equality. But that single broad goal masked considerable variations in approach. Although the authors repeatedly addressed the relationship between racial and economic inequality, they analyzed that relationship in myriad ways.[69]

Several of the contributors emphasized the historical continuities that characterized discrimination in industry. Frederick D. Patterson, president of Tuskegee Institute, described "the underselling of the Negro" "just as during slavery," occurring "for the purpose of keeping him in economic bondage." International Brotherhood of Red Caps president Willard S. Townsend felt that "[i]nequalities in our economic order" resulted from the American economic structure, rather than from "individual or stereotyped collective prejudices." Discriminatory encounters were not "a series of isolated and unrelated incidents, but are part and parcel of the whole organized pattern to keep America, economically, half free and half slave."[70]

Others ruminated particularly on the relationship between economic and political equality. Logan himself placed "[e]quality of opportunity" and "[e]qual pay for equal work" as the top two "irreducible fundamentals of first-class citizenship for all Negroes." He suggested, "The growing force of organized labor provides the Negro with a golden opportunity if he can participate in it on a truly democratic basis." W. E. B. Du Bois, one of the founders of both the NAACP and the Pan-African Congress and a giant among African American intellectuals and activists, noted that "economic equality is today widely advocated as the basis for real political power: men are beginning to demand for all persons, the right to work at a wage which will maintain a decent standard of living." And Charles H. Wesley, president of Wilberforce University, took as the starting point for his essay President Roosevelt's Four Freedoms speech. Wesley described how African Americans "have wanted freedom from want." "The Negro wants freedom to work and to maintain, with others, the accepted American standard of living."[71]

A. Philip Randolph, president of the Brotherhood of Sleeping Car Porters and organizer of the March on Washington Movement, declared that "the biggest problem confronting Negroes today is economic, that is, getting work and wages to buy food, clothing and shelter." Randolph recommended direct action techniques as well as political action to gain "the right to work": "The struggle of all oppressed peoples shows that economic action requires the supplementation of political action." Red Caps president Townsend also planned to use political action to create economic change. He called for "an integrated and planned postwar economy in order to convert our vast industrial power for an all-out conquest of domestic poverty, in a practical realization of the Four Freedoms." He recommended certain items including: nationalizing economic resources; extending "government responsibility into the fields of health, education, and housing"; broadening Social Security coverage and price and rent controls; enforcing minimum wages and maximum hours; and expanding trade unions. He also wanted anti–poll tax legislation, a permanent FEPC, and other programs directed at ending segregation and discrimination against African Americans in all aspects of economic, social, and political life.[72]

These African American leaders and civil rights activists assumed that legal nondiscrimination alone would not solve the problems of black workers. The goal for many became "full employment." Black lawyer and activist Pauli Murray thought it "obvious" in 1945 that "job discrimination based upon racial or religious prejudice is subsidiary to the more pressing issue of full employment. When jobs are plentiful, all kinds of economic discrimination are minimized. . . . The basic problem to be solved, therefore, is the problem of full employment." In the unstable reconversion economy, the problem appeared acute. In 1946, Weaver wrote that "no group [could] hope for job protection unless there [were] enough jobs for all." Because "employment opportunities for any group cannot be secured without regard for the volume of total employment," he warned, "one of the most serious consequences of mass unemployment is the fact that it will create an economic situation in which gainful employment for the Negro can and will be interpreted as a menace to insecure white workers."[73]

Ruchames, writing about the FEPC in 1953, saw the same problems Weaver had seen seven years earlier. The "discriminatory attitudes and practices" of white Americans, he predicted, "will continue for some time and will become more insistent and demanding once large-scale unemployment and suffering begin to appear." In order for black workers to achieve the right to nondiscriminatory work, it had to be linked to a governmentally provided right to work. Almost a decade after the war ended, then, Ruchames made essentially the same observation African American workers had long offered the NAACP: race discrimination in employment was both a racial problem and an economic one.[74]

It was also potentially a legal one. Like the rural farmworkers who wrote to the NAACP from the South, industrial workers across the country invited the association's lawyers to find legal solutions to their compound problems. Whether they complained about "discrimination solely on the basis of race" or the need for survival, the indignities of segregation and harassment or the bread-and-butter problems of wages and hours, they all asked lawyers to intercede. They lamented their inability to exercise, as one black painter told a recalcitrant union official, "citizenship rights, privileges, obligations and liabilities devolved upon colored men as well as white men." Black workers asserted their "full Rights" and expressed their gratitude to the NAACP at having "men of our race who have taken [interest] enough in us to look after us." They asked the NAACP for help, for investigations, and most pointedly, for legal intervention that would give perpetrators "trouble for discrimination or what."[75]

Consider Shirley May Codrington. When she complained to the NAACP about her inability to find a clerical position in New York City in 1947, she challenged NAACP lawyers to provide her with a job, with economic freedom, with citizenship itself. "As a citizen born in the United States," she wanted to know, "am I not entitled to rights of life, liberty and the pursuit of happiness?" She did not think she was asking for much. She wanted "the privilege of existing, not living, just merely existing." She understood "that conditions as far as positions are concerned are rather difficult" but reminded the NAACP that, "lest you forget, we too live by Bread and Water." She connected political freedom and economic advancement, racial subordination and economic duress. "I am making this plea to you and other civil minded persons to SHOW me and other young people like me the democracy that you taught us during our High School years. SHOW us the resulting economic freedom that you say can only be derived by education. . . . *SHOW ME AMERICA!*"[76]

◆ ◆ ◆

FOUR

The Work of Civil Rights in the Department of Justice

The Thirteenth Amendment to the federal Constitution . . . establishes the most basic of all civil liberties—the right to be free.

Robert Carr, *Federal Protection of Civil Rights: Quest
for a Sword,* 1947

CIVIL RIGHTS LAWYERS in the United States Department of Justice
(DOJ or Justice Department) tried to respond, if somewhat indirectly,
to Shirley May Codrington's challenge to make America live up to its
democratic ideals. When Attorney General Frank Murphy created the
new Civil Liberties Unit (CLU) in the Criminal Division in 1939, he announced the novel proposition that an "important function of the law
enforcement branch of government is the aggressive protection of
fundamental rights inherent in a free people." For the first time in
American history, a unit of the federal government was specifically responsible for pursuing "a program of vigilant action in the prosecution
of infringement of these rights."[1]

At the time, it was not at all clear how the lawyers in the new unit
were supposed to practice law on the basis of such ambiguous language as "fundamental rights." Although that language echoed some
descriptions of substantive due process, Murphy most certainly did not
have in mind *Lochner*-era rights to contract and property. Rather, he
and his lawyers initially understood "fundamental rights" to include
New Deal rights, the rights of organized labor, and related First
Amendment rights of free speech and assembly. Reporting on
Murphy's creation of the unit, the *New York Times* concluded that although "many cases affecting civil liberties will arise as a result of the
conflict between labor and industry, officials said the field would not
be confined to labor matters." Viewed in the context of the 1930s—a

decade saturated with discussion about and protection of the rights of workers—it seems fitting that at its creation the first federal governmental unit devoted specifically to protecting civil rights was deeply concerned with labor's rights.[2]

World War II and its domestic repercussions led to a shift in the priorities of the Civil Liberties Unit that mirrored shifts in national civil rights understandings. In 1941, the unit's name changed to the Civil Rights Section (CRS). Victor Rotnem, chief of the unit, explained that "Civil Liberties Unit" was too easily confused with the American Civil Liberties Union (ACLU, which shared much of the CLU acronym) and therefore implied too close a connection with labor. The new name, Rotnem thought, sounded less "radical" than the old. To the extent that "civil liberties" and "civil rights" had distinctive meanings in the 1940s—the former referring to labor and speech rights and the latter to Reconstruction protections for African Americans—the name change reflected a shift in the CRS's focus. The vocal protests of African Americans like Codrington had created a new political imperative for DOJ lawyers to attend to the rights claims of African Americans. The "civil rights" appellation reflected that new attention. So too did the CRS's increased pursuit of involuntary servitude, lynching, police brutality, and voting rights cases on behalf of African Americans.[3]

Still, the name change and new agenda were hardly a complete repudiation of all that went into the creation of the unit in the 1930s. The CRS maintained its original commitment to the rights of labor and reworked, rather than rejected, labor rights into its new civil rights practice during the 1940s. Unlike the most prominent interactions of labor and race rights in the national political arena during the war, however, the CRS's reworking of civil rights did not take the form of protecting black workers from discrimination in industry. The complaints of both black agricultural and industrial workers offered the CRS opportunities to combine its original commitment to labor with the new wartime race imperative. But the CRS lawyers found that complaints from black agricultural workers provided the better foundation for their own legal practice.

When black farmworkers complained that they were being held in slavery, that their debts kept them hostage, that the conditions of their lives were appalling by mid-twentieth-century standards, they invoked the Thirteenth Amendment's prohibition on slavery and involuntary servitude. Prosecutions under that amendment seemed particularly promising to the lawyers in the CRS for institutional, political, and doctrinal reasons.

Institutionally, the CRS's emphasis on agricultural over industrial workers reflected a kind of division of labor within the federal government. Federal agencies like the Fair Employment Practice Committee (FEPC), the National Labor Relations Board (NLRB), and the War Labor Board (WLB) had the capacity, if not always the will, to protect black industrial workers. Black agricultural workers, however, had no place else to turn.

Involuntary servitude cases were also promising politically. The continued existence of involuntary servitude in the South was shocking to many Americans, including many white southerners. It was thus more politically palatable for an administration partially beholden to southern white Democrats to undertake Thirteenth Amendment prosecutions than for it to target civil rights violations that more directly challenged segregation. At the same time, African Americans possessed long-held and deeply felt convictions that slavery and involuntary servitude were illegal, unconstitutional, and just plain wrong. Those convictions, and the complaints in which black workers expressed them, placed additional political pressure on the CRS to take Thirteenth Amendment cases.

Finally, CRS lawyers experienced fewer doctrinal constraints when they prosecuted cases under the Thirteenth Amendment than under other constitutional provisions. Since the early twentieth century, the Justice Department had had success prosecuting some types of involuntary servitude. Although the target in the 1940s grew much larger than the debt-based peonage the Supreme Court had denounced earlier, the CRS used these long-established precedents as a sound foundation on which to build. With this fortuitous convergence of institutional specialization, ideological commitments, political expediency, rights consciousness, and doctrinal opportunities, the CRS attorneys made peonage and involuntary servitude a critical target of their civil rights lawyering.

The Thirteenth Amendment practice the CRS consequently created offers a glimpse into the construction of civil rights in a time of political opportunity and doctrinal uncertainty. Section lawyers had come of age as liberals during the *Lochner* era, but they rejected many of its most fundamental tenets. Instead, they looked to a variety of pasts for inspiration, for constitutional authority, and for the frameworks with which to build a new federal program to protect civil rights. Although involuntary servitude cases were not the sole focus of the CRS in the 1940s, they were at the conceptual fulcrum of its developing civil rights practice. More so than lynching, police brutality, or voting cases, Thirteenth Amendment cases offered the government lawyers the chance to work out the integration of the rights they had inherited and the rights they hoped to vindicate. At a time when the rights of laborers and the rights of African Americans both appeared robust and deserving of federal protection, the Justice Department lawyers positioned black agricultural workers at the center of their Thirteenth Amendment prosecutions. They attempted to create a civil rights practice that took seriously black agricultural workers' claims to be free from both racial and economic oppression.

By the time Frank Murphy created a separate administrative unit to protect civil rights in 1939, the Criminal Division of the Justice Department had been prosecuting infringements of the rights of industrial and agricultural workers for several years. These precursor cases arrived at DOJ after thorough investigation by the Senate's La Follette Civil Liberties Committee. Although Congress had tried to protect industrial workers under the National Labor Relations Act (NLRA) in 1935, employers were convinced that the Supreme Court would invalidate that law as it had other New Deal legislation. This conviction led them to resist workers' attempts to organize. Senator Robert La Follette, Jr., of Wisconsin and his committee worried that the powers of the newly created NLRB were too uncertain to protect organizing workers from violence and intimidation. Congressional hearings and criminal prosecutions seemed more effective methods of safeguarding industrial workers, not to mention the agricultural workers excluded altogether from the NLRA's protections.[4]

The committee's sensational hearings, the DOJ's path-breaking prosecutions, and the encouragement of labor leaders, black civil rights organizations, and other liberal and left-leaning organizations spurred Murphy to create the Civil Liberties Unit. It was a natural initiative for the new attorney general. As a liberal governor of Michigan, Murphy had negotiated with, rather than forcefully suppressed, sit-down strikers in the auto industry. He was also a "darling" of the labor-oriented ACLU. Perhaps encouraged by President Franklin Roosevelt himself, Murphy saw the unit as a way "to stimulate in our people a disposition to rediscover and embrace the civil liberties."[5]

Shortly after Murphy created the CLU, his assistant attorney general in charge of the Criminal Division, Brien McMahon, took a first stab at defining the new unit's responsibilities. When appointed in 1936, McMahon was, at thirty-two, among the youngest assistant attorneys general in the department's history. A Democratic Party loyalist and Yale-trained lawyer from Connecticut, McMahon did not have any particular experience with labor issues prior to joining the department. Yet he had been deeply involved in some of the La Follette Committee cases, and his early, foundational writings on the unit reflect his understanding that "civil liberties" were infused with labor concerns.[6]

In a memo to his attorney general written just after the creation of the CLU, McMahon included eighteen "types of legal situations" in which the unit would act against government officials. The Civil Rights Act of 1866 and 1870 made it a crime for anyone to deprive a person of federal constitutional or statutory rights "under color of law." By 1939, that "color of law" statute had been codified as Section 52 of the criminal code. In defining what precisely comprised such federal rights under Section 52, McMahon listed some race-related items—police brutality, lynching, voting, and jury discrimination—that sound familiar to modern ears. But those issues were numerically and thematically overwhelmed by a wide variety of labor-related transgressions. Some explicitly concerned the rights of laborers, like instances where government officials "effect peonage or slavery," "break up picket lines," and "prohibit picket lines from forming." An even greater number consisted of the kinds of repressive tactics government officials used (often at the behest of private employers) against both industrial and agricultural workers trying to organize and bargain. Thus, the memo suggested that the unit take action where officials "break up meetings, private or public, with or without violence"; where they "prevent meetings in proper places"; where they "prevent speakers from addressing meetings" and individuals from distributing leaflets and pamphlets; and where they "prevent, interfere with, or intimidate persons in the act of petitioning the Government for redress of grievances."[7]

McMahon reinforced this labor focus when he set forth the circumstances under which private individuals (as opposed to government officials) could become targets of the unit's investigation. Another section of the Civil Rights Act of 1870, by McMahon's time known as Section 51 or "the conspiracy statute," criminalized conspiracies by private parties to violate federal constitutional or statutory rights. McMahon listed three "rights affirmatively best[ow]ed by the Federal Government" protected from private infringement. First, wrote McMahon, was the "[r]ight of workers in interstate commerce to organize;" second was the "[r]ight of persons to benefits" under New Deal legislation like Social Security, the Works Progress Administration (WPA), and the Public Works Administration (PWA); and last on the list was the "[r]ight to vote in national elections." Dominant in McMahon's mind, then, were the rights of workers to organize and the related economic rights of receiving work, welfare, or a minimum subsistence from the government.[8]

Finally, in discussing the "functions" of the new unit, McMahon described whom he saw as the unit's allies and collaborators among both private organizations and other governmental units. As to the former, he expected the unit to cooperate with the ACLU and the special Bill of Rights Committee of the American Bar Association (ABA). Although the NAACP and other African American organizations had urged and applauded the creation of the unit, McMahon did not mention them. As to governmental units, he hoped to work with the La Follette Civil Liberties Committee, the NLRB, the Social Security Board, and the administrators of the WPA and PWA. From the kinds of harms the new unit would redress to the agencies with which it saw itself in sympathy and partnership, the memo clearly indicates that the rights of labor and economic security were to be the focus of the unit's activities.[9]

In a number of public addresses and publications, other DOJ officials reinforced McMahon's labor focus. When McMahon left the department for private practice later in 1939, O. John Rogge replaced him. Rogge, a farm boy from near Springfield, Illinois, attended the University of Illinois and then Harvard Law School. Thirty-five years old when he arrived at the Justice Department, Rogge was known as "a warm advocate of the New Deal" who had worked as a lawyer in various parts of the Roosevelt administration since 1934. Rogge's appointment as assistant attorney general elicited surprise in Chicago, however, where some remembered that he had voted for Socialist candidates in the 1932 elections.[10]

A few months after Murphy created the new unit, Rogge told a committee of the ABA: "One of the types of situation which the civil unit will watch closely concerns labor. . . . We propose to enforce the 1870 [Civil Rights Act] to the fullest extent, to the end that labor may organize and secure the power of collective bargaining and all other rights." Rogge also spent the better part of a 1939 article entitled "Justice and Civil Liberties" discussing labor. Significantly, Rogge emphasized that agricultural workers should receive no less protection than industrial workers. He saw "no distinction in principle" between cases involving industrial workers "and those of organized intimidation of tenant farmers, to deprive them of benefits under Federal agricultural aid acts, or similar activities directed against citizens on Federal relief rolls." Repression against agricultural workers had figured prominently in the La Follette Committee hearings, and they figured prominently in the the government lawyers' initial understanding of their mandate as well. "Labor," Rogge made clear, included both agricultural and industrial workers, and both categories deserved federal protection.[11]

District of Columbia native Henry A. Schweinhaut became the first chief of the new unit. According to Wendell Berge, who took charge of the Criminal Division as of 1941, Schweinhaut was "a rapid worker and a good tactician" of "exceptional ability" with a "ready capacity to adjust himself to new situations." Schweinhaut too stressed the vindication of labor's rights. "Recent federal legislation," he wrote, "has made federal beneficiaries of some classes of people who have in the past been particularly subject to private intimidation through thugs and vigilantes." The only example he gave of such a beneficiary was "[i]ndustrial labor, . . . which had previously been denied protection . . . against lawless interference with its efforts to organize." Labor "now has acquired through the Wagner Act under certain circumstances a federally protected right to organize for collective bargaining." As the "beneficiary" of federal legislation, labor became as well the beneficiary of new civil rights protection from the executive branch.[12]

The unit's early prosecutions reinforced the notion that labor rights played a key role in its lawyers' initial understanding of their mandate. Although the lawyers made efforts to prosecute lynch mobs, most of the early cases they deemed within their purview dealt with labor, not racial, issues. The lawyers used the threat of prosecution to convince coal operators in violence-torn Harlan County, Kentucky, to negotiate with organizing coal miners. They helped the United Mine Workers (UMW) receive recognition as the workers' exclusive bargaining agent, gain the release of 200 mine workers from jail, and lower the bail for several others.[13]

The CRS also became involved in a suit the ACLU and the Congress of Industrial Organizations (CIO) initiated against Jersey City's Mayor Frank "I am the law" Hague for repressing the free speech of workers and their advocates. In *Hague v. CIO,* the CRS prepared an amicus brief for the Supreme Court. In what would become a pattern of tension between the unit and the Solicitor General's Office over the filing of amicus briefs, however, then Solicitor General Robert Jackson dissuaded the unit from filing it. In addition, the lawyers investigated labor suppression across California and secured an indictment against a cotton mill for violating NLRA rights.[14]

From early on, the unit intervened on behalf of black and white southern sharecroppers and tenant farmers. In 1936, even before the creation of the unit itself, the department had used an antislavery statute from the Reconstruction era to prosecute Paul Peacher. As the town marshal of Earl, Arkansas, Peacher arrested striking black sharecroppers, charged them with vagrancy, and made them work on his plantation. Two years later, the DOJ successfully prosecuted two additional cases under the 1867 Peonage Act. The department also investigated a large-scale, interracial farmworker protest in Missouri. Landlords hoping to keep New Deal subsidies to themselves and to lower labor costs by mechanizing their crop production evicted tenants in large numbers. By the end of 1938, hundreds of sharecroppers, most of them black, who had been evicted from their farms protested by setting up makeshift homes on major highways in Missouri. Planters and law enforcement officers evicted the protestors from their temporary highway dwellings. Although the department ultimately found no federal violations to prosecute, the FBI report that resulted sided generally with the sharecroppers rather than the planters, and the department publicized those findings. The *St. Louis Post-Dispatch,* the *Cape*

Giradeau Southeast Missourian, the *New York Daily Worker,* and the *Memphis Commercial-Appeal* gave substantial coverage to the report.[15]

Once the unit had its own designated lawyers in 1939, it took more aggressive action on behalf of farmworkers. That same year, the unit's first agricultural prosecution targeted a town marshal and two citizens who arrested three Southern Tenant Farmers' Union (STFU) organizers in Arkansas without a warrant and then beat two of them. The following year, the CRS prosecuted a farm security administrator. The administrator had attempted to force two African Americans in Alabama to surrender a Farm Security Administration loan because he thought them impudent. That grand juries refused to indict in both cases reflected one of the key obstacles facing the new unit. Juries frequently refused to indict or convict employers for labor-related violations, and when civil rights victims were black and perpetrators white, all-white juries routinely and defiantly nullified DOJ prosecutions.[16]

None of these cases—protecting farmworkers and coal miners, the CIO and the STFU—created earth-shattering legal precedents. They nonetheless show that as Murphy and his lawyers went about constructing their civil rights practice, labor and its rights composed a major part of their activities. In its inception and early years, the Civil Rights Section established deep roots in the protection of the rights of organized and organizing labor.

After Murphy, McMahon, Rogge, and Schweinhaut's initial burst of energy for federal civil rights protection in 1939 and 1940, leadership flagged briefly. During Robert Jackson's short tenure as attorney general in 1940 and 1941—crowded between his posts as solicitor general and Supreme Court justice—he failed to distinguish himself in the civil rights realm. As a Roosevelt insider from 1934, Jackson had attacked big business and defended the New Deal. And later, as a Supreme Court justice, Jackson authored opinions in such individual rights cases as the peonage case of *Pollock v. Williams,* the flag-salute case of *West Virginia State Board of Education v. Barnette,* and the right to travel case of *Edwards v. California.*[17]

But those decisions were still in the future when Jackson briefly served as attorney general in the early 1940s. In that role, he did not generally favor intrusive executive branch action into civil rights; he shied away from using law enforcement to campaign for particular causes. Jackson believed that there was "an ever present danger of overstepping in investigations, of publicity tending to prejudge the accused, of wandering beyond the realm of criminal acts into that of unpopular opinion, of exceeding the proper bounds of Federal power." Perhaps Jackson's early career as a small-town lawyer in upstate New York had convinced him that private attorneys were better equipped to handle the responsibility of protecting civil rights. He contrasted the eight lawyers of the Civil Rights Section with the 160,000-strong private bar in the United States: "Every failure of civil rights is at bottom a reflection on the legal profession. . . . If this bar is properly functioning it should be an adequate guarantee of the civil rights of every citizen." As section lawyer Albert Arent later put it, Jackson "paid very little attention to our work and the old guard [in the department] made it frustrating for us."[18]

It fell to Jackson's successor, Francis Biddle, to reinvigorate the federal civil rights project on the eve of America's entry into World War II. Biddle grew up in a prominent Philadelphia family. Like the president under whom he served, he was educated at Groton and Harvard. A post–law school clerkship with Justice Oliver Wendell Holmes in 1912 revealed to Biddle the worth of public service. "After my winter with Holmes," he later wrote, "I would never altogether shrink back into the bundle of small class platitudes and prejudices with which I had left Harvard."[19]

During the next three decades, Biddle's numerous posts in state and federal government gave him both insights into the need for and confidence in the capacity of government to intervene actively into economic relationships. During a stint on a state coal and iron investigatory commission, Biddle was struck by "the conditions of virtual peonage under which the Pennsylvania miners lived . . . in the dismal little company towns." As chair of another state committee in 1936, Biddle wrote and defended in court the Pennsylvania State Housing Authority Act and a state statute regulating the retail and wholesale prices of milk. He described how a "horrified judge" saw "a new social plan which was concerned with the public economy rather than the public health." "*A new social plan,*" mocked Biddle, "that was a dreadful idea, particularly if it was concerned with the public economy!"[20]

Biddle's first appointment to federal service reflected and reinforced his interest in labor and heightened his commitment to the federal protection of labor rights. In 1934, he served as chairman of the first National Labor Relations Board. Biddle attempted to enforce the board's findings and to develop a body of law protecting workers' rights to organize under the National Recovery Act's Section 7(a). The Justice Department under Homer Cummings stymied his efforts on both counts.[21]

In 1940, when Biddle gained a more effective voice in law enforcement as solicitor general, he used it on behalf of both labor rights and the rights of African Americans. As the administration's foremost legal advocate, Biddle defended the New Deal in fifteen cases and won them all. Most significantly, in 1941, he argued for, and the Supreme Court upheld, the Fair Labor Standards Act. Biddle also broke new ground for the Solicitor General's Office when he decided not to represent the Interstate Commerce Commission (ICC) as it defended segregation on interstate railroads. Instead, Biddle submitted a brief agreeing with the NAACP's challenge to the ICC's regulations permitting segregation.[22]

United States Attorney General Francis Biddle at his desk, circa 1941. (© Bettmann/CORBIS.)

When President Roosevelt appointed Biddle attorney general in September 1941, Biddle was, in the words of *New York Times* reporter Cabell Phillips, "as near fulfilling President Roosevelt's prescription for highly placed public servants as any man in the New Deal." "The most inescapable fact about Francis Biddle," Phillips reported, "is his liberal philosophy." Even before the attack on Pearl Harbor on December 7 of that year, Biddle told Phillips "that the most important job an Attorney General can do in a time of emergency is to protect civil liberties." Biddle worried that the fear and apprehension of war would lead Americans "to vent our dammed-up energy on a scapegoat" like "some one [*sic*] whose views are contrary to our own, . . . some one [*sic*] who speaks with a foreign accent, or . . . a labor union which stands up for what it believes to be its rights."[23]

Two of Biddle's friends and political associates joined him at the helm in 1941. Berge replaced Rogge as head of the Criminal Division, and Rotnem replaced Schweinhaut as head of the Civil Rights Section. In each instance, the new official was more active on civil rights than his predecessor. Berge, a member of the "Biddle crowd," was from a Nebraska family of active Democrats with "Populist" leanings. After law school at the University of Michigan, he worked in private practice in New York before joining the Antitrust Division of the DOJ. Rotnem, the new chief of the CRS, was a Minnesotan of Norwegian descent who attended his state university and Harvard Law School. He was a humorous man who once described his ambition as "longevity." In the early 1930s, Rotnem worked under Jerome Frank in the Legal Division of the Agricultural Adjustment Administration (AAA). When Secretary of Agriculture Henry Wallace purged members of what he referred to as "the extreme liberal group" in the AAA—"trouble makers who let their social theories stand in the way of the major task of restoring farm prosperity"—Rotnem was among them. He was, according to one of his colleagues, "a crusader who conceived of the Civil Rights Section as a social as well as a legal operation."[24]

Like the political appointees who managed them, the Civil Rights Section's lawyers in the 1940s came from all backgrounds. Some were elite lawyers from elite law schools, whereas others went to their state or hometown law schools. Frank Coleman even trained himself using the Blackstone's *Commentaries* and Virginia Code he bought from the widow of a local attorney. The lawyers of the Civil Rights Section shared a liberal outlook. They were pro-labor but not Communists, though some had greater ties to the left than others. As a young man, Albert Arent had attended a socialist summer school and had had personal ties to socialist Norman Thomas and his family. Fred Folsom's brother was a "devout Communist" and the author of such books as *Impatient Armies of the Poor: The Story of Collective Action of the Unemployed, 1808–1942*. Folsom himself thought "we ought to work out our problems through our democratic system" and generally described his family as "liberal thinking." The lawyers were "western liberals" like Folsom, northeastern Jews like Sydney Brodie, and southern progressives like Coleman. They were Democrats and New Dealers, quite a few of whom identified, and were identified with, the liberal wing of the party. A number had worked in other New Deal and wartime agencies known for liberal tendencies, such as the Reconstruction Finance Corporation and the Office of Price Administration.[25]

For the most part, the lawyers joined the CRS out of a commitment to civil rights. To be sure, some chose the section only after being rejected by more prestigious divisions of the DOJ, like Antitrust. As CRS lawyer Henry Putzel later described, civil rights was "a field that was real easy to get into" because it was "the ugly duckling of the Criminal Division" and "a little group off the mainstream." But the majority chose to work in the Civil Rights Section because they were, again in Putzel's words, "dedicated" and "committed." Maceo Hubbard, the CRS's only African American lawyer, came to the DOJ in 1946 seasoned as chair of the Philadelphia Legal Committee of the NAACP and as a staff member of the Fair Employment Practice Committee. Eleanor Bontecou, the only woman lawyer, had worked in the anti–poll-tax movement and on other suffrage issues with black intellectual and activist Ralph Bunche and prominent race relations expert Gunnar Myrdal before joining the CRS in 1943. The commitment of Hubbard, Bontecou, and Jewish CRS lawyers like Arent was not merely abstract: they had all "endured" prejudice and discrimination in their own lives. Those outside the CRS "looked upon [the section's lawyers] as 'do-gooders' and what-not, and it didn't[,] at that time, lead to anything outside the Department," Bontecou recalled. "A young attorney wouldn't make his reputation or be asked by a good law firm to come in. . . . [I]t wasn't exactly a lark."[26]

For these "working stiffs," as Folsom called them, who did the hard work of bringing cases and creating precedents, the support of political appointees was critical to success. When the Civil Rights Section made decisions about whether to pursue cases, they first met among themselves, then had their decisions "cleared beyond us by the head of the Criminal Division," and then sometimes by the attorney general. In Bontecou's estimation, the CRS "went to the Attorney General more than most sections." The cases were "red hot potatoes" and "[i]t was essential to have the Department behind us." "Of course," she said, "we didn't send anything up without very careful preparation. You realize we always had hanging over us that this must be done with the greatest caution and restraint. You can't just go ahead—for that reason some of the civil rights people thought we were pretty poor fish."[27]

Biddle's commitment to civil rights was apparent to his staff. "You always know if the Attorney General is interested in backing what you are doing," Bontecou asserted. "You know it in a lot of ways that you can't exactly write down. He made a good many speeches on the subject, and wrote a book. He had a well-known interest in the field. . . . Then when cases did go up to him, he voted on the side of the civil rights activities rather than against it." Because of the fact that Biddle was "very, very interested in this field and kept in touch with us very closely," the CRS went to him both as "a matter of course [and as] a matter of sensitivity of the subject."[28]

As Biddle's wartime civil rights lawyers got their bearings, they found that New Deal labor legislation continued to provide significant legal authority. Yet even as labor remained politically salient and legally promising, World War II also highlighted the problems African Americans endured in Jim Crow America. As the Roosevelt administration struggled to balance its concern for African American rights with its desire not to antagonize too completely its white Democratic allies in the South, the Civil Rights Section refocused its labor rights practice. Peonage cases, it turned out, offered the CRS a way to join labor and race rights, to protect African Americans in a politically palatable way, and to build on doctrinal strengths.

Within the Civil Rights Section as without, labor rights remained prominent during World War II. The wartime economy heightened attention to labor market participation and any obstacles to it. The Roo-

sevelt administration continued to signal to the Civil Rights Section
lawyers that labor rights remained politically salient as well as legally
appealing. Roosevelt pronounced "freedom from want" as part of his
Four Freedoms in 1941. Three years later, his "Economic Bill of
Rights" continued the trend of publicizing the importance of economic rights in general, and the rights of labor in particular. As Bontecou recollected, the only "clearly defined rights" the CRS could protect in the early 1940s were those at issue in peonage cases, voting
cases, and "cases involving the rights specifically given in various New
Deal statutes—the National Labor Relations Act and a few others.
Those acts defined the rights and we could bring a case when they
were violated."[29]

Indeed, into the war, Biddle was pleased that legislation from the
late New Deal provided just the kind of authority he had sought as
chair of the first NLRB. Biddle thought that the "rights of individuals
protected by federal law" now included collective bargaining under
the NLRA, as well as the "right to wages under the Fair Labor Standards Act, rights under the Agricultural Adjustment Administration
Act and the Social Security Acts, rights to the use of housing projects
constructed under the Lanham Act, rights of returning soldiers to
reemployment under the Selective Service Act." He applauded these
expansions of federal jurisdiction. Because "all these are rights now secured by federal laws directed against individual as well as against state
interference," Biddle's lawyers could broaden their legal efforts.[30]

Of all of this legislation, section chief Rotnem saw the NLRA as
having the greatest impact: "[A]t long last, men who work can, and
what is more[,] increasingly have organized themselves in to unions of
their own choosing to enable them to bargain collectively." Federal
protection for those rights was particularly important because Rotnem
thought that without governmental intervention laborers were inherently subordinate to their employers. Rotnem described using Section
51's conspiracy statute in conjunction with rights granted under the
Fair Labor Standards Act "against greedy employers and unscrupulous
union leaders who have conspired to deprive the workers of those
rights." And he interpreted the NLRA as unequivocally pro-labor. He
quoted Senator Robert F. Wagner, its chief champion, as describing
the "measure [as] deal[ing] with the subtler forms of economic pressure [that] . . . can be directed against a worker by an employer who

controls his job." Biddle and Rotnem, like Murphy, McMahon, and Schweinhaut before them, repeatedly warned that DOJ jurisdiction in labor cases "has been sustained and it can be exerted again whenever it is necessary to prevent the industrial unrest which is the result of constant violation of the rights of the workers."[31]

Even as the CRS lawyers remained committed to labor's rights, several developments in the early 1940s changed their approach to labor cases. Once the Supreme Court validated the NLRA, the NLRB began successfully exercising control over labor disputes. As a result, the need for the Civil Rights Section to use the unwieldy statutory apparatus of the late nineteenth century diminished. With the twentieth-century administrative mechanisms of the NLRB, its expertise in labor issues and the details of the NLRA, and the sheer volume of labor disputes, the board was far better equipped than the eight criminal lawyers at the Department of Justice to protect labor's new statutory rights. Moreover, as many employers became resigned to the authority of the NLRB (and other wartime labor agencies like the WLB) and union leaders became more conventional and bureaucratic, the kind of violence that had occasioned DOJ intervention also began to drop off.[32]

Just as the NLRB began regularly to enforce the rights of industrial labor, the Roosevelt administration began to realize how low African American morale had fallen. Attorney General Biddle and his lawyers thought black civil rights "peculiarly acute" because of the nation's "reiterated insistence on democratic equality of opportunity, irrespective of race, and the total nature of this war compared to the last." Section lawyer Coleman feared that "many of our own citizens [would] become cynical and disillusioned about fighting on the seven seas and in every foreign land in the name of ideals which . . . were being trampled under foot at home." He and his colleagues believed that the federal government had to respond to African American demands "that the constitutional paper guarantees of individual freedom be made real in action." Coleman thought "[w]ar had brought a pressure to substitute the technique of enforcement for that of promise."[33]

The key for the Civil Rights Section was to figure out which violations of black civil rights it could most fruitfully pursue. The systematic and multifaceted nature of Jim Crow provided a plethora of targets from which to choose: the anachronism of peonage; the horror of lynching; the officially sanctioned violence of police brutality; the reality of disfranchisement; the pervasive discrimination in war industries; and the state, local, and privately mandated racial segregation that touched every aspect of life in the South and many aspects of life outside the region.

In choosing their targets, both Roosevelt and his lawyers hoped to alter the political landscape of the white South without alienating southern white Democrats completely. Even before World War II, Roosevelt had commenced a campaign to undermine conservative white control over the southern Democratic Party. He had appointed to the Supreme Court a number of justices who were favorable to both the New Deal's labor program and to the civil rights of minorities. Likewise, in 1938, Roosevelt initiated a "purge campaign" to replace conservative southerners in Congress with more liberal ones. Although he was successful with some campaigns in Florida and Kentucky, he failed in his efforts against three named southern democrats—Walter George of Georgia, "Cotton Ed" Smith of South Carolina, and Millard Tydings of Maryland.[34]

In addition to these efforts, the Roosevelt administration used the CRS lawyers to make cautious but clear inroads into southern racial prerogatives. That said, neither Roosevelt nor his Justice Department was prepared, politically or doctrinally, to take on the entire system of racial segregation. To do so looked politically dangerous. Southern Democrats were still critically important to Democratic Party power. Perhaps more pressing, to challenge segregation directly would be "unsafe" in light of racial tensions then roiling American cities, a 1943 Justice Department memo warned. Overcrowding, inadequate housing, and job competition had set both northern and southern race relations on edge. The DOJ mainly worried about the South. "So long as the South feels the Federal government means to regulate its intimate relations with the Negro, the South will fight any Federal intervention. This flame can easily be fanned into a terrible conflagration."[35]

So instead of state-mandated segregation, the CRS pursued more politically acceptable cases on behalf of African Americans. The department took those cases that directly advanced the liberal Democrats' political agenda, like election fraud and voting rights cases. More importantly for the development of new civil rights understand-

ings, the CRS tried to prosecute especially shocking abuses, like peonage and involuntary servitude, lynching, and police brutality. Peonage in particular allowed the CRS to navigate safely between the prerogatives southern whites most cherished and the rights claims African
Americans most urgently pressed.

As a general matter, DOJ lawyers had good reason to believe that
white southerners would tolerate more government intervention into
employment relationships of all kinds than into social matters of any
kind. Whites were hardly receptive to black economic advancement, as
white hostility to FEPC hearings amply illustrated. But they were less
recalcitrant on economic issues than on issues more closely linked to
"social equality" and miscegenation. Sociologist and political scientist
R. M. MacIver found that "[w]hites on the whole are considerably
more concerned to maintain the lower social status of the Negro than
to deny him a measure of economic opportunity. . . . Advances along
this line do not encounter the emotional block that guards the system
of social segregation." And Gunnar Myrdal's pathbreaking book, *An
American Dilemma,* pointed out that "the Negro's own rank order [was]
just about parallel, but inverse, to that of the white man." African
Americans, according to one 1944 study, were "most wrought up about
economic opportunity" and "relatively less concerned about social discrimination." The priorities of white liberals, like those in the wartime
CRS, matched the priorities of black workers: although they might disagree on many issues, most opposed economic discrimination.[36]

Within the realm of work-related claims, Thirteenth Amendment
protection against peonage and involuntary servitude—rather than
the more politically prominent race discrimination in war industries—
ultimately proved more politically profitable for CRS litigation in the
1940s. Institutional considerations played an important role in that
precedence. Just as the general acceptance of the NLRB took pressure
off the CRS to prosecute NLRA cases, the creation of a routine administrative complaint procedure in the FEPC obviated CRS involvement
in industrial discrimination cases. The FEPC's enforcement of its
nondiscrimination mandate was grossly inadequate. But as the FEPC
grew to maintain fifteen field offices and 128 full-time staff members,
it dwarfed the handful of lawyers in the Civil Rights Section. African
American industrial workers protesting employment discrimination
thus had recourse in the administrative mechanisms of the FEPC

rather than the clumsier criminal enforcement of the Civil Rights Section. Moreover, industrial workers could complain about union discrimination to the NLRB or about unequal pay for equal work to the WLB. African American agricultural workers who complained of peonage and involuntary servitude, however, could realistically hope for a response from no part of the federal government other than the Civil Rights Section. The paltry protection the government offered black industrial workers looked formidable compared to the protection available to black agricultural workers.[37]

To the extent that Civil Rights Section lawyers addressed the problems of African American industrial workers during the war, it was largely by advising the president on the future of the FEPC. When the committee ran into political trouble in 1943 for allegedly overreaching, the president called upon Biddle and Rotnem to assist in its reorganization. Like many black and white advisors to Roosevelt, Rotnem was critical of the committee's modus operandi. He thought the FEPC "justified its own existence . . . with violent publicity" and "needless arousing of race tensions" that "imped[ed] or stopp[ed] the orderly integration of Negroes into industry." Perhaps unsurprisingly, Rotnem suggested the FEPC would do better if it operated more along the lines of the Civil Rights Section: with less publicity and greater enforcement powers, with less roiling of the pot of race hatred and more emphasis on placing African Americans into jobs and industries. Although the president ultimately chose to emphasize education and persuasion over stringent enforcement mechanisms, he embraced Biddle and Rotnem's recommendation to make the FEPC larger.[38]

The CRS also turned to Thirteenth Amendment claims because of the seriousness of the claims themselves. In addition to having fewer institutional resources at their disposal, agricultural workers usually complained of more shocking and compelling civil rights violations than their industrial counterparts. The black shipyard workers who received a hearing from the FEPC complained that union discrimination relegated them to low-paying, unskilled laborers' jobs. The black workers who traveled to Florida to work in the sugar cane fields, by contrast, complained to the DOJ of living in filthy, inhuman conditions; being locked up so they could not escape; and being threatened with death if they tried.

The relative outrage incidents of involuntary servitude produced affected their political attractiveness for three reasons: involuntary servitude horrified many white southerners, provoked extreme opposition from African Americans, and made an excellent target for DOJ lawyers trying to raise black morale during World War II. First, southern whites were less opposed to peonage cases than industrial discrimination. Like lynching cases, peonage cases were often sensational, full of horrible images and pitiable victims. Although Justice Department lawyers complained that peonage cases were difficult to win because the main witnesses were black, illiterate, and often afraid to testify, peonage victims nonetheless often made sympathetic complainants. When workers protested that their employers beat them with cat-o'-nine tails, shackled them to beds, and threatened them with death, even some white southerners committed to segregation became "outraged local citizens" and reported the incidents. As Bontecou later put it, "[T]he person who violated this law was terribly unpopular in the community."[39]

The most vocal southern defenders, like Congressman John E. Rankin of Mississippi, saw even the cases the department did pursue as akin to "a Gestapo for the persecution of the white people throughout the South." But many whites did not deem these cases as threatening as attacks on segregation itself. To the extent that discrimination in industry implicated segregation as well as inequality, peonage complaints were less likely to provoke an all-out defense from a relatively unified white South.[40]

At the same time, African Americans complained about peonage in especially strong and demanding terms because of their unique antislavery rights consciousness. Just as whites could hardly bring themselves to condone the brutalities of peonage, African Americans did not hesitate to claim their constitutional rights to avoid such a fate. They complained explicitly about "violat[ions] under the Federal Civil Rights statute and under the Thirteenth Amendment to the Constitution." Although the Supreme Court had repudiated expansive visions of the Thirteenth Amendment in the late nineteenth century, it had never denied the amendment's force to prohibit slavery and peonage altogether. By contrast, any rights claim directly challenging segregation had to contend with both the *Civil Rights Cases* and *Plessy v. Ferguson*. Short of direct attacks on those long-standing precedents, challenges to segregation would have to prove both that the state perpetrated the harm and that separate was not equal. African Americans perceived that the federal government was better able to protect them from the most extreme forms of involuntary servitude than to attack segregation after the *Civil Rights Cases* and *Plessy*. They consequently backed their claims to be free from involuntary servitude with a unique, seventy-five-year-old entitlement.[41]

That the basic outlines of federal protection against slavery and involuntary servitude were clear enough for laypeople to understand and assert added to the power of peonage complaints. As Civil Rights Section lawyer Brodie explained in the early 1950s, "[T]he public cannot be expected to be familiar with the extremely technical body of law under the Fourteenth Amendment and the limited boundaries of federal jurisdiction in the field of 'due process of law.'" By contrast, "forced labor as such falls within the federal jurisdiction by virtue of the broad grant of rights in the Thirteenth Amendment." Brodie found an increase in cognizable peonage complaints due to "increased awareness by the public of the Government's interest and its powers in this area, and the experience acquired by its personnel."[42]

Once the government began prosecuting and publicizing peonage cases in earnest in the early 1940s, rights consciousness rose apace. Thus, one NAACP branch member wrote to an employer alleged to have held an African American in servitude: "It APPEARS that [y]ou took advantage of him due to his skin being black and yours white, which in some instance have been going on in this Country for low these many years. However allow us to call your attention to the fact that this is a strict violation of the Law." He emphasized his point. "That is to subject any HUMAN BEING TO SLAVERY OR PEONAGE and the person or persons that commits or commit such acts charges can be filed against them in Civil or Criminal Federal Court of The U.S. and if found guilty will be fined accordingly." Another complaint informed the "Most Excellent President" that when he took his oath of office, he pledged to "up hold the Constitution of the U.S.A. . . . I am sure that the thirty one million negroes in the United States want this [slavery] fully investigated. And I do know that if You, just speak the words and these shackles will fall off these people leggs."[43]

Advocates and civil rights organizations across the nation reinforced the urgency with which African American agricultural workers made Thirteenth Amendment claims. Bob Wirtz was secretary of the Chicago International Labor Defense, a Communist-led popular front organization. In 1941, he peppered his policy statement for the newly formed Abolish Peonage Committee with references to "Nazi tyranny," "Hitlerism," and the "institution of human slavery [that] is an expression of Hitlerism in our country." The Abolish Peonage Committee suggested that "the unity of the American people today can be extended by a vigorous campaign to seek out and prosecute every violation of those United States statutes which make peonage a crime." Peonage cases "would strengthen the faith of millions of Negro people in the democracy for which they are loyally fighting against the aggressor fascist powers." With a similar outlook but quieter rhetoric, political scientist Howard Devon Hamilton commented after the war—referring to Joseph Stalin's Soviet Union as well as Adolf Hitler's Germany—that "the revival of slavery on a large scale by the totalitarian regimes in the new form of slave labor camps for ethnic and political 'unregenerates' has shaken [the] comfortable thought" that "slavery and involuntary servitude [were] evils which were wiped out in the Nineteenth Century."[44]

Others did not think it necessary to refer to the war when urging the DOJ to pursue involuntary servitude cases. William Henry Huff, the black lawyer who crusaded with the Abolish Peonage Committee during the war, frequently reminded the Department of Justice of Assistant Attorney General Rogge's statement that "there were adequate laws on the statute books with which to stamp out peonage." Huff saw it as his duty to "point . . . out those laws to the department, together with cases that have been successfully prosecuted under and by virtue of those laws."[45] Throughout the early 1940s, the NAACP also served as a spur to government action and a conduit for worthy cases. The NAACP would investigate potential peonage cases, sometimes in conjunction with the socialist-affiliated Workers' Defense League, and then it would press the CRS to prosecute. Bontecou called Thurgood Marshall "a regular client."[46]

These entreaties fell on sympathetic ears. The very brutality of involuntary servitude made it an attractive public relations tool. Federal officials hoped that publicizing Thirteenth Amendment prosecutions would enhance both the United States' international standing and the morale of African Americans domestically. When United States attorneys or FBI agents recommended closing peonage investigations, Assistant Attorney General Berge often sent them missives ordering the cases reopened. The archives reveal numerous instances in which he wrote in boilerplate language to U.S. attorneys that they needed to investigate further because of the importance of safeguarding the rights of African Americans.

Berge sent such a letter in a peonage case where an African American man in Louisiana alleged that he was forced to work on the farm of a white man. Berge pointed out that the case was "but one of many in which members of the Negro race have been the victims. Enemy propagandists have used similar episodes in international broadcasts to the colored race, saying that the democracies are insincere and that the enemy is their friend." He informed the U.S. attorney that the president had instructed "that lynching complaints shall be investigated as soon as possible; that the results of the investigation be made public in all instances, and the persons responsible for such lawless acts vigorously prosecuted." And he emphasized that the attorney general had "requested that we expedite other cases relating to Negro victims." Although lynching, as the most sensational of cases with African American victims, was the only type of case mentioned in the memo, Berge sent the same or similar letters in connection with peonage cases.[47]

Indeed, media coverage of at least one Thirteenth Amendment case confirmed the strategy. In 1943, the CRS obtained a conviction in *United States v. Skrobarczyk.* According to the *Corpus Christi Times,* the case involved a father and daughter who had "enslav[ed] a feeble-minded negro worker on their farm." "The Skrobarcyk [*sic*] trial and its conclusion undoubtedly will be said in the future to have given a decisive setback to the enemy propaganda machine in the United States." The trial made clear that "the negro, no matter what his station in life, has the protection of the laws of the land." From the president to the attorney general to FBI agents and DOJ lawyers alike, federal officials sought to take, win, and publicize cases with black victims in order "to draw the fire from Axis propaganda, which stem[med] from racial conflicts within the United States."[48]

As a result of both the vehemence with which African Americans pressed involuntary servitude cases and the tepidness with which white southerners resisted them, Thirteenth Amendment cases were ideal candidates not only for improving the lives of southern black agricultural workers but also for improving black morale. In considerable measure, the power of the stories themselves spurred the Department of Justice to action in involuntary servitude cases. The civil rights lawyers clearly saw peonage, along with lynching and election law violations, as "obvious Federal prerogatives" demanding intervention.[49]

Peonage and involuntary servitude cases occupied an important position in the CRS's practice not only because they integrated the CRS's historical concern with labor and its wartime preoccupation with African American rights. Their importance stemmed also from the doctrinal opportunities they provided the CRS lawyers. In the wake of the constitutional transformations of the New Deal, the lawyers explicitly saw themselves as experimenting with new forms of federal civil rights protection. Biddle contrasted the 1940s favorably with the *Lochner* era, pleased that of late "the Supreme Court has generally not felt it necessary to yield to the temptation to substitute its views" of civil rights statutes for those of Congress.[50]

With the present doctrinally open and the recent past largely repudiated, the Civil Rights Section lawyers searched for inspiration and authority in the constitutional understandings of the more distant past. One contemporary commentator described how, in order to create a basis for the unit's authority, Biddle and his lawyers began "combing the statutes, . . . exploring the interstices of the Constitution, searching for national authority." Indeed, Rotnem's reputation as an "original thinker" led his superiors to consider him well suited to the creativity the Civil Rights Section demanded.[51]

Unsurprisingly, the lawyers turned to the period of constitutional ferment that followed the Civil War. When section lawyers Albert Arent and Irwin L. Langbein drafted a thirty-page memo on potential legal authorities, Reconstruction amendments and statutes appeared to offer far more promising prosecutorial power than the original rights-creating part of the Constitution, the Bill of Rights. As Robert Carr, the CRS's first historian, put it in 1947, "[T]he Bill of Rights operates in every way to curtail federal activity, not to encourage it. . . . [T]here is no *express* grant of power to protect civil liberties, or even to enact criminal statutes and provide for the punishment of criminals." CRS lawyers saw the Reconstruction-era amendments and statutes as "constitut[ing] the sole source of the power of the Federal Government to protect individual rights against encroachment by the States and, in some instances, by individuals." They adopted Justice Stephen J. Field's dissenting view in the *Slaughter-House Cases:* Reconstruction had, as Rotnem put it, "drastically altered the earlier balance of power between the states and the Federal government." Attorney General Biddle contrasted the federalist balance struck at the founding with the post–Civil War federalism. In the earlier era, men who were taken by a "resentment and fear of government" ensured that federal power would be both less important than state power and negative in its protections of individual rights. In contrast, lawmakers during Reconstruction invested affirmative protections in the national government. "The National Government rather than the States became at that time the proponent of liberal doctrine."[52]

In declaring that the "balance of State and Federal power was materially altered" by the Reconstruction amendments, Biddle found historical support for his aggressive federal program of civil rights. Federal power was not new during World War II; he was restoring it to the rightful place it had briefly held, and then lost, during Reconstruction. In describing how it was only a "divided court" that "whittled down" the power of the Reconstruction amendments and statutes, Rotnem similarly attempted to undermine the nineteenth-century Court's authority and resurrect "Congress' own theory of the scope of its powers under the 13th and 14th Amendments." As Coleman, special assistant to Attorney General Biddle, complained in 1944, "In the long years when the bar and bench were busily developing the great body of law which extends the protection of the Fourteenth Amendment to the property rights of corporations, these [civil rights statutes] for the most part lay dormant." The unit thus aimed, in Biddle's words, to reestablish the Reconstruction statutes as "effective instruments for the protection of individuals' rights."[53]

One set of historically narrow but nonetheless promising instruments the lawyers found when they looked back to the postbellum era was the Thirteenth Amendment and its enforcement legislation. By the turn of the twentieth century, the Supreme Court had read the Thirteenth Amendment as a narrow rule against slavery-like forms of involuntary servitude. It did not see the amendment as the capacious mandate for federal protection of equality and freedom that at least some of its supporters had imagined it to be. In the *Slaughter-House*

Cases, the *Civil Rights Cases,* and *Hodges v. United States,* the Court eliminated from the amendment's scope protection against a whole host of labor- and race-related harms beyond slavery and involuntary servitude themselves. By so limiting the Thirteenth Amendment, those cases actually reinforced the amendment's central prohibition on involuntary servitude.[54]

The Court's reading of the Peonage Act of 1867, passed on the basis of congressional power granted in section 2 of the Thirteenth Amendment, was similarly narrow but vital. The act declared that "the holding of any person to service or labor under the system known as peonage is hereby declared to be unlawful, and the same is hereby abolished." The act imposed criminal penalties on all violations. When the Court upheld the act in the early twentieth century, it defined peonage as a form of involuntary servitude in which an employee was forced to work out a debt to an employer. Only where "compulsory service in payment of a debt" existed did the Court recognize a violation of the statute. That recognition was nonetheless the result of hard-fought legal battles by progressive southern attorneys and the Justice Department under Theodore Roosevelt.[55]

As CRS lawyers reviewed the statutes under which the Department of Justice had authority to prosecute civil rights violations, they found the Peonage Act to be a familiar relic from an earlier era of experimental federal power. They hoped it could form a promising wedge with which to broaden federal authority at mid-century. Despite its limitations, the Peonage Act remained, in Carr's words, one of the "more usable value[s] that carried over from the post–Civil War experiment."[56]

The act was especially valuable in light of the severe doctrinal constraints under which the CRS lawyers labored in other areas of its practice. As federal prosecutors, the CRS lawyers could bring only cases that implicated federal, as opposed to state, rights. Much as the end of the *Lochner* era opened up opportunities for new constitutional frameworks, it did not instantly broaden the category of federal rights the Justice Department could protect. Section lawyers still had to contend with the detritus of many of the Supreme Court's late-nineteenth-century interpretations of the Reconstruction amendments. A memorandum the unit sent to U.S. attorneys in May 1940 cautioned that "the underlying conception of the Federal Government as one of delegated powers operating against a background of reserved States' rights leave[s] the Federal Constitution largely unconcerned with the social and governmental situations which give rise to civil liberties problems."[57]

In particular, the continuing vitality of *Plessy v. Ferguson* and the *Civil Rights Cases* proved doctrinally problematic. Even as the lawyers saw themselves as "[p]ioneering in the field of theory as well as of action," they hesitated, for doctrinal as well as political reasons, to challenge *Plessy*. It was their understanding that "only where a state fosters discrimination in fact by requiring unequal accommodations would we have clear authority to intervene under the civil rights statute. . . . The mere requirement of segregation . . . does not seem at this time to be a deprivation of rights guaranteed under the Fourteenth Amendment." Expanding positive precedents like the early twentieth-century peonage cases seemed less daunting than chipping away at or challenging head on negative precedents like *Plessy*.[58]

The *Civil Rights Cases'* state action requirement proved equally limiting. Even after the New Deal Revolution, the Fourteenth and Fifteenth Amendments protected individuals only against government action. Injuries and discriminations perpetrated by private individuals presented tricky problems for prosecution. The CRS lawyers felt that they had to confine their prosecutions to state actors or find adequate constitutional authority for prosecuting civil rights violations perpetrated by private individuals. "The courts have held," section lawyer Brodie wrote, "that privately enforced segregation is not prohibited." Even when the CRS lawyers used the Reconstruction-era conspiracy statute (Section 51), the state action requirement still haunted them. They still could not reach rights—like those under the Fourteenth and Fifteenth Amendments—guaranteed only against the state.[59]

The Thirteenth Amendment, however, did not present the state action problem that plagued the Fourteenth and Fifteenth Amendments, many Reconstruction statutes, and the Bill of Rights. The Thirteenth Amendment declared that "neither slavery nor involuntary servitude . . . shall exist within the United States." "In sharp contrast" to the state action requirement in the Fourteenth and Fifteenth Amendments, Rotnem wrote, "is the Thirteenth Amendment, . . . a general prohibition which applies not only against the States and the federal government but also against all individuals who seek to enslave others." Biddle described in 1944 how "the application of the criminal sanctions to the protection of civil rights has come to be restricted mainly to cases in which State officials participate, or misuse their power, or to situations involving rights granted directly to individuals and guaranteed against individual infringement by the Federal Constitution or laws." For some time, the latter was limited to the Thirteenth Amendment and a few narrow statutory rights.[60]

Thus, although the department struggled to gain jurisdiction over election fraud, lynching, and police brutality, it harbored no doubts about peonage. The CRS lawyers viewed lynching in particular, however sensational and abhorrent, as a poor candidate for federal prosecutions. It was difficult to demonstrate that state officials were actively involved, and without such involvement, the CRS worried it would not have jurisdiction. Consequently, the CRS staff spent a lot of time theorizing ways around the state action requirement. Rotnem and Biddle both tried to find circumstances in which state inaction could be construed as action. Using the "inaction theory," the conspiracy statute (Section 51), and the "color of law statute" (Section 52), as well as a host of academic theories parading across the pages of law reviews in the 1940s, the department attempted to reach as many violations of African American civil rights as possible.[61]

As the war progressed and successful civil rights prosecutions began to accrue, Rotnem proudly announced that the civil rights statutes created "[p]owers much greater than most people realize reach[ing] all the way down to the source of many of our most difficult problems— the behavior of the local enforcement officials." As Rotnem's statement indicates, however, the Fourteenth Amendment-based statutes still could not usually reach private individuals. Indeed, after *Screws v. United States,* the Supreme Court not only required state action, but it would uphold prosecutions under Section 52 of the criminal code only where the state official intended to violate the victim's constitutional rights. From *Screws* on, such prosecutions would prove even more difficult.[62]

The unique character of the Thirteenth Amendment converged with the lawyers' various political incentives to attend to the claims of African American agricultural workers. The decision to prosecute involuntary servitude cases during the 1940s thus resulted from myriad overlapping motivations: the pressures of unions and civil libertarians; the CRS's early association of civil rights with labor rights; Biddle's early experiences with labor rights at the National Labor Relations Board; the demands of African Americans in organized protest organizations and on their own; the doctrinal requirements of civil rights enforcement in the 1940s; the CRS lawyers' hope that they could dampen wartime charges of American hypocrisy by protecting African Americans; and the Roosevelt administration's cautious challenge to the white southerners in its own party.

As a result of these disparate pressures, what had been a rather small set of harms redressable under the Thirteenth Amendment earlier in the century took on far greater importance during World War II. Indeed, after a thirty-year hiatus, the Supreme Court decided three Thirteenth Amendment cases during the war. Although one of those was entirely the product of private legal initiative, the CRS was involved in both of the other two. *United States v. Gaskin* represented a successful CRS peonage prosecution. In *Taylor v. Georgia,* the Justice Department wrote an amicus brief to the Court. Because that case was privately initiated, the department was not a party to the original case. Its decision to submit an amicus brief for the first time in a civil rights case made clear that it was, however, a very interested party.[63]

These Supreme Court cases represented only a small portion of the CRS's Thirteenth Amendment practice. When hundreds of young black workers appealed to the DOJ after they found themselves in peonage on Florida sugar plantations, for example, the CRS directed FBI agents to gather interviews and evidence from victims across the South. The agents hunted down witnesses and victims through the maze of the armed services. No fewer than twenty agents worked on the case at one point or another. No fewer than 100 youths gave interviews. As the words of men and women who had called on the government as victims became the bedrock on which the government founded its case, the lawyers convinced a grand jury to indict the sugar company with involuntary servitude and peonage. When a judge quashed that indictment, the CRS tried again. When the second all-white jury refused to indict, the CRS accepted defeat in the case.[64]

Defeats were not uncommon, but the Civil Rights Section continued to commit its resources and energy. The sugar case was only one of many involuntary servitude investigations and prosecutions the section undertook during the 1940s. Again and again, when Civil Rights Section lawyers discussed their mandate, the right to be free from involuntary servitude played a prominent role. As Rotnem observed, "Probably no single constitutional provision is the basis of so many complaints to the Department" as the Thirteenth Amendment. One of his fellow section lawyers likewise noted, "No small part of the work of the Civil Rights Section is that concerned with the enforcement of the right secured by the Thirteenth Amendment, the right of persons to be free of involuntary servitude." And a section chief concluded in the early 1950s that "the importance of these relatively old laws, designed to eradicate every form of compulsory labor, cannot be overemphasized."[65]

FIVE

◆ ◆ ◆

A New Deal for Civil Rights

> We cannot be content with a civil liberties program
> which emphasizes only the need of protection
> against the possibility of tyranny by the Govern-
> ment. . . . We must keep moving forward, with new
> concepts of civil rights to safeguard our heritage.
> The extension of civil rights today means not protec-
> tion of the people *against* the Government, but pro-
> tection of the people *by* the Government.
>
> President Harry Truman, speech at the Lincoln
> Memorial, June 29, 1947

IN 1947, ROBERT CARR WROTE *Federal Protection of Civil Rights: Quest for a Sword.* A political science professor at Dartmouth and the executive secretary of President Harry Truman's 1946 Committee on Civil
Rights, Carr hoped to publicize the work of the "unique and little-
known agency" called the Civil Rights Section (CRS). Carr organized
this first history of the section around a metaphor Supreme Court Justice Robert Jackson used in the 1944 peonage case of *Pollock v.
Williams.* Jackson described two ways to protect those caught in involuntary servitude. "Congress," Jackson declared, "raised both a shield
and a sword against forced labor because of debt." When victims of peonage found themselves imprisoned on charges of accepting advances
under false pretenses, or breaking parole by leaving a particular job,
they invoked the shield of federal law. They defended themselves "by
requesting a federal court to invalidate the state action that is endan-
gering [their] rights." When the federal government brought prosecutions against individual perpetrators of peonage, however, it raised a
sword against them. It "[took] the initiative," Carr described, "in protecting helpless individuals by bringing criminal charges against persons who are encroaching upon their rights."[1]

Adopting Jackson's metaphor, Carr concluded that in recent years the federal government, in the "tentative and experimental work" of the CRS, had taken up the sword not only in peonage cases but also in civil rights cases generally. "Government has traditionally been regarded as the villain in the civil rights drama," he wrote. "The government threat remains, but threats from other sources are extremely serious. They can and should be met by government action." Carr saw "the great achievement of the CRS" as making "[t]his new role of government [seem] to be inescapable."[2]

Carr's choice to describe the CRS's achievements through the lens of its peonage and involuntary servitude prosecutions is telling. As the section's lawyers directed civil rights cases across the country from their perch in Washington, D.C., these Thirteenth Amendment violations made up the conceptual core of the section's civil rights practice. Unlike the section's other practice areas—lynching, police brutality, and voting rights cases—its Thirteenth Amendment cases uniquely responded to the combined racial and economic harms about which African American farmworkers complained. These cases built on New Deal protections for free labor and economic security and responded to wartime imperatives for racial justice. In pursuing involuntary servitude cases, the CRS lawyers aspired to a civil rights framework that assumed the government was responsible for eliminating some of the worst and most fundamental aspects of Jim Crow.

The section's Thirteenth Amendment cases during and after World War II did not, however, comprise a single plan for a new civil rights doctrine. Rather, the CRS lawyers expanded the long-standing federal interest in peonage in three related but distinct directions. First, they reconceptualized Thirteenth Amendment violations from a narrow contractual understanding of peonage to a "federally-secured right to be free from bondage." As Carr observed, this conceptual shift suggested that affirmative federal power could and should be used to protect not only New Deal economic security but also African Americans' right to the "safety and security of the person": the right to be free from bondage, lynching, and police brutality.[3]

Second, the CRS expanded the Thirteenth Amendment from focusing on individual employment relationships to mandating the elimination of legal obstacles to African American free labor writ large. The CRS lawyers used the Thirteenth Amendment to deepen what had been the New Deal's equivocal commitment to free labor within a unified national economy. The National Labor Relations Act (NLRA) offered labor rights to industrial workers, but it largely accommodated the desire of southern whites to exclude many African Americans. So the CRS attacked the emigrant-agent, enticement, and other laws that restricted the mobility of black farmworkers. With these attacks, the CRS suggested that the Thirteenth Amendment should protect African Americans in the South from more than simply the chattel slavery it most centrally proscribed. The Thirteenth Amendment could guarantee free labor for those workers excluded from New Deal labor protections.

Finally, section lawyers expanded their understanding of the core economic problem of involuntary servitude. No longer were debt, violence, and legal coercion the sole indicia of unconstitutional servitude; extreme forms of economic coercion were also constitutionally problematic. Here too the CRS's use of the Thirteenth Amendment filled in the legislative gaps of the New Deal. Just as the NLRA had left many African Americans without labor rights, the New Deal's guarantees of economic security in the Fair Labor Standards Act (FLSA) and the Social Security Act (SSA) also excluded many African Americans. In attacking the poor conditions in which African American agricultural and domestic workers lived as problematic under the Thirteenth Amendment, the CRS lawyers indicated that such workers were entitled to a version of the economic rights to minimal living standards that FLSA and the SSA offered industrial workers.

Each expansion of the Thirteenth Amendment's protections built on a different strain of New Deal liberalism and represented a different promise for civil rights. Where the New Deal had emphasized labor and economic rights and assisted African Americans only partially and incidentally, these novel involuntary servitude prosecutions aimed to bring African Americans within the New Deal rights framework. Following changing trends within the involuntary servitude complaints of African Americans themselves, the CRS lawyers went about expanding the meaning of involuntary servitude—and the accompanying protection of the Thirteenth Amendment—in order to make the Constitution serviceable for African Americans in the post–New Deal era.

When the Civil Rights Section took up peonage cases during World War II, it did so at least in part because of their familiarity. During the

early twentieth century, the Department of Justice (DOJ) had prosecuted southern officials under the Peonage Act of 1867. In the 1905
case of *Clyatt v. United States* and the 1914 case of *United States v.
Reynolds*, the Court upheld the Peonage Act and indictments under it.
Moreover, in the privately litigated case of *Bailey v. Alabama*, the Court
invalidated a state contract labor law similar to those of many southern
states. The law presumed a criminal intent to defraud when an employee accepted an advance from an employer but broke his labor
contract without repaying his debt to his employer. The Court declared that the "plain intention" of the Thirteenth Amendment "was
to abolish slavery of whatever name and form and all its badges and incidents; to render impossible any state of bondage; to make labor free,
by prohibiting that control by which the personal service of one man is
disposed of or coerced for another's benefit, which is the essence of involuntary servitude." These cases, as well as lower court victories in succeeding decades, provided the wartime Civil Rights Section with a
sturdy basis for peonage prosecutions.[4]

At the same time, these *Lochner*-era precedents constrained the
kinds of Thirteenth Amendment cases the section could optimistically
pursue in the 1940s. For the previous forty years, the Supreme Court
had seen itself as intervening sporadically into private relationships to
ensure the contractual freedom of the parties. This approach held
true for peonage cases. The problem in *Bailey*, as the Court saw it, was
that the Alabama law functionally required specific performance for
the breaking of a labor contract. Although decided under the Peonage
Act and the Thirteenth Amendment, the language and logic of contract law and contract rights pervaded the opinion.[5]

Many instances of forced labor during the first half of the century did
not involve contracted debt—as where employers maintained immobility through violence or threats of violence. Nonetheless, both during
and after the *Lochner* era, the debt element of peonage kept enforcement of the Thirteenth Amendment closely tied to its contract-based
interpretation. Every successful federal involuntary servitude prosecution before 1937 involved contractual indebtedness. All three involuntary servitude cases that reached the Supreme Court during World
War II—*Taylor v. Georgia*, *United States v. Gaskin*, and *Pollock v. Williams*—
conformed to the conventional definition of peonage. All three involved contracted debt. All three arose under the Peonage Act of 1867.[6]

During World War II, however, the CRS lawyers began to unshackle the Thirteenth Amendment from the contract-based framework of the *Lochner* era. Attorney General Francis Biddle refused to tie the Peonage Act to an outdated conception of servitude from a half century past. Rather, he saw it as "a living law, used to eliminate the various indirect methods by which many persons of low economic status in many of the States have been forced to labor for a particular employer against their will."[7]

The prosecutions the CRS pursued during the war put into practice this more expansive understanding of peonage and involuntary servitude and revitalized the Thirteenth Amendment. One DOJ prosecution exemplifies how radical even small changes in the definition of peonage seemed at the time. In *Pierce v. United States,* a federal appeals court upheld a conviction under the Peonage Act only slightly removed from the classic case of peonage. It found a violation where the employer contrived the alleged debt to keep control over his employees. Without entering into a formal contract, the employer bought goods for his employees. He then refused to allow them to leave his employ without repaying him for the goods. Removing contract but not the guise of debt from consideration, the court stated, "In a prosecution for peonage, the law takes no account of the amount of the debt, or the means and method of coercion. It is sufficient to allege and prove that a person is held against his will and made to work to pay a debt."[8]

This shift provoked a vociferous response from Judge Joseph Chappell Hutcheson, Jr. He protested that in the absence of a contract, a peonage prosecution must fail. The evidence showed "merely that . . . [the defendant] claimed [the victims] owed him and, so claiming, subjected them, by threats and putting in fear, to involuntary servitude." Hutcheson complained that the "statutes have been on the books since 1867 and many cases have been tried under them. No case until this one has ever held that, *absent a contract,* law or usage requiring service in payment of a debt, a condition of peonage is made out." Hutcheson thought that it would "do violence to [the statute's] plain meaning and established construction" to understand it after 100 years "to cover any case of involuntary servitude except one which constitutes peonage."[9]

Pierce just barely broadened the definition of peonage, but it represented the first tiny step in the far more fundamental conceptual change that Carr would identify three years later in *Federal Protection of Civil Rights: Quest for a Sword.* In fact, even before the *Pierce* opinion was published, Attorney General Biddle instituted a policy to expand the use of the Thirteenth Amendment beyond the specific, timeworn cases of peonage proper and beyond prosecutions under the Peonage Act itself. Circular No. 3591 exhorted CRS lawyers and U.S. attorneys to pursue cases of involuntary servitude without the element of debt. Biddle requested that United States attorneys "defer . . . prosecutions under the peonage statute in favor of building the cases around the issues of involuntary servitude and slavery . . . disregarding entirely the element of debt." To underscore the change in approach, Biddle changed all existing case titles from "Peonage" to "Involuntary Servitude and Slavery."[10]

To accomplish this shift from peonage to involuntary servitude, the CRS lawyers not only reinterpreted the Peonage Act but also revitalized other statutory weapons from the recent and distant past. For example, the section put to use the 1932 Lindbergh Law, a federal kidnapping law passed after the abduction of Charles Lindbergh's infant son. An employer who brought an unwilling employee across state lines in order to return him or her to servitude violated the federal law, and the section successfully prosecuted such individuals.[11]

In 1943, section attorney Fred Folsom saw even greater promise in a slave kidnapping law from 1866. That statute prohibited, among other things, the holding of a person as a slave. It had been mobilized twice earlier: unsuccessfully in 1908 and successfully in 1937. The latter case established slavery when workers lived in something resembling a "chicken house" with bars over the windows. Their landlord used "armed guards . . . and dogs" to keep them from leaving. In an article called "A Slave Trade Law in a Contemporary Setting," Folsom explained why he favored the "little known statute." It provided a basis for prosecution in cases in which debt was not the mechanism of forced immobility. Folsom contended that the word "slave" was not limited to African Americans held in the chattel slavery of the antebellum South. Rather, " 'slave' [should] be construed to mean a person so far subjected to the will of another that he is held to labor or service against his will." Folsom "prefer[red] to consider the act as framed for post bellum conditions, in the light of the war amendments, and as using the word slave as meaning a person in a state of enforced or extorted servitude to another."[12]

Most significantly, for the first time since the passage of the Thirteenth Amendment, the Department of Justice used conspiracy and other general civil rights laws to prosecute involuntary servitude cases not based on an underlying debt. Once the Civil Rights Section lawyers read the Thirteenth Amendment as establishing a "federally-secured right to be free from bondage," the Reconstruction criminal civil rights statutes could provide far broader authority for prosecution than the Peonage Act alone. Section 51 of the criminal code criminalized all conspiracies to violate rights guaranteed against private interference, and Section 52 criminalized all governmental violations of constitutional rights. Because the Thirteenth Amendment lacked a state action requirement, it protected the right to be free from bondage against all comers. Just as the CRS lawyers could use general civil rights statutes to protect unionizing workers, so too they could use the same statutes to protect isolated and virtually enslaved workers in the rural South. These statutes enabled the department to obtain convictions in cases in which debt was not an issue at all, so long as the perpetrators were either state officials or private individuals involved in a conspiracy.[13]

Even before Biddle made it a policy to use these general civil rights statutes, the CRS had begun experimenting with a variety of statutory cocktails. The celebrated prosecution of the notorious William T. Cunningham in Oglethorpe County, Georgia, offers a prime example. As anti-peonage crusader William Henry Huff and others publicized, Cunningham had provided his workers with so little food that they frequently went hungry. He threatened to beat them with a pistol if they could not keep his pace. And he hunted his terrified, escaping workers all the way from Georgia to Chicago, where he convinced the police to arrest them. Cunningham's indictment included counts of conspiracy to deprive the farmworkers of the right to be free from slavery and involuntary servitude under Section 51 and counts of holding them as slaves under Folsom's slave kidnapping law, as well as the traditional counts of peonage under the 1867 act.[14]

The changes in involuntary servitude prosecutions were even more apparent after Biddle made his new policy position explicit in Circular No. 3591. When peonage and other forms of servitude coexisted, the section increasingly emphasized elements other than debt. When the

CRS prosecuted Albert Sydney Johnson for peonage in response to numerous complaints from his "terrorized" sharecroppers, for example, Biddle emphasized how Johnson had "threaten[ed] to kill them if they left his place, and lent color to these threats by always carrying a gun, a revolver, and a pair of brass knuckles."[15]

The section's attempted prosecutions of the United States Sugar Corporation during the war illustrate the change even more dramatically. The investigations into the servitude of the young black men working in the Florida cane fields temporally straddled Biddle's change in policy. As the case titles altered from "Peonage" to "Involuntary Servitude," so too did the emphasis of the FBI's questions and the lawyers' analyses of their trial evidence. Before Biddle's circular, questions and memos had focused on the amount and details of the debts the youngsters owed the sugar company. Afterward, the lawyers wrote memos organizing their investigative reports by references to threats, shootings, and beatings, among other things.[16]

Harvesting sugarcane at the United States Sugar Corporation, Clewiston, Florida, 1939. (Farm Security Administration, Office of War Information Photograph Collection, Library of Congress.)

The expansion from peonage to involuntary servitude continued even after Biddle left office following Franklin Roosevelt's death. President Harry S. Truman appointed his attorneys general and assistant attorneys general—like Texan Tom Clark, Rhode Island politician J. Howard McGrath, and Theron Lamar Caudle from North Carolina—more for their loyalty to the Democratic Party than for their commitment to civil rights. That said, especially in the immediate postwar years, Truman impressed upon them the importance of civil rights protection. "I emphasized this so much," Truman recalled, "that Tom Clark thought I was 'hipped' on the subject—and I was."[17]

Truman's attorneys general and assistant attorneys general appointed section chiefs to run the CRS who were more southern than the staff lawyers and section chiefs under FDR. Staff attorneys would not describe section chief Turner L. Smith, a state legislator from Albany, Georgia, as liberal, but they did find him "generally of a frame of mind to accept the rights of all people." He had intervened on behalf of African American victims of civil rights violations in his hometown before moving to Washington. And his fear that he would appear biased in favor of southern whites led him to work hard toward even-handedness. According to his staff lawyers, Arkansan A. B. Caldwell was deeply "dedicated" to civil rights and served as chief of the section from the end of the Truman years into the Eisenhower administration.[18]

Even when impetus from the top for civil rights waned, however, involuntary servitude cases did not suffer. Under Attorney General McGrath, the CRS went eighteen months without a section chief. With one of the "working stiffs," attorney Leo Meltzer, acting as chief, the section's Thirteenth Amendment practice continued apace. McGrath finally filled the position in 1950 with George Triedman, a Democratic crony from his home state. The Washington Post reported that Triedman "had no experience in civil rights matters." His qualifications for the job were merely that "he [was] a long-time friend" of McGrath's, and McGrath believed he could "do a capable job." Even then, McGrath instructed his attorneys to continue with their previous policies toward civil rights. As personnel changed during the decade after the war—sometimes rapidly, as when, from 1947 to 1950, four assistant attorneys general and five chiefs or acting chiefs led the section—the work of peonage and involuntary servitude cases continued relatively unaffected.[19]

In fact, section lawyers under Truman reinforced the shift from peonage to involuntary servitude, from the Peonage Act to the multiplicity of constitutional and statutory prohibitions that they could use
to enforce the Thirteenth Amendment. A 1948 recodification of the
peonage statutes brought the CRS even closer to achieving its goal of
"destroying the system of involuntary labor," as Brooklyn-born section
lawyer Sydney Brodie put it. As part of the modernization of the
seventy-five-year-old criminal laws, the language of the "slave trade"
gave way to the more contemporary language of "involuntary servitude." The more significant substantive change to the statutes was, as
section attorney Henry Putzel, Jr., later noted, that "[u]nder the new
provision, . . . holding a person to a condition of involuntary servitude
is made a crime apart from the existence of any debt." The section
lawyers thought these revisions would ideally enable prosecutors to use
a single statute to attack non-debt-based involuntary servitude. They
would no longer need to resort to the somewhat clumsy combination
of the Thirteenth Amendment and the criminal civil rights laws they
had used in the early 1940s.[20]

These developments—the shift from peonage to involuntary servitude, from use of the peonage statute to a host of other statutory
tools—reflected a larger transformation in conceptualizing and enforcing civil rights during the late 1930s and 1940s. As Carr's use of the
shield-and-sword motif suggested, the *Lochner*-era conception of civil
rights as a constraint on government action no longer occupied the
field. A new positive liberty in which the federal government acted as
wielder of the sword had grown up beside it.

The New Deal itself had begun this transformation. "Security" in the
economic sense was the watchword of the federal government's attack
on the Depression of the 1930s. New Deal legislation attempted to provide such economic security (mostly for white men) through unemployment insurance, public works projects, Social Security, relief, the
protection of unions, and other economic and social welfare programs. The New Deal thus demonstrated that the exercise of government power, rather than its restraint, might serve to safeguard the
vulnerable. Attorney General Biddle made this very point in a lecture
he delivered at the end of 1942. He acknowledged that the Founders
were most concerned with a limited government. He argued, however,
that after the Industrial Revolution, Americans came to realize that

"the powers of unregulated business had to be checked by transferring much of their control from private to public hands."[21]

The Truman administration reinforced this new emphasis on the government's use of the civil rights sword. When Truman created his groundbreaking Committee on Civil Rights in 1946, he declared the end of complacency "with a civil liberties program which emphasizes only the need of protection against the possibility of tyranny by the Government." Modern conditions required the creation of "new concepts of civil rights to safeguard our heritage." The "extension of civil rights today," Truman announced, "means not protection of the people *against* the Government, but protection of the people *by* the Government."[22]

In its final report, Truman's committee described how increased national authority for protecting civil rights extended the "positive governmental programs designed to solve the nation's changing problems." The Supreme Court had found in the Constitution a "basis for governmental action at the national level . . . for such policies as the control of prices; regulation of agricultural production; requirement of collective bargaining; social security benefits for millions of people; prohibitions of industrial monopolies" and more. The committee built on those interpretations, and it "reject[ed] the argument that government controls are themselves necessarily threats to liberty. . . . [F]reedom in a civilized society is always founded on law enforced by government."[23]

Truman and his committee also rejected the notion that the new governmental duty to provide security began and ended with economic security. Invoking FDR's identification of "freedom from fear" as one of the Four Freedoms, the committee's report made clear that fear did not stem from economic hardship and uncertainty alone. It grew as well out of the personal insecurity of living as a racial minority in a society that publicly and privately, systematically and informally, oppressed such minorities. As a result, freedom from fear now required not only the economic safety net the New Deal had provided mostly to white workers but also freedom from involuntary servitude, lynching, and police brutality for African Americans.[24]

By the late 1940s and early 1950s, then, the New Deal's catchphrase of "economic security" had mutated in some contexts into the "security of the person" or "the safety and security of the person." The phrase drew on a venerable but long-submerged understanding of civil rights, with common law roots traceable to William Blackstone's 1765 *Commentaries*. There, Blackstone defined personal security as "a person's legal and uninterrupted enjoyment of his life, his limbs, his body, his health, and his reputation." The American roots of the concept went back to the 1866 Civil Rights Act and the Freedman's Bureau Bill of the same year. The very first of the Reconstruction-era civil rights statutes guaranteed all citizens the same "full and equal benefit of all laws and proceedings for the security of person and property" that white citizens enjoyed. When African American civil rights reemerged as a national political issue in the 1940s, the "security of the person" reemerged with them. It was a central component of the report of the President's Committee on Civil Rights in 1947. And it was the phrase used to describe the category of harms that included involuntary servitude and peonage, lynching, and police brutality in the only casebook on civil rights in existence in 1952.[25]

Freedom from involuntary servitude was a staple component of "the security of the person" and an ideal site for implementing this New Deal approach to civil rights. As CRS lawyer Brodie noted, precisely because the victims of peonage were often "defenseless or without capacity to pursue [their] personal remedies," the government needed to "act on its own initiative." Although the DOJ had done so in its prosecutions in the early twentieth century, its cases had remained limited by the Supreme Court's image of peonage cases as essentially exercises in contract law. During World War II, the CRS lawyers rejected the essence of *Lochner*-era peonage cases as the occasional interference of courts into private contracts. Instead they focused on a direct, ongoing relationship between the executive branch of the federal government and its citizens. Vindicating a citizen's rights against private violations was institutionally, doctrinally, and culturally different from enforcing the narrow terms of the Peonage Act. When the CRS expanded the "security" of the New Deal to include the "safety and security" of African Americans, they recognized that private as well as public power supported Jim Crow and the economic, social, and political disabilities it perpetuated.[26]

As the 1940s progressed, CRS lawyers continued to expand their attacks on involuntary servitude, to broaden the Thirteenth Amendment, and to apply other New Deal protections to African American laborers. During the war, the CRS had first expanded its involuntary servitude prosecutions to include mechanisms of servitude beyond debt. The section's second expansion represented an even more dramatic departure from *Lochner*-era peonage cases. The lawyers deemphasized the Thirteenth Amendment's focus on the individual employer-employee relationship for a broader attack on the southern political economy that made such relationships possible.

Even as conventional indicia of immobility like debt and violence remained important to the wartime Civil Rights Section, Biddle and his staff began to explore the effects of less individualized obstacles to free labor. They shifted focus from a given laborer to the southern labor market itself—to the structural, legal obstacles to labor mobility in the South. The South's low-wage, work-intensive, and under-industrialized economy was rooted in the legacy of slavery and the ability to exploit African Americans both politically and economically. As a result, the southern labor market had long remained separate from that of the rest of the nation. The Great Migration of the interwar period, the weak labor market of the Depression, the partial creation of a national labor market during the New Deal, and mobilization for the war effort went some of the way toward national economic integration.

In many ways, however, the South still operated as a separate labor market. Even as the New Deal took steps to integrate the southern economy, it largely accommodated the racial hierarchies of the region's labor market. The NLRA, the FLSA, and the SSA all exempted from coverage the agricultural and domestic work that most African Americans in the South performed. The National Recovery Administration failed to eliminate regional wage differentials, and its local administrators maintained racial differentials through discriminatory implementation. Locally administered federal relief agencies similarly catered to the southern system by customarily cutting from the rolls workers needed for agricultural work during planting and harvesting seasons. And the Agricultural Adjustment Act even strengthened the economic power of white planters at the expense of white and black tenants and sharecroppers. Without addressing these New Deal biases and attacking the southern labor market as a whole, the CRS lawyers realized, it would be difficult to undermine effectively individually coercive labor relationships.[27]

Roosevelt himself initiated the assault on the separate southern labor market in the late 1930s. The attack was part of his newfound will to make inroads into the conservative Democratic monopoly of the South. In a letter to his Conference on Economic Conditions of the South in 1938, he described the region as "the Nation's No. 1 economic problem." He believed the Democratic Party had to change the South's "feudal system" and called for the region's integration into the national economy. Presaging the approach Supreme Court Justice Jackson and Attorney General Biddle would take toward peonage and involuntary servitude during the war, Roosevelt described the South's economy as "vitally and inexorably linked with that of the Nation." He proclaimed, "Nationwide thinking, nationwide planning and nationwide action are the three great essentials to prevent nationwide crises for future generations to struggle through."[28]

Shortly after the president politically attacked state-level impediments to national economic integration, the Supreme Court's 1941 decision in *Edwards v. California* made them seem increasingly constitutionally vulnerable. Fresh from his post as attorney general, Justice Jackson wrote the opinion striking down a 1937 California statute that prohibited anyone from bringing an "indigent person" into the state. The law had aimed to prevent masses of poor and desperate migrants from the Dust Bowl of Oklahoma, Texas, Arkansas, and Missouri from flooding California's labor camps and overwhelming its relief efforts.[29]

The Court interpreted the Constitution as "framed upon the theory that the peoples of the several states must sink or swim together, and that in the long run prosperity and salvation are in union and not division." The Court described care for the needy as a federal, rather than solely a local, concern. California overstepped its constitutional bounds because its statute hindered such national unity and attempted to legislate where only Congress had authority under the commerce clause. In a concurrence, Justice William O. Douglas agreed with the result, but on different grounds: the constitutionally protected but textually nebulous right to travel. He thought that allowing an exception to the right to travel would undermine "national unity" and "introduce a caste system utterly incompatible with the spirit of our system of government." It would relegate the poor "to an inferior class of citizenship."[30]

A few years later, section lawyer S. P. Meyers saw the obvious implications of *Edwards* for the legal obstacles to free labor that pervaded the southern states. African American agricultural workers repeatedly complained about these obstacles, southern statute books unabashedly published them, and legal scholars increasingly criticized them. They included nineteenth-century enticement, emigrant-agent, and vagrancy statutes as well as wartime "work or fight" ordinances that gave police officers and sheriffs authority to arrest and put to work anyone who appeared unemployed. In particular, Meyers thought it possible after *Edwards* that the Supreme Court would strike down a Florida emigrant-agent statute similar to a Georgia statute upheld in 1900. Several legal scholars agreed that these and other southern restrictions on interstate mobility for work had become "vulnerable to a challenge of constitutionality." The tighter wartime labor market made the problem seem even more acute. Wrote one legal scholar, "Constitutional rights of citizens and mobilization of manpower for war production are threatened with serious interference by state legislation designed to restrict the removal of workers to other states for employment."[31]

Over the course of World War II, top Justice Department officials grew increasingly committed to such unfettered regional and national mobility. Biddle's comments about the Detroit race riot in the summer of 1943—in which thirty-four people, mostly blacks, were killed after a scuffle at a city park—suggested that he had not always endorsed a completely unrestricted national labor market. President Roosevelt had asked Biddle to investigate the riot's causes and to recommend preventive measures for the future. Biddle, like others, blamed the riot on overcrowding due to the large number of migrants who had crammed into Detroit for war work. He suggested that "careful considerations be given to limiting, and in some instances putting an end to, Negro migrations into communities which cannot absorb them."[32]

When Biddle's confidential memo to the president found its way to the press, it stirred up a furor. The NAACP, the National Urban League, and other African American organizations, as well as black newspapers across the country, attacked Biddle as "not the liberal he had been thought to be." They condemned the proposed migration restrictions for their "appalling" "inequity and injustice." Biddle clarified that he did not intend to keep African Americans in the South. Rather, he proposed to use federal power to match both black and white migration with manpower needs and local absorption capacities.[33]

Within a year, Biddle's thinking had changed considerably. By the

time Justice Jackson penned the opinion in the 1944 peonage case of
Pollock v. Williams, Biddle had set himself squarely behind efforts to
create a unified labor market unimpeded by southern attempts to control the region's black laborers. Even if the war required some federal
manpower coordination, he thought restrictive state laws would undermine rather than facilitate that effort.[34]

In *Pollock,* the Court invalidated Florida's contract labor statute. Like
the laws the Court had struck down more than thirty years earlier in
Bailey v. Alabama and less than two years before in *Taylor v. Georgia,* the
Florida law made it a crime for a laborer to leave a job without repaying an advance from his employer. In Pollock's case, he had bor-
rowed five dollars. Although *Pollock* still contained the element of contracted indebtedness, the Court's expansive language indicated a
broader view of unconstitutional involuntary servitude. Where the
Bailey opinion had emphasized the constitutionality of various mechanisms of enforcing contracts, *Pollock* emphasized the relationship between this particular law and the labor market as a whole.[35]

Justice Jackson could not fathom the purpose behind a law meant to
legally bind employees to particular employers. Rather, he saw "the
right to change employers" as the worker's prime "defense against oppressive hours, pay, working conditions, or treatment." He maintained
that when "the master can compel and the laborer cannot escape the
obligation to go on, there is no power below to redress and no incentive
above to relieve a harsh overlordship or unwholesome conditions of
work." Jackson warned that the "[r]esulting depression of working conditions and living standards affects not only the laborer under the
system, but every other with whom his labor comes in competition."
Laws such as Florida's contract labor statute, Jackson cautioned, not
only imposed immobility on particular individuals but also depressed
the labor market as a whole and infringed on the rights of all workers.[36]

Justice Department lawyers took Justice Jackson's observations and
ran with them. They saw, as did the black agricultural workers who
wrote to them, that many state and local laws were designed to keep
the southern labor market impermeable. So long as such laws continued to restrict some laborers in their bargaining power, laborers of
all kinds and in all regions of the nation would not be truly free.
Echoing Jackson, section lawyer Brodie discussed in 1951 the "de-
pressing effect of slave labor upon our society and economic system."

He described "the detriment suffered by the public as well as by the individual victim who is forced to work for another against his will [as] serious and substantial." A United States attorney from Alabama was even more specific about the relationship between peonage and the labor market. The purpose of using contract labor laws to obtain labor, he explained, was to get individuals "to work for less money than labor could be obtained ordinarily in the open market."[37]

Biddle and the lawyers in the Justice Department thus read *Pollock* and the other wartime cases as "substantially strengthen[ing] the federal guaranty of freedom from involuntary servitude." According to Biddle, *Pollock* placed "the right to freedom from involuntary servitude on so broad a base that the way has been opened to an attack on the 'enticing labor' and 'emigrant agent' statutes, and some of the vagrancy statutes and 'work or fight' orders." The department had learned from experience that such laws had "proved to be in reality indirect means of enforcing involuntary servitude, especially against Negro farm hands and laborers." These laws were the very ones that minimized African American mobility, that made employment recruitment impracticable in the South, and that closed off the channels of information necessary to facilitate widespread migration for work.[38]

In its second departure from pre–Civil Rights Section efforts at ending peonage, then, Biddle targeted laws that did not necessarily create a particular employment relationship from which exit was difficult but rather those that made exit difficult from any employment relationship. He thought that prohibiting involuntary servitude meant far more than stopping a particular employer from directly coercing a particular employee. It meant protecting truly free labor, even in the South and even, "especially," for southern African Americans. The CRS thus attacked the "work or fight" laws about which many African Americans complained during the war.[39]

In addition, CRS lawyers and U.S. attorneys during and after the war made wholesale, rather than retail, efforts to eliminate peonage by ensuring that justices of the peace, county sheriffs, and local prosecutors knew when they were violating the Thirteenth Amendment. United States attorneys lobbied legislatures to repeal contract labor statutes like those the Supreme Court had struck down. They tried to educate law enforcement officials by speaking at events like annual meetings of the Georgia Peace Officers Association. And they repeatedly wrote local officials about laws the Supreme Court had held unconstitutional. They told the officials to "read [the *Pollock* opinion] in full, so that you will understand the ruling of the Supreme Court."[40]

By 1945, Biddle had concluded that the Thirteenth Amendment "guaranteed that there should not only be an end to slavery, but that a system of completely free and voluntary labor should be maintained throughout the United States." The "free and voluntary labor" to which Biddle referred had its roots in both the Civil War era and the New Deal. To many Reconstruction congressmen, the Thirteenth Amendment not only ended slavery but mandated "free labor" as the opposite of slavery and servitude. Although they did not necessarily agree on a single definition of free labor, the term carried connotations of the right to pursue a calling, the dignity of labor, and the autonomy of the individual. It also embraced the opportunity to find jobs, to advance economically, and to receive a just compensation for labor. This ideal provided part of the basis for *Lochner*-era liberty of contract, and it persisted with some force even after the *Lochner* era ended.[41]

What made labor free for the CRS lawyers during and after World War II differed substantially from what made it free in the free-labor ideology of Reconstruction and in the freedom-of-contract jurisprudence of the *Lochner* era, however. The New Deal transformed the essence of free labor into rights to organize, bargain, and strike. "The tendency of modern economic life toward integration and centralized control," an early version of the NLRA stated, "has long since destroyed the balance of bargaining power between the individual employer and the individual employee, and has rendered the individual, unorganized worker helpless to exercise actual liberty of contract, to secure a just reward for his services, and to preserve a decent standard of living." In order for the free-labor ideology of the Reconstruction and *Lochner* eras to become a reality in the industrial United States, workers had to have the right to act collectively.[42]

Workers who could not move physically or occupationally to exert market pressure were poor candidates for labor organization, however. The immobility created by southern statutes posed a barrier to organization and bargaining. It therefore posed a barrier to the full and effective implementation of New Deal free labor principles. The ability to protect oneself from coercion by exercising the right to strike and the right to work for minimum wages under minimally acceptable conditions had become the means by which American workers would resist labor exploitation. They were the means by which workers could protect themselves against the kind of involuntary servitude the Thirteenth Amendment prohibited. Contemporary commentator Howard Devon Hamilton recognized this when he included "resistance to organization and movement of agricultural labor" among the obstacles that workers faced in violation of "the Thirteenth Amendment's objective of a system of completely free and voluntary labor throughout the United States."[43]

The Civil Rights Section's Thirteenth Amendment practice thus targeted for constitutional protection precisely those workers the New Deal left unprotected and unions left unorganized. From the beginning, the CRS had included both industrial and agricultural workers in its purview. But while the NLRA provided a relatively secure statutory basis for industrial workers' rights and the FEPC promised nondiscrimination in industrial employment, agricultural workers lacked clear statutory or administrative rights. For one thing, New Deal legislation failed to live up to the national promise its roots in the commerce clause suggested when it excluded agricultural and domestic work in order to maintain southern support and obtain Supreme Court approval. For another, even where the NLRA applied in the South, local law enforcement used involuntary servitude, shored up by both legal and extralegal authority, to quash attempts at union organization.[44]

When Biddle announced his plans to attack the statutes that kept the southern economy separate and oppressive, he drew on these unrealized New Deal aspirations for a free national labor market. National markets, national regulation, and union organization were the key to free labor. So long as a dual labor market persisted, the full promise of the New Deal's labor protections could never be effectuated. Biddle thus moved toward a position in which the prohibition on involuntary servitude could include not only direct physical and legal coercion by the employer but also the larger legal framework that structured southern, especially agricultural, employment. Biddle and his staff took the old, abolitionist, free-labor ideology, transformed it from the *Lochner* era for service in the post–New Deal era, and tried to make it constitutionally foundational.

As the nation put the war behind it, the Civil Rights Section expanded its interpretation of the Thirteenth Amendment in yet a third way. Once predictions of a postwar recession largely fell flat, the CRS began to suggest that black agricultural and domestic workers who had not shared significantly in either the wartime economic boom or the nation's postwar prosperity might also find some measure of economic security in the Thirteenth Amendment. More than a decade after the New Deal promised Social Security and unemployment insurance for most Americans, these African American men and women were still denied rights to the most basic economic security. As the Civil Rights Section turned its attention to the conditions in which these workers lived and worked, its cases suggested that no worker in the United States, not even those excluded by political compromise, could constitutionally endure such extreme economic privation. The lawyers suggested that the Constitution itself might protect workers unable to take advantage of New Deal economic rights, just as it might protect those unable to take advantage of New Deal labor rights.

As the section lawyers increasingly defined involuntary servitude in terms of economic coercion in the late 1940s, they drew on changing academic, political, and popular meanings of peonage and involuntary servitude. These meanings stemmed from the social and economic "realities" of involuntary servitude, which the turn-of-the-century Supreme Court had failed to acknowledge in its attention to contract. Political scientist Hamilton, for example, defined peonage "[i]n every day parlance" as "used loosely to cover almost any variety of forced labor, or simply exploited labor." Moreover, Hamilton extended his discussion of the Thirteenth Amendment from peonage proper to "peonage-like conditions," condemning the latter as those in which "men get sick or die from overwork or bad conditions." He discussed how contract workers were "farm[ed] out" to other employers during slack periods and how Mexican workers endured "hideous living conditions and . . . low wages." To Hamilton, peonage encompassed all of these coercions and indignities.[45]

In the mid-1940s, press releases by organizations like the NAACP similarly spoke of "virtual slavery." A local NAACP branch requested FBI involvement in a case in which teenage boys from Brooklyn had been lured to a farm in upstate New York. When the boys "complained and asked to be taken home," they were "told if they wanted to leave they'd have to walk." Neither the reporter who wrote about the case nor the NAACP saw the permission to leave as fatal to the youths' claims of peonage. Rather, they emphasized that the young men had "worked like peons . . . for little or no money" in "conditions of practical peonage." Although the lawyers in the NAACP's national legal department emphasized to its branches the importance of forced immobility in making out legal claims, the conditions of the work, the hardship it entailed, and the inadequate pay sufficed to demonstrate "practical peonage" among nonlawyers.[46]

Similarly, the common practice among farmers and employers of selling the debt of their employees to one another began to appear beyond the bounds of the legitimate employment relationship. The practice had long escaped legal notice as "just another of those cases where two white men are squabbling over colored help." But when the Senate held hearings on involuntary servitude and union organizing in the lumber industry in Laurens County, Georgia, it brought new national concern to the practice. The incredulity with which Macon attorney Thomas W. Johnson testified is apparent even in transcription: "They actually buy the debts from each other. If one Negro wants to go and work for somebody else and it is satisfactory with the man for whom he is working at the moment, the man with whom he wants to work buys the debt from the other man." The sale of debt may arguably have enhanced worker mobility more than if the debts had been nontransferable. The practice—and the related perception that some African American workers "belonged" to particular employers— nonetheless offended the sensibilities of those interested in ending involuntary servitude.[47]

Complaints to the Department of Justice and to organizations like the NAACP reflected these changes in the meaning of involuntary servitude. Male agricultural laborers began to protest their lack of amenities, rather than the violent means by which they were forced to work. They "wore rags" and slept in "chicken house[s]" or on "old rusty cot[s]."[48]

Moreover, a new group of workers began to complain about involuntary servitude in similar terms. Female domestic workers like Elizabeth Coker, Polly Johnson, and Dora Jones also complained about the poor conditions of their working lives, their isolation from American freedom, and their exclusion from America's plenty. They emphasized lack of pay, degrading conditions, and work too onerous for their sex, but they rarely mentioned forced immobility. In fact, Polly Johnson testified not that she was kept by force, but that "she was not allowed to leave [her employer's] premises except when her employer sent her to the store and then she had to return within a given period." Because she could leave her workplace and home unaccompanied, the essence of her servitude was not in the force by which she was held, but rather the conditions that ensured that she would indeed "return within a given period." At the heart of such complaints was the sense that these women, as Coker put it, had "never enjoyed any of the privileges of a free person."[49]

These metaphorical meanings and nonlegal understandings of terms like "slavery," "peonage," and "involuntary servitude" led the Civil Rights Section to try to expand the Thirteenth Amendment in one final way in the postwar period: to protect African American workers from such shocking conditions. Section lawyers took up Fred Folsom's suggestion to use the slave kidnapping law to reach such complaints. Folsom himself had had in mind cases involving legal coercion as well as unacceptable conditions, but the "virtual slavery" prosecutions the section eventually pursued under Folsom's reclaimed statute went far beyond that.[50]

The watershed case came in 1947. Though it occurred in California rather than Georgia or Alabama, the implications for the South were clear. For years, Helen Roberts had fretted about the way her parents, Elizabeth and Alfred Wesley Ingalls, treated their servant, Dora Jones. When Roberts learned that her parents had forced Jones to sleep in a car outside a hotel equipped with rooms for maids, she finally went to the authorities. After an extensive investigation, the Department of Justice prosecuted the case under the slavery statute. The jury heard testimony for eighteen days. Although it could not agree as to the guilt of Alfred Ingalls, it convicted his wife of holding Jones in slavery.

Judge Jacob Weinberger decided that the *Ingalls* case was novel and important enough to warrant the publication of his opinion denying Elizabeth Ingalls's motion for a new trial. The threats the judge described as having prevented Jones from exercising her "free will" for thirty years were considerably different from earlier indicia of forced immobility. Although Elizabeth Ingalls threatened Jones with imprisonment, it was for an adulterous affair that had occurred thirty-eight years prior (with Ingalls's first husband) and the abortion that resulted. Elizabeth Ingalls also told Jones that "she was not bright, mentally, and could not make her way in the competitive world and would—if not sent to prison—be committed to a mental institution."

The court took seriously Jones's subjective perception of her options, rather than any objective harm that would come to her. "It appears that these threats and numerous others acted effectively upon the servant to hold her against her free will in the service of the defendant."[51]

More significantly, because the case was prosecuted under the slave kidnapping law, the conditions of Jones's life were central to the court's description of the harm. The essence of slavery for the court was the subjection of the will of one individual to that of another. In proving Jones's subjection to Elizabeth Ingalls, the trial court emphasized the conditions of Jones's life in a way never before discussed in a published opinion. For more than twenty-five years, Jones had been "required to arise at an early hour in the morning and perform practically all of the household labor in connection with the maintenance of the Ingalls household. She was forbidden to leave the household except for the commission of errands and performed drudgery of the most menial and laborious type." All this, he noted, was performed "without compensation, . . . days off[,] . . . or vacation[s]." Jones's "quarters were among the poorest in the several homes occupied by the defendant during this period of years." Her board "was of a substantially lower standard than that common to servants generally."[52]

After detailing additional poor treatment, the court concluded that "the servant, Dora L. Jones, was a person wholly subject to the will of defendant; that she was one who had no freedom of action and whose person and services were wholly under the control of defendant and who was in a state of enforced compulsory service to the defendant." The facts of Jones's life spoke for themselves: an individual exercising her free will would simply not have countenanced such treatment. That Jones had opportunities to leave and did not suggested all the more that she was indeed "wholly subject to the will of the defendant" with no "freedom of action" of her own. She was, as the *Los Angeles Times* put it, "a 20th century slave."[53]

The chain of reasoning that led to a conviction in *Ingalls* differed greatly from that which had led to peonage convictions less than a decade earlier. In the intervening period, promising complaints began to include not only physical restraint and imprisonment but also the quality of the victims' lives and the conditions of their work. By 1952, *Ingalls* represented an acute example of modern slavery and involuntary servitude. In discussing the question whether "slavery" and "involuntary servitude" should be considered the same thing, CRS lawyer Brodie concluded that because *Ingalls* had been such an extreme case, it had not "disposed of the problem." "The sordid facts of the case actually established more than mere unwilling labor, service rendered another because of duress, fear, threats or intimidation," Brodie wrote. Even someone with "privileges such as going home after work, receiving some remuneration, maintaining a form of private life," privileges that Jones most certainly did not enjoy, might still "clearly be in a condition of involuntary servitude" even if not slavery itself.[54]

Elizabeth Ingalls's sentence was also groundbreaking. Prior to *Ingalls*, criminal prosecutions of involuntary servitude, like criminal prosecutions generally, primarily aimed to vindicate the government itself. The perpetrator's fine and prison term served as restitution owed for violating the laws of the nation. In a departure from the past, Judge Weinberger required Elizabeth Ingalls to provide restitution to Jones herself in the amount of $6,000. This was above and beyond Elizabeth Ingalls's suspended prison sentence and a $2,500 fine she had to pay the government. The harm, then, was not only against the government but also against Jones personally. The case had made much of the Ingallses' failure to pay Jones, and the sentence provided her with remuneration for her work.

As *Ingalls* drew headlines, waves of similar complaints hit the department. Whereas in 1946, CRS attorney Meltzer had described Polly Johnson's case as "not the ordinary type of peonage or involuntary servitude situation," by 1948 such cases were legion. One complainant explained that news coverage of the *Ingalls* case led her to speak out about a case in the very same California town where the Ingallses had been exposed. Her allegations—that a woman held the daughter of her mother's former slave in a shack and paid her no wages—closely mirrored those in *Ingalls*. Other complaints alleging that families caring for the "feeble-minded," the blind, and the disabled were actually holding them in servitude poured in from concerned neighbors, family members, and organizations. They described, almost uniformly, how the victims worked long, hard hours with little or no pay other than paltry room and board and some clothing to wear. For the complainants, the lack of schooling these victims received, and the lack of modern amenities they could access, indicated that such workers lacked freedom in the modern, postwar sense of the word.[55]

The Civil Rights Section attempted to respond to these complaints with legal action. In addition to *Ingalls,* the department brought charges to a grand jury against Elizabeth Coker's employers. Despite evidence that Coker's employers had held the young woman without pay and forced her to perform strenuous work under inhumane conditions, the all-white jury refused to indict.[56]

Sometimes, however, it was not the jury but the very nature of the crime—the complete subjection of the victim's will to the perpetrator—that made prosecution virtually impossible. Mary Wright had lived on the Meirses' New Jersey farm for twenty-six years. She had left it only in "very isolated instances" in the company of one of the Meirses. When the NAACP first contacted her, she told them that she wanted to leave but was afraid. Just as the Ingallses had claimed to be Jones's benefactors, so too the Meirs family claimed that Wright was of subnormal intelligence and needed their care. The CRS lawyers determined that Wright had indeed been held in involuntary servitude, but they ultimately found prosecution untenable. The problem was that after the initial investigation, Wright changed her story. She told an FBI agent that "she liked living at the Meirs[es'] farm and did not want to leave; that no one had ever forced her to remain on the farm nor had any one threatened [her] with trouble if she tried to leave; that she had received a small salary weekly for the past three years; and that the Meirs family buys her clothes, furnishes her room and board, and pays for all her medical and dental expenses." The U.S. attorney could only conclude that her change in attitude resulted from "the psychological effect upon the victim of her years in the situation in which she now finds herself." Because of that attitude, he concluded, any prosecution would fail.[57]

A number of the victims, however, remained steadfast in their claims of involuntary servitude and slavery, or they wavered only briefly, as Jones had done at moments in the investigation of the Ingallses. Some even insisted, following the court-ordered restitution in Jones's case, that their employers owed them salaries they had never received. Where criminal cases failed to provide restitution, they brought civil lawsuits. Pauline Anderson and Elsie Jensen sued their employers, claiming conditions similar to Jones's and hoping to recover for the lost wages and damage their servitude had inflicted. Some farmworkers followed suit. After the federal government successfully prosecuted George Stark for holding Francisco Rodriguez in slavery from 1941 to 1947, Rodriguez initiated a civil suit for damages. When Stark's supporters pleaded for the federal government to release him from prison so that he could testify in the civil case, the department declined. "It is indeed regrettable," wrote Assistant to the Attorney General Peyton Ford, without much apparent regret, "that Stark finds himself a defendant in a suit for damages filed by the victim in the criminal case of which he was convicted."[58]

In the postwar decade, the CRS saw some success in cases like *Ingalls*. Yet the section lawyers still thought the nineteenth-century statutes on which they were forced to rely somewhat cumbersome and outdated. At times, though the conditions in which some people lived seemed "shocking," U.S. attorneys and the lawyers in Washington lamented that they were "only a violation of the laws of civilized society and not the laws of the Federal Government." In one such case that arose a few months after the victory in *Ingalls*, Assistant Attorney General T. Vincent Quinn concluded that the victim was "clearly" being held as a "virtual slave." He was "embarrassed," however, to find that he could not prosecute an individual who merely held a slave without conspiring or aiding another, without the existence or allegation of a debt, and without carrying that person away to be held as a slave within the statute of limitations. Even though the 1948 recodification of the criminal code facilitated prosecution of what political scientist Hamilton called "peonage-like conditions," CRS lawyers like Putzel thought that "further clarifications [were] still in order."[59]

In 1951, both the Senate and the House considered legislation to bolster the legal tools for eliminating involuntary servitude. As part of the House consideration of the bill, Civil Rights Section Chief George Triedman—the McGrath appointee with little interest in civil rights—testified before a subcommittee about the need for further changes to the involuntary servitude statutes. Complaints of forced labor conditions kept "coming up and hitting us constantly," Triedman reported. He and his attorneys found themselves "powerless to go forward" with prosecutions under the laws as they then stood. They were "frustrated with a situation where a condition exists like this." Although the section had few attorneys and no need "to borrow any more work," it nonetheless pursued wider jurisdiction in involuntary servitude cases. An omnibus civil rights bill that included "modernization" of the involuntary servitude statutes was pending in 1951, but Triedman sought additional legislation specifically remedying defects in those laws. "[T]here are actual cases of happenings that have come across my table as well as [those of] members of my section and there are no other laws to meet them," Triedman explained. "That is what prompted us, even at this late date, even after 75 years, to come in and see if we can modernize them a bit."[60]

The cases Triedman brought to Congress's attention illustrated how much the section's view of involuntary servitude had changed between 1939 and 1951. The classic case of peonage—of the poor black man in the rural South held for debt in either agricultural or rural nonagricultural work (like timber or sugar refining) by violence, threats of violence, and arrest—had given way to a far broader understanding about who was forced to work and how. Of the four prototypical cases Triedman described to the committee, only two conformed to the traditional image of involuntary servitude: one employer held his worker through violence and another through threats of arrest. The other two both involved female victims. One had never even worked for the alleged perpetrator. The other was a domestic laborer. Triedman spent a considerable part of his testimony describing the women's plight and the federal law's inability to help them.[61]

The newly prominent cases of domestic worker servitude and the newly identified forms of coercion at issue in these and other cases represent the CRS's final departure from past practice on two levels. First, these cases expanded yet again who was entitled to federal protection. It is hardly surprising that more than a decade after the New Deal had mandated minimum wages and conditions under the FLSA, the majority of Thirteenth Amendment complaints about substandard living conditions and a lack of wages came from black agricultural and domestic workers, often in the South. Such workers could not appeal to the Department of Labor or the Social Security Administration.

Instead, the CRS used its Thirteenth Amendment practice to complement the gaps in the New Deal's economic protections. The CRS aimed to protect not just industrial and agricultural workers, but all workers. The section included domestic workers normally thought to occupy a private sphere immune from governmental intervention. These workers lived with their employers; they traveled with them; like Jones, they spent the night in cars while employers slept in hotels. Al-

though Triedman tried to assure his congressional audience that his
bill "would effect no radical change in existing law and would not extend the jurisdiction of the Department to any new situation or type of
case," his domestic worker example belied those reassurances. Such
examples were revolutionary, as they indicated a willingness to use federal law to intrude into relationships of household labor, relationships
that Congress had deemed local, private, and off-limits to the federal
government.[62]

Exactly what such workers were protected from constituted the
second major departure of the domestic workers' cases from the section's past peonage practice. The economic coercion that ensured immobility in such cases—evidenced not by violence or force of law but
by the individual's apparent inability to save herself from objection-
able conditions—had never before received systematic federal attention. But the New Deal's partial promise to provide economic security
to the American people had wrought a revolution in expectations
about work, working conditions, and free will. Against the backdrop of
promised federal protection for minimum wages, maximum hours,
collective bargaining, and free movement within the labor market, a
person choosing his or her employment would obviously not choose to
work very long days under squalid and dehumanizing conditions. The
baseline was a low one. As the judge had suggested in *Ingalls,* Jones was
properly compared to other domestic workers who were not enslaved,
not to some middle-class or even working-class ideal. It was not, however, necessary for the conditions to deteriorate so far that the victims
became slaves without any free will at all before the federal government could intervene. Rather, as section lawyer Brodie made clear in
1951, the label of "involuntary servitude" could attach even to those
who (unlike Jones) enjoyed some measure of personal and economic
autonomy.[63]

In a series of lectures at the University of Virginia Law School on
"Democratic Thinking and the War" in 1942, Francis Biddle described
the "democratic hopes and democratic faith" that were the ultimate
aims of American involvement in WWII. He rooted those aims in the
Four Freedoms and the Atlantic Charter. The charter, he reminded his
audience, did not "stop with a guaranty of political integrity. Access to
trade and raw materials, improved labor standards, economic advance-

ment and social security were among the 'common principles.'" The first phase of the American heritage had protected "individual men and women against tyrants and the tyrant state." The second and more recent phase would protect "individual men and women against what Senator Wagner has called 'social and economic conditions in which human beings cannot be free.'"[64]

Biddle did not see how his assertions could cause much controversy. He pointed out that this "bold democratic faith [was] affirmed not only by liberals but by groups that we think of as properly conservative." Rights to economic security, just wages, and labor organization were no longer marginal aspirations. Rather, Biddle said with some sharpness, "All this is implicit in the Atlantic Charter and the authoritative statements of our ends that have already been made. Those who do not find it there have not yet learned to read."[65]

The speech is quite revealing. It not only illuminates Biddle's views on the aims of the war but also provides a commentary on the Civil Rights Section's Thirteenth Amendment practice in the 1940s and early 1950s. In viewing black workers' rights under the Thirteenth Amendment in the context of the New Deal, the Atlantic Charter, and the Four Freedoms, Biddle and his lawyers did not think that they were going too far out on a limb. Even as organized labor became embattled against a conservative Congress and the Cold War narrowed acceptable political and economic discourse, labor and economic rights remained relatively mainstream, as Biddle emphasized in his speech. The lawyers in the CRS and the DOJ were not members of the Communist Party, nor did they identify with Communism. Some had sympathy with left ideas, but by and large they were conventional liberal Democrats. Some, like Biddle, were more committed to the federal protection of rights than others, like Triedman or McGrath. Overall, they thought about the legal problems they faced squarely within liberal, New Deal understandings of civil rights and the role of the federal government in protecting them. They did not think that "a planned economy" that would deliver economic security was identical to socialism. As Biddle said, denying the charge, "all economy is planned." He derided as an "oversimplified choice" the common depiction of socialism and laissez-faire as diametrically opposed economic systems.[66]

Thus, the idea that labor and economic rights were critical to postwar democracy, that the federal government had an obligation to protect these rights, and that they might be constitutionally grounded were not the oddball ideas of a marginal and marginalized left. These ideas were contemplated in the most exclusive corridors of government power and academic deliberation. They drew on and constructed historical narratives that brought them within the fold of American heritage and tradition.

By the same token, the CRS lawyers approached the civil rights of African Americans as the mainstream liberal Democrats they were. Certainly, Biddle's equivocation about African American migration and Rotnem's rancor about the FEPC reflected the ambivalence about dramatic racial change many white liberals felt at the time. Moreover, the political and institutional affiliations of the CRS lawyers, and especially their leaders, prescribed circumspection. They were political actors in a party and a system that required caution as well as action in addressing the rights of African Americans.

Within this context, the Thirteenth Amendment provided an appropriate constitutional starting point for the section's hybrid civil rights. The amendment had ended African chattel slavery as a system of both labor exploitation and racial caste. The Supreme Court had curtailed the amendment's most expansive aspirations in both directions, and the system of Jim Crow that eventually replaced slavery served both slavery's economic and its social functions. Yet the amendment's heritage, reworked and reinterpreted, remained part of its meaning during and after World War II. And when the Civil Rights Section lawyers unearthed the amendment, they unearthed as well the potential of challenging the whole racial and economic complex of Jim Crow.[67]

Perhaps ironically, changes in the political climate of the late 1940s and early 1950s aided the lawyers in their Thirteenth Amendment practice. The Cold War menace of totalitarianism abroad made government officials and ordinary Americans alike more rather than less acutely aware of the imperative that the United States maintain the most basic freedom of its people. In 1948, the United Nations Universal Declaration of Human Rights included a provision that stated, "No one shall be held in slavery or servitude; slavery and the slave trade shall be prohibited in all their forms." The Workers' Defense League thrust involuntary servitude further into the international limelight when it created an International Commission of Inquiry into Forced Labor and persuaded the United Nations to create a Committee on Slavery in 1949. Indeed, even as domestic anti-Communism and political machinations somewhat lessened political pressure to attend to civil rights and made the CRS hesitate to prosecute some types of cases in the late 1940s, the CRS continued to prosecute peonage cases.[68]

Moreover, people beyond the confines of the Department of Justice recognized that the Thirteenth Amendment spoke to more than the most extreme forms of coerced labor. In 1952, political scientist Howard Devon Hamilton followed Carr's lead in highlighting the Thirteenth Amendment. He wrote optimistically in the *National Bar Journal* about how the 1948 revisions to the nineteenth-century peonage statutes would improve the Department of Justice's ability to enforce the law against "peonage-like conditions" and labor exploitation. He noted that the Workers' Defense League and the National Farm Labor Union were actively publicizing and pursuing cases of forced labor. Commenting on the Supreme Court's 1944 opinion in *Pollock v. Williams,* he wrote, "One can only conclude that the Supreme Court, zealous to protect civil rights, particularly of the weak, has placed freedom from involuntary servitude in the same class as the 'fundamental liberties' of the First Amendment, against which any impinging statute is denied the usual presumption of constitutionality."[69]

Hamilton was not alone in his enthusiasm. In the decade after World War II ended, law review articles discussing the Thirteenth Amendment, slavery, peonage, and involuntary servitude proliferated. Into the 1950s, legal scholars remarked specifically on the need for a more robust Thirteenth Amendment jurisprudence. In 1951, Jacobus tenBroek explored the roots of the Thirteenth Amendment in the context of debates about the Fourteenth Amendment and its abilities to protect African Americans. The same year, prominent legal realist Robert Hale wrote an article called "Some Basic Constitutional Rights of Economic Significance," which canvassed the relationship between various clauses of the Constitution and economic rights. Unsurprisingly, he began with the Thirteenth Amendment's prohibition on slavery and involuntary servitude.[70]

By the early 1950s, then, much had changed from the *Lochner* era. Once limited to enforcing the narrow terms of the Peonage Act, the

CRS had greatly expanded the Thirteenth Amendment's purview and seemed poised to protect some of the nation's most "fundamental liberties." In slightly different ways, each of the section's three expansive interpretations of the Thirteenth Amendment showed how African Americans could benefit from the new conceptions of positive rights. The first understood New Deal promises of "security" to encompass the "safety and security of the person," including peonage and involuntary servitude. The second expanded the New Deal's free labor protections to the South and to the African American agricultural and domestic workers purposefully restricted by state laws and purposefully unprotected by federal ones. And the last expanded New Deal rights to economic security to the same two groups legislatively excluded from such protections.

In the process of developing these Thirteenth Amendment interpretations, the cautious initiatives with which the CRS had begun to challenge Jim Crow took on new meaning. The section's involuntary servitude cases seemed to set a standard of minimal treatment and shore up the ability of workers to choose their work, to join with other workers, and to exercise power vis-à-vis employers. And they did so for not just any workers, but for the poorest, most excluded workers—African American workers in relationships most reminiscent of chattel slavery, of subjection and coercion. The most uncivilized brutality did not seem to be the only target. Debt and violence were off-limits. So too might be the myriad formal and informal, legal, psychological, and economic methods of coercion that white southerners used to maintain the hierarchical, racialized political economy of Jim Crow. Immanent in the experimental work of the Civil Rights Section was a civil rights that could simultaneously address the combined public and private, racial and economic system of Jim Crow.

The lawyers of the CRS did not always and self-consciously understand their work in this way. Their civil rights practice reflected all of the complexities they faced in their particular historical moment. But by exploring the possibilities for protecting black workers with the new, positive rights the New Deal had begun to vindicate, the CRS helped foster a definition of civil rights that included rather than excluded labor freedom and economic rights alongside racial equality. As the Civil Rights Section cast about for a way to integrate the past and the present, it turned to the Thirteenth Amendment to combine the labor-oriented civil rights of the 1930s with the race-oriented conceptions that gained prominence during the 1940s. The lawyers built upon the initial labor pedigree of the section, and they took the New Deal rights of industrial workers as a jumping-off point for addressing the day-to-day problems and complaints of black agricultural and domestic workers. During a period in which the meaning of postwar civil rights remained unknown, involuntary servitude prosecutions pointed toward a new civil rights looking toward the future but deeply, indelibly marked by the past.

◆ ◆ ◆

SIX

Work and Workers in the NAACP

> The peculiar position of Negro workers [is that they are beset] with problems arising from their relationship not only with employers and government but also from their relationship with white workers and the Negro middle class.
>
> Memorandum from Walter R. Ming, Jr., to Walter White, June 5, 1941

IN DECEMBER 1943, Thurgood Marshall, special counsel of the National Association for the Advancement of Colored People (NAACP), flew on short notice to San Francisco, California, to assist a group of African American shipyard workers fighting for their jobs in area shipyards. Like the black workers who had traveled from New York City to Portland, Oregon, in search of shipyard employment two years earlier, the men who called on the NAACP in late 1943 were doing battle with both the shipyards and the International Brotherhood of Boilermakers. The day before Marshall arrived, the Marinship Corporation had barred from employment 430 African American workers who had refused to pay dues to a segregated and powerless auxiliary of the union. Like other area shipyards, Marinship had signed a closed-shop contract with the union—an agreement to hire only union members—and the union claimed that the black workers had lost their good standing when they refused to pay their dues.

The crisis garnered so much local attention that Marshall appeared on a radio show to discuss it. He told his audience that, "as a negro and an attorney" of the NAACP, he saw "the right of the negro to nondiscriminatory employment" and the right to vote as the two most pressing long-term problems of African Americans. "When those problems are solved," he predicted, "other questions will settle themselves." The African American boilermakers' complaint, Marshall later explained, was "the type of case which must be filed."[1]

At the same time the lawyers in the Civil Rights Section of the Department of Justice were busy using the complaints of African American agricultural workers as the basis for an evolving Thirteenth Amendment practice, the NAACP lawyers were committing themselves to what Marshall called the NAACP's "nation-wide fight against discrimination in defense industries." That commitment was something of a departure from the NAACP's priorities and practice before World War II. Since its creation in 1909, the NAACP had been ambivalent about how much and what kind of attention to give the special concerns of black workers—agricultural or industrial. During its first two decades, the association did not emphasize those problems. When it did expend energy on the claims of workers, it responded more to the problems of black agricultural workers in the South—especially peonage—than to those of industrial workers across the nation. The economic crisis of the Depression pushed the NAACP to take more aggressive and wide-ranging action on behalf of poor and working African Americans. Those activities nonetheless remained outside of both the association's central agenda and its increasingly important legal work. With the onset of World War II, however, the NAACP as a whole began to pay more attention to industrial workers. The NAACP lawyers began to view their problems, though not the problems of agricultural workers, as promising foundations for legal action.[2]

Before World War II, the difficulties African Americans faced in their working lives were at the periphery of the NAACP's agenda. Established on the heels of race riots in Springfield, Illinois, in 1908, the association's founders hoped to halt and reverse the legalization of racial inequality in the early twentieth century. The black elites who joined with white elites to lead the NAACP embraced the "uplift ideology" of the Progressive Era. They simultaneously advocated cross-class racial solidarity and reinforced class lines within African American society. Because of their privileged socioeconomic status, the African American leaders of the association were well prepared for their positions—they were far better educated than most African Americans, and their professional training and status specially enabled them to marshal resources and plan attacks on Jim Crow. They embodied W. E. B. Du Bois's notion of the "talented tenth" of African Americans who should lead the race. The founders hoped to represent the race despite the fact that their lives largely were unrepresentative of the lives of most African Americans.[3]

For these black elites, work-related problems did not constitute the primary disabilities of living in Jim Crow America. Certainly, black teachers, lawyers, doctors, and other elites faced barriers to entry in the professions, salary differentials, and other challenges. But to a considerable extent, their professional success depended on Jim Crow; it lay in serving a relatively captive black community. Instead, black elites largely experienced the wrongs of Jim Crow in their personal and political lives—with limited access to government, restaurants, hotels, theaters, and other social, cultural, and political institutions. They profited from it (in the short run, at least) in their professional lives.[4]

Obtaining employment for African Americans was nonetheless among the goals listed in the NAACP's certificate of incorporation. Early on, however, the NAACP came to an informal arrangement with the National Urban League by which the two organizations divided the pursuit of African American advancement into legal and economic inequality. The NAACP focused on the former, and the Urban League on the latter. As one speaker at the NAACP's 1914 annual conference put it, "[T]his Association is concerned with 'Legal Equality' only, and proposes to let 'Economic Equality' take care of itself." That speaker overstated the division of labor, but the statement characterized the NAACP's basic orientation.[5]

When the specific concerns of black workers did capture the NAACP's attention during its first twenty years, they were more often the problems of agricultural than industrial workers. Although black agricultural workers made up less than 5 percent of NAACP membership anywhere, their problems were attractive to the two major constituencies of the early NAACP—black elites and white philanthropists. For the black elites, the dire need of black agricultural workers made them ideal candidates for uplift. For the white philanthropists who provided much of the NAACP's early funding, what NAACP executive director James Weldon Johnson called "the vicious evils of peonage" were more shocking—and attacking them was less threatening—than the problems of industrial workers.[6]

As a result, the *Crisis*, the NAACP's official organ, published more articles on the plight of southern black agricultural workers than any other labor-related subject in the association's first decade of existence. Throughout the 1920s, the NAACP conducted a "nation-wide campaign against mob violence and peonage." It produced numerous press releases on peonage cases across the South, it wrote letters to presidents and attorneys general, and it organized its branches to hold mass meetings protesting peonage conditions. The NAACP also occasionally used legal methods on behalf of farmworkers, especially when they faced criminal prosecution for asserting themselves against whites. These cases not only provided much-needed defense services to southern African Americans, but they also offered excellent vehicles for publicizing some of the most flagrant harms of Jim Crow.[7]

The horrific violence and extreme poverty many southern agricultural workers faced lent easily to investigation, publicity, and public condemnation. The claims of industrial workers required more nuanced solutions and elicited more tentative and ambivalent responses from the NAACP. A few issues were easy: when the conflict between black and white industrial workers resulted in violence, investigation and publicity seemed as appropriate as in peonage and lynching cases.[8]

But beyond such incidents, the NAACP was not at all clear about what it should or could do to help black industrial workers. Like other black elites of the time, NAACP leaders sometimes embraced voluntarist approaches like developing black businesses and cooperatives. Although union organizing offered a theoretically powerful approach to improving the lot of African American workers, most unions in the early twentieth century were defined as much by the race of their membership—white—as by their class composition. With the Urban League working with employers to increase African American employment, unions largely segregated and hostile to black workers, and many African American workers in turn hostile to unionization, the NAACP had no obvious agenda to pursue on behalf of industrial workers. Even when the association gained working-class members during a major organizing drive between 1916 and 1920—the association grew to 274 branches and gained 90,000 new members—the problems African American laborers faced in their working lives remained largely peripheral to the NAACP's goals.[9]

The fact that black industrial and agricultural workers were both relatively marginal to the early NAACP had long-term consequences for the association's litigation agenda. In 1929, the Garland Fund, a left-leaning foundation looking to fund labor organizing among African Americans, created a committee to help the foundation decide how best to do so. The NAACP-dominated committee unsurprisingly suggested that the NAACP was the best recipient of the funds. But the fit was not perfect. The committee struggled unsuccessfully to find a way for the NAACP adequately to integrate labor issues into the proposed use of the funds. "[T]he Negro as a Negro suffers disabilities which the white laborer does not face," the committee ultimately explained. It was therefore necessary first to change "these precedent conditions" before black organizations could tackle "[t]he subsequent problem of organizing the Negroes." The NAACP, in other words, planned to treat African American workers as any other African Americans. It would leave their distinctively work-related problems for another day or another organization.[10]

The Garland Fund nonetheless offered the NAACP a grant, which financed the writing of what became known as the Margold Report. The report grew into something of a blueprint, much modified over the years, for the NAACP's litigation focus for the next several decades. True to the grant proposal that funded its writing, the report contained scant mention of labor-related legal action on behalf of either agricultural or industrial workers. It focused instead on challenges to segregated and unequal education, unequal teachers' salaries, and racially restrictive covenants that excluded African Americans from buying and renting property in covered areas. Ironically, the organization that tried to push the NAACP to take on labor issues instead helped the association clarify that, at least for its own legal agenda, labor and litigation did not mix.[11]

Just at the moment the Margold Report shied away from litigation on behalf of black workers, however, the Depression and the New Deal spurred the association to rethink its relationship to poor and working-class African Americans. The Depression heightened the nation's awareness of the plight of both black and white farmworkers. As new labor and left-leaning organizations like the Southern Tenant Farmers' Union (STFU) and the Workers' Defense League (WDL) arose to assist farmworkers, the NAACP gained allies and energy in combating peonage.[12]

In general, however, the rise of leftist organizations in the fertile ground of the Depression proved complicated for the NAACP. A prime example was the NAACP's legendary fight with the International Labor Defense (ILD) over the legal representation of the nine young African American men almost "legally lynched" for rape in Scottsboro, Alabama. That dispute initiated a long-lasting enmity that shadowed the association's relationships with organizations to its left. The rise of the ILD, the National Negro Congress, and other left-leaning organizations spurred the NAACP to compete self-consciously for black loyalty and membership, in part by adopting parts of the programs and techniques of such organizations.[13]

In a very different way, the rise of the Congress of Industrial Organizations (CIO) also strengthened the NAACP's commitment to addressing the problems of African American workers. The long-dominant American Federation of Labor (AFL) consisted of affiliated unions that were craft based and often racially discriminatory in both policy and practice. In contrast, the CIO was composed of industrial unions that made early, though inconsistent, attempts to persuade African Americans of their opposition to racial discrimination. Within a year of the CIO's creation in 1935, the NAACP was taking a more positive approach to the unionization of black workers.[14]

A rising generation of black intellectuals centered at Howard University also challenged the NAACP to make economic issues more central to its agenda. These "Young Turks," as Du Bois called them, blamed the NAACP's race-based approach on its middle-class leadership and membership base. Political scientist Ralph Bunche, for example, lambasted the NAACP for "elect[ing] to fight for civil liberties rather than for labor unity. . . . [I]t has never reached the masses of Negroes, and remains strictly Negro middle-class, Negro-*intelligentsia*, in its leadership and appeal." Fellow Howard political scientist Emmett Dorsey agreed. He concluded that the NAACP "has not and cannot develop an economic program because such a program must necessarily stress labor solidarity and fundamental social reforms. Such a program is incompatible with the Association's middle class and thoroughly racial philosophy."[15]

Even association insiders and sympathizers thought the NAACP's middle-class membership constrained its labor activism. In 1935, assistant secretary Roy Wilkins chalked up the lack of working-class membership in the association to "differences in interests and in levels of society." Charles Hamilton Houston, the black lawyer who would shortly become the NAACP's first full-time legal counsel, saw that absence as a problem. He argued at the NAACP's 1933 annual conference that the way to increase membership was for "the Negro professional group" to offer "real brotherhood to the masses" and convince them "that it is not exploiting them."[16]

As a result of these various pressures—the Depression itself, internal and external critiques, challenges from left-leaning organizations and from other African Americans—by 1932 the association was "becoming convinced that it is because [African Americans] are poor and voiceless in industry that we are able to accomplish so little with what political power we have." The annual conference concluded "that what the Negro needs primarily is a definite economic program." Press releases about the 1933 annual conference describe how "[a] discussion of the alleged left or radical movement of Negroes in this country" led to "resolutions . . . dealing more than ever before with the economic status of the Negro." "In the United States," Houston recognized in 1935, "the Negro is economically exploited, politically ignored and socially ostr[a]cized."[17]

No single program materialized to help poor and working-class African Americans in the 1930s, but the NAACP took a number of steps toward that end. Through articles in the *Crisis* and resolutions at its annual conferences, the NAACP urged unions to cease their deeply ingrained and long-standing discrimination against African Americans. Together with the National Urban League and local boycott organizations, the association appealed to employers to do the same. As the New Deal increased federal involvement in the economy, the NAACP saw that new involvement as a political opportunity. It tried to convince President Franklin Roosevelt, federal administrators, and local functionaries to implement New Deal programs without discrimination. And it lobbied hard but unsuccessfully to amend the National Labor Relations Act (NLRA) to require the withholding of certification to any union that discriminated on the basis of race.[18]

The NAACP's embrace of such activities was doubly qualified, however. First, even during the Depression, the "work of the Association in the economic field [was] conducted," in the words of one NAACP report, "as an incidental phase of its civil liberty program." Economic issues, although addressed, never displaced the NAACP's core concerns with the legal and political disabilities of the race. Second, when the NAACP did intervene on behalf of African American workers, they did so largely in the economic and political realms. Although some black lawyers thought they could use litigation to address the problems of African American industrial workers during the 1930s, the NAACP generally found no place in its litigation practice for labor issues. The NAACP viewed the NLRA, for example, as a law that needed revision in the political process, not as a law that needed interpreting through the legal process.[19]

In those years, even when legal cases related to labor issues, the NAACP staff largely declined to view them that way. Litigation on behalf of African American teachers who received lower salaries than white teachers was, from the start, part of the NAACP's campaign for educational opportunity, not part of a larger assault on racial wage differentials. Only rarely, as when Houston tried to secure more funding from the labor-oriented Garland Fund, did anyone in the NAACP spin "[t]he drive for equalization of teachers' salaries" as "a fundamental drive against wage differentials." Even then, Houston was forced to acknowledge that "no attempt has been made to discuss the general relation of the educational program to the whole struggle of labor to organize and obtain greater security and higher living conditions."[20]

Indeed, part of the association's zeal for teacher salary equalization cases was its desire to encourage membership among teachers, who were a bulwark of the NAACP's middle-class constituency. By describing litigation that improved the salaries of teachers as improving the quality of education for all black children, the NAACP avoided the class implications involved in pursuing employment discrimination cases only on behalf of middle-class teachers. As a result, the teachers' equal-pay-for-equal-work campaign did not lead to a wholesale application of the argument to workers. It led instead to other education-related litigation on the road to *Brown*.[21]

As the NAACP broadened its agenda in the 1930s to appeal to working-class African Americans, its nascent legal practice remained impervious. In 1939, the NAACP created a series of pamphlets setting forth the (mostly legal) procedures for branches to take toward a variety of problems. They included criminal defense, exclusion from jury service, the right to vote, police brutality, and equalizing educational opportunities. Labor issues were nowhere to be found.[22]

World War II fundamentally transformed the role of black workers in the NAACP. As the NAACP's lawyers developed a sustained legal agenda and the association clarified its vision of its future, black industrial, but not agricultural, workers came to play a more significant role. New legal tools available to assist black industrial workers—at both the federal and state level—looked doctrinally and strategically promising to the NAACP lawyers. And the large-scale migrations of African Americans to cities and higher-paying jobs made them more likely candidates for NAACP membership. As the fortunes of industrial workers rose within the NAACP, agricultural workers lost what little legal attention they had once garnered. When the World War II "back to peonage" campaign created opportunities for NAACP legal action on behalf of agricultural workers, the lawyers did not seize them.

In part, the NAACP's legal department was able to tackle the problems of black industrial workers during the war simply because it was able to take on more cases. Prior to hiring Houston in 1934, the NAACP had had no full-time lawyer on its staff. It had relied on a national legal committee made up of prominent lawyers for both legal advice and representation. Moreover, its legal cases had focused more on generating publicity that would bring the association funding and

Roy Wilkins, Walter White, and Thurgood Marshall, circa 1950s. (© CORBIS.)

members than on generating incremental legal precedents that would doctrinally challenge Jim Crow.[23]

Hiring Houston fundamentally changed the nature and direction of the NAACP's legal agenda. As a former Washington lawyer, Houston brought to the NAACP the experience of a practiced litigator. He saw the value of challenging Jim Crow through the accumulation of beneficial legal precedents. As a former dean of Howard Law School, Houston was committed to having black lawyers represent black clients and to attacking Jim Crow in education.[24]

In 1936, Thurgood Marshall joined Houston as a full-time NAACP lawyer. In 1938, Marshall took over the management of the NAACP's litigation strategy when Houston returned to private practice. Born in Baltimore to a sleeping-car porter and a sometime teacher, Marshall grew up as part of the black middle class. He attended historically black Lincoln University, and he was a student of Houston's when Houston was dean of Howard Law School. After graduation, Marshall practiced law privately in Baltimore, though he spent much of his time on ad hoc work for the NAACP. Parlaying that work into a full-time job, Marshall essentially made the NAACP his only client.[25]

By the end of 1945, Marshall had convinced the association to hire at least five attorneys, plus nonattorney assistants. Among the handful of lawyers Marshall took on during the war was Prentice Thomas, whom he hired in 1942. Thomas came from Kentucky, and his professional experience mostly involved agricultural labor. When asked for his biography for publicity purposes, Thomas apologized to Marshall for not having "a 'respectable' biography." The one Thomas provided described how he had worked with the STFU and the WDL. Both organizations had socialist roots and close ties with the American Socialist Party. Thomas also had connections to the Highlander Folk School, which its enemies called a "Communist Party training school," and he was a Quaker conscientious objector during World War II.[26]

It soon became clear that the NAACP's developing agenda did not match Thomas's more left-leaning and agricultural bias. Marshall himself had been a member of the board of the American Civil Liberties Union (ACLU) and a member of the left-leaning Lawyers Guild when Houston hired him in 1939. Still, Thomas's various affiliations were further to the left than Marshall's. Moreover, Thomas's "personal interest . . . in the unorganized and unskilled workers, of whom . . . Ne-

groes constitute the greatest number" placed him at odds with his
fellow lawyers and NAACP leaders. After planning a conference on
farm labor that would "give notice that the NAACP is on the job,"
Thomas had to withdraw the suggestion. Thomas's superiors were not
satisfied with his work, and they did not approve of his proposed projects. Houston, who remained a close legal advisor to the NAACP even
after he returned to private practice, suggested that Thomas instead
look into labor legislation before Congress and make a study of unions
barring African Americans from membership. "Until further notice,"
executive secretary Walter White wrote Thomas, "I would like to see
before they are sent out all letters you may write involving policy or to
persons in official or semi-official positions except on routine matters." After little more than a year on the NAACP's staff, Thomas ten-
dered his resignation.[27]

Whether Thomas's agenda or what his superiors deemed his defi-
cient performance weighed more heavily in the association's dissatis-
faction with his work, the NAACP chose to replace Thomas with two
staff members more interested in industrial than agricultural workers.
Marshall invited Marian Wynn Perry to join his legal staff. Perry was,
according to Wilkins, "a progressive liberal, left of center" New York
lawyer. She joined the legal department from work in private practice,
in unions, and in the Department of Labor, as well as with the Lawyers
Guild. Clarence Mitchell, a nonlawyer who joined the political office,
had previously served on the Fair Employment Practice Committee
(FEPC). He led the lobbying aspects of the NAACP's labor program as
its first labor secretary in 1945. He mobilized against employment discrimination by the federal government, lobbied for permanent federal
and state fair employment practice laws, and worked toward an executive order barring discrimination in government employment.[28]

As this change in personnel indicates, the differences of opinion
and approach between Thomas, the other lawyers, and the NAACP
leadership during World War II did not include whether the association should accept labor cases. They agreed, as Thomas put it, that "it
is most important that the NAACP extend its activity in the field of
labor relations." They differed, rather, on what kind of labor cases the
association should accept.[29]

In significant part, the decision to accept industrial but not agricultural cases was rooted in the lawyers' evolving approach to litigation in

the early 1940s. In 1939, the NAACP formally separated the legal department from the rest of the association for tax purposes. It created the NAACP Legal Defense and Educational Fund (still referred to as the legal department). The bylaws of the new corporation stated that its purpose was "[t]o render legal aid gratuitously to such Negroes as may appear to be worthy thereof, who are suffering legal injustices by reason of race or color and unable to employ and engage legal aid and assistance on account of poverty." Early in the 1940s, Marshall interpreted the bylaws to allow the legal department to take cases in the event of injustice because of race or color, a denial of due process (in

NAACP lawyer Marian Wynn Perry. (Library of Congress.)

criminal cases), or a likelihood that the case would establish precedents that would benefit African Americans substantially.[30]

Even as the bylaws remained the same, NAACP lawyers transformed
"injustice because of race" into "cases involving race discrimination
and cases that are of national importance to the Negro race." The new
gloss specified that the type of "injustice" that would warrant NAACP
legal intervention was "discrimination" rather than inequality, personal insecurity, or other manifestations of racial and economic "injustice." The touchstone of the legal challenge to Jim Crow became the
fact that whites singled blacks out for discriminatory treatment, not
the related fact that blacks lived in conditions of material inequality
and insecurity. In particular, the lawyers hoped to challenge discriminatory denials of voting rights, as well as attack the half-century-old
Supreme Court precedents sanctioning segregation (in *Plessy v. Ferguson*) and requiring state action (in the *Civil Rights Cases*).[31]

The industrial workers' cases the legal department began to pursue
in the 1940s, like the education, transportation, housing, and voting
cases it also undertook, facilitated progress toward those doctrinal
goals. New federal and state regulatory developments offered possible
sites for both moving toward the attack on *Plessy* and challenging the
state action doctrine that immunized unions and private employers
from lawsuits. On the federal level, the most significant new opportunity, the FEPC, definitionally excluded agricultural workers. It was limited to federal employees, those working for private industries contracting with the federal government, and those in war and war-related
industries. On the state level, the passage of fair employment legislation
in New York and New Jersey, and the relative ease and thrift of bringing
cases near the legal department's New York City headquarters, further
accentuated legal opportunities outside the agricultural South.[32]

Once the NAACP defined the problem as racial discrimination
rather than inequality or insecurity, it essentially defined the farmworkers' problems out of its litigation agenda. Like the Justice Department, the NAACP received many letters from black farmworkers in the
rural South. Had the legal department so chosen, it might have concluded that these complaints also fit some interpretations of its bylaws.
Because the NAACP never developed the agricultural complaints into
legally cognizable claims that could serve as the basis for litigation, the
nature of the harms and entitlements embodied in these letters remained nascent and largely unarticulated.

Instead, the NAACP lawyers haphazardly and unsystematically tried to transform farmworkers' claims into those more commensurate with the rest of its legal agenda. In response to a peonage complaint from Florida in 1941, for example, Marshall took the opportunity to shift the ground to terrain on which he was more comfortable: "This is merely one more on a long line of cases which justify our continued action to secure the right to vote for Negroes in Southern states, in order to compel the law-enforcement authorities in these states to give Negroes the equal protection of the laws to which they are entitled." A peonage complaint became an occasion for promoting voting rights.[33]

The reality, however, was that the lawyers could not reduce the farmworkers' claims to the legal claims of racial discrimination the lawyers now privileged in their practice. These claims were intimately and inextricably bound up with both the racial hierarchies and economic exploitation of Jim Crow. A strategy focused solely on black agricultural workers as workers—needing minimum wages, pensions, unemployment insurance, or unions and collective bargaining—was unlikely to make much headway so long as it failed to take account of the constant surveillance and political disabilities of black farmworkers. It was equally unlikely that a litigation strategy whose goal was solely to wipe out racial discrimination and segregation would get the farmworkers very far. The integration of unions or employers would have provided little help in the agricultural South. The most significant union around, the STFU, was already integrated, but it faced overwhelming difficulties in challenging the political and economic power of the planters. And the employer who was also landlord and banker had ways other than racially differentiated wage structures for maintaining dominance.

Not only doctrinal opportunities but also sympathetic judges and amenable lawyers were more readily available outside the rural South. It was generally easier to win cases outside the region, and winning was important both in itself and for morale. The geographical realities of the black bar in particular reinforced the lawyers' shift away from agricultural cases. The NAACP relied heavily on local counsel. In the 1940s, most black lawyers were concentrated in cities, especially in Washington, D.C., and the North. In 1937, Arthur Shores of Birmingham became the first African American admitted to the Alabama bar in twenty years, and a decade later only four black lawyers practiced in the entire state. But at least southern cities were home to some

black lawyers. In the rural areas of the South, black lawyers were almost nowhere to be found, and white lawyers saw little appealing in
the cases of poor black farmworkers.[34]

The greater availability of legal assistance in the North and in cities
generally might suggest that urban, and especially northern, African
Americans had greater access to the courts on their own and therefore
less need for NAACP lawyers. Indeed, most of the industrial employment cases the legal department pursued during the decade had com-
petent counsel other than the legal department. The NAACP had neither the human nor the financial resources to pursue more than a few
of the hundreds of complaint letters it received. At times, the NAACP
distinguished between those types of cases it would take and those it
would not by determining if another lawyer, institution, or government agency could address the issue. But as the legal department increasingly took control over the NAACP's legal agenda, it found cases
brought by others in areas in which it was independently interested a
spur to involvement—not a deterrent. Individual African Americans
with grievances they could not afford to bring to court were thus often
utterly without legal resources and a real shot at developing the law. By
contrast, those with some resources who could get the case to court
were more likely to have the NAACP intervene and obtain redress. As
rural southerners more often fell into the former category, the legal
department's approach to alternative legal assistance reinforced the
disappearance of southern agricultural cases from its docket.[35]

The lawyers' doctrinal and strategic choices favoring industrial over
agricultural workers converged with demographic and institutional
pressures affecting the NAACP as a whole. Even though African Americans had been leaving southern agriculture in large numbers since
World War I, the NAACP had not considered African American industrial workers particularly fruitful targets for membership before the end
of the 1930s. Until World War II, the NAACP had been highly attuned to
the fact that most African Americans still lived in the agricultural South.

By the 1940s, however, the NAACP shared the sense of many that the
rural South was the past, the industrial South, North, Midwest, and
West the future. *Crisis* articles about migration no longer focused on
the conditions that African Americans left behind; instead, they focused on those created in destination cities, like scarce and substandard housing, crowded schools, and unemployment. Whereas NAACP

labor secretary Mitchell saw "broad national issues" involved when auto workers struck in Detroit, the strike of tobacco workers in North Carolina raised only local concerns. Agricultural southerners no longer peopled the NAACP's imagination about who constituted the nation and where it was headed. The NAACP did not ignore the rural South altogether during the 1940s, and the lawyers sometimes took cases originating there. But neither the association in general nor the lawyers specifically paid much attention to the particular problems southern agricultural workers faced in their working lives.[36]

Not only the problems of southern agricultural workers but also those organizations and individuals that had most frequently attended to them seemed increasingly relegated to the past. As American anti-Communism gained momentum during the 1940s, the association became more skittish about cooperating with Communist-affiliated organizations. Marshall still occasionally asked the WDL to help investigate peonage cases to refer to the DOJ. Nonetheless, like White and Wilkins, Marshall distanced himself from peonage cases championed by more left-wing groups such as the ILD and the People's Council. As even Marshall hesitated to collaborate with some of the groups who advocated most vociferously for agricultural workers, the work-related claims of farmworkers moved further to the periphery of the NAACP's agenda.[37]

Instead, the NAACP focused its efforts to bring in working-class members on industrial workers. Increasing numbers of African American workers were moving north, joining unions, registering to vote, gaining greater personal freedom, and crucially, beginning to earn wages that might enable them to afford membership dues. The NAACP, like the Democratic Party, began to recognize that the growing African American working class could be a profitable new constituency. In particular, the NAACP believed strengthening ties with mainstream organized labor would attract more working-class members. After a major strike at the River Rouge plant of the Ford Motor Company unified the NAACP and the United Automobile Workers in 1939, labor leaders frequently spoke at the NAACP's annual conventions, and the NAACP frequently sent representatives to union-related activities.[38]

As NAACP leaders watched the number of African American union members swell, they saw new potential for synergies between NAACP litigation and membership. The NAACP had always seen its legal cases as generating publicity, members, and money for the association as a whole. For much of its prewar history, funding from elite and middle-class African Americans and wealthy, philanthropic whites was crucial to the NAACP's financial well-being. These sources of income did not necessarily map perfectly onto particular legal priorities. Still, the NAACP had focused its energies on cases (such as teacher salary and graduate education cases) that both benefited and helped to create the black middle class, as well as on shocking issues like lynching and involuntary servitude that garnered support from liberal whites. The NAACP lawyers had thus given some hearing to the complaints of workers "on the lowest rung of our economic ladder" (as farmworker advocate and NAACP board member Alfred Baker Lewis called them) not due to their own power in the association, but because of the racial solidarity embodied in uplift ideology and the power of wealthy whites outraged by their plight.[39]

By 1946, the influence of both that ideology and those benefactors was on the decline precisely because membership had become the association's financial mainstay. Between 1940 and 1946, the NAACP grew from 355 branches and a membership of 50,556 to 1,073 branches and a membership of about 450,000. The association's budget grew from $54,300 in 1930, composed of a combination of contributions and membership dues, to more than $319,000 in 1947, entirely from membership dues. As the NAACP's income increased during the war, so too did the legal department's budget—from $4,000 in 1941 to $63,000 by 1944.[40]

The new composition of the NAACP's membership—and the expectation that the legal department's cases and that membership would continue to support each other—reinforced the legal department's independent doctrinal and strategic reasons for preferring the cases of industrial to agricultural workers. Even as the NAACP made the legal department a formally separate entity in 1939, the two organizations continued to share members of the boards of directors, office space, and most significantly, financial resources for more than a decade. At times, Marshall found the financial arrangement frustrating, as he thought the NAACP was getting the better end of the deal. The association had "reaped the reward upon a number of legal victories for which it [had] not paid a great deal of its own treasury."[41]

Marshall's frustrations notwithstanding, White emphasized the need to make the legal department's cases responsive to the new members who partly made the lawyers' work possible. Like his assistant secretary, Roy Wilkins, and many of the other NAACP leaders, White came from a relatively privileged background. Born to a postal worker and a teacher, White had been groomed at Atlanta University for a place in the black elite. He understood from personal experience why it was important to fight discrimination in places of accommodation that excluded middle-class and elite African Americans despite their ability to pay. But by World War II he had also come to believe that such legal challenges "failed to attack problems of employment and the like which affect the lives and destinies of persons who are not financially able" to frequent nice restaurants and theaters. White thought that the NAACP needed to broaden its reach from the middle-class litigation it had historically pursued. With this broader agenda in mind, when Marshall hired more lawyers in 1943, White trusted that the new lawyers' work would, "combined with that of ourselves in selling that work to the public, bring in added revenue."[42]

Indeed, Marshall did his part in "selling" the legal department's work to the NAACP's new industrial "public." The San Francisco boilermakers provide a case in point. When they first began their protests in 1943, the NAACP's San Francisco branch was so nonoperational that the black workers created their own protest organization. Once Marshall joined the effort on their behalf, however, Joseph James, the "president" of the almost defunct branch and one of the key organizers of the workers, arranged for a merger of the boilermakers' organization and the NAACP branch.

The problem was that not all of the boilermakers who benefited from the NAACP's legal efforts joined the association initially. This prompted Marshall to write James about the need for him to prevail upon his colleagues. Marshall urged James to "explain to [the workers] that if they do not pay for the case it might be necessary to use the funds sent to the association by soldiers." Those soldiers, Marshall added, "earn about one-tenth of the money they earn, . . . are constantly up against the proposition of being killed and . . . are, nevertheless, sufficiently interested in the advancement of their people to send money from India, China, France, Italy, Africa, and other theaters of war." Marshall made clear that the NAACP expected workers who profited from its legal action to pay for such benefits by becoming members and supporting the association. By May 1946, the San Francisco branch had grown from near extinction to 900 members.[43]

By the same token, as the NAACP responded to its new working-class members, those members came to feel that one of the benefits for which they paid was the provision of legal counsel. One of the very soldiers Marshall invoked in his letter to James felt that the NAACP had accepted contributions "under conditions other than honorable" when the NAACP did not take the action he requested. Moreover, the president of the Newark, New Jersey, branch reported that "many members of this branch are beginning to protest against investigating so many cases of non-members, while cases of members (when the time does arrive) find . . . a depleted treasury and no means of carrying on the work that they have given their money to for such protection." The legal department certainly did not feel compelled to take the case of every member who complained—in fact, the department made clear that it, not the branches, not the members, made litigation policy. Nonetheless, the synergies between membership and litigation meant that the NAACP's orientation toward a recently prosperous industrial working-class constituency affected its resource-allocation decisions on a broader level.[44]

That farmworkers were less successful at exerting such pressure compounded the other dynamics displacing them from the lawyers' legal agenda. When farmworkers were members—or when those middle-class patrons through whom they sometimes spoke were members—they emphasized their membership in an attempt to secure a legal response. A local branch official writing on behalf of a black agricultural worker pointed out, in all capital letters, that "87% of our membership comes from the County of this incident—THE FATHER OF THIS YOUNG MAN SOLICITED AROUND FIFTY MEMBERS IN OUR MEMBERSHIP DRIVE." Agricultural workers rarely made such claims, however, and most could not credibly make them. The secretary of a branch in Wando, South Carolina, lamented that "some of the people are willing to join but they don't have the money."[45]

Thurgood Marshall's most explicit reply to agricultural workers who complained about their working lives was that their concerns were "purely private" and did "not come within the rules of the association."

Occasionally, the legal department showed greater interest in agricultural complaints, as when the confrontation between planters and farmworkers rose to such a level of violence that death ensued. Those conflicts that ended in the death of the landlord and the trial of the defendant without proper safeguarding of his (or more rarely, her) rights could lead the legal department to try to ensure that the defendant received due process during his criminal proceedings. Those that ended with the death of the African American could at times fall under the largely nonlegal rubric of lynching, against which the NAACP had long crusaded. Still, by the 1940s, the NAACP rarely became as involved in such cases as it had earlier, and it usually limited itself to investigating and referring them to state and local authorities.[46]

Indeed, a common legal department response to agricultural complaints in the 1940s was to refer them to NAACP branches, other organizations, other NAACP departments, and governmental agencies. For example, the national legal office relegated many involuntary servitude cases to the branches, even though the branches often had insufficient resources to pursue the cases or had a difficult time investigating them if the offense crossed state lines. At still other times, the lawyers treated the issues raised in agricultural complaints as political rather than legal problems and forwarded the complaints to the NAACP's political staff in the Washington Bureau.[47]

The NAACP's treatment of the cotton wage ceiling issue, for example, was basically an extended game of hot potato between the legal and political offices. After the secretary of agriculture imposed draconian wage ceilings on cotton in 1945, the STFU began pursuing legal action immediately. However, its legal efforts were poorly researched, poorly written, and quickly rejected by the courts on technical grounds. Throughout 1945 and 1946, NAACP board member Alfred Baker Lewis and H. L. Mitchell, cofounder of the STFU, tried to get the NAACP—with its greater "resources, legal ability, and ability to reach the daily papers than . . . the STFU"—to take ownership of the case. Involvement initially looked promising, as Lewis had obtained a resolution of support from the NAACP's board.[48]

From relatively early on, however, Lewis had a hard time getting either the political or the legal staff to follow through on the board's stated commitment. Each NAACP department thought the issue belonged to the other. "Because of the complexity of the problem involved and our work on other cases at the moment," lawyer Edward Dudley told the STFU, the legal department could not support the initial lawsuit. Instead of legal action, Marshall suggested that Leslie Perry of the Washington office put political pressure on the Department of Agriculture. For his part, Perry told a skeptical Lewis to wait for the outcome of the STFU's legal case before lobbying the secretary. In the end, the entirety of the NAACP's efforts consisted of Leslie Perry contacting two government officials and lawyer Marian Wynn Perry offering the STFU "supporting action" in additional litigation that never occurred. Lewis "confess[ed] defeat by the invincible inertia of the National Office."[49]

The conflict between the NAACP's lawyers and lobbyists over the wage-ceiling issue reveals not only the jurisdictional issues that were beginning to divide the legal and political departments of the association but also the (relatively limited) action the NAACP would take when it deemed an agricultural complaint worthy of response: referral to the appropriate government agency. Prominent examples of how the NAACP served as a conduit between a complainant and the government occurred in the peonage and involuntary servitude context. Frequently, the NAACP lawyers and branches investigated peonage cases enough to ensure their veracity, and then they recommended that the Civil Rights Section of the Department of Justice prosecute.[50]

For the most part, the possibility of private litigation does not seem to have occurred to the legal department, even under the most obvious circumstances, and even in light of highly publicized peonage cases brought by private parties other than the NAACP. In one case Marian Wynn Perry described as "present[ing] a situation about as close to peonage as one can get," she wondered "whether there is any action that can be taken." Her answer: "It certainly would not be legal action but perhaps an investigation and some publicity might help these poor souls." In another case involving the very labor contract law the Supreme Court would strike down in the "shield" case of *Taylor v. Georgia* shortly thereafter, the legal department did not consider the possibility of taking legal action. At other times, the NAACP knew of the possibility of private litigation but left it unpursued. Although the legal department saw the importance of involuntary servitude cases and could envision legal action regarding them, that action was not its own. As NAACP lawyers contemplated their attack on racial inequality in the 1940s, labor-related inequality as experienced by African Americans working in southern agriculture stood outside the strategy they were developing.[51]

By contrast, the NAACP's lawyers took on three primary sets of cases on behalf of black industrial workers in the first half of the 1940s. First and most important were the boilermakers cases. When Marshall flew to San Francisco in 1943, he stepped into an ongoing national controversy within the boilermakers' union about racial inclusion and equality. In 1938, the International Brotherhood of Boilermakers adopted bylaws establishing separate African American auxiliaries. And in 1941, as African Americans crowded into San Francisco and other shipyards for war work, the union entered into closed-shop contracts—restricting employment to union members—with a number of West Coast shipyards. Combined, these two actions forced black workers to choose between losing their jobs and joining powerless segregated auxiliaries. Although many African American workers chose union membership and celebrated when the union began referring them to the shipyards for jobs in the wake of federal hearings on the issue, they later condemned the auxiliary unions. After helping the workers file largely ineffectual complaints with the federal government, the NAACP, the Lawyers Guild, and the private lawyers with whom they worked eventually succeeded in obtaining several favorable state court decisions.[52]

The white boilermakers' recalcitrance toward African American inclusion and equality offered the NAACP legal opportunities not only in San Francisco but also across the nation. Both lawyers and non-lawyers in the NAACP spent time and energy addressing the problem. NAACP attorney Edward R. Dudley traveled to upstate New York to talk to the black workers and to Providence, Rhode Island, to try a case with Marshall. Although the NAACP received assistance from other organizations, like the Urban League, the NAACP took the lead. While on the NAACP's staff, Prentice Thomas was involved in boilermakers' crises in Portland, Oregon, and Vancouver, Washington. Roy Wilkins, then assistant secretary of the NAACP, attended several meetings in Portland in 1942, and even executive secretary Walter White traveled across the country to Portland to support the black shipyard workers.[53]

The second set of cases represented a much more localized effort. Passed in 1945, New York's Ives-Quinn Law was the first fair employment practice law at the state level: it prohibited private employers and unions from discriminating on the basis of race. Passage of the law invited NAACP legal assistance in two ways. First, it gave the NAACP lawyers an opportunity to file amicus briefs in *Railway Mail Ass'n v. Corsi*. In *Corsi*, the United States Supreme Court upheld the constitutionality of the New York law as it applied to union discrimination against due process and equal protection challenges.[54]

Second, the law provided an administrative forum in which the NAACP lawyers could bring complaints of employer and union discrimination before the New York State Commission Against Discrimination (SCAD). Marshall himself was not convinced that SCAD cases were important for his developing litigation agenda. They were too piecemeal, too individualized, and not particularly likely to create generative precedents. Because of pressure from the New York branch and the ease of pursuing such local cases, however, he did not object that Marian Wynn Perry spent much of her time on SCAD complaints. She brought cases challenging, for example, discrimination in the merchant marines and New York tunnel construction projects, as well as the Pennsylvania Railroad's practice of replacing black mechanics hired during the war with returning white veterans with less seniority. Together with other minority advocacy organizations, Perry pressed SCAD to restructure whole workplaces and take proactive steps toward eliminating discrimination.[55]

In the third set of cases, the NAACP lawyers assisted in litigation that longtime NAACP supporter and lawyer Charles Hamilton Houston championed on behalf of African American railroad workers against white railroad unions. Because the black trainmen could afford private counsel, Marshall and Houston agreed that Houston would lead the charge with Marshall offering support. These cases challenged contracts between the white unions and the railroads that had the effect of eliminating African Americans as firemen on locomotive railroads. Before the Supreme Court, the African American workers and the NAACP argued successfully that the Railway Labor Act's (RLA) grant of exclusive representation to a bargaining agent selected by a majority of workers prohibited that agent from discriminating against a minority.[56]

That the NAACP leaders and their lawyers saw the problems of these workers as invitations to legal action represented a sea change in the association's approach to both its economic agenda and its litigation strategy. In 1943, Marshall asserted that employment discrimination was more important than all other issues facing African Americans, except for the right to vote. As late as 1946, he saw cases like the San Francisco boilermakers' as "definitely within the purview of the program of the N.A.A.C.P." Industrial workers had become promising candidates for membership and their problems promising foundations for an evolving legal attack on Jim Crow.[57]

◆ ◆ ◆

SEVEN

Litigating Labor in the Wartime NAACP

The right to work is the right to live. Take it away or
circumscribe it and trouble is inevitable.

Crisis, July 1945

WHEN THE NAACP LAWYERS decided that the time was ripe to take on
the cases of black industrial workers, they moved somewhat outside of
their doctrinal comfort zone. The Margold Report, the blueprint for
the NAACP's legal work since 1930, had said almost nothing about
such cases. Nonetheless, the pressures to attend to segregation and discrimination in industrial labor—and the opportunities the cases offered—were too great to ignore. Wartime political dynamics brought
popular support for black industrial workers. They led as well to more
expansive and promising doctrinal opportunities. And the institutional demands toward taking the cases of black workers were considerable.

Yet because the lawyers' embrace of labor cases represented an entrepreneurial and pragmatic response to these forces, it was always
somewhat reluctant and provisional. Even as the lawyers added labor
to their litigation agenda in the 1940s, they continued to pursue the
kinds of cases that had long bedeviled the black elite and constituted
the mainstay of the association's legal agenda: cases in education,
transportation, housing, and voting. And by the time the legal department decided in 1950 to make an all-out attack on *Plessy v. Ferguson* in
education, the lawyers once again rejected labor cases as a viable site of
constitutional contestation.

That said, when the NAACP lawyers pursued labor litigation in the
early to mid-1940s, they exploited every possible doctrinal opportunity
the cases presented. Because of their inexperience with treating

workers' complaints as potential legal cases, the lawyers found them-selves creating their labor litigation agenda from scratch. To some ex-tent, the knowledge the lawyers had gained in their other practice areas applied to industrial labor cases. The labor cases were different, however. In particular, it was difficult to disentangle the claims of black industrial workers, like those of black agricultural workers, from the economic components of Jim Crow.[1]

The centrality of economic issues to the NAACP's wartime labor liti-gation both exposed frictions within the legal department's evolving antisegregation agenda and created unique opportunities for doc-trinal experimentation. As the NAACP lawyers went about the work of litigating the claims of black industrial workers, they faced three im-portant legal and strategic issues: how to sue the private actors—both employers and unions—that often violated the rights of African Amer-ican workers; what kinds of constitutional arguments might succeed; and how to navigate between seeking economic advancement within segregated workplaces and maintaining a principled commitment to desegregation. The lawyers' creative and entrepreneurial approach to each of these issues revealed that both relevant legal doctrine and the lawyers' own agenda remained in considerable flux. It produced doc-trinal and material benefits for both the NAACP and black industrial workers. And it pointed toward a civil rights practice and a civil rights law that would take seriously the economic as well as the political and social components of Jim Crow.

The targets the legal department pursued in its labor cases during World War II—the railroad unions, the boilermakers' unions, and a host of private employers in New York—would not have been subject to liability for race discrimination just a few years earlier. Private actors generally had not been vulnerable to Fourteenth Amendment chal-lenges since the 1883 *Civil Rights Cases* limited the Fourteenth Amend-ment to actions undertaken by governments. Because much of the in-equality black workers faced was a product of private action, not state or federal law directly, the workers' complaints offered opportunities for the NAACP lawyers to challenge the *Civil Rights Cases*' state action requirement. When the lawyers accepted the doctrinal challenge, they found ways to attack the private as well as the public manifestations of Jim Crow.

In part, the lawyers' choice of targets reflected the larger trend in the mid-1940s toward the weakening of the state action requirement. Various cases in the Supreme Court, from the NAACP's own white primary case of *Smith v. Allwright,* to the police brutality case of *Screws v. United States,* to *Marsh v. Alabama*—where the Court considered a privately owned company town to be a state actor for purposes of a First Amendment violation—suggested that the requirement was in some disorder. Scholars in the 1940s identified connections between these disparate cases and concluded, "There are possibilities . . . that the rights guaranteed by the 14th Amendment may be extended over areas previously considered wholly private."[2]

Labor-related cases offered a particularly vital arena in which to break down—or find ways around—the state action requirement in the 1940s. State action in labor-related race cases existed without doubt only in government jobs themselves. Such jobs, of course, grew in number as the administrative state expanded during the New Deal and the war. Despite the federal government's frequent official statements of nondiscriminatory policy, claims of discrimination against it, as well as against state and local governments, were not hard to find.[3]

Beyond government employment, however, the doctrine was uncertain. In 1945, Pauli Murray, an African American civil rights and labor activist who had just completed law school at Howard University and a year of graduate study at the University of California at Berkeley, considered the issue in an article entitled "The Right to Equal Opportunity in Employment." "As to what degree of action or inaction by the state is embraced in the constitutional prohibition against arbitrary interference with the right to work," Murray wrote, "there seems to be some question." Drawing on an influential article about state action in the context of racially restrictive covenants on housing, Murray theorized that legislative, administrative, and even judicial action amounting only to enforcing private contractual agreements might come within "the constitutional ban."[4]

Changes in legal thought, forms of governance, and Supreme Court doctrine in the 1930s had set the stage for these wartime arguments for private liability. As legal academics proliferated books and articles exposing the theoretical instability of categories like "public" and "private," federal responses to the Depression concretely exposed the messiness of reality. Public works projects melded public and private as the federal government became a quasi-employer. Regulations governed the private market and delegated power so as to make private actors more public.[5]

The Supreme Court's own changing constitutional doctrine reinforced and further transformed basic assumptions about the distinction between private, constitutionally immune conduct and public, constitutionally liable conduct. In a 1934 case upholding a New York regulation of milk prices, the Court abandoned long-standing doctrine allowing regulation only of those entities "affected with a public interest." After *Nebbia v. New York,* any entity a statute regulated was so affected and could therefore find no refuge in constitutional due process protections. Finally, the Supreme Court's validation of the National Labor Relations Act (NLRA) decisively interred one of the most fundamental of *Lochner*-era assumptions—that employers were completely free to hire and fire whom they liked—by banning discrimination against union members.[6]

To the extent that the NLRA began the process of undermining a private employer's "*absolute* discretion in matters of hiring, firing, and labor policies on the job," Murray thought the next step was to argue for "freedom from discrimination on a racial or religious basis." New Deal labor legislation had not prohibited discrimination on the basis of race. But Murray was not alone in thinking that the federal government's increased intervention into the wartime economy could make unions and many private employers newly liable—as a statutory if not a constitutional matter—for race discrimination. As political scientist Louis Kesselman put it in 1946: "The old argument that employment is a private affair between the employer and the worker could not be maintained in a period of national emergency when the continued existence of the country depended upon maximum utilization of the labor force."[7]

The NAACP lawyers' arguments in *Railway Mail Ass'n v. Corsi* exemplified these trends. In supporting the application of New York's pioneering antidiscrimination law to labor unions, the legal department urged the Supreme Court to recognize the legitimacy of state interference in the labor market. The Court's validation of the New York law confirmed that it had created constitutional space within which states could regulate the employment relationship. As Professor E. Merrick Dodd pointed out just after the decision in 1945, "Whatever might have been thought to be the law in the days when liberty of contract was treated by the Supreme Court as an almost absolute constitutional privilege," since the end of the *Lochner* era, "a union's claim that anti-discrimination laws infringe its constitutional liberties is a palpable anachronism." The new, much more liberal view of potential private liability was "a natural consequence . . . of the increase in the economic power of unions and of the Supreme Court's increasing recognition . . . that to refuse to treat the economic power of particular private groups as a constitutional justification for their regulation is in effect to substitute private government for government of, by and for the people." In a similar vein, rising young labor law scholar and University of Toledo law professor Clyde Summers saw unions as exercising power analogous to legislatures. Assuming that a union "is engaged in governmental action when it makes a collective bargaining agreement, then it can no more discriminate in that agreement as to terms of employments than could the legislature in passing a statute regulating working conditions."[8]

That New York's law dealt with discrimination in the labor market was neither accidental nor incidental. The economic power of private actors required governmental regulation. Indeed, Dodd pointed out, since employers wielded even more economic power than unions, they too might be regulated. Each time Marian Wynn Perry filed a complaint with New York's State Commission Against Discrimination, then, she expanded the realm of private statutory liability for work-related discrimination. Each time the New York legal apparatus intervened on behalf of an African American worker, it undermined the private prerogative of employers and unions. As state laws prohibiting private discrimination in employment grew more widespread after *Corsi*, that prerogative withered further. By 1946, New Jersey, Wisconsin, Indiana, Utah, and the city of Chicago had statutes like New York's. In a fast-growing number of states, the state action requirement was losing salience.[9]

Besides using state statutes, the legal department found success arguing that federal legislation, such as the NLRA and the Railway Labor Act (RLA), created federal obligations on the part of formally private but regulated entities. In the 1930s, the NAACP had tried unsuccessfully to amend the NLRA to prohibit race discrimination by unions. In the 1940s, however, Charles Hamilton Houston, Thurgood Marshall, and Marshall's legal staff saw that administrative and judicial tribunals might interpret the legislation as enacted to require nondiscrimination just the same. In the railroad union cases of *Steele v. Louisville & N.R. Co.* and *Tunstall v. Brotherhood of Locomotive Firemen*, the NAACP supported Houston's arguments that the unions were state actors for constitutional purposes.[10]

The Court did not go as far as the lawyers would have liked. But it did hold that federal regulation of the unions under the RLA bound the unions to a statutory duty of fair representation. Unions could not simultaneously gain exclusive power of representation under the RLA and use it to eliminate minorities from the best jobs in the railroad industry. Federal regulation and protection brought with them the legal—if not the constitutional—obligation not to discriminate.

Poster of FEPC Executive Order in a defense plant with Robert C. Weaver, chief of Negro Employment and Training Branch of Labor Division, Office of Personnel Management, and Lawrence Cramer, executive secretary of the President's Committee on Fair Employment Practice, circa 1942. (Farm Security Administration, Office of War Information Photograph Collection, Library of Congress.)

Murray pointed out the hybrid public-private status of unions as understood in *Steele* and *Tunstall:* "For purposes of its collective bargaining functions, [a union] is akin to a governmental agency and has analogous power and obligations, but for purposes of membership it remains a private organization immune from judicial regulation in the public interest."[11]

Federal intervention into the wartime economy created additional opportunities for finding liability against formally private actors in the employment context. The Fair Employment Practice Committee (FEPC) prohibited discrimination by all private firms engaged in production related to the war effort. Political scientist Kesselman opined that the FEPC movement "mark[ed] a milestone in Negro history" because it "supplemented the theory that economic rights can be obtained principally by activity in the economic sphere . . . with an all-out drive to gain the support of the states and the national government in the elimination of racial discrimination in employment." Although the FEPC lacked the power to subpoena witnesses or to enforce its findings without calling on the president for punitive action, it represented yet another governmental intervention into the private employment relationship, yet another erosion of the immunity of private actors for discrimination.[12]

The existence of the FEPC also suggested the growth of a new federal public policy condemning discrimination on the basis of race that ultimately might bind private actors. For example, defense contracts between the federal government and private firms supplied a basis for litigation arguing that private employers had to refrain from discriminating. "There is no law as such which contains a nondiscrimination clause in the matter of employment under the National Defense Program," Marshall acknowledged just prior to the creation of the FEPC. "However, the Advisory Council of the National Defense Commission has issued a statement of policy against such discrimination and it is up to Negroes to see to it that the firms awarded contracts under the National Defense Program live up to the spirit of this policy."[13]

Once the FEPC offered more convincing evidence of this national policy, Marshall attempted to implement it in several lawsuits on behalf of San Francisco's African American shipyard workers. The NAACP lawyers argued in a 1943 federal suit that government contracts with the shipyards entitled the "plaintiffs [to] a federal right under those contracts and that those rights and contracts are paramount to any private agreement between the Boilermaker's Union and Marinship [the company]." Although the federal courts did not agree in that case, the lawyers achieved success on other grounds in a series of state suits they subsequently filed against the California boilermakers' union. In *James v. Marinship Corp.*, the lawyers argued that a union could not maintain both a closed shop and a closed union. The unions replied that they were entitled to operate their private association immune from legal regulation.[14]

The California Supreme Court vindicated the NAACP and the black workers. It cited both *Steele* and *Smith v. Allwright* as recent instances in which courts had prohibited discrimination by those who were not formally state actors. But the crux of the court's holding did not transform the union into a state actor per se. Instead, the California Supreme Court concluded that the unions were subject to legal regulation as businesses affected with a public interest. Although the court did not go so far as the Supreme Court's opinion in *Nebbia* to completely undermine that category, the court used an expansive definition of such "businesses". In particular, it rejected legal doctrine going back to 1890 that had allowed unions to "claim the same freedom from legal restraint enjoyed by golf clubs or fraternal associations." Instead, the *James* court analogized a union holding a labor monopoly to such classic businesses affected with a public interest as innkeepers and common carriers, which at common law had special duties to serve all comers on reasonable terms. The union's "asserted right to choose its own members does not merely relate to social relations; it affects the fundamental right to work for a living," the *James* court announced. "Where a union has . . . attained a monopoly of the supply of labor by means of closed shop agreements and other forms of collective labor action, such a union occupies a quasi public position similar to that of a public service business."[15]

Like other businesses affected with a public interest, unions—unlike churches, fraternal orders, and golf clubs—were bound by the public policy of the state. As the California Supreme Court explained, nondiscrimination, as set forth in President Franklin Roosevelt's executive order creating the FEPC, constituted California's public policy. The *James* court therefore concluded that the union's actions violated not the Fourteenth Amendment, but the public policy of the state of California. In *Williams v. International Brotherhood of Boilermakers*, another NAACP boilermakers case, the same court established that even unions without a local monopoly were affected by a public interest and would be held to the same common-law standard.[16]

Betts v. Easley, a similar 1946 case involving railroad workers brought by an NAACP branch, represents the most far-reaching example of how labor cases enabled lawyers to attack the constitutional immunity of private actors under the *Civil Rights Cases*. The Kansas Supreme Court concluded that federal regulation had actually transformed the union from a regulable actor into a government actor. Because the union held the exclusive power of representation of relevant railway employees under the provisions of the RLA, the court ruled that "[t]he acts complained of are those of an organization acting as an agency created and functioning under provisions of Federal law." The *Betts* court unequivocally found the union to be a state actor under the Fifth Amendment. It thus went even further than the California court in *James* and *Williams* and the United States Supreme Court in *Steele* and *Tunstall*. It demonstrated that courts were amenable to expanding state action beyond formally public actors.[17]

The NAACP lawyers' use of legal doctrine in their 1940s labor cases was, like their arguments about private liability generally, entrepreneurial and pragmatic. By the time of the NAACP's victory in *Brown*, the equal protection clause of the Fourteenth Amendment had become the constitutional text of choice in civil rights cases on behalf of African Americans. In the early 1940s, however, the long-revered, if somewhat discredited, right to work rooted in the due process clause of the Fifth and Fourteenth Amendments offered a resource in labor cases that appeared at least as promising, if not more so, than the equal protection clause. As the NAACP lawyers experimented with both equal protection and right-to-work arguments in their industrial labor cases, they took advantage of new uses for an old civil rights framework. They also highlighted, rather than submerged, the unique work-related aspects of the claims of black industrial workers.

The judicial rejection of *Lochner*'s right to work was neither clean nor complete. Many state courts, and a few lower federal courts as well, continued to adhere to the kinds of substantive due process rights commentators had eulogized at the end of the *Lochner* era. These cases invoked nineteenth-century notions of free labor and emphasized "the right to engage in a gainful occupation and to seek to better one's economic position" as being "of basic importance to the individual." To some judges and legal commentators, the right to work stood for much of what it had in Justice Stephen J. Field's dissent in the *Slaughter-House Cases,* in the foundational right-to-work case of *Allgeyer v. Louisiana,* and in *Lochner* itself: the individual's right to work unimpeded by governmental regulation.[18]

In their labor-related litigation in the 1940s, the NAACP lawyers considered variations on this work-based notion of civil rights. In 1942, for example, while still on the NAACP's staff, Prentice Thomas approved of a lawyer's plan to challenge discrimination by a federally funded company under the Fifth Amendment. The hitch was that the lawyer "would have to prove that the right to work is a property right," Thomas explained. "Our Legal Committee has been considering the same approach in these cases of discrimination, but we have not arrived at any agreement as a basis."[19]

Marian Wynn Perry also recognized that *Lochner* and its ilk provided substantial doctrinal resources in labor cases. A memo she wrote about challenging the discriminatory and segregative practices of the United States Employment Service (USES) later in the decade illustrates her understanding of the relevant legal doctrine. Perry not only argued that it was "illegal for the federal government itself to sanction racial discrimination in employment," but she also invoked Supreme Court recognition of "the fundamental nature of the right to work." Quoting *Allgeyer,* Perry argued that the Fourteenth Amendment "embrace[d] the right of the citizen . . . to live and work where he will; to earn his livelihood by any lawful calling; to pursue any livelihood or avocation." The bulk of the argument rested on *Allgeyer* and the proposition "that state action discriminating against workers on the ground of color is a violation of the 14th Amendment *in that it restricts the liberty guaranteed by that Amendment without due process of law.*"[20]

Thomas and Perry, who both stood somewhat to the left of Marshall and the other NAACP lawyers, were hardly outliers in the department for suggesting the potential of substantive due process arguments in labor cases. When the NAACP lawyers filed their state court briefs in the boilermakers cases, they had apparently "arrived at . . . agreement" on Thomas's argument that the laborer's rights in his work (whether sounding in property or liberty) could form the doctrinal basis for work-related race cases. In a boilermakers case in Providence, Rhode Island, the association's brief stated that "the right of laborers to organize unions is an exercise of the right of every citizen to pursue his calling, whether of labor or business . . . or of the right guaranteed by the constitution of acquiring, possessing, and protecting property." The NAACP's California Supreme Court brief in *James* quoted the New Jersey Supreme Court: "Everyone must be left free to pursue his lawful calling; that is fundamental." The *James* brief also argued that the New Jersey court, among numerous others, had recognized that "the right to earn a livelihood is a property right guaranteed by the Fifth and Fourteenth Amendments to the United States Constitution." As late as 1948, in *Takahashi v. Fish and Game Commission,* the NAACP lawyers cited *Allgeyer* and relied on the right to work in their brief on behalf of Japanese American fishermen denied fishing licenses in California.[21]

Whereas some post-*Lochner* lawyers and judges used substantive due process to harken directly back to a preindustrial, pre-regulatory era, the NAACP lawyers thought that unions potentially enhanced, rather than necessarily undermined, the right to work. The NAACP lawyers linked the old right to work with the protections of the interventionist New Deal state by explicitly connecting the common law to constitutional and statutory law. They argued in *James* that "the arbitrary exclusion of qualified workers from a union means the deprivation of a livelihood for persons who are willing and able to earn their livelihood by the sweat of their brow."[22]

These arguments capitalized not only on the lingering right to work from the *Lochner* era but also on the prominence labor rights gained in the 1930s and continued to enjoy in the 1940s. The NAACP feared at the time, and scholars have argued then and now, that the NLRA would hurt African Americans by giving greater power to exclusionary and discriminatory white unions. But the NAACP lawyers' arguments in the boilermakers cases reveal that they were sympathetic to the NLRA, that they thought it could theoretically help black workers, and that combining it with the right to work was one way of realizing that theoretical possibility. That the NLRA protected the right to work, rather than abridged it, meant that even protected unions should not be allowed to violate the rights of African Americans to work. The lawyers viewed "[t]he underlying problem" much as Summers did in

1947: how to give "the worker the greatest possible protection against exclusion by a union with the least possible dangers to the independence and effectiveness of the union." The NAACP made clear that the black workers preferred union organization to an open shop, but that the right to work limited the protection that the New Deal could offer to discriminatory unions.[23]

The NAACP lawyers' right-to-work rhetoric and arguments met with considerable success in the state courts. In deciding *James* in the NAACP's favor, the California Supreme Court repeatedly referenced the "fundamental right to work for a living," the "constitutional right to earn a livelihood," and the "fundamental" fact that "[e]veryone must be left free to pursue his lawful calling." In *Williams,* the same court emphasized "the fundamental right to work" and the kind of "unlawful interference with a worker's right to employment" that union discrimination created. In the railroad workers *Betts* case, the Kansas Supreme Court explicitly linked substantive due process and union participation. Among the injuries that the due process clause redressed was "the denial to a workman, because of race, of an equal voice in determining issues so vital to his economic welfare." The court refused to be "blind to present-day realities affecting labor in large industrial plants," and it concluded that because "[t]he individual workman cannot just 'go it alone,'" collective bargaining was necessary.[24]

Commentators analyzed the problem in similar terms. Note that despite the title of Murray's 1945 article—"The Right to Equal Opportunity in Employment"—she did not begin with the plight of African Americans in the United States generally or with the principle of racial nondiscrimination. Rather, she began with the statement, "The interest in freedom from discrimination in employment is part of the broader interest in freely disposing of one's labor." The courts, she said, "have been profuse in their verbal homage to the idea that the right to work is an inalienable and natural right, a logical extension of the right to life and pursuit of happiness, inherent in the guarantees of the Federal Constitution, and rooted in the common law." Murray cited *Lochner* and derived the right to work from both the Fifth and Fourteenth Amendments. The "broad over-all problem of security in our time is the right to employment," she concluded. "This interest is on a par with the right to existence itself." Summers agreed. "The right to work is uniformly recognized as essential," he wrote in 1947, "for it involves not only the right to live but the right to follow one's chosen occupation."[25]

Taken together, Murray's and Summers's articles, the memos of Perry and Thomas, the briefs of the other NAACP lawyers, and the judicial analyses of the NAACP's cases are revealing. They demonstrate the extent to which the NAACP's most successful legal arguments in the union discrimination cases were based on a substantive reading of the due process clause and closely related common-law doctrine rather than on the equal protection clause. The cases vindicated the substantive right to work (as it happened, without racial discrimination) as much as, if not more than, the substantive right to be free from racial discrimination (as it happened, in the context of work). Because the complaints of African American workers concerned, at base, the right to work, they enabled the lawyers to invoke arguments specifically about work. And because the lawyers invoked the right to work, they enabled black workers to make headway against discrimination within labor unions and the private labor market.

The lawyers further facilitated their attack on private labor market inequality by taking a flexible approach to the pervasive tension between pursuing economic advancement within segregation and attempting to end segregation altogether. When John Grantham wrote to the NAACP about the segregated shipyard at the Sun Shipbuilding and Dry Dock Company of Chester, Pennsylvania, he wavered between criticizing his employer for having segregated its workforce and for having offered black workers inadequate opportunities within the segregated yard. Grantham's ambivalence encapsulated that of black workers, the NAACP, and the NAACP's lawyers about the goals of labor-related legal action in the 1940s. Throughout the decade, African American workers and their advocates clashed over whether to seek economic advancement within segregation or to pursue desegregation without compromise. In labor cases as in education cases, those directly affected frequently sought advancement rather than await the end of segregation. And in labor cases as in education cases, black leaders increasingly disagreed.[26]

Consider the Sun Ship controversy. Grantham was not the only person to bring the all-black shipyard to the NAACP's attention.

Herman Laws, leader of the local branch of the NAACP in Chester, explained to NAACP assistant secretary Roy Wilkins that economic advancement was itself a step in the right direction. Likening the shipyard situation to teaching in segregated schools, Laws thought that it would be foolish and harmful to force black workers to await the end of segregation idly rather than take segregated opportunities for advancement and higher pay. "The problem," he analogized, "is whether to let colored teachers teach segregated now or remain idle until the mixed democratic idea is fixed in the public mind."[27]

Laws's reference to teachers was astute. Around the time he was writing, the NAACP lawyers were involved in suits to equalize teacher salaries. These suits arose mostly within segregated systems, and the claimants requested equalization of salaries rather than desegration as relief. Despite Laws's attempted analogy, the national leadership of the NAACP, along with other national organizations and some black newspapers, took a somewhat harder line on the Sun Ship's segregated yard. The NAACP publicly condemned "Jim-Crow Shipbuilders," and executive secretary Walter White scolded Laws. White reminded Laws that the NAACP had been founded to "oppose segregation . . . without compromise."[28]

That antisegregation position was not as doctrinaire or absolute in the early 1940s as it became at the end of the decade, however. In fact, both the NAACP as an organization and its lawyers in their litigation strategy took opportunities to improve the economic prospects of black industrial workers even when such progress required accommodating segregation. In response to the pleas of longshoremen Adolphus Braithwaite and Alphonso Morris for greater opportunities for segregated work, for example, Marshall wrote to the president of the International Longshoremen's Association to ask the union to allot to "Negro gangs" more work on the New York City and New Jersey piers.[29]

The West Coast boilermakers' union litigation offers the most revealing instance of how the NAACP eventually softened its position on segregation and embraced the possibilities that labor cases offered for economic advancement. When Wilkins first traveled to Portland, Oregon, to assist black shipyard workers in 1942, supporters of the auxiliary unions told him how thousands of African Americans in San Francisco had joined the unions and obtained skilled work for high wages. Despite the economic benefits workers in the auxiliaries obtained, Wilkins presumed that the NAACP would "stand pat for non-segregated unions with Negroes having all rights and privileges enjoyed by whites. That is the only position we can take."[30]

Three years later, however, after several lawsuits and appeals aimed at eliminating the boilermakers' Jim Crow auxiliaries, NAACP leaders and attorneys applauded when the California Supreme Court took a middle position between acceptance and condemnation of the segregated auxiliaries. In *James* and *Williams*, the court decided that the boilermakers' union would have to choose between a closed shop and a closed union. The white boilermakers could enjoy either a market monopoly with racial nondiscrimination (if not inclusion) or give up that monopoly in order to retain their discriminatory and segregative practices.[31]

These decisions mirrored and drew upon National Labor Relations Board (NLRB) opinions around the same time. In a series of cases during the war, the NLRB entertained "grave doubt whether a union which discriminately denies membership to employees on the basis of race may nevertheless bargain as the exclusive representative in an appropriate unit composed in part of members of the excluded race." Although the NLRB explained in *In re Larus & Brother Co.* in 1945 that it felt powerless to force unions to admit black members, it could and did order employers to reinstate the excluded workers. The California Supreme Court cited *Larus* in *Williams* for the proposition that unions with closed-shop contracts could not "compel the discharge of employees who are discriminatorily denied membership."[32]

At the time, the NAACP and its lawyers viewed this choice between a closed union and a closed shop as a step in the right direction. The NAACP issued a press release announcing the decision. Marshall called the *James* case "a splendid victory" that would create "a blue print for labor unions in regard to Negro and other minority groups." He predicted that *Williams*, echoing both *James* and *Larus*, would have "a sweeping effect." Despite the fact that unions could still choose to segregate and discriminate, they could not eliminate the jobs of African Americans in the process, and that was cause for celebration.[33]

Even in the late 1940s, not all of the NAACP's lawyers deemed segregation an evil to be avoided always and in every context. Especially if segregation seemed likely to benefit African American workers materially, some of the NAACP lawyers equivocated. Labor secretary Clarence

Mitchell and labor lawyer Perry disagreed, for example, about the advantages of attacking the discriminatory and segregationist practices of USES. Mitchell wanted to challenge the USES, whose discrimination had intensified once the Truman administration returned the employment services to state control after the war. Mitchell analogized to the association's emerging anti-segregation stance in education cases, arguing that "wherever there is segregation there also is discrimination." Although Perry agreed to explore the legal basis for such a challenge, she disagreed about its potential benefits. She concluded that separate was not necessarily worse for African Americans, at least in the context of employment agencies. She thought "that the Negro gets better service in the Negro office when he applies for Negro jobs because there are no whites competing with him for those jobs."[34]

Thus, although neither the NAACP leadership nor its lawyers explicitly supported segregation, its lawyers recognized that the antisegregation principle at times conflicted with the practical needs of working African Americans. The NAACP's labor cases highlighted the tension between the two goals, and navigating between them was neither easy nor straightforward. Through the mid-1940s, however, the lawyers did not deem it necessary to choose one over the other. They were reluctant to commit wholeheartedly to a desegregation strategy in labor just as they generally hesitated to commit to a strategy of no-holds-barred, across-the-board desegregation in the 1940s. In the education context, the NAACP lawyers realized in 1945 that they faced a choice between equalization and a direct attack on segregation. They generally opposed trying to enforce equality within segregation explicitly, and the association rhetorically reaffirmed its principled opposition to segregation throughout the 1940s. But pragmatism counseled pursuing material advancement within the confines of segregation, and the lawyers postponed the choice in their litigation strategy until 1950. It was not until the 1951 annual conference that commitment to desegregation became a tenet of the association and that activities countenancing segregation became subject to disciplinary action.[35]

By the end of World War II, the NAACP had made considerable progress in industrial labor cases. More African Americans were employed in industry due to the association's interventions. The destructive combination of the closed shop and the closed union seemed destined

for extinction. Courts and administrative agencies increasingly constrained the private prerogatives of unions to use their regulatory bargaining monopoly with unbridled discretion. Law—state and federal,
administrative, statutory, constitutional, and common—had gone some
distance toward protecting African Americans in the labor market.

There was still much to do, however. Labor-related cases—technical,
painstaking, and limited in their potential impact—were difficult to
pursue. Houston, champion of labor litigation in his private practice,
recognized in 1944 that the remaining questions could not all "be
fought out in the courts because the courts are too slow and litigation
is too expensive." A single case would not change the position of black
industrial labor, let alone destabilize Jim Crow more generally. Yet the
same was true of the NAACP's education cases at the end of the 1940s
and the beginning of the 1950s. As White explained in 1950 after the
NAACP's Supreme Court victories in several graduate education cases,
"Our legal staff . . . inform[s] us that many score—possibly several
hundred—legal actions may have to be initiated and fought to secure
Southwide compliance in every professional and graduate school of
every Southern state." Even once the NAACP obtained initial victories,
White counseled, it would still have to bring contempt proceedings for
noncompliance and additional cases for lower levels of education.[36]

Numerous people within the NAACP's orbit commented on the
possibilities for expanding the wartime precedents in the mid-1940s.
Work-related cases, the push toward desegregation, the search for
more state action, the protection of more categories of workers—all
these areas begged for further attention and litigation. Mitchell continued to push the NAACP's lawyers to work toward desegregation and
nondiscrimination in USES. Union discrimination cases continued to
look promising for future doctrinal development. Marshall himself followed up on the boilermakers' victories in *James* and *Williams* with letters to twenty-five apparently discriminatory unions informing them of
the cases and urging them to cease discriminating. The next step in
union cases, according to Herbert Resner, a San Francisco attorney
with whom Marshall had collaborated in the boilermakers cases, was to
"press for a decision that there is no economic security at all for Negro
workers unless they are full members of the union which has the contract and the jurisdiction over the job in question." Murray agreed.
"Does it not follow," she asked, "that this obligation [to abstain from

discriminatory activity] can only be met in practical fact by opening the organization's membership without restriction because of race, creed, color, national origin or ancestry?"[37]

A number of civil rights and labor advocates thought the Supreme Court's RLA cases of *Steele* and *Tunstall* were the key to further development of the law. The CIO suggested that the way to proceed was to get the NLRB not to certify a discriminatory union as the sole collective bargaining agent for a class of workers. Although the NLRB had taken steps in this direction, it still refused to deem either exclusion or segregation as violations per se of the duty of fair representation. In fact, although the NAACP's legal department did not ultimately take the lead, cases challenging the NLRB's claimed lack of power to regulate union membership arose with some regularity in the postwar period. Other lawyers pursued analogous cases under the RLA.[38]

In particular, Houston and his law partner in private practice, Joseph C. Waddy, vigorously followed up on the railroad cases that had brought them success in *Steele* and *Tunstall*. Houston aimed to "establish the principle that a railroad union has no right to represent a nonmember minority worker unless it gives him the same chance to elect the officials who conduct the collective bargaining process, censure and remove them as possessed by the union members." In the late 1940s and into the early 1950s, Houston and Waddy tried to make that principle a reality. "If we win these cases," Houston exclaimed, "the Jim-Crow union membership will be nothing but an empty shell." Houston thought that such precedents in the railroad context could apply "to every other public utility: gas, electricity, telephone and telegraph, bus lines and air lines, every industry affected with a public interest."[39]

For Houston, the goal was not simply the end of formal discrimination in unions and employment. He also aimed to overturn the 1906 Supreme Court precedent of *Hodges v. United States*. *Hodges* limited Thirteenth Amendment protection for African Americans prevented from working at their chosen calling by private white citizens. Houston was convinced that "keeping a man down to certain limited jobs in restricted places is nothing but a refined form of involuntary servitude and . . . lawyers must keep digging until they find a way to make the United States Supreme Court change [the] view it took in *Hodges*."[40]

Houston thus hoped to go beyond expanding *Steele* and *Tunstall*. His focus on *Hodges* was explicitly derived from the Thirteenth Amend-

ment as well as the Fourteenth, and it went to the very heart of constitutional protection for African Americans' right to work. He proposed
that even private action not officially sanctioned by federal or state regulation could be constitutionally problematic. Houston made the
target not simply the formal, state-mandated segregation of *Plessy* but
also the violations of black workers' ability to make a living left unredressed in *Hodges*. He thus indicated that the gap between the
NAACP's doctrinal orbit and that of the Civil Rights Section of the Department of Justice was not quite as wide as it might seem.

Echoing Houston's substantive concerns, Summers was optimistic in
1947. Summers acknowledged that "[e]ven to suggest that there is a
constitutional right to join a union might seem preposterous," but
"with the present pace of constitutional law it is not amiss to discuss the
possibilities." The constitutional hurdle of deeming previously "private" unions to be state actors, he concluded, "is not insuperable." The
Chicago Defender was hopeful not only about private liability, but also
about the possibility of undermining segregation altogether on the
basis of the recent precedents. The paper generalized the statutory victories over railroad discrimination in *Steele* and *Tunstall* to the possibility of ending Jim Crow entirely. It seemed that the Court had "dis-
covered that whatever is segregated and Jim Crowed cannot be equal
in the true sense. . . . It opens the way for striking new powerful blows
against Jim Crow in American life."[41]

EIGHT

Eliminating Work from the NAACP's Legal Strategy

This Association is concerned with "Legal Equality" only, and proposes to let "Economic Equality" take care of itself.

> Charles J. Bonaparte, 1914 NAACP Annual Conference

AS WORLD WAR II ENDED, the possibilities for labor litigation appeared robust. The cases that the NAACP pursued in the first half of the decade had, in the view of the NAACP lawyers, "go[ne] far to protect the right of the Negro worker not to be discriminated against" by either employers or unions. From the vantage point of the immediate postwar period, labor, education, transportation, and residential segregation cases all offered possibilities for deepening the attack on racial inequality. Indeed, the economic components of labor-related cases offered a variety of doctrinal opportunities for finding both constitutional violations and liable defendants and for attacking both the public and the private components of Jim Crow.[1]

Even as the lawyers pursued labor cases in the mid-1940s, however, they also began to set their sights more narrowly on state-mandated segregation, especially in education. Postwar political, institutional, and doctrinal developments expedited these emerging choices and led the legal department largely to turn away from the labor-related claims of industrial workers. During the late 1940s, the NAACP, labor unions, and the non-Communist Democratic coalition were defending themselves against Republicans, southern Democrats, and anti-Communist attacks. In that political climate, the kinds of arguments the NAACP lawyers had made with some success earlier in the 1940s increasingly conflicted with both the association's and the legal department's goals, constraints, and commitments.

By the time Thurgood Marshall and his team embarked in earnest on their attack on Jim Crow at the end of the 1940s, they had clarified all three questions left open earlier in the decade: the lawyers would challenge state-mandated segregation without also challenging the *Civil Rights Cases'* state action requirement; they would do so on the basis of the equal protection clause of the Fourteenth Amendment; and the goal of the litigation strategy would be to overturn *Plessy's* validation of segregation rather than procure material advancement within the confines of segregation. The combined result of these three decisions was to leave intact the economic aspects of Jim Crow and to virtually eliminate the particular concerns of African American workers from the legal department's practice of civil rights law.

In the broadest strokes, the lawyers' marginalization of the cases of black industrial workers was merely the flip side of their decision to initiate such cases in the first place. When the war created a national momentum toward eliminating "economic discrimination," the association and its lawyers joined the crusade. In the aftermath of the war, the economy, the national political landscape, the NAACP's institutional position within that landscape, the legal department's position within the association, and the legal department's doctrinal goals all changed. The claims of industrial workers no longer appeared as promising.

Economically, the end of the war meant the end of the wartime boom. World War II had broken a decade-long depression, and in pursuing labor-related litigation in the early to mid-1940s, the NAACP had wanted African Americans to benefit from economic growth without facing racial discrimination. The method was race based, but the goal was at least partly economic. The workers who complained to the NAACP wanted nondiscriminatory access to jobs and unions, but they also simply wanted jobs. Where the two goals—one economic and one racial—conflicted, the NAACP and the workers who sought its help sometimes agreed and sometimes disagreed on which goal should be paramount. Although the NAACP and its lawyers opposed explicit and intentional efforts by employers to segregate their workforces, they were nonetheless pleased with rulings they obtained in union discrimination cases that countenanced segregation but allowed for economic advancement. In cases like *James v. Marinship* and *Williams v. International Brotherhood of Boilermakers,* the courts had required unions either to open their doors to African Americans or to open their previously closed shops. The NAACP embraced these cases because they enabled African Americans to obtain jobs, even though the decisions continued to tolerate segregation.

When the war boom faded, however, many Americans, especially African Americans, lost their wartime jobs in the reconversion to domestic production. Desirable jobs were no longer in great supply. Returning soldiers complicated hiring and promotion with questions of seniority and service, which played (usually purposefully) to the benefit of white workers. The ability to work for an open-shop employer alongside the white union members of a segregated union meant little when employers had not only ceased hiring but had begun laying off workers in large numbers. These economic developments did not lessen African American workers' needs for legal counsel—in fact, they arguably increased those needs—but they did undermine the perceived choice between striving for economic improvement and advancing the doctrinal attack on segregation. Only the latter seemed to offer much promise in light of fears about the immediate postwar economy.[2]

The political changes that accompanied the end of the war also affected the NAACP's institutional position and approach to labor litigation. The rising Cold War and domestic anti-Communism put the NAACP and other civil rights groups on the defensive far more than it did the lawyers in the Civil Rights Section of the Department of Justice. Anti-Communist attacks somewhat tempered the CRS's ambitions, but as a general matter, the legal work of the CRS flew under the political radar of southern conservatives who tainted all racial change with the brush of Communism.[3]

The NAACP, however, was an organization publicly committed to racial equality. As such, it made an easy target for anti-Communists who were also segregationists. As a result, even as activists and scholars remained optimistic about expanding wartime labor litigation precedents, as early as 1947, African American activists began to mute their demands for fear of seeming too radical. The NAACP in particular pulled back from some relatively aggressive interventions it had previously made into the international arena, especially its efforts to connect domestic civil rights to the human rights the newly established United Nations had begun to protect. In addition, the NAACP hunkered down at home. Executive secretary Walter White and assistant secretary Roy Wilkins spent considerable energy in the late 1940s scanning news reports and challenging alleged links between the NAACP, race advocacy, and Communism. They assiduously avoided associating with organizations with potentially subversive tendencies. Worried about the National Lawyers Guild's defense of Communists, Marshall resigned from the organization. And in 1950, Wilkins and Marshall led a successful effort at the NAACP's annual convention to pass the association's first resolution putting the organization on record "as unequivocally condemning attacks by Communists and their fellow-travelers upon the Association and its officials . . . in order to safeguard the good-name of the Association." The resolution called for the expulsion of branches "under Communist or other political control and domination."[4]

These responses to potential Communist "infiltration" stemmed not only from the political dangers of being associated with Communism during the Cold War but also from the association's long-standing ideological and institutional antipathy to Communism and Communist organizations. From its inception, the NAACP had been a largely "liberal" organization committed to eliminating racial discrimination and segregation within the context of the American legal system. Accordingly, when White and Wilkins responded to anti-Communist attacks in the late 1940s, they emphasized that the NAACP intended not to revolutionize American society wholesale but rather to encourage Americans to live up to fundamental American promises of equality and freedom. NAACP administrative assistant Madison S. Jones protested to the House Un-American Activities Committee in 1949 that "there has never been any question of the loyalty of the Negro to the United States."[5]

The NAACP's liberal, anti-Communist commitment to the legal reform of Jim Crow enabled it to capitalize on new political opportunities the Cold War created. Critical international attention on the United States' racial practices, along with competition between the Soviet Union and the United States for the allegiance of people of color the world over, actually assisted some forms of civil rights advocacy. The NAACP and other civil rights groups referenced the international implications of segregated housing and education in their rhetoric and their legal strategies, and government officials found the arguments at least somewhat persuasive.[6]

These arguments were less appealing in labor-related litigation for both political and institutional reasons. Politically, the declining fortunes of organized labor sapped black industrial workers' claims of some of their national imperative. When, during World War II, the NAACP and its lawyers had advocated on behalf of black workers, they had drawn support from the vitality of workers' rights and labor unions generally. The rights of black workers to share in the economic opportunities that other workers enjoyed had taken the center stage of civil rights debates. After the war, the Civil Rights Section lawyers continued to press labor and economic rights in their Thirteenth Amendment practice, and other government officials and academics continued to advocate for them as well. Nonetheless, labor's coattails had lost some length. Passage of the 1947 Taft-Hartley Amendments to the National Labor Relations Act (NLRA)—which restricted some strikes and boycotts, validated state right-to-work laws, and required anti-Communist loyalty oaths—both signaled and led to some decline in

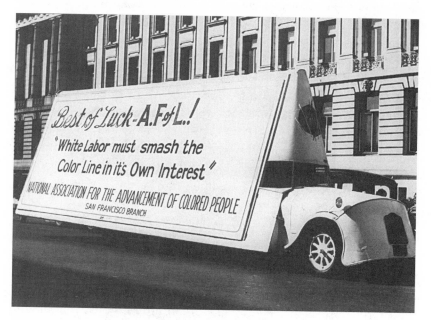

In a parade in Detroit circa 1944, a moving billboard sponsored by the NAACP congratulates the American Federation of Labor's stand against race discrimination. (© CORBIS.)

the fortunes of organized labor. To the extent that the NAACP's lawyers (other than Prentice Thomas and Marian Wynn Perry) had embraced workers' cases at least in part because of their political traction during the war, waning popular support meant less impetus to pursue those cases.

Indeed, changes in the NAACP's institutional position pushed the legal department away from further litigation in the labor cases in which it had seen the most success earlier in the decade—those against unions. Even as the lawyers lost the political impetus to attend to the claims of black workers, the association as a whole deepened its alliance with organized labor in the aftermath of World War II. As the NAACP became a central part of the liberal, pro-labor but anti-Communist Democratic coalition, its early 1940s affiliation with unions became a much tighter alliance. Civil rights groups such as the NAACP and labor unions were both on the defensive against red-baiting Republicans and southern Democrats. They turned to each other for support. In 1947, White wrote William Green of the American Federation of Labor (AFL) about the "vital and mutual interest" of the NAACP and the AFL in "anti-lynching bills [and] fair employment practice legislation" as well as their "unwholesome twin"—"the drive to shackle the labor movement with the Taft-Hartley Act." The NAACP's legislative agenda included items dear to both the NAACP and organized labor. The unions and the NAACP each embraced the goals of the other, and they shared what White called a "common fight for justice."[7]

As witness to these new relationships, the NAACP made the International Longshoremen's Association a life member and A. Philip Randolph of the Brotherhood of Sleeping Car Porters a vice president. The NAACP also appointed powerful liberal anti-Communist labor leaders Philip Murray of the United Steel Workers and Walter Reuther of the United Auto Workers to its board. In 1949, the NAACP, other black civil rights organizations, and labor organizations created a permanent interracial lobbying coalition, the Leadership Conference on Civil Rights.[8]

The NAACP's new institutional relationship with unions tended to replace, rather than augment, earlier litigation-based relationships with individual African American workers. The NAACP targeted unions aggressively for financial as well as political support, thereby reducing its reliance on the membership of individual black workers. In 1948, the NAACP made the decision to double its membership dues from $1 to $2. For at least the 40 percent of African Americans earning less than $200 per year,[9] the increase was substantial. The association expected the increase to reduce its membership by one-third, but they underestimated its effect. As a result of both the dues increase and postwar economic retrenchment, the association shrank from its postwar peak of 420,000 to 248,000. The most dramatic losses occurred in branches in cities that had attracted many working-class African Americans to war industries. In Detroit, for example, the NAACP branch decreased from about 25,000 during World War II to 5,162 in 1952. These figures indicate the NAACP's lack of commitment to those at the economic bottom of its membership. The association seemed to prefer a smaller group of wealthier members, along with support from organized labor, to a larger group with a wider range of economic ability.

What happened on a financial level happened on a programmatic level as well. When the NAACP allied with organized labor in the political realm, it largely stopped litigating on behalf of individuals or groups in labor-related cases. The NAACP's increasingly intimate political alliance with mainstream organized labor proved complicated for the NAACP's labor-related litigation in the late 1940s. The defensive posture of organized labor made the NAACP hesitate to appear hostile to labor, lest the NAACP unwittingly aid organized labor's— and hence its own—political enemies. Although labor secretary Clarence Mitchell sometimes criticized segregated unions, he generally approached unions about their internal affairs cautiously and with considerable diplomacy. Most of his time was focused not on union discrimination but on the fight for a permanent, legislative Fair Employment Practice Committee (FEPC) and for a second-best solution of interim executive orders. On those matters, organized labor was a strong ally of the NAACP.[10]

The NAACP lawyers themselves saw the delicacy of the association's relationship with unions. They became skittish about siding with one union against another when the unions competed to organize the same group of workers. In 1943, the legal department had written an amicus brief on behalf of a Congress of Industrial Organizations (CIO) union in a representation fight with the AFL's boilermakers.

The department argued that if two bargaining units were proposed, one of which would be represented by a nondiscriminatory union, the other by a discriminatory union, the National Labor Relations Board (NLRB) should certify the nondiscriminatory unit. By 1948, however, Marian Wynn Perry was leery of raising "the constitutional issue of the right of [the NLRB] to certify as the sole collective bargaining agent any union which either refused to admit Negroes to membership or placed them in segregated locals with limited voting power." She hesitated to "be in the position of taking sides in a battle between the AF of L, CIO, or an independent union." Organized labor as a whole was a critical, and politically vulnerable, part of the Democratic coalition to which the NAACP gave allegiance. That coalition would lose strength if the NAACP lawyers took sides in union disputes.[11]

Union discrimination cases that once seemed appealing now looked institutionally problematic to the NAACP and its lawyers in another, even more fundamental way. Recall the NAACP's jubilation at the 1945 decisions of the California Supreme Court in *James* and *Williams*. The cases, like the NLRB's *Larus* decision, had given unions the choice of opening their closed shops to nonunion workers or opening their closed unions to African American workers. By 1949, however, *Larus* had become a case, according to Mitchell, "with which we are in vigorous disagreement." The benefit *Larus* offered African Americans, an open shop if not an open union, was no longer one the NAACP could accept. The NAACP's political and institutional situation had changed considerably since the beginning of the war: the open-shop movement was undermining labor, with whom the NAACP was in a much closer alliance. Indeed, the association and its lawyers took pains to ensure that no one mistook its arguments about union discrimination for attacks on unionism per se.[12]

The NAACP's two most labor-oriented staff members, labor secretary Mitchell and lawyer Perry, strategized about how best to get the word out that the NAACP was not antiunion, and especially not against closed shops. "We have a responsibility," Perry wrote to Mitchell in 1947, "to keep the Negro community from getting confused on this issue." After years of facing closed union shops and closed white unions, Perry and Mitchell assumed that there was "strong feeling in the Negro community that the closed shop is harmful to Negroes, and we know there is enough evidence of misuse of this to warrant such a fear on the part of the Negro people." Indeed, the lawyers' own arguments in their briefs to the California courts in the wartime boilermakers cases had suggested just such a strategic, if not principled, hostility to the closed shop.[13]

Mitchell and Perry consequently felt that they had to convince the NAACP's own members, other African Americans, and the public at large that the NAACP supported closed shops when unions came under attack after the war. The association aimed to target discriminatory and exclusionary unions where necessary rather than condemn unionism itself or eschew its potential benefits for African Americans. "[I]t is a delusive misstatement of fact," Mitchell explained in congressional hearings, "to say that the elimination of the closed shop will cut down discrimination against any minority." Echoing the NAACP lawyers' arguments in the boilermakers cases, Mitchell made clear his belief in the protective power of unions and in the possibility of addressing their shortcomings through other means: "[T]he remedy for this type of discrimination is contained in the enactment of fair employment practice legislation rather than by taking from workers—colored and white alike—the protection of various forms of union security which have operated for their benefit."[14]

With suits against labor unions institutionally and politically problematic for the NAACP, its lawyers might have turned to other kinds of litigation on behalf of industrial workers. From a doctrinal perspective, the regulation of unions made them particularly vulnerable to legal liability. But there were certainly other viable defendants for labor-related litigation. New York and an increasing number of states with fair-employment-practice laws offered up the possibility of private employer liability. President Harry Truman's 1948 executive order prohibiting discrimination in federal employment gave impetus to claims against federal agencies and officials. Challenges to government-sanctioned practices of discrimination were still available as well.

By the late 1940s, however, the NAACP's lawyers essentially returned to their Depression-era position that "labor" issues—separate from "race" issues—were not appropriate for legal action. Even though Marshall had seen the boilermakers cases as "definitely within the purview of the program of the N.A.A.C.P." as late as 1946, he was already pulling back from any legal department commitment to labor-related litigation that same year. In answering the question, "where and how shall we attack" segregation, Marshall stated: "By fighting for legislation we can secure equal job opportunities for Negroes and we will have broken down segregation a little bit." In contrast, Marshall thought, legal battles could achieve equal education and destroy restrictive covenants. Although the fight for legislation was clearly legal in some sense—trying to establish laws to prevent discrimination—both the goals (statutory remedies) and the form of NAACP activity (lobbying) set labor issues apart from the constitutional goals of Marshall's litigation agenda. Labor-related activities were for the lobbyists, not the litigators, of the NAACP.[15]

In fact, when Perry, the lawyer hired to pursue labor litigation during the war, resigned from the NAACP for personal reasons in 1949, Marshall did not replace her. By 1950, labor issues had become essentially the purview of Mitchell, the NAACP's labor secretary in Washington, to the general exclusion of involvement by the legal office in New York City. Although both Mitchell and his successor, Herbert Hill, tried to involve the NAACP lawyers in labor-related cases into the 1950s, they only occasionally succeeded.[16]

Indeed, around the same time the legal department largely excised labor cases from its practice, it also began to flex its institutional muscle. By the early 1950s, the legal department's tax-exempt status and successful fundraising had made it more financially flush than the NAACP itself. That caused some tensions between the two entities and gave Marshall greater institutional power. Marshall began to argue that the NAACP board had no authority to make decisions for the lawyers. By 1952, he underscored the organizational separation that had begun so tentatively in 1939 by no longer referring to his "outfit" as the legal department of the NAACP. Instead, he called it the NAACP Legal Defense and Educational Fund, Inc., or, a little later, the "Inc. Fund." By the end of 1952, the lawyers had moved into their own space and taken greater control over their litigation strategy. Although the two organizations remained deeply involved with one another—with overlapping boards, for example—even much of that involvement had ended by 1956. This gradual institutional separation both reflected and solidified the division between the politics of labor-based discrimination and the legal team's litigation strategy.[17]

For Marshall and the lawyers who remained in the legal department after Perry's 1949 departure, then, the new alliance with labor proved liberating as well as limiting. Where once the NAACP leadership had expected the legal team to take on labor-related cases as a spur to increase membership among African American workers, now the association's legislative activities would suffice. So long as both African American workers and the NAACP had remained hesitant to embrace unionism fully, the association had found other means, such as litigation, to convince working-class African Americans of the benefits of NAACP membership. As the NAACP's legislative agenda increasingly converged with that of organized labor, and its political alliance with unions grew even closer, those activities and relationships freed the legal department to pursue litigation toward achieving the goals with which its lawyers were historically and fundamentally concerned—desegregating transportation and graduate education (and eventually all education) and eliminating racially restrictive covenants.

When the legal department turned away from industrial workers' claims in the late 1940s, it did so not only for external political and institutional reasons but also for its own doctrinal ones. In the years following the war, the legal department's lawyers began clarifying their doctrinal goals. In particular, the lawyers set their sights clearly and resolutely on the fifty-year-old precedent of *Plessy v. Ferguson*. When the Supreme Court decided the case in 1896, *Plessy* had received little public attention and much less opprobrium from African Americans than the *Civil Rights Cases* had in 1883. Yet *Plessy* had come to epitomize for the NAACP the essence of Jim Crow. The equal protection clause, long thought "the usual last resort of constitutional arguments," as Justice Oliver Wendell Holmes put it in 1927, was the terrain on which African Americans had lost much of the federal protection that the Civil War and Reconstruction had promised. It was the terrain on which the legal department would try to win it back.[18]

The lawyers' increasingly single-minded pursuit of *Plessy* represented a departure from the war era. In the first half of the 1940s, labor cases brought success because Thomas, Perry, Marshall, and the other lawyers sought creative ways of finding liable defendants, of constructing legal arguments for constitutional violations, and of negotiating between the sometimes conflicting goals of desegregation and economic advancement. As Marshall and his lawyers (minus the labor-oriented Thomas and Perry) began to clarify their doctrinal agenda in the late 1940s, their goal became overturning segregation in government agencies on the basis of the equal protection clause. "The 'separate but equal' doctrine of *Plessy v. Ferguson*," the lawyers announced at the NAACP annual conference in 1949, "must be exposed and overruled."[19]

By 1950, the lawyers deemed the timing right for their attack on *Plessy* in segregated education. Marshall won three Supreme Court victories that year. In particular, the graduate education cases of *Sweatt v. Painter* and *McLaurin v. Oklahoma* represented the NAACP's first Supreme Court victories in education since 1938. Marshall viewed these cases as "replete with road markings telling us where to go next." Those markings pointed to a direct attack on *Plessy* in the education context. Other signs pointed in the same direction. Teacher salary and graduate education cases had reached their limits, and educational equalization cases had become untenably expensive. Moreover, both the political climate and the NAACP membership seemed increasingly receptive to the direct attack. Although challenges to the direct attack remained both within and outside of the association, by 1950, the course was largely set.[20]

Once Marshall fixed his sights on *Plessy*, the labor cases that had once held out legal as well as institutional promise fell by the doctrinal wayside. Each of the three opportunities the industrial workers' cases had offered was at best orthogonal to and at worst in direct tension with the lawyers' pursuit of *Plessy*. The key doctrinal target became *Plessy*'s sanction of state-mandated segregation, not the *Civil Rights Cases*' removal of the problem of private discrimination from constitutional scrutiny. The critical doctrinal advance would be reinterpreting the equal protection clause, not obtaining favorable precedents of whatever constitutional ilk. And the goal was formal, state-mandated desegregation, not economic advancement or material equality. For the NAACP lawyers, the legal challenge to Jim Crow increasingly referred only to public discrimination and segregation, not the private racial and economic hierarchies that also constituted Jim Crow.

As the NAACP lawyers committed themselves to the attack on *Plessy*, then, they left for another day the challenges to private discrimination they had begun to undertake during World War II. The legal department's wartime labor cases had targeted a variety of defendants—federal and state governmental entities, labor unions, and private employers. In fact, by the late 1940s, the *Civil Rights Cases*' state action requirement seemed even more fundamentally vulnerable than it had at mid-decade. In *Shelley v. Kraemer* in 1948, the Supreme Court vindicated theories that judicial action could constitute state action for Fourteenth Amendment purposes. In that case, which addressed racially restrictive covenants on housing, the Court (with urging from the NAACP lawyers) found state action in the judicial enforcement of an entirely private agreement between private parties. As Pauli Murray had pointed out in 1945, if the judicial imprimatur of the state could transform a purely private property transaction into state action, then the field was clearly open for claims of race discrimination against private companies and unions.[21]

The continued existence of the state action requirement, and the continued vitality of the *Civil Rights Cases*, thus did not itself rule out labor cases for the NAACP. In fact, if challenging, overturning, or marginalizing the *Civil Rights Cases* had been part of the lawyers' goals, the labor cases would have provided an excellent opportunity for continuing the progress of *Steele, Tunstall, Larus, James, Williams,* and *Betts.* To be sure, finding obvious state actor defendants, such as those in public grade-school education, was easier than pursuing some defendants in labor cases. And the Cold War and the NAACP's alliance with organized labor made the most vulnerable nongovernmental actors—unions—unappealing defendants after World War II.

Numerous other labor-market participants remained potentially liable for labor-related discrimination cases, however. Federal and state government entities with pay disparities, discriminatory hiring and promotion practices, and segregated and discriminatory facilities presented no state action difficulties whatsoever. Mitchell's commitment to challenging the expenditure of federal funds on segregated state employment services and to confronting the state services themselves similarly raised no state action obstacles. Private employers in the ever-increasing number of states with fair employment practice laws also remained vulnerable to legal sanction. Creating federal constitutional liability for private employers (or some subset of them) might have been attainable through the same doctrinal dexterity the NAACP's lawyers had displayed during the war.

The clear doctrinal goal of the legal department in the late 1940s, however, became the challenge to *Plessy,* not the *Civil Rights Cases.* The NAACP's participation in *Shelley* was reactive, not proactive: Marshall thought the attack on racially restrictive covenants in the late 1940s premature. He became involved because other lawyers had brought cases that he thought might make bad precedent without his help. Indeed, success in *Shelley* did not make the NAACP lawyers any more inclined to seek out private liability. The NAACP largely followed up the case with arguments about extending *Shelley* to other aspects of government discrimination in housing rather than extending its broad state action analysis to other forms of private liability.[22]

Still, attacking *Plessy* did not have to mean leaving the *Civil Rights Cases* intact. Challenging segregation was likely facilitated by abandoning creative approaches to state action, thereby isolating the segregation issue. But the lawyers might have taken on both segregation and state action, both the public and the private underpinnings of Jim Crow. That they chose not to do so in labor cases reflected not only their determination about the relative importance of *Plessy* and the *Civil Rights Cases*. Their choice reflected as well the fact that throughout the association's history, neither the NAACP as a whole nor the NAACP lawyers were primarily concerned with material inequality in the labor market.

Recall that an NAACP-dominated committee had explained to the Garland Fund in 1930 that "the Negro as a Negro suffers disabilities which the white laborer does not face." Twenty years later, the NAACP lawyers' attack on *Plessy* indicated that they still thought it was necessary first to change "these precedent conditions" before addressing the economic problems of African American workers. Such economic problems, although certainly created by and part of Jim Crow, were not what the NAACP lawyers thought of as the essence of the problem. Rather, they deemed state-mandated segregation—rather than state-supported private segregation and discrimination—the crux of American racial subordination. That basic assumption stemmed from a discounting of the problems of working African Americans and of the fundamentally economic as well as racial hierarchies embedded in Jim Crow.[23]

Indeed, the NAACP lawyers further marginalized labor-related litigation by deciding that *Plessy*'s interpretation of the equal protection clause was their key constitutional target. The NAACP's most successful legal arguments in labor cases had been rooted in substantive due process and common law precedents. Although the equal protection clause buttressed and provided context for some of the arguments, both liability for private actors and vindication of the right to work largely turned on the due process clause, state and federal statutory law, and the common law. In the boilermakers cases, the California Supreme Court relied on substantive due process and the common law of common carriers. In the New York State Commission Against Discrimination cases, state statutory and administrative remedies provided the basis for liability. In *Steele* and *Tunstall*, it was federal statutory law.

By the late 1940s, however, equal protection was the doctrinal foundation, and a nondiscrimination framework was the primary goal. In part, this equal protection focus resulted from the lawyers' expertise at reading legal tea leaves. Even as state courts and some lower federal courts vindicated substantive due process claims, the Supreme Court increasingly relegated those claims to the doctrinal scrap heap. The Supreme Court made clear in the latter half of the decade that arguments based on the right to work no longer garnered much support when they conflicted with an emerging antidiscrimination norm. In *Railway Mail Ass'n v. Corsi*, the union argued that it should be allowed to exclude African Americans because New York's Ives-Quinn Law "offends the due process clause of the Fourteenth Amendment as an interference with its right of selection to membership and abridgement of its property rights and liberty of contract."[24]

The Court rejected that old reading of the Fourteenth Amendment as inconsistent with a newer, antidiscrimination reading. Citing *Steele*, the Court commented: "We have here a prohibition of discrimination in membership or union services on account of race, creed or color. A judicial determination that such legislation violated the Fourteenth Amendment," the Court pronounced, "would be *a distortion of the policy manifested in that amendment*[,] *which was adopted to prevent state legislation designed to perpetuate discrimination on the basis of race or color.*" In concurrence, Justice Felix Frankfurter described the claim as "devoid of constitutional substance" and suggested that using the Fourteenth Amendment against state prohibitions on race discrimination "would stultify that Amendment." The Court treated as incoherent, at least as applied to labor-related cases, the simultaneous vindication of a due process clause emphasizing the right to work and an equal protection clause emphasizing nondiscrimination. It explicitly sided with the latter.[25]

In 1949, the Court also rejected substantive due process claims to the right to work in a different kind of case. The state right-to-work laws passed in the wake of Taft-Hartley essentially prohibited closed union shops by promoting the rights of workers to work without being forced to join a union. These laws represented a more extreme, explicitly antiunion manifestation of the *Lochner*-based arguments that the NAACP legal department itself had made in its union cases earlier in the decade. Both the unions challenging the right-to-work laws and the nonunion workers defending them invoked substantive due process. The former claimed the right to contract freely for a closed shop, and the latter claimed the right to work without having to join a union.

Unlike the state courts, which received these substantive due process arguments favorably, the United States Supreme Court rejected *Lochner* reasoning as a basis for either upholding or invalidating state right-to-work laws. In one such case, a union could not persuade the Supreme Court of its arguments for the vitality of the liberty of contract issue—the unions' alleged right to contract with employers for a closed shop. Nor did the Court countenance the antiunion workers' due process right to work without joining a union. In *Lincoln Federal Labor Union v. Northwestern Iron and Metal Co.*, the Court refused to "return . . . to the due process philosophy that has been deliberately discarded." It chose instead to reduce the question of the validity of right-to-work laws entirely to the principle of antidiscrimination. These laws, and the Court's approach to them, placed the right not to join a union on the same moral plane as the right to join one and equated discrimination against union members with discrimination against nonmembers. Even for labor cases in which racial discrimination was not at issue, then, the Court began applying a framework taken from a nondiscrimination norm, rather than from the substantive right to work.[26]

That the Supreme Court perceived a conflict between the equal protection and the due process clauses did not mean the NAACP lawyers could not obtain traction with due process arguments elsewhere. It was not easy to determine which doctrinal stars were ascending and which were descending out of the mixed signals of courts and commentators. The California Supreme Court's decision in *Williams*, for example, postdated *Corsi*, indicating that the state courts took a different approach to the continuing vitality of the right to work. But as the NAACP followed the Supreme Court's growing emphasis on nondiscrimination over the substantive right to work, it simultaneously reinforced that very trend.

As the NAACP lawyers targeted *Plessy*, they not only retreated from their attacks on the private labor market and their earlier use of the right to work; they also retreated from their earlier goal of economic advancement within segregation alongside doctrinal advancement toward desegregation. Indeed, in 1951, the NAACP passed a resolution that for the first time made opposition to segregation a tenet of the association. The annual conference resolved that the association "is opposed to racial segregation" and "requires all branch officers, members and attorneys to refrain from participation in any cases or other activities which in any manner seek to secure 'equality' within the framework of racial segregation." The resolution authorized the board of directors to take disciplinary action against anyone within the association acting inconsistently with the policy. Gloster Current, director of branches, sent a missive to the branches criticizing those who "embraced the separate but equal theory and have, in the past, embarrassed a number of branches by so stating their views specifically and creating division with the community."[27]

That the NAACP did not pass such a resolution until 1951 is telling. Certainly, NAACP staff and members had vetted the question of the association's position on segregation many times in the past, most famously in the 1934 *Crisis* episode in which W. E. B. Du Bois suggested that he could countenance self-segregation. Du Bois's resignation from the NAACP that same year signaled at least in part that his reluctance to embrace integration as the ultimate and only goal was out of step with those holding greater institutional power. And between 1934 and 1951, the association publicly reaffirmed that it opposed segregation, even while practically trying to make strides toward racial progress within its confines. The lawyers similarly had long held the end of segregation as their goal, though they accepted, and even celebrated, interim and incomplete victories within the framework of *Plessy*.[28]

Nonetheless, it was not until more than fifteen years after the Du Bois episode that the association affirmatively made actions inconsistent with desegregation disqualifying for NAACP staff and its members. The 1951 resolution recognized that some members had "embraced the separate but equal theory" and finally committed the

NAACP definitively to integration. It made clear that past efforts at economic advancement while tolerating segregation were at an end.[29]

In this new context, the legal department's most successful labor cases no longer looked so successful. The *Larus/James/Williams* approach of giving unions the choice of a closed shop or a closed union offered the NAACP very little by way of doctrinal development toward undermining *Plessy*. The NAACP's changed doctrinal goals, no less than its changed political and institutional constraints, made *Larus* a case "with which we are in vigorous disagreement." According to Mitchell, by 1949 the cases stood for the proposition "that unions could segregate colored persons into auxiliaries and B-class locals without violating the National Labor Relations Act." Even though *Larus* itself seemed to legitimate only separate unions that were equal in every respect, "separate but equal" was no longer enough for the NAACP. Once the lawyers decided to make an all-out attack on segregation, countenancing victories within the framework of Jim Crow became deeply problematic.[30]

Indeed, cases that highlighted material inequalities even in the context of challenging segregation became problematic for the NAACP lawyers. The premise of *Plessy* was that a racial distinction, on its own, with no material inequality to accompany it, was only harmful if African Americans allowed it to be. In order to demonstrate that racial distinctions were inherently harmful—in labor cases as in education cases—Marshall needed to find, or construct, instances of formal separation unaccompanied by material inequalities. The stigma of such formal separation—ultimately supported by sociological and psychological evidence—became the essence of Jim Crow's injury. The lawyers' decision to target *Plessy* reflected, once again, the legal department's return to the Margold Report and the stigmatic manifestations of Jim Crow visible to elite black lawyers in their daily lives.[31]

Some labor cases lent themselves to claims of stigma. Union discrimination cases such as *Larus* offered up suitable doctrinal vehicles to argue what Marshall ultimately argued in *Brown*—"that there is no such thing as 'separate but equal.'" Once the workers in a separate African American local enjoyed all the rights white union workers enjoyed, the question would become whether the mere fact of separation violated equal protection. Then lawyers could isolate and attack the intangible stigmatic harm of separate unions. *Larus* and cases like it were no longer attractive as an institutional and political matter, however, because of the NAACP's ties with organized labor. And they were not attractive because of their complicated state action status and amenability to due process arguments. Consequently, the most obvious labor cases in which to apply the new doctrinal approach proved unsatisfactory.[32]

Other labor cases the lawyers had pursued in the early part of the decade were less amenable to the new doctrinal claims of stigma. The injuries of Jim Crow in the labor market could rarely be confined to such intangibles, as material harms systematically resurfaced. In 1949, for example, Mitchell announced his opposition "to any makeshift plan which establishes certain job categories or shifts which are given over to colored people." The problem, as he saw it, was not the intangible harm of segregation; it was the fact that such segregation was inseparable from material harm: "Always in such arrangements we find that the worst possible spots go to the non-whites." Although similar issues pervaded the NAACP's school desegregation cases, by the early 1950s, the lawyers' graduate education precedents had gone a long way toward isolating intangible educational harms even where material inequalities persisted. Because of the structure of the workplace and the pervasive economic inequalities of the private labor market—as well as the NAACP lawyers' political, institutional, and cultural aversion to labor cases—imagining the labor case (especially outside the union discrimination context) that would allow the NAACP lawyers to isolate the intangible harm was no easy task. Ultimately, it was a task they did not undertake.[33]

By the late 1940s, the NAACP had come a long way from its roots in progressive ideology and its financial base in philanthropic donations. It had embraced labor unions and created a labor secretary. During World War II, its lawyers had championed the rights of African American industrial workers with some vigor. They had seen such cases as opportunities for both doctrinal development and material advancement. And their efforts had met with some success.

But the moment that would make the association's legacy was the moment in which its lawyers returned to its roots in middle-class life and the Margold Report. As the NAACP lawyers targeted *Plessy* in earnest, labor-related cases disappeared from their litigation agenda.

In the postwar era, the legal department sometimes, but not always, included employment discrimination among the targets of its litigation strategy. Although labor cases were not prominent on the agenda at the NAACP's first lawyers' conference in 1949, for example, they nonetheless were on the agenda. At the time, the legal department was not actively involved in much labor litigation, but its lawyers were still "committed to putting greater emphasis on fighting to remove employment discrimination of both labor and management."[34]

By the NAACP's annual convention in 1950, much had changed since Marshall had described labor cases as one of the NAACP's two top litigation priorities in 1943. Marshall organized his second annual legal conference to take stock of recent Supreme Court victories and decide on next steps. Labor secretary Mitchell wrote to Marshall to submit three labor-related items for consideration at the 1950 legal conference. Following on the wartime labor litigation efforts, Mitchell hoped to discuss the possibility of bringing court actions to deny federal protection to segregated unions, to challenge segregated and discriminatory government employment services, and to enforce in court nondiscrimination clauses in government contracts. Recognizing that time was scarce, Mitchell asked that Marshall consider at least one recommendation.[35]

Marshall's reply was less than encouraging. He intended to focus the conference on education, where *Plessy* seemed to be close to collapse after the graduate education victories earlier that year. If time remained after the lawyers had exhausted the question of how to deepen the attack on education, they might consider Mitchell's suggestions. Perhaps, Marshall mused, the labor secretary's points could "possibly come in on the discussion of the extent to which the recent Supreme Court decisions will be used." Marshall thus relegated labor issues to what was left over—in both time and the course of doctrinal development.[36]

In 1951, Marshall held another legal conference. No labor issues appeared in the minutes of the conference. The lawyers came up with a list of "the types of cases that would have priority": public education, transportation, health, housing and recreational facilities, public gatherings, and all places of public accommodation. Labor and employment did not make the list. The agenda for the 1950 legal conference and the resolution and priorities that eventually emerged in 1951 show

how marginal labor and employment issues were to the legal department's agenda as it embarked in earnest on its attack on segregation.
Even on the agenda Mitchell proposed, the scope of labor issues was
quite narrow, limited as it was to discrimination and segregation by
unions, employers, and employment services. The problems black
agricultural workers faced, which had once concerned the NAACP,
were long gone even from the labor secretary's agenda. Although reform of employment services would help some agricultural workers,
Mitchell's suggestions were largely geared toward industrial workers.[37]

More fundamentally, the exchange between Mitchell and Marshall
reinforced that labor issues were political rather than legal, more
properly addressed by the NAACP's labor secretary than its legal
counsel. The possibility that labor-related cases would provide a site
for the lawyers' attack on *Plessy* had largely disappeared by 1950.
Making *Plessy* the target—and interpreting *Plessy* as requiring the isolation of intangible harm—both compelled and liberated the NAACP to
transform its class interests in integrated graduate schools, railroad
dining cars, and middle-class neighborhoods into an apparently class-
less modern civil rights. This new civil rights would prove fundamentally unable to redress the economic hierarchies of Jim Crow America.

NINE

◆ ◆ ◆

Brown and the Remaking of Civil Rights

> The basic law dealing with race relations in the
> United States is fairly well settled.
>
> Jack Greenberg, *Race Relations and American Law,*
> 1959

IN 1952, THE FOREWORD to Thomas Emerson and David Haber's pioneering treatise described the field of civil rights as deeply "unsettled." Seven years later, Jack Greenberg, a ten-year veteran of the NAACP's legal team, came to the opposite conclusion. Greenberg acknowledged the existence of "sectors of indecision" within the field. He was confident, however, that "in all situations we can identify the relevant, fundamental principles" governing civil rights law. Indeed, Greenberg's very terminology—his equation of "civil rights" with "race relations"—indicated how much had changed. Between 1952 and 1959, civil rights doctrine had evolved from a state of disarray to one of considerable clarity.[1]

The pivotal moment in that transformation was the Supreme Court's 1954 decision in *Brown v. Board of Education.* The NAACP's victory in *Brown* fundamentally changed the scope of civil rights lawyering and the constitutional imagination. Like all cases, *Brown* reflected a partial view of the social reality that produced it.[2] Generally, at each step in the litigation process, parties, lawyers, and judges filter out factual scenarios, sites of legal contestation, doctrinal theories, and experienced harms. By the time a case reaches the Supreme Court, the complexities not only of social life but also of the lawyering process itself have been winnowed into neat legal questions. Those questions represent only a small slice of the social milieu and legal practice that generated and nurtured the original complaint.

This process of doctrinal distillation was particularly powerful in the years leading up to *Brown*. The multiplicity of the civil rights practices of the 1940s reflected both the unsettled nature of legal doctrine and the complexity of challenging a seventy-five-year-old racial and economic caste system. As lawyers transformed into legal claims attacks on the unwieldy thing called Jim Crow, they chose particular cases, particular legal theories, and particular formulations of injury that they thought legal doctrine could remedy. As a result, the civil rights case that took the definitive step toward undermining Jim Crow would, as *Brown* did, both embody a legal understanding of what Jim Crow was and begin to define the constitutional response to it. In so doing, that case would, as *Brown* also did, elide the forms of civil rights and understandings of Jim Crow that lawyers had chosen to filter out of the litigation process.

The *Brown* litigation thus represented several critical choices the NAACP lawyers had made for a decade, supported from the late 1940s on by lawyers in the Justice Department's Office of the Solicitor General (OSG or SG's office). The lawyers culled from the diversity of 1940s civil rights practice equal protection claims focused on state-imposed segregation in public education. And they extracted from the multilayered system of Jim Crow the psychological wounds such segregation inflicted. In the end, the NAACP's legal department created a litigation strategy devoid of the myriad labor-oriented civil rights complaints of the prior fifteen years and the material harms they had sought to redress.

The iconic image of Jim Crow the Supreme Court's decision in *Brown* projected and the civil rights framework it inaugurated helped shape the contours of civil rights law for decades to come. *Brown*'s invalidation of school segregation did not, as Greenberg recognized, create a single, coherent approach to civil rights; nor did it purport to colonize the entire field. The Court's purposefully brief opinion left many questions about the future of civil rights doctrine and enforcement unanswered.[3]

Even so, *Brown* represented a key moment in the history of American civil rights doctrine and constitutional understandings. *Brown* consolidated a critical shift in control over the Justice Department's civil rights agenda away from the labor-based civil rights practice of the Civil Rights Section (CRS) and toward a more equal-protection-based approach within the OSG. It validated the NAACP's *Plessy*-oriented litigation strategy and reinforced key elements of that strategy for the lawyers' future efforts. And it set on its path the legal and intellectual framework that continues to dominate how lawyers and laypeople alike think about civil rights.

When *Brown* reached the Supreme Court, it represented the culmination of the NAACP's long-term litigation strategy. In particular, it vindicated the lawyers' 1950 decision to attack *Plessy v. Ferguson* directly in the context of public education. Even though material inequalities pervaded segregated education, the lawyers had made it their mission to tackle the principle of segregation itself. In 1950, the legal team convinced the Court that even intangible inequalities in segregated graduate education violated *Plessy v. Ferguson*'s "separate but equal" command. The lawyers then turned their attention to proving that such inequalities were inevitable in grade-school education as well. They succeeded wildly in *Brown*. The Court concluded that "[s]eparate educational facilities are inherently unequal," that attending legally segregated schools deprived African American schoolchildren of educational benefits by making them feel inferior to whites, and that "[a]ny language in *Plessy v. Ferguson* contrary to this finding is rejected." With *Brown*, the lawyers achieved their major doctrinal goal of establishing the constitutional harm of government-enforced segregation in the absence of any accompanying material inequality.[4]

Brown also enshrined as the supreme law of the land and as a new cultural icon a civil rights devoid of the hallmarks of both the CRS's and the NAACP's 1940s labor-related civil rights practices. Neither the legal strategies those practices had employed nor the image of Jim Crow they had reflected survived the filtering process of the school segregation litigation.

Consider the constitutional basis for the decision in *Brown*. As the NAACP lawyers constructed their legal theories on the road to *Brown*, they came to understand *Plessy* as the lynchpin of Jim Crow. Because *Plessy* had legitimated segregation in the face of an equal protection clause challenge, *Brown* had to delegitimate it on the same basis. The equal protection clause "precludes a state from imposing distinctions or classifications based on race and color alone," the NAACP accordingly argued. The "doctrine of 'separate but equal,'" the United States elaborated in an amicus brief, "is an unwarranted departure . . . from the fundamental principle that all Americans, whatever their race or color, stand equal and alike before the law."[5]

Without much fanfare, the Court embraced the NAACP's and the government's constitutional reasoning. Concluding that "in the field of public education the doctrine of 'separate but equal' has no place," Chief Justice Earl Warren held that the plaintiffs had been "deprived of the equal protection of the laws guaranteed by the Fourteenth Amendment." The Court went out of its way to clarify that its decision was based on the equal protection clause alone. "This disposition makes unnecessary any discussion whether such segregation also violates the Due Process Clause of the Fourteenth Amendment."[6]

Indeed, when the Court found itself forced to look beyond the equal protection clause, it did so only reluctantly. *Bolling v. Sharpe* was a companion case to *Brown* from Washington, D.C. Because the district was not a state, the Fourteenth Amendment's command that "[n]o State shall . . . deny . . . the equal protection of the laws" did not apply there. The Court seemed somewhat flummoxed by the fact that the Fifth Amendment, which did apply to the district, "does not contain an equal protection clause." Forced to rely on that amendment's due process clause, the Court concluded that "the concepts of equal protection and due process, both stemming from our American ideal of fairness, are not mutually exclusive. . . . [D]iscrimination may be so unjustifiable as to be violative of due process." Due process thus did not function as an independent source of constitutional analysis. Rather, as the Court had previously done in cases like *Hirabayashi v. United States* and *Korematsu v. United States,* it imported equal protection concerns into the due process clause in order to scrutinize federal racial classifications. Even where due process provided the doctrinal basis for decision, then, equal protection provided the conceptual framework.[7]

This dominance of equal protection was not foreordained. Because civil rights lawyers in the 1940s had not targeted *Plessy* exclusively, they had not viewed the equal protection clause as the only constitutional basis for their arguments. The lawyers in the Civil Rights Section, for example, often avoided the equal protection clause. Instead, they exploited a variety of understandings of the Thirteenth Amendment in their involuntary servitude and peonage cases. For both political and doctrinal reasons, the government lawyers had avoided challenging

Plessy directly. Politically, attacking *Plessy* and the segregation it legitimated would have alienated powerful southern elements of Franklin
Roosevelt's Democratic coalition. Doctrinally, the lawyers chose instead to expand upon favorable precedents, like those concerning peonage. Moreover, the labor pedigree of the CRS, the lawyers' political
interest in peonage cases, and the lawyers' responsiveness to complaints opened up arguments rooted elsewhere in the Constitution.
When farmworkers like Col. Elton D. Wright VI wrote to the federal
government that they were "only asking for rights" under the Constitution not to work at a "low wage unfair and inhuman treatment," it was
the Thirteenth Amendment rather than the Fourteenth that could answer their prayers for relief.[8]

Even within the NAACP's legal department during the 1940s, the
equal protection clause had not reigned alone. To be sure, the lawyers
launched equal protection claims on behalf of workers as well as students. But the workers who complained to the NAACP had wanted
economic advancement as much as racial nondiscrimination. As the
New York City longshoremen had told the NAACP, the issue for them
was less the segregation of work on the city's piers than "the chance to
make a fair living" at all. More often than not, arguments based on
the right to work—rooted in the Fifth and Fourteenth Amendments'
due process clauses as well as the common law—accompanied and
even dominated equal protection arguments in these cases. The
NAACP had revamped the right to work from its *Lochner* roots for service in the New Deal era. It had capitalized on the unique doctrinal
resources the right to work offered in labor cases. *Brown*'s exclusive attention to the equal protection clause submerged these arguments, as
well as the Thirteenth Amendment claims of the CRS.[9]

Just as the *Brown* litigation and opinion filtered out some of the core
constitutional arguments of the 1940s, so too they painted only a partial picture of the harms of Jim Crow. Once again, the focus on *Plessy*
was partly responsible. More than a half-century before the school segregation litigation, the *Plessy* Court had concluded that if "the enforced separation of the two races stamp[ed] the colored race with a
badge of inferiority," it was only because "the colored race [chose] to
put that construction upon it." As the lawyers embarked on their attack on *Plessy*, they felt they had to prove the contrary. They had to
show that the state's act of segregation, rather than African Americans'

own assumptions, placed upon the latter the "badge of inferiority." In order to do so, the lawyers had to isolate the harm of state-mandated segregation from the larger milieu of private and public discrimination and inequality that pervaded Jim Crow America. That, in turn, required the NAACP to bracket the question of material inequality that had marked both labor and education cases in the 1940s. Contrary to *Plessy*, state racial classifications alone, they argued, caused African Americans intrinsic harm.[10]

Worried that the Court would not accept a mere assertion that such classifications violated the Constitution, the NAACP looked for a way to prove how these state rules stigmatized African Americans. The "badge of inferiority" about which Homer Plessy had complained referred to his reputation. By 1954, a therapeutic ethos had taken such hold of American culture that psychological had replaced reputational harm as the natural form of the stigma argument. In the late 1940s and 1950s, concern with the development of personality and the healthy psyche had become an American preoccupation. In 1946, Congress passed legislation creating the National Institute of Mental Health. Between 1950 and 1960, the number of psychiatrists in the United States almost doubled to 12,000. The White House held conferences with titles like "A Healthy Personality for Every Child." That culture shapes, and damages, personality became a tenet of modern American psychology. The psychologizing of race in particular led to studies on both the psychological causes of racism and the effects of racism on the human personality.[11]

Drawing on these trends and especially the growing body of social science data on race and psychology, the NAACP introduced evidence and testimony in the lower courts about how school segregation psychologically damaged African American children. They used so-called doll studies that black social scientists Kenneth and Mamie Clark had conducted in the South. The Clarks showed African American children black and white dolls. When asked which was the nice doll, or the one the child would like to play with, the child would point to the white doll. When asked by a psychologist to identify with a doll, the child would point to a black doll. According to the Clarks, these identifications revealed psychological damage. These studies, the NAACP argued in both the lower courts and the Supreme Court, revealed that even under conditions of material equality, "unconstitutional inequality inheres in the retardation of intellectual development and distortion of personality which Negro children suffer as a result of enforced isolation in school." In a lengthy appendix to its Supreme Court brief, the NAACP also submitted a statement by a long list of social scientists expert in "race relations." They emphasized the sense of "inferiority and . . . personal humiliation segregation caused in children."[12]

Taking its cue from the NAACP, the Court set to one side the continuing material inequalities in the segregated school systems under attack. It cited "findings below that the Negro and white schools involved have been equalized, or are being equalized, with respect to . . . 'tangible' factors." The Court then explicitly embraced the NAACP's stigma argument as to "intangible" factors. To separate black children "from others of similar age and qualifications solely because of their race generates a feeling of inferiority as to their status in the community that may affect their hearts and minds in a way unlikely ever to be undone," the Court concluded. "Whatever may have been the extent of psychological knowledge at the time of *Plessy v. Ferguson,* this finding is amply supported by modern authority." In what would become an infamous footnote, the Court then cited several of the studies that purported to prove school segregation's psychological harm to children.[13]

Enshrined in constitutional law, then, was *Brown*'s image of a Jim Crow that had as its central harm the psychological injury of inferiority. That harm and the harms highlighted in the 1940s labor cases could not have been more different. Stigmatic harm was not unimportant to the workers who complained to the NAACP, but they more often emphasized the economic harms that segregation entailed: less work, worse work, inadequate salaries, and economic insecurity and lack of advancement. The NAACP's labor cases had attempted to redress both the stigmatic and the material components of the workers' claims. In the West Coast boilermakers cases, for example, the NAACP aimed to desegregate the all-white boilermakers' unions. The lawyers nonetheless celebrated when their litigation efforts produced more and better jobs without achieving union desegregation.

The Civil Rights Section's Thirteenth Amendment practice focused even more directly on the material, attending as it did to the most economically deprived African Americans. The agricultural and domestic workers who came to the attention of the federal government also sought dignitary relief. They complained that they did not share in any of the "privileges of a free person." But for the most part their material needs were more urgent. They worked "long, hard hours" for little or no pay; they lacked adequate food, shelter, and clothing; and they lacked the ability to leave such conditions. The first task of the CRS, then, was to free these workers from their servitude, to open up labor markets and provide government protection. When the NAACP pressed, and the *Brown* Court accepted, stigmatic harm as the essence of Jim Crow, the image of civil rights the Court projected eclipsed the deep and abiding material inequalities that characterized the nation's caste system for most African Americans.[14]

The NAACP further marginalized material injury in *Brown* by emphasizing the specific harms of government-imposed segregation. The NAACP's decision to attack *Plessy* without also trying to undermine the state action requirement of the 1883 *Civil Rights Cases* privileged the place of governmental action in the maintenance of Jim Crow. The problem as *Plessy* had defined it in 1896 was whether "[l]aws permitting, and even requiring" segregation violated the Fourteenth Amendment. *Plessy* did not involve the constitutionality of privately created discrimination, segregation, and inequality. By challenging only *Plessy,* and therefore only state action, the NAACP parsed the public from the private aspects of Jim Crow. Public education provided an ideal locus for attacking *Plessy* alone, as it ensured that the state action requirement would not constitute a barrier to success. Once the NAACP demonstrated that the challenged public school segregation was in each instance enforced by law—an uncontroversial fact on its face—it met its burden of proving state action.[15]

And yet the NAACP, the United States, and the Court all treated state action not only as a technical jurisdictional requirement in the school segregation litigation but also as a substantive component of the harm of Jim Crow. Throughout the course of the litigation, the NAACP linked psychological stigma directly to governmental action. Neither the NAACP nor its experts denied the force of privately sanctioned segregation, but they emphasized that the legitimacy of the law enhanced Jim Crow's harm. Because segregation was often based on the myth of black inferiority, the NAACP argued, when "the state enforces segregation, the community at large is supported in or converted to the belief that this myth has substance in fact." The NAACP's experts acknowledged the difficulty of assigning causation to state-enforced segregation itself. Legal segregation was, after all, "only one feature of a complex social setting." They nonetheless claimed that "enforced segregation gives official recognition and sanction to [the] other factors of the social complex, and thereby enhances the effects of the latter in creating the awareness of social status differences and feelings of inferiority." The experts stressed that they were "not here concerned with such segregation as arises from the free movements of individuals which are neither enforced nor supported by official bodies." The United States echoed the sentiment in its own brief to the Supreme Court. It stated, "The constitutional right invoked in these cases is the basic right, secured to all Americans, to equal treatment before the law." The government emphasized that "[t]he cases at bar do not involve isolated acts of racial discrimination by private individuals or groups."[16]

The Supreme Court also treated state action as not only a jurisdictional requirement but also a significant component of the harm itself. The Court quoted the Kansas court in *Brown* as finding that "the impact [of segregation] is greater when it has the sanction of the law; for the policy of separating the races is usually interpreted as denoting the inferiority of the negro group." The Court did not rule out the possibility that the private aspects of Jim Crow might be constitutionally problematic. But it emphasized the sanction of government as a critical part of the harm of segregation.[17]

This emphasis on state-derived harm represented yet another partial reflection of the civil rights practices of the 1940s. The NAACP's choice to abide the public-private line was something of a departure from both the CRS's and the NAACP's own approach to the state action question in the 1940s. One of the attractions of the Thirteenth Amendment for the CRS lawyers was that it had no state action requirement. Alone among the Reconstruction-era amendments, the Thirteenth Amendment provided constitutional authority to redress private wrongs. The complaints farmworkers and domestic workers presented to the Civil Rights Section revealed how difficult it was to disaggregate private from public harm. When a planter apprehended an "escaped" worker, brought him before a court, obtained a conviction, brought him back to work on his plantation, and kept him there through violence and threats of imprisonment, the line between public power and private, between the state's contributions to Jim Crow and the individual's, blurred to the point of extinction. When the Civil Rights Section attacked Jim Crow, it did so with cognizance of the line between public and private but with no intention of abiding by it. The CRS's Thirteenth Amendment practice had epitomized the 1940s "extension of civil rights," as President Harry Truman had put it, from "protection of the people *against* the Government [to] protection of the people *by* the Government."[18]

So, too, when the NAACP's legal department took on labor cases in the 1940s, it purposefully attempted to undermine the line between state and private action. Responsibility for the problems that plagued black industrial workers no less than those that plagued agricultural or domestic workers lay with both public and private actors. The problems resulted not only from discriminatory referrals from the United States Employment Service, discriminatory government training programs, and discriminatory government hiring. The obstacles industrial workers faced resulted as well from the decisions of private employers, many of whom had contracts with the federal government. Their problems stemmed from the decisions of co-workers and unions, which the government also sanctioned in important ways. Deeming the state action doctrine vulnerable, the NAACP lawyers targeted unions, private employers, and government agencies alike. They seemed to view as significant the straitjacket the *Civil Rights Cases* imposed on potential racial equality no less than that imposed by *Plessy*. Whereas the attacks of the lawyers in the 1940s targeted both the private and the public aspects of racial and economic subordination, the Court's iconic construction of Jim Crow in *Brown* privileged the harms inflicted specifically by the state.

The NAACP's litigation choices similarly transformed the role of education in *Brown*, elevating it from a background condition of the litigation into an important substantive component of the case. By the time the Court issued its opinion in *Brown*, education had become the paradigmatic site for the reproduction of Jim Crow and the crucial battleground for a new civil rights. The education context—and the children who inhabited it—infused the case with its particularities. At every turn, education affected the doctrinal arguments as well as the image of Jim Crow and the embodiment of its victims.

The specific attributes of educational inequality had long made an impression on the NAACP's litigation strategy. From the association's early school equalization cases to its teacher salary cases to its graduate school cases, the nitty-gritty facts of education had been omnipresent. The cases, like many of the complaints that initiated them, dwelt at length on the lack of school buses, the outdated textbooks, the underpaid teachers, and the shotgun segregated black law schools operating in basements with only a few part-time professors. Without "substantial equality in . . . educational opportunities," the Court had concluded in *Sweatt v. Painter,* it could not find the *Plessy* standard satisfied.[19]

When the NAACP lawyers decided that satisfying *Plessy* would no longer satisfy them, the strategic burdens on education grew more substantial. To be sure, especially at the trial level, the parties continued to haggle over the magnitude of the material inequalities between white and black schools. But the direct challenge to *Plessy* raised two strategic problems that required education to do more work than simply provide a site for revealing such inequalities. First, as the NAACP's social science experts recognized, it was not easy to prove that the psychological damage they had observed stemmed from segregated education. It could have stemmed instead from the many other formal and informal indignities and inequalities African American children endured. One way to solve that problem was to demonstrate the importance of education as a site for the production and maintenance of the American caste system in toto. If education played a major role in American life, then it must also play a major role in fostering the feelings of inferiority the social scientists had documented.

Second, the NAACP needed to address hard questions about the expectations of the Fourteenth Amendment's framers regarding segregated schools. After the initial oral arguments but before rendering a final decision in *Brown,* the Court ordered the parties to prepare additional briefs concerning the original intent and historical understanding of the Fourteenth Amendment. The lawyers' efforts to find evidence that the framers intended to outlaw segregation in public education in 1867 yielded at best nothing definitive and at worst evidence that the framers accepted the segregated education then scattered across the nation. One way the NAACP neutralized the historical evidence was to suggest that education in the 1950s meant something wholly different—and far more important—to Americans than it had in the 1860s. Education in general, and especially in the South, had not yet become an essential public good after the Civil War. Both the NAACP and the United States thus attempted to reframe the question away from whether school segregation existed in the nineteenth century to whether, "under the far different conditions existing today," school segregation violated the Constitution.[20]

Toward both these ends—proving that segregated education was the specific cause of psychological damage and the primary American institution for racial and civic indoctrination—the NAACP waxed eloquent about the "basic function of the public school" as the instruction of "each succeeding generation in the fundamental traditions of our democracy." Again the NAACP drew on the trend toward psychologizing America's race problem. In particular, it relied on the growing intercultural education movement. The movement suggested that interracial contact in schools was critical to counteracting the societal pressures toward racism that undermined democracy. "The public school," the NAACP argued, "even more than the family, the church, business institutions, political and social groups and other institutions, has become an effective agency for giving to all people that broad background of attitudes and skills required to enable them to function effectively as participants in a democracy." It emphasized how " 'education' comprehends the entire process of developing and training the mental, physical and moral powers and capabilities of human beings." Schools provided opportunities "to develop citizenship skills and to adjust . . . personally and socially in a setting comprising a cross-section of the dominant population."[21]

The Court embraced this privileged role of education. "Today," it announced, "education is perhaps the most important function of state and local governments." Education was not only "the very foundation of good citizenship." It also promoted democracy and acculturation to American ways of life. The Court echoed the NAACP in describing education as "a principal instrument in awakening the child to cultural values . . . and in helping him adjust normally to his environment." Education prepared African Americans "for later professional training," and it was essential to success in life. The Court described education as so distinctive that when it overruled *Plessy* in *Brown*, it did so only "in the field of public education."[22]

In this way, education moved from litigation context to "the most important function of state and local governments." The effect was to

make African American children the focus of the Court's opinion in
Brown. These children became the central and iconic figures representing the casualties of legal segregation. Drawing on the graduate
education cases, the Court argued that considerations of intangible inequality applied "with added force to children in grade and high
schools." In that context, separation "generates a feeling of inferiority
as to their status in the community that may affect their hearts and
minds in a way unlikely ever to be undone." The victims of Jim Crow in
Brown were grade-school children, and the salient harms were to their
psychological well-being and their capacity for citizenship. As the *New
Republic* editorialized just after *Brown*, "Above the [political] tumult
will remain the children themselves."[23]

The emphasis on schools and schoolchildren is striking from the
perspective of pre-*Brown* civil rights practice. As an initial matter, black
support for desegregated primary education was fairly weak before
Brown, and white opposition to educational desegregation passionate
and unyielding. In contrast, African Americans felt more ardently and
whites less so about black economic advancement.[24]

In part, this stemmed from the centrality of labor to pre-*Brown* civil
rights. Between the end of the *Lochner* era in the 1930s and the eve of
Brown, the worker had been the central figure of American civil rights.
When the *Lochner* era disintegrated, legal commentators thought
workers, not racial groups, would be the next beneficiaries of Supreme
Court protection. Moreover, into the 1940s—when the rights of
African Americans joined those of workers as critical civil rights issues
on a national level—lawyers and commentators referred to laborers as
"weak and unpopular minorities" in the same terms as racial and religious groups.[25]

The black worker in particular came into his own with the start of
World War II. The rights of black workers drew support from both the
rights of white workers and the wartime economic imperative for total
mobilization. Discrimination against the black industrial worker had
been the focus of what Thurgood Marshall identified during World
War II as the most significant problem facing African Americans other
than being denied the right to vote. These workers suffered from the
"feeling[s] of inferiority" that afflicted schoolchildren. But more immediately, they suffered from depressed wages, inadequate work, unacceptable working conditions, segmented labor markets, and segre-

gated accommodations on the job. The central rights of the NAACP's 1940s labor cases, in contrast to the rights the lawyers purposefully isolated and highlighted in *Brown,* were those of the black worker to obtain a job and make a living.

In the Civil Rights Section's Thirteenth Amendment practice, black workers also dominated the stage. In the government's approach, however, the central figure, the prototypical litigant, was an African American agricultural or domestic rather than industrial worker. These workers were poor. They were usually physically, politically, economically, and psychologically isolated from the rest of the world. They enjoyed few of the benefits of modern American life. Their hopes for civil rights protection focused largely on escaping poverty and improving upon their limited opportunities for a livelihood. Recall Robert Hammond's complaint to the NAACP: "we live's in a free house such as it is, but you can't live in the free house with nothing to eat one half of the time and no shoes and cloth to wear in the winter."[26]

Because *Brown* concerned education, the labor-market context that had marked both complaints like Hammond's and the cases they generated in the 1940s was predictably absent in the Court's opinion. There could be no language about the fundamental right to work, the right to work as the right to live, or the centrality of work to American life. The fact that *Brown* was an education case accordingly reinforced the doctrinal and cultural imprint of *Plessy* on *Brown.* Without challenging work, the due process right to work disappeared as a readily available constitutional resource in the case. The obvious need to challenge private as well as public action dissipated. And material harms receded behind psychological ones. Although many of the schoolchildren who would benefit from *Brown* were poor and isolated, the NAACP ensured as a matter of litigation strategy that it was their psychological rather than their material well-being that concerned the Court in *Brown.* Their economic circumstances were beside the point.

Brown thus constructed a partial and particular image of Jim Crow—as a problem of state-mandated segregation causing psychological harms. It divorced the seventy-five-year-old caste system from its economic roots, from its material inequalities, from the farmworkers who complained about their immobility and the industrial workers who complained about their inability to make a living. Because the complaints of the workers—agricultural, domestic, and industrial—depicted Jim Crow as a system of both racial oppression and economic exploitation, so too did the cases lawyers had pursued in response. In cases on behalf of black workers, the Civil Rights Section and the NAACP's legal department took seriously both the economic and the racial aspects of workers' problems. They targeted material inequality and privation. They challenged the practices of private individuals, groups, and institutions as well as those of governments and state actors. And they used a variety of constitutional texts and statutory and administrative authorities to do so.

By the time *Brown* reached the Court, the NAACP had already bracketed material harms. The stigmatic understanding of state-imposed harm the Supreme Court embraced instead brought with it clear class implications. Working-class and poor African Americans no less than middle-class and elite African Americans suffered psychologically from Jim Crow. And middle-class and elite blacks suffered as well from stunted economic opportunities and inequalities. But the focus on both stigma and state action in *Brown* subordinated the material to the psychological. In doing so, it subordinated the problems most acute for working African Americans to those most acute for the more privileged of the race.

With banner headlines, newspapers announced the end of segregated education and the end of an era. The new era *Brown* initiated was one of upheaval and change, though not always in predictable directions. The Court's decision in *Brown* led to some desegregation of public schools, especially in border states that had already begun moving slowly toward desegregation before 1954. It led to scattered desegregation that affected rather small numbers of schoolchildren elsewhere in the South as well. *Brown* inspired hope among African Americans who had long resisted Jim Crow. And it galvanized Congress to pass the first national civil rights legislation since 1875. At the same time, *Brown* radicalized southern whites and led to massive and even violent resistance to the changes *Brown* itself had inaugurated.[27]

The era *Brown* ended was not only the era of judicially legitimated segregation. It was also the era of civil rights experimentation in the face of Jim Crow. As lawyers and legal academics implemented, expanded upon, and made sense of both what *Brown* effectuated and what it purposefully left undone and unsaid, they responded not only to the opinion itself but also to developments outside the Supreme Court. Together, the opinion in *Brown* and nonlegal historical developments made some constitutional arguments more culturally available than others. The Cold War—in both highlighting racial injustice for diplomatic purposes and narrowing domestic discourse by fostering anti-Communism—limited and structured how legal professionals understood *Brown*. So too did the larger world of domestic politics, especially as the southern hold on Congress loosened and national civil rights legislation supplemented constitutional change. And as lawyers increasingly came into contact with participants in the broader civil rights movement, the challenges that movement generated and the foundational symbols and myths it propagated affected the lawyers' work as well.

Within this larger context, *Brown* exerted a substantial gravitational pull. Its consequences for the future of civil rights practice and doctrine were both immediate and long term. When lawyers sought guidance about the best strategies for the continued development of civil rights law, they turned neither to *Lochner*-era holdovers nor to New Deal conceptions of rights. Instead, they drew on *Brown* as both a doctrinal and a cultural resource.

Within the Department of Justice itself, *Brown* magnified and institutionalized changes in the federal protection of civil rights that had been brewing since the late 1940s. When Attorney General Frank Murphy established the Civil Rights Section in 1939, it had been the sole locus of civil rights activity within the Department of Justice. The portfolio of the CRS was relatively open ended. The lawyers had considerable leeway to set their own civil rights agenda. Criminal prosecutions were the mainstay of their work and required approval only from the assistant attorney general for the Criminal Division and occasionally from the attorney general himself.

The lawyers supplemented their trial work with appeals and amicus curiae briefs in privately initiated civil rights cases. They viewed briefs from the government acting as a "friend of the court" as underscoring the importance of civil rights cases and signaling to the courts that federal executive will stood behind the rights claims of the private parties. Both appeals and amicus briefs required additional approval from the Justice Department's Office of the Solicitor General. That small, elite group of lawyers decided when the United States would appear in the Supreme Court and the federal appeals courts. The OSG sometimes rejected the amicus requests of the Civil Rights Section as too political or precedent setting. Beginning with the wartime peonage case of *Taylor v. Georgia,* however, it began to approve them. For the early years of the section's existence, then, the CRS's civil rights agenda dominated both its own criminal prosecutions and the Justice Department's interventions into civil rights cases initiated elsewhere.[28]

Two simultaneous developments in 1947 led the SG's office to take a new and sustained interest in civil rights cases that would eventually eclipse the CRS's approach to civil rights within the Justice Department. First, President Truman's Committee on Civil Rights published *To Secure These Rights.* This final report on the committee's work assessed the state of civil rights in the United States and recommended steps for the future. The report praised the efforts of the Civil Rights Section. It nonetheless lamented that without more potent legislative tools and greater resources, the CRS would not be able to address the wide range of civil rights violations the committee had identified. Due to the power of white southerners in Congress, the committee's recommendations for civil rights legislation seemed unlikely to succeed in the short term. Its calls for greater Justice Department civil rights activity fell on more sympathetic ears in the OSG. Philip Perlman, Truman's solicitor general and political advisor, saw greater involvement in civil rights cases as potentially valuable for the upcoming 1948 election. A higher profile in civil rights litigation promised to improve Truman's low opinion-poll ratings, the Democrats' appeal to critical black voters, and the bleak Democratic prospects for retaining the presidency.[29]

At the same time the report spurred Perlman and his lawyers to look for civil rights opportunities, Under Secretary of the Interior Oscar L. Chapman offered them one. Chapman was concerned about the effects of racially restrictive covenants on Native Americans. He suggested that the Justice Department take action in *Shelley v. Kraemer* and its companion cases then pending in the Supreme Court. Perlman was primed for the call: *To Secure These Rights* had specifically mentioned restrictive covenants as an area in which the Justice Department should intervene. Moreover, civil rights organizations like the NAACP, the ACLU, and the American Jewish Congress, among others, also urged federal action in those cases. The day after the committee's report was released, Perlman announced his intention to file an amicus brief in *Shelley*.[30]

Shelley was the turning point in the institutional geography of the DOJ's civil rights work. Although the CRS was involved in seeking input from other federal agencies, Philip Elman, an OSG lawyer with friends at the various civil rights organizations, took charge of writing the brief. Elman later described the victory in *Shelley* as putting the SG's office "in business looking for Supreme Court civil rights cases in which to intervene as amicus curiae." As the NAACP racked up high-profile legal victories in the late 1940s and early 1950s, the OSG not only allowed amicus briefs in civil rights cases to proceed but also saw them as part of its own agenda. The SG's office wrote and submitted amicus briefs in *Sweatt v. Painter* and *McLaurin v. Oklahoma*, the graduate education cases the NAACP litigated, and in *Henderson v. United States*, an NAACP case challenging segregated and unequal dining facilities on railroads.[31]

By the time *Brown* and its companion cases reached the Supreme Court for the first time in 1952, the SG's office had created a second locus of civil rights in the DOJ. The contours of that civil rights approximated the anti-*Plessy* agenda of the NAACP far more closely than it did the agenda of the CRS. It was not that the OSG and the NAACP agreed on every legal theory, every tactical move, in the civil rights cases they pursued. They most certainly did not. The OSG did not even limit itself to NAACP cases themselves. But as to the kinds of cases that warranted attention and the broad outlines of a litigation strategy for civil rights, the OSG took the NAACP's lead.[32]

By 1949, the CRS was no longer involved in either the decision to act as amicus curiae in civil rights cases or in the preparation of the amicus briefs themselves. Between 1949 and 1956, the CRS did not file a single amicus brief. The lawyers in the OSG, especially Elman and his colleague Robert Stern, had gained their own expertise in civil rights cases. They had their own ideas about which ones were worthy of pursuit.[33]

At the critical moment in the creation of modern civil rights, then, the OSG overtook the CRS as the definitive voice of the Department of Justice, and hence the executive branch, on questions of civil rights law. That remained largely constant even after Dwight Eisenhower's election to the presidency in 1952. Despite President Eisenhower's own misgivings about racial change, the Republican appointees to the DOJ who replaced Truman's Democrats largely accepted the civil rights agenda that had preceded them. The supplemental briefs they submitted after the Court requested reargument in *Brown* in 1953 opposed segregation more equivocally than had the Truman briefs. But at oral argument, Assistant Attorney General J. Lee Rankin made clear that the United States still backed the NAACP in opposing school segregation.[34]

The Supreme Court's vindication of the OSG's approach to civil rights in *Brown* amplified these changes in the civil rights practice of the DOJ. The lawyers in the Civil Rights Section still pursued involuntary servitude, police brutality, and lynching cases—cases combining the issues of race, labor, and economic security and protecting the safety and security of the person. Even so, those cases began to make way for a whole new litigation agenda. The question the lawyers asked themselves was no longer what the future of civil rights should look like. Rather, they began to ask what their place would be in the new regime the NAACP, the OSG, and the Supreme Court had set in motion.

The CRS lawyers embraced the new civil rights, though with some reluctance about letting go of the past. By the time the OSG took over the federal civil rights agenda from the CRS, the CRS's origins in the labor struggles of the 1930s had been largely lost to history everywhere but in the CRS itself. In the spring of 1954, as the OSG lawyers were awaiting the Supreme Court's decision in *Brown,* the lawyers in the CRS approached them for permission to file an appeal. In *United States v. Bailes,* a federal district court in West Virginia dismissed an indictment the CRS had procured in a labor rights case under the National Labor Relations Act (NLRA). The judge had concluded that the National Labor Relations Board (NLRB) had exclusive jurisdiction over violations of the NLRA. The dismissal undermined one of the CRS's foundational beliefs from the Harlan County case on—that it had jurisdiction to prosecute violations of labor rights. But when the CRS lawyers pushed the OSG vigorously for permission to appeal, the OSG declined the request. The OSG deemed the assertion of jurisdiction in labor cases a "broad expansion of federal criminal jurisdiction" that would deluge the Department with labor complaints. In response, the lawyers of the Civil Rights Section chided the OSG lawyers for being "wholly unaware of [the CRS's] repeated efforts to apply the civil rights statutes to rights secured by the Labor Act." When the solicitor general nonetheless refused to authorize the appeal, the CRS was forced to accept defeat.[35]

The CRS lawyers' commitment to protecting their historical vision of federal civil rights enforcement notwithstanding, the new, higher profile of civil rights reinvigorated the CRS's role within the department. As the CRS lawyers experimented with a number of ways to assist the NAACP and local black communities in post-*Brown* school desegregation efforts, they cooperated with lawyers in the DOJ's OSG, Civil Division, and Office of Legal Counsel. By 1956, the Civil Rights Section was once again submitting amicus briefs. Now, however, they were in school desegregation rather than peonage, labor, or police brutality cases. The implementation of desegregation dominated the civil rights agenda in the DOJ, and the questions were how aggressively and with what tools to pursue it.[36]

The answer to those questions changed considerably as a result of the passage of federal civil rights legislation after *Brown*. The Civil Rights Act of 1957 disappointed civil rights proponents, as it remained hampered by the continuing power of white southerners in Congress. In particular, the new law lacked authorization for the attorney general to sue for injunctive relief in civil rights cases. Even the voting rights protections that survived the House and Senate were greatly watered down.[37]

From the perspective of the CRS, however, the Civil Rights Act was revolutionary: It finally granted the attorney general authority to expand the seven or so lawyers of the Civil Rights Section into their own Civil Rights Division. The creation of the division institutionalized the changes *Brown* had initiated. The new division doubled in size in 1958 and again in 1959, bringing the number of lawyers from seven to twenty-eight in just two years. A few of the lawyers of the CRS continued the work of the section in other parts of the Justice Department. Henry Putzel migrated with the CRS's traditional interest in voting rights to head a new Voting and Elections Section. Maceo Hubbard, the only black lawyer, became chief of the new Due Process Unit (called the Constitutional Rights Unit after 1960). Hubbard and his lawyers continued to enforce the Reconstruction criminal statutes that had once provided the mainstay of the Justice Department's civil rights work. But their work was marginal within the Civil Rights Division, and responsibility for a number of labor statutes had been transferred elsewhere.[38]

Other former CRS lawyers scattered elsewhere in the division. A. B. Caldwell, who had served as chief of the CRS between 1952 and 1957, lost his status as chief and became an assistant to the assistant attorney general of the division. A lawyer with whom Caldwell had worked on a 1955 school desegregation case complained about Caldwell's fate. The lawyer had been impressed with Caldwell's work, and he worried that the government lawyer had been "shunted into virtual oblivion" in the new division.[39]

Rather than bolster the CRS's traditional activities, the division applied its increased funding and personnel to a new civil litigation agenda. That agenda seemed to take the rights of African Americans, to the exclusion of other groups the CRS had previously protected, like workers in general, as its core. The division increasingly focused on the racial segregation and discrimination claims that had occupied the lawyers in the NAACP and then the OSG. The proliferation of grassroots civil rights protests among African Americans in the early 1960s reinforced the new directions. Where in the past, the section had avoided racial discrimination and segregation cases, the new division, still with caution, embraced them.[40]

By 1964, in fact, the CRS's labor legacy had been so far submerged under the weight of *Brown* and subsequent developments that the Justice Department's Civil Rights Division was seen as an unlikely agent of aggressive enforcement of employment discrimination laws. The Civil Rights Act of 1964 finally prohibited as a legislative matter the kind of employment discrimination the NAACP lawyers had first attacked through litigation in the early 1940s. During congressional wrangling over the institutional location of the new prohibitions, civil rights activists pushed Congress to give authority to bring lawsuits to the newly created Equal Employment Opportunity Commission. Congress, however, decided to lodge that power instead in the Civil Rights Division. With the history of the CRS's long-standing commitment to protecting the rights of black workers forgotten behind *Brown*'s momentum, Congress thought DOJ would be less aggressive. In public memory at least, the DOJ had come far from its origins in a civil rights that targeted both economic and racial oppression, far from its role as pioneer in federal civil rights protection. It had become the place where laws against employment discrimination would rest in underenforced peace.[41]

Unsurprisingly, *Brown*'s victory proved somewhat less transformative for the NAACP than for the CRS. *Brown* served primarily to reinforce the decisions—both institutional and doctrinal—the NAACP lawyers had been making for some time. On an institutional level, *Brown* precipitated a further split between the NAACP and its lawyers that conclusively divorced the lawyers' legal agenda from the particular concerns of working-class African Americans. On a doctrinal level, it laid the groundwork for further inroads against state-enforced segregation.

Among the white South's responses to the NAACP's school desegregation campaign was an attack on the NAACP as an organization. Southerners and their governments charged the lawyers with ethical violations, passed statutes intended to hamper the lawyers' ability to bring cases, and instituted aggressive campaigns to shut down the NAACP's operations. As part of these attacks, and in response to pressure from southern congressmen, the Internal Revenue Service (IRS) began to take a close look at the relationship between the NAACP lawyers and the NAACP. The work of the lawyers, formally incorporated since 1939 in the NAACP Legal Defense and Educational Fund (the Inc. Fund), was tax-exempt. The NAACP's lobbying work was not. If the formal separation of the organizations masked the reality of a single, relatively integrated one, the Inc. Fund could lose its tax-exempt status. Indeed, even after the greater physical and programmatic separation in 1952, the boards of the two organizations had remained intertwined, and the lawyers had occasionally contributed financially to branches they represented in litigation.[42]

By 1956, the lawyers and the NAACP felt they needed to cut ties to a much greater extent to satisfy the IRS. Robert Carter, an NAACP lawyer with a more working-class perspective than his colleagues, had sometimes clashed with Thurgood Marshall. He moved to the NAACP as its general counsel. Marshall and the rest of the lawyers remained with the Inc. Fund. Although some connections remained, Marshall resigned as special counsel of the NAACP, and the Inc. Fund resolved that no one could be a member of both the NAACP and the Inc. Fund boards. The impetus for the split came from the IRS, but Marshall had sought just such independence for several years. He later recalled that the government had done the lawyers "a favor" by instigating the separation.[43]

The consequences for any future labor litigation agenda in the Inc. Fund were substantial. The membership of the NAACP, the lay African Americans who had grounded the litigation program of the lawyers at least somewhat, remained with the NAACP. This further attenuated the lawyers' ties with what Marshall called the "little Joes." Also with the NAACP went the labor department and its ferocious director since 1951, Herbert Hill. Hill and Clarence Mitchell, who had advanced to the head of the NAACP's Washington Bureau, continued their multi-pronged campaign for nondiscrimination in employment and unions. Carter sometimes assisted their efforts, bringing lawsuits and filing claims before the NLRB. As the NAACP and the Inc. Fund finally split, then, the last remnants of the 1940s labor litigation migrated away from the purely litigative work of the Inc. Fund to the coordinated negotiation, lobbying, and litigation efforts of the NAACP. Although employment discrimination was occasionally on the Inc. Fund's radar screen in the decade after *Brown*, its lawyers expended little energy litigating on behalf of black workers.[44]

On a doctrinal level as well as an institutional one, the victory in *Brown* fortified the lawyers' previous choices. Before the Inc. Fund and NAACP split in 1956, the NAACP and its lawyers together capitalized on *Brown* in the most obvious and necessary way: by trying to make *Brown*'s promise of school desegregation a reality. Days after the Supreme Court's first decision in *Brown*, the NAACP held a massive strategy conference in Atlanta. The NAACP mobilized and expanded local NAACP chapters. Both the lawyers and the nonlegal staff educated black communities about the benefits and risks of attempting desegregation. Despite the Court's failure to specify in *Brown* exactly what school boards had to do to comply with the decision, the NAACP set forth its own procedures for black communities across the South to begin the legal process of desegregation. Once local attempts at negotiation for desegregation failed, the lawyers assisted in the filing of lawsuits. These efforts continued after the Court's disappointing opinion in *Brown v. Board of Education II* required only that desegregation proceed "with all deliberate speed."[45]

At the same time, the lawyers followed and reinforced other central characteristics of *Brown*. In particular, the class implications of at least some of the Inc. Fund's cases came into sharper relief in the post-*Brown* years. Many of the cases—challenging segregated public transportation and beaches, for example—benefited African Americans across a wide, though still hardly complete, socio-economic spectrum. But the lawyers puzzled over why so many of their challenges to segregated golf courses originated with complaints from dentists, for example. The dentists, some of the lawyers surmised, sought status equivalent to doctors, and golf was a route to such status. Or perhaps, they thought, dentists just had enough free time for the pastime. Either way, the Inc. Fund pursued the cases. As Inc. Fund lawyer Jack Greenberg later summarized their reasons, "Dentists had rights too, any defeat of segregation contributed to its ultimate destruction, and last, but not least, these middle-class professionals were then the mainstay of the civil rights movement."[46]

More substantively, the cases the NAACP and the Inc. Fund pursued largely followed and reinforced *Brown*'s emphasis on the state's role in the perpetuation of Jim Crow. The NAACP's recreational facilities, public library, and public transportation cases successfully challenged government-enforced segregation. Although these new cases by definition extended beyond *Brown*'s emphasis on education, they remained within the equal-protection-based, antisegregation, traditional state action parameters of *Brown*.[47]

The ability to reach beyond state action was a secondary goal, less theorized and less coordinated than the first. The Inc. Fund occasionally challenged segregation where state action was uncertain. Shortly after *Brown*, the lawyers challenged the segregation of a Louisville, Kentucky, amphitheater that had been leased by the city to a private party. When the Court remanded the case "for consideration in the light of the Segregation Cases . . . and conditions that now prevail," it suggested that the Court, like the NAACP, viewed *Brown* as perhaps effecting a broader understanding of state action. In a subsequent case challenging segregation in a restaurant leased from the city of Wilmington, Delaware, the Inc. Fund's Louis Redding again succeeded in convincing the Court to strike down segregation where it resulted from something less than a direct command from government.[48]

Indeed, when Greenberg wrote about the state of the law concerning race relations in 1959, he considered the state action problem at some length. He thought there was a need for greater clarity about the state action requirement and predicted "considerable activity" on the question. Still, he gave no indication that such activity was high on the agenda of the Inc. Fund. Rather than take any ownership of the issue, he found it "impossible to predict what will move people to file suits, the manner in which cases will be handled, and what encouragement will be offered by the course of decision."[49]

When the lawyers forayed into the question of state action in the early 1960s, their efforts were largely reactive rather than proactive. Responding to the student sit-ins and widespread protests of the new decade, the Inc. Fund coordinated the defenses of those arrested and provided many with counsel. Although these cases often turned on whether the quashing of demonstrations involved the requisite level of state action, the protestors and local prosecutors set the agenda. The Inc. Fund lawyers accordingly found it difficult to build and follow the kind of coherent litigation campaign they had mounted in the school segregation cases.[50]

Where the lawyers could control their agenda in the 1960s, they did so largely by expanding other parameters set by *Brown*. The lawyers continued to bring school desegregation cases, as well as cases challenging segregation in other areas, like hospitals and public accommodations. Sometimes these required creative state action arguments. For the most part, however, the lawyers began to challenge not only state-enforced segregation but also state-created racial classifications of all kinds. In 1964's *McLaughlin v. Florida*, for example, the lawyers challenged prohibitions on, and criminal penalties for, interracial cohabitation. They argued that "race is constitutionally an irrelevance" and cited *Hirabayashi v. United States* and *Korematsu v. United States*. The Court struck down the law. It viewed the case "in light of the historical fact that the central purpose of the Fourteenth Amendment was to eliminate racial discrimination emanating from official sources in the States." Fully twenty years after the Court's decisions in *Hirabayashi* and *Korematsu*, the Court embraced its own suggestion that racial classifications be subject to the "most rigid scrutiny."[51]

A few years later, in *Loving v. Virginia*, the Inc. Fund lawyers challenged a statute prohibiting interracial marriage. Again, the NAACP cited *Korematsu*. Again, the Court struck down the statute, finding it to "rest solely upon distinctions drawn according to race." It quoted *Korematsu* and *Hirabayashi* and concluded that racial classifications had long been considered " 'odious to a free people' " and subject "to the 'most rigid scrutiny.' " In both cases, the Inc. Fund moved from arguing the principle that the equal protection clause prohibited segregation to arguing that all racial classifications were at least suspect under the Constitution. The Court agreed.[52]

In the decade after *Brown,* then, undermining the constitutionality of state racial classifications was the Inc. Fund's main goal, and the growing civil rights movement itself essentially constituted its new constituency. The lawyers continued to allot little time to the kinds of work-related cases they had pursued in the 1940s. Only after passage of the Civil Rights Act of 1964 prohibited race discrimination in employment did the Inc. Fund reenter the realm of work and economic inequality. Together with the NAACP, the Inc. Fund lawyers once again capitalized on national momentum and new statutory tools for work-related civil rights. It was after that point, recalled Greenberg, that it "became apparent that black poverty was inextricably wound up" with what he considered "classic civil rights issues."[53]

Brown's impact on the law reverberated past the bar itself and into the legal academy. As *Brown* came under attack both within and without the academy, legal scholars spent considerable effort analyzing and justifying the Court's decision in the case. As is their wont, such scholars not only commented on but refined and systematized the emerging legal doctrine. In so doing, they reinforced the aspects of *Brown* most at odds with the labor-infused civil rights of the 1940s and the complex understanding of Jim Crow it reflected.

By the time scholars began responding seriously to *Brown,* the Court—largely in response to the NAACP's follow-up litigation—had given a few additional hints about the meaning and scope of its purposefully vague and incomplete opinion in *Brown.* It appeared that, much as the Court had emphasized education, the new civil rights doctrine actually eschewed all state-enforced segregation. With critics already skeptical about *Brown*'s doctrinal footing, the Court's unexplained extension of *Brown* added to their doubts. In 1959, legal scholar Herbert Wechsler published an influential article called "Neutral Principles." He was unable to find such principles to justify *Brown.* Wechsler likened the judicial activism he saw in *Brown* to that practiced by the reviled *Lochner* Court.[54]

Wechsler hit a raw nerve among liberal legal scholars who supported both the New Deal and racial equality. During the 1940s, the Civil Rights Section's and the NAACP's labor cases had linked the New Deal and racial equality by addressing the rights of African Americans as in some ways an extension of New Deal protections for labor and economic rights. *Brown* itself largely eclipsed that possibility as a historical if not an analytical matter. Instead, scholars felt they had to find other ways to defend *Brown* and distinguish it from *Lochner.* Louis Pollack, one such scholar, turned to *Carolene Products'* footnote four to provide *Brown* with a more secure doctrinal pedigree and constitutional rule than the Court had given it. *Carolene Products* suggested that the courts scrutinize government action involving "discrete and insular minorities" more stringently than other action, especially that involving economic regulation. The invocation of *Carolene Products* echoed the Court's citation of *Hirabayashi* and *Korematsu* in the Washington, D.C., school segregation case of *Bolling v. Sharpe.* And it presaged the Court's similar citations in *McLaughlin* and *Loving.* Race was different, Pollock argued, and it justified a different level of judicial scrutiny.[55]

Pollock's theory, eventually embraced by the Court, the bar, and the legal academy, finally interred any linkage of economic and labor rights with racial rights. The reemergence of *Carolene Products* doctrinally separated economics from race and justified judicial interference with the latter but not the former. Substantive due process—striking down economic legislation—was problematic. *Carolene Products'* protection of racial minorities—striking down racial segregation and classification—was not. Although the Court had articulated the basis for treating race differently as early as 1938, it did not actually establish such a rule until *McLaughlin* in 1964. It was not until after *Brown* that the legal academy saw the jurisprudential advantages of such bifurcated constitutional review.

More generally, academic treatments of civil rights and constitutional law winnowed out the diversity of approaches that had characterized the pre-*Brown* years. Before and just after *Brown,* treatises and casebooks reflected considerable variety in both the subjects they included within the field of civil rights and the way they analyzed those subjects. Legal scholars treated "civil rights" as encompassing issues like involuntary servitude and labor rights as much as racial segregation; they saw rights as falling into categories like "the security of the person" as much as "discrimination"; and they described the vindication of civil rights as an affirmative responsibility of government as much as the responsibility of private litigants.

As scholars began a gradual but unmistakable process of filtering out many of these subjects and schematic approaches, they drew not only on *Brown* itself. Over the decade that followed *Brown,* subsequent cases (many brought by the Inc. Fund), the rise of the civil rights movement, and legislative developments all contributed to the transformation. To an extent, these developments reinvigorated some aspects of pre-*Brown* civil rights. The pivotal civil rights protest of 1963 was called the March on Washington for Jobs and Freedom. The Johnson administration's War on Poverty tried to attack economic deprivation in part out of a recognition of the continuing connection between racial and economic inequality. And Title VII of the 1964 Civil Rights Act legislatively prohibited discrimination in the private labor market and labor unions as well as among state actors themselves.

Even so, these developments often reinforced, rather than undermined, the image of Jim Crow and racial harm that *Brown* depicted. Media representations of the 1963 March on Washington largely forsook the protest's economic emphasis for Martin Luther King, Jr.'s, focus on formal color-blindness—in which people would "not be judged by the color of their skin but by the content of their character." The War on Poverty took as its mission the redress of economic inequality not for its own sake but rather as a cause of the psychological alienation that underlay rising racial violence across the nation. And Title VII prohibited "discrimination on the basis of race" in the same terms as it prohibited discrimination in education and public accommodations. The law addressed work-related inequality as simply an ordinary manifestation of the general problem of race discrimination. Title VII, like *Brown* itself, submerged the substantive right to work that had been a hallmark of the pre-*Brown* years for the antidiscrimination paradigm that was a hallmark of the post-*Brown* era.[56]

Moreover, these and other developments remained largely separate from constitutional law itself. Title VII was not constitutionally mandated. The *Civil Rights Cases,* with their state action requirement, remained good constitutional precedent. And attempts to translate legislative and social movement momentum for protection of the poor into constitutional guarantees ultimately failed.

As legal scholars increasingly converged on a general framework for making sense of the constitutional law of civil rights, then, that framework was predominantly the one *Brown* had set into motion in 1954. This is apparent in changes in succeeding editions of civil rights and constitutional law casebooks and treatises. In their seminal 1952 treatise, for example, Thomas Emerson and David Haber's first chapter was entitled "The Right to the Security of the Person." It discussed the lynching, police brutality, involuntary servitude, and other cases that made up the mainstay of the CRS's 1940s civil rights practice. Where the first chapter of the treatise covered harms in that category, the final chapter discussed "discrimination." The two separate chapters not only covered different types of civil rights, they also revealed the multiple forms of civil rights practice in the pre-*Brown* era. The chapter on discrimination featured privately litigated cases, often brought by the NAACP, against mostly government actors. By contrast, "The Right to the Security of the Person" focused on the increasing power of the federal government affirmatively to protect Americans from civil rights violations. Each approach to civil rights had its own place, its own arena in the 1952 edition. Moreover, even within the chapter on discrimination, no single area of law dominated. Emerson and Haber divided the discussion into housing; a combined grouping of "Education, Transportation, and Public Accommodations"; and employment. Education and employment filled around the same number of pages (37 and 33, respectively) out of the 180 on discrimination.[57]

By the second edition in 1958, *Brown*-induced changes were apparent. As a result of legal developments relating to civil rights coming "thick and fast," Emerson and Haber doubled in size and expanded to two volumes. Significantly, discussion of the school segregation cases and resistance to them received their own new sections. They constituted almost 100 pages of the now 290 devoted to discrimination. Employment increased only to 61 pages. By the third edition, in 1967, the changes were even more dramatic. Although the authors retained a section on the security of the person, they subsumed it under the larger heading "Discrimination," which filled the entire second volume. The security of the person no longer offered an independent approach to civil rights.[58]

Milton Konvitz, a former NAACP lawyer and professor at Cornell's School of Industrial and Labor Relations, also modified his *Bill of*

Rights Reader to reflect the emerging post-*Brown* scholarly synthesis. In both the 1954 and 1960 editions, Konvitz reflected the pre-*Brown* tendency to consider labor rights civil rights. He included independent sections titled "Freedom from Race Discrimination" and "Freedom of Labor." The first issue in "Freedom of Labor" was peonage, and the main case was *Pollock v. Williams.* Even within the chapter on discrimination, *Brown* did not initially make its weight felt. Education was represented only by *Brown,* just as the sections on "Equality of Job Opportunities," "Equality in Interstate Transportation," and property issues each received only one or two cases. By 1965, however, "Freedom of Labor" had been eliminated altogether, and six education cases dwarfed the other categories within the regnant chapter titled "Freedom from Race Discrimination."[59]

The popular constitutional law casebook of Paul G. Kauper, a University of Michigan law professor, was slower to change, but change it did and in the same direction. Both the 1954 and the 1960 editions included a chapter titled "Substantive Rights: Freedom of the Person" that began, like Konvitz's "Freedom of Labor" chapter, with the main case of *Pollock v. Williams.* Kauper included multiple chapters on the various "substantive" due process rights of property ownership, business enterprise, and vested interests. And he included a separate final chapter titled "Freedom from Discrimination" that included *Brown* and other race-based equal protection cases. Among them was the labor-related case of *Takahashi v. Fish and Game Commission.*[60]

In the third and fourth editions in 1966 and 1972, Kauper filtered out these heterogeneous understandings of civil rights. By the third edition, he omitted *Pollock* as a main case and discussed involuntary servitude only in a note in "Substantive Rights: Freedom of the Person." By the fourth edition, he eliminated the chapter on freedom of the person altogether. Kauper excluded any significant discussion of the labor case of *Takahashi* as well. He also consolidated the many chapters on substantive due process into a single chapter and moved them to the end of the book. Perhaps most significantly, Kauper edited his main, introductory chapter on due process and equal protection subtitled "Some General Considerations." He included there for the first time the race-based equal protection cases that had previously occupied their own chapter. By 1972, they had become the definitive individual rights cases, as opposed to one subset of the subject.[61]

The changes in these three casebooks were representative of the field. Treatise and casebook authors eliminated sections on the freedom of the person; they condensed or eliminated discussions of *Pollock v. Williams* and involuntary servitude; and they eliminated chapters on freedom of labor altogether. Work-related civil rights were largely reduced to the question of job discrimination under the equal protection clause, akin to discrimination in other arenas. As early as 1959, Greenberg could describe peonage as "outside the main channels of job discrimination" in contrast to "discrimination in government employment," which was "[s]quarely in these channels." Moreover, although the Supreme Court had largely undermined substantive due process by the late 1930s, casebooks did not lessen their attention to the category until after *Brown* had made the equal protection clause the obvious new constitutional provision of choice. One typical casebook renamed its "Substantive Due Process" chapter "Economic Affairs—Power to Regulate." As "discrimination," "equal protection," and "equal opportunity" came to dominate scholarly conceptions of civil rights, cultural space for and conceptual clarity about substantive due process began to shrink.[62]

As scholars winnowed out the varieties of pre-*Brown* civil rights, they converged on a race-based, privately litigated, equal-protection-oriented civil rights framework that *Brown* had inaugurated. It was not until the post-*Brown* years privileged a race-focused equal protection clause, and contrasted stringent judicial review of government actions affecting racial minorities with deferential review of actions affecting the economy, that race and labor truly diverged in constitutional law. It was not until then that constitutionally grounded civil rights became squarely rights against the government, in contrast to both rights against private power and rights protected by the government. It was not until then that it would become clear how partial the victory in *Brown* was and how much of Jim Crow would remain intact in the face of the new civil rights *Brown* had helped construct.[63]

These developments were still largely immanent and unformed in the days just after the Supreme Court decided *Brown* in May of 1954. *Brown* represented the culmination of years of hard work by the NAACP lawyers and a tremendous victory for both those lawyers and African Americans generally. The constitutional energy it unleashed served as the driving force for a major revolution in civil rights doctrine. Absent from that new energy, however, was the legacy of the labor-related civil rights practices of the 1940s: the African-American worker, the rights of labor more broadly understood, and the use of constitutional texts other than the equal protection clause—like the Thirteenth Amendment and the due process clause—as foundational resources for promoting civil rights.

The disappearance of the African American worker as a relevant legal character, work as a relevant doctrinal category, and the 1940s labor practices of the CRS and the NAACP as relevant historical resources for constitutional civil rights has had major ramifications. At least in part because of the decisions described in this book, our imagination of the civil rights plaintiff, the civil rights complaint, and the scope of constitutional civil rights protections is significantly different today. We take for granted, fifty years after *Brown,* that the crux of legally cognizable racism in the United States is the psychological, stigmatic, and symbolic injury of state-sanctioned racial classification.

That abstracted notion of harm might well have looked odd from the perspective of the poor and the working-class African Americans who complained to the CRS and the NAACP about the problems they endured living and working in Jim Crow America. To them, Jim Crow was a system of both racial hierarchy and economic oppression. Although workers would, and did, benefit from the decision in *Brown* and those that followed, those benefits did not reach all of the harms black workers faced under Jim Crow. Even after both legislative and doctrinal developments after *Brown* went some distance toward treating work as an appropriate site for government intervention and civil rights advancement, the constitutional framework largely remained the one created in *Brown.* That framework left the material, private-labor-market side of Jim Crow not only unredressed but also unaddressed. Without recognizing both the formal and the informal, the legal and the customary, the public and the private aspects of Jim Crow, constitutional law was unlikely effectively to undermine the entirety of the harms black workers experienced.

To be sure, the *Brown* decision did not by itself cause the narrowing of constitutional discourse. That narrowing is also a product of how judges, lawyers, constitutional theorists, historians, and laypersons think about *Brown.* The myth that ours is a negative constitution, committed to protecting rights against, rather than rights protected by, the government, remains vibrant in part because we have erased the affirmative protections the CRS sought to implement in the 1940s. And the myth that a race-oriented, equal-protection-based civil rights immediately replaced *Lochner*ism flourishes because it ignores the alternative frameworks with which both the CRS and the NAACP experimented before *Brown*.

These myths limit our imaginations—lay and professional, scholarly, lawyerly, and judicial—about the possibilities for constitutional redress of material inequalities. They are a product of the canonization of a *Brown*-inspired, race-based understanding of civil rights that has served to mask alternatives that black working-class clients and their lawyers once proposed. This book serves as a reminder of what *Brown* has erased. It opens up the future of constitutional understandings of civil rights by revealing the contingencies in their pasts.

Notes

Acknowledgments

Index

Notes

273

NAACP Papers   *Papers of the NAACP,* ed. August Meier (Frederick, Md., 1982), microfilm

Introduction

1. Corwin Johnson, FBI Report, Memphis, Tenn., July 27, 1942, 2, file 50–18–15, RG 60, National Archives (hereafter cited as DOJ Files). U.S. Employment Service, flyer advertising United States Sugar Corporation employment, DOJ Files, 50–18–15. James H. Morrow, Jr., FBI Report, Birmingham, Ala., Nov. 20, 1942, 4, 5, DOJ Files, 50–18–15.
2. Ousley Perkins to J. Edgar Hoover, Feb. 16, 1942, DOJ Files, 50–18–15.
3. Johnson, FBI Report, Memphis, Tenn., July 27, 1942, 5 (statement of James Moffett), 17 (statement of Harvey Lee Branner), DOJ Files, 50–18–15; John E. Keane, FBI Report, Memphis, Tenn., Mar. 11, 1942, 11 (statement of Vernon Lawhorn), DOJ Files, 50–18–15. See John L. Glasser, FBI Report, Birmingham, Ala., June 23, 1942, 5 (statement of Johnnie Grey), DOJ Files, 50–18–15; Corwin Johnson, FBI Report, Memphis, Tenn., July 27, 1942, 17, DOJ Files, 50–18–15; William Gerard Bedell, FBI Report, Birmingham, Ala., May 8, 1943, 6 (statement of Ollie Rogers, Jr.), DOJ Files, 50–18–15.
4. Letter from Robert S. Glasgow, Jr., Mar. 4, 1942, DOJ Files, 50–18–15.
5. Herbert R. Northrup, "An Analysis of the Discriminations against Negroes in the Boiler Makers Union" [Draft Brief] at 2, Hill v. Int'l Bhd. of Boilermakers (R.I. Super. Ct. filed Dec. 16, 1943), file 6–7333 of 18-BU-COS-WP, in *Papers of the NAACP,* ed. August Meier (Frederick, Md., 1982), microfilm, pt. 13C, rl. 2:23–40, 24 (hereafter cited as *NAACP Papers*). NAACP, "NAACP Aids Coast Shipyard Workers," news release, Dec. 3, 1943, in *NAACP Papers,* pt. 13C, rl. 1:42.
6. Direct Examination of Sidney Wolf at 201, In re Or. Shipbuilding Corp. (F.E.P.C. Portland, Ore., Nov. 15–16, 1943), in *Selected Documents from Records of the Committee on Fair Employment Practice: RG 228, National Archives,* ed. Bruce Friend (Glen Rock, N.J., 1971), microfilm, rl. 13. See NAACP, "War Production Board: Labor Division," news release, Jan. 24, 1942, in *NAACP Papers,* pt. 13C, rl. 1:27.
7. The canonical article is Robert Korstad and Nelson Lichtenstein, "Opportunities Found and Lost: Labor, Radicals, and the Early Civil Rights Movement," *Journal of American History* 75 (1988): 786–811. For additional contributions to the literature, see Chapter 1, note 48.
8. Brown v. Board of Education, 347 U.S. 483 (1954). See, for example, Richard Kluger, *Simple Justice: The History of* Brown v. Board of Education *and Black America's Struggle for Equality* (New York, 1977); James T.

Patterson, Brown v. Board of Education: *A Civil Rights Milestone and Its Troubled Legacy* (New York, 2001); Mark V. Tushnet, *The NAACP's Legal Strategy against Segregated Education, 1925–1950* (Chapel Hill, N.C., 1987); Mark V. Tushnet, *Making Civil Rights Law: Thurgood Marshall and the Supreme Court, 1936–1961* (New York, 1994); Peter H. Irons, *Jim Crow's Children* (New York, 2002); Michael Klarman, *From Jim Crow to Civil Rights: The Supreme Court and the Struggle for Racial Equality* (New York, 2004); Derrick Bell, *Silent Covenants:* Brown v. Board of Education *and the Unfulfilled Hopes for Racial Reform* (New York, 2004); Gerald Rosenberg, *The Hollow Hope: Can Courts Bring About Social Change?* (Chicago, 1991); J. Harvie Wilkinson, *From* Brown *to* Bakke: *The Supreme Court and School Integration, 1954–1978* (New York, 1979); John Howard, *The Shifting Wind: The Supreme Court and Civil Rights from Reconstruction to* Brown (Albany, N.Y., 1999); David Armor, *Forced Justice: School Desegregation and the Law* (New York, 1995); Jack Greenberg, *Crusaders in the Courts: How a Dedicated Band of Lawyers Fought for the Civil Rights Revolution* (New York, 1994); Andrew Kull, *The Color-Blind Constitution* (Cambridge, Mass., 1992); Constance Baker Motley, *Equal Justice . . . under Law: An Autobiography* (New York, 1998); Jennifer Hochschild, *The New American Dilemma: Liberal Democracy and School Desegregation* (New Haven, Conn., 1984). For new narratives on civil rights before *Brown,* see, for example, Kenneth Walter Mack, "Race Uplift, Professional Identity and the Transformation of Civil Rights Lawyering and Politics, 1920–1940" (Ph.D. diss., Princeton University, 2005); Tomiko Brown Nagin, "Black Ambivalence about Legal Liberalism: A Pragmatically Conservative Path to Civil Rights, Atlanta, 1895–1979" (manuscript, University of Virginia Law School, n.d.); Wendell E. Pritchett, "A National Issue: Segregation in the District of Columbia and the Civil Rights Movement at Mid-Century," *Georgetown Law Journal* 93 (2005): 1321–1333; Wendell E. Pritchett, "Working along the Color Line: The Life and Times of Robert Weaver" (manuscript, University of Pennsylvania Law School, n.d.).

9. An extensive literature addresses the relationship between litigants, lawyers, and legal change. See, for example, Michael W. McCann, *Rights at Work: Pay Equity Reform and the Politics of Legal Mobilization* (Chicago, 1994); Barbara Yngvesson, *Virtuous Citizens, Disruptive Subjects: Order and Complaint in a New England Court* (New York, 1993); Hendrik Hartog, "The Constitution of Aspiration and 'The Rights That Belong to Us All,' " in *The Constitution and American Life,* ed. David Thelen (Ithaca, N.Y., 1988), 353–374; Patricia Ewick and Susan S. Silbey, *The Common Place of Law: Stories from Everyday Life* (Chicago, 1998). On the

relationship between lawyers, judges, and laypeople in constitutional law specifically, see Larry D. Kramer, *The People Themselves: Popular Constitutionalism and Judicial Review* (New York, 2005); Robert Post and Reva Siegel, "Popular Constitutionalism, Departmentalism, and Judicial Supremacy," *California Law Review* 92 (2004): 1027–1043. Regarding the power of stories in the law generally, and of victims' stories in particular, see Carol J. Greenhouse, "Citizenship, Agency, and the Dream of Time," in *Looking Back at Law's Century,* ed. Austin Sarat, Bryant Garth, and Robert A. Kagan (Ithaca, N.Y., 2002), 184–209, 196; Richard Delgado, "Storytelling for Oppositionists and Others: A Plea for Narrative," *Michigan Law Review* 87 (1989): 2411–2441; Austin D. Sarat and William L. F. Felstiner, *Divorce Lawyers and Their Clients: Power and Meaning in the Legal Process* (New York, 1995); Kim Lane Scheppele, "Foreword: Telling Stories," *Michigan Law Review* 87 (1989): 2073–2098; Vicki Schultz, "Telling Stories about Women and Work: Judicial Interpretations of Sex Segregation in the Workplace in Title VII Cases Raising the Lack of Interest Argument," *Harvard Law Review* 103 (1990): 1749–1843.

10. In viewing Jim Crow as both a racial and an economic system, I draw on Robert Rodgers Korstad, *Civil Rights Unionism: Tobacco Workers and the Struggle for Democracy in the Mid-Twentieth-Century South* (Chapel Hill, N.C., 2003); Eric Arnesen, *Brotherhoods of Color: Black Railroad Workers and the Struggle for Equality* (Cambridge, Mass., 2001); Thomas J. Sugrue, "Affirmative Action from Below: Civil Rights, the Building Trades, and the Politics of Racial Equality in the Urban North, 1945–1969," *Journal of American History* 91 (2004): 145–173.

11. Civil Rights Cases, 109 U.S. 3 (1883); Plessy v. Ferguson, 163 U.S. 537 (1896).

12. Lochner v. New York, 198 U.S. 45 (1905). See Eric Foner, *Free Soil, Free Labor, Free Men: The Ideology of the Republican Party before the Civil War* (New York, 1970), 11–51; Civil Rights Act of 1866, ch. 31, 14 Stat. 27 (1866). For the argument that African Americans benefited from the Court's protection of contract and property rights, see David E. Bernstein, *Only One Place of Redress* (Durham, N.C., 2001).

13. See, for example, Barry Cushman, *Rethinking the New Deal Court: The Structure of a Constitutional Revolution* (New York, 1998).

14. On struggles between legal professionals over constitutional interpretation, cf. Pierre Bourdieu, "The Force of Law: Toward a Sociology of the Juridical Field," *Hastings Law Journal* 38 (1987): 805–853.

15. I am not claiming here that any particular argument became analyti-

cally unavailable. As an analytical matter, a variety of arguments is always available. See, for example, Duncan Kennedy, "The Structure of Blackstone's Commentaries," *Buffalo Law Review* 28 (1979): 205–382; Mark Kelman, *A Guide to Critical Legal Studies* (Cambridge, Mass., 1987). Rather, I am suggesting that historically, some arguments are more culturally available in a particular time and place. See, for example, Morton J. Horwitz, *The Transformation of American Law, 1870–1960: The Crisis of Legal Orthodoxy* (Oxford, 1992).

16. Thurgood Marshall, address, annual meeting of the NAACP, Jan. 3, 1956, in *NAACP Papers*, pt. 1, supp. 1956–1960, rl. 1:508.

1. Transition, Uncertainty, and the Conditions for a New Civil Rights

1. "Civil Liberties—A Field of Law," *Bill of Rights Review* 1 (1940): 7–8, 7.
2. Lea S. VanderVelde, "The Labor Vision of the Thirteenth Amendment," *University of Pennsylvania Law Review* 138 (1989): 437–504, 473–474 (quoting Representative John A. Bingham); Godlove S. Orth, Cong. Globe, 38th Cong., 2d Sess., pt. 1, 142–143 and William D. Kelley, Cong. Globe, 38th Cong., 1st Sess. 2987, quoted in Jacobus ten-Broek, "Thirteenth Amendment to the Constitution of the United States: Consummation to Abolition and Key to the Fourteenth Amendment," *California Law Review* 39 (June 1951): 171–203, 178. See generally Michael Vorenberg, *Final Freedom: The Civil War, the Abolition of Slavery, and the Thirteenth Amendment* (New York, 2001).
3. Slaughter-House Cases, 83 U.S. 36, 69 (1873) (emphasis added).
4. Robert J. Kaczorowski, *The Politics of Judicial Interpretation: The Federal Courts, Department of Justice, and Civil Rights, 1866–1876* (New York, 2005), 158–159; Civil Rights Cases 109 U.S. 3, 24 (1883). See also *Ex parte* Virginia, 100 U.S. 339, 346–347 (1879); Civil Rights Act of 1875, ch. 114, 18 Stat. 335.
5. Hodges v. United States, 203 U.S. 1, 16 (1906); United States v. Cruikshank, 25 F. Cas. 707, 712 (C.C.D. La. 1874), aff'd, 92 U.S. 542 (1876).
6. 203 U.S. at 16.
7. 109 U.S. at 11, 17.
8. Plessy v. Ferguson, 163 U.S. 537 (1896). See Michael J. Klarman, *From Jim Crow to Civil Rights: The Supreme Court and the Struggle for Racial Equality* (Oxford, 2004), 17–60.
9. Cruikshank, 92 U.S. 542; United States v. Reese, 92 U.S. 214 (1876). See also Williams v. Mississippi, 170 U.S. 213 (1898); Giles v. Harris, 189 U.S. 475, 488 (1903).
10. U.S. Const. amends. XIV, §1, V; Lochner v. New York, 198 U.S. 45

(1905). On antebellum free labor ideology, see, for example, Eric
Foner, *Free Soil, Free Labor, Free Men: The Ideology of the Republican Party Before the Civil War* (New York, 1970), 11–51. The term "substantive due
process" was not used during the *Lochner* era itself. After the New Deal
Revolution, it was used derogatively. To the extent possible, I mean to
use the term in its "analytical" capacity and do not mean to adopt the
"normative jurisprudential" connotation. G. Edward White, *The Constitution and the New Deal* (Cambridge, Mass., 2000), 243–245. For
different views on the *Lochner* era, compare John Hart Ely, *Democracy
and Distrust: A Theory of Judicial Review* (Cambridge, Mass., 1980);
Arnold M. Paul, *Conservative Crisis and the Rule of Law: Attitudes of Bar
and Bench, 1887–1895* (Ithaca, N.Y., 1960) with Owen Fiss, *Troubled Be-
ginnings of the Modern State, 1888–1910* (New York, 1993); Howard
Gillman, *The Constitution Besieged: The Rise and Demise of Lochner Era Police Powers Jurisprudence* (Durham, N.C., 1993); Morton J. Horwitz, *The
Transformation of American Law, 1870–1960: The Crisis of Legal Orthodoxy*
(New York, 1992), 3–230; Michael Les Benedict, "Laissez-Faire and Liberty: A Reevaluation of the Meaning and Origins of Laissez-Faire Constitutionalism," *Law and History Review* 3 (1985): 293–331. On the debate itself, see Gary D. Rowe, "*Lochner* Revisionism Revisited," *Law and
Social Inquiry* 24 (1999): 221–252. For two very different middle positions, see Charles W. McCurdy, "The 'Liberty of Contract' Regime in
American Law," in *The State and Freedom of Contract*, ed. Harry N.
Scheiber (Stanford, Calif., 1998), 161–197; David E. Bernstein,
"*Lochner* Era Revisionism Revised: *Lochner* and the Origins of Fundamental Rights Constitutionalism," *Georgetown Law Journal* 92 (2003): 1–
60. See, for example, Adkins v. Children's Hospital, 261 U.S. 525
(1923).

11. Charles Wallace Collins, *The Fourteenth Amendment and the States: A Study
of the Operation of the Restraint Clauses of Section One of the Fourteenth
Amendment to the Constitution of the United States* (Boston, 1912), 46–47,
68, 145–146. See also Brook Thomas, ed., *Plessy v. Ferguson: A Brief History with Documents* (Boston, 1997), 21. The early cases on freedom of
speech include Stromberg v. California, 283 U.S. 359 (1931); Near v.
Minnesota, 283 U.S. 697 (1931); Fiske v. Kansas, 274 U.S. 380 (1927).
Early family-related cases include Meyer v. Nebraska, 262 U.S. 390
(1923); Pierce v. Society of Sisters, 268 U.S. 510 (1925). Period cases
protecting the procedural due process rights of criminal defendants include Brown v. Mississippi, 297 U.S. 278 (1936); Norris v. Alabama, 294
U.S. 587 (1935); Powell v. Alabama, 287 U.S. 45 (1932); Aldridge v.
United States, 283 U.S. 308 (1931); Moore v. Dempsey, 261 U.S. 86

(1923). The Court also sporadically protected the voting rights of African Americans. See, for example, Nixon v. Condon, 286 U.S. 73 (1932); Nixon v. Herndon, 273 U.S. 536 (1927); Guinn v. United States, 238 U.S. 347 (1915). But see Grovey v. Townsend, 295 U.S. 45 (1935).

12. Buchanan v. Warley, 245 U.S. 60, 76 (1917). See, for example, "Recent Decisions: Constitutional Law—Equal Protection—Refusal to Admit Negro to State Law School," *Fordham Law Review* 8 (1939): 260–263; Morroe Berger, *Equality by Statute: Legal Controls over Group Discrimination* (New York, 1952), 60.

13. National Labor Relations Act, ch. 372, 49 Stat. 449 (1935) (codified as amended at 29 U.S.C. §§151–169 [2000]); Fair Labor Standards Act, ch. 676, 52 Stat. 1060 (1938) (codified as amended at 29 U.S.C. §§201–219 [2000 & Supp. II 2002]); Social Security Act, ch. 531, 49 Stat. 620 (1935) (codified as amended at 42 U.S.C. §§301–1397jj [2000 & Supp. II 2002]); Wickard v. Filburn, 317 U.S. 111, 120 (1942); Steward Mach. Co. v. Davis, 301 U.S. 548, 578–598 (1937); NLRB v. Jones & Laughlin Steel Corp., 301 U.S. 1, 49 (1937); W. Coast Hotel Co. v. Parrish, 300 U.S. 379, 398–400 (1937). Robert E. Cushman, "Constitutional Law in 1938–1939: The Constitutional Decisions of the Supreme Court of the United States in the October Term, 1938," *American Political Science Review* 34 (1940): 249–283, 249. Despite extensive academic debates about the timing, causes, and legal and political significance of the end of the *Lochner* era, there is general consensus that change occurred. Compare Barry Cushman, *Rethinking the New Deal Court: The Structure of a Constitutional Revolution* (New York, 1998); White, *Constitution and New Deal;* Merlo J. Pusey, *Charles Evans Hughes* (New York, 1951); Felix Frankfurter, "Mr. Justice Roberts," *University of Pennsylvania Law Review* 104 (1955): 311–317; Paul A. Freund, "Charles Evans Hughes as Chief Justice," *Harvard Law Review* 81 (1967): 4–43 with Bruce Ackerman, *We the People: Transformations* (Cambridge, Mass., 1998); Edward S. Corwin, *Constitutional Revolution, Ltd.* (Claremont, Calif., 1941); Robert G. McCloskey, *The American Supreme Court* (Chicago, 1960); Alpheus Thomas Mason, *The Supreme Court: Vehicle of Revealed Truth or Power Group, 1930–1937* (Boston, 1953); Benjamin F. Wright, *The Growth of American Constitutional Law* (Boston, 1942). See generally Laura Kalman, "Law, Politics, and the New Deal(s)," *Yale Law Journal* 108 (1999): 2165–2213; AHR Forum, "The Debate over the Constitutional Revolution of 1937," *American Historical Review* 110 (2005): 1046–1115.

14. See Stephen Gardbaum, "New Deal Constitutionalism and the Un-

shackling of the States," *University of Chicago Law Review* 64 (1997): 483–566, 566, 485–491.

15. C. Gordon Post, "Civil Rights and the Role of the Republican Party in the Post-War World," *Bill of Rights Review* 2 (1942): 201–208, 202.

16. Frank Coleman, "Freedom from Fear on the Home Front," *Iowa Law Review* 29 (1944): 415–429; Frederick Bernays Wiener, "Justice, Labeled and Boxscored," *Washington Post,* Sept. 28, 1947, B2; President's Committee on Civil Rights, *To Secure These Rights: The Report of the President's Committee on Civil Rights* (Washington, D.C., 1947), x, 13. See generally Robert E. Cushman, "Constitutional Law in 1944–1945: The Constitutional Decisions of the Supreme Court of the United States in the October Term, 1944," *American Political Science Review* 40 (1945): 231–255; Robert E. Cushman, "Constitutional Law in 1945–1946: The Constitutional Decisions of the Supreme Court of the United States in the October Term, 1945," *American Political Science Review* 41 (1947): 248–270.

17. Robert E. Cushman, "Civil Liberties," pt. 5 of "Ten Years of the Supreme Court: 1937–1947," *American Political Science Review* 42 (1948): 42–52, 42; Robert J. Harris, "Constitutional Law in 1948–1949," *American Political Science Review* 44 (1950): 23–46, 46.

18. Walter F. Dodd, *Cases and Materials on Constitutional Law: Selected from Decisions of State and Federal Courts,* 3rd ed. (St. Paul, Minn., 1941), xxiii–xxv; Robert M. Hutchins, foreword to *Political and Civil Rights in the United States: A Collection of Legal and Related Materials,* by Thomas I. Emerson and David Haber (Buffalo, N.Y., 1952), iii–iv. See also Dodd, *Cases and Materials,* 5th ed. (St. Paul, Minn., 1954), xxii–xxiii; Dodd, *Cases and Materials,* 4th ed. (St. Paul, Minn., 1949), xxi–xxii; Dodd, *Cases and Other Authorities on Constitutional Law: Selected from Decisions of State and Federal Courts,* 2nd ed. (St. Paul, Minn., 1937), xxiii; Dodd, *Cases and Other Authorities* (St. Paul, Minn., 1932), xxiii; Noel T. Dowling, *Cases on Constitutional Law,* 4th ed. (Brooklyn, N.Y., 1950); Dowling, *Cases on Constitutional Law,* 3rd ed. (Chicago, 1946), xx; Dowling, *Cases on Constitutional Law,* 2nd ed. (Chicago, 1941), xix–xx; Dowling, *Cases on Constitutional Law* (Chicago, 1937), xv.

19. *Encyclopaedia of the Social Sciences,* 1930 ed., s.v. "Civil Rights." (The quoted language remained unchanged in the 1937 and 1944 editions of the *Encyclopaedia*); Henry Campbell Black, *A Law Dictionary Containing Definitions of the Terms and Phrases of American and English Jurisprudence, Ancient and Modern,* 2nd ed. (St. Paul, Minn., 1910), s.v. "Liberty," quoting Allgeyer v. Louisiana, 165 U.S. 578, 589 (1897); see also Coppage v. State of Kansas, 236 U.S. 1, 14 (1915).

20. Robert E. Cushman, "Some Constitutional Problems of Civil Liberty,"

Boston University Law Review 23 (1943): 335–378, 361; "Civil Rights," in Edward C. Ellsbree, *Corpus Juris,* vol. 11, ed. William Mack and William Benjamin Hale (New York, 1917), 796, 799–814, 800; "Civil Rights," in *American Jurisprudence,* vol. 10, ed. Willis A. Estrich (San Francisco, 1937), 893–920, 894–895. See, for example, Wilkerson v. Rahrer, 140 U.S. 545, 555 (1891); Adair v. United States, 208 U.S. 161, 172–173 (1908); *Buchanan,* 245 U.S. at 81. Throughout the book, I try to use these terms as did the sources I describe. Where necessary, I use the terms "civil liberties" and "civil rights" in their more distinctive meanings.

21. Hamilton v. City of Montrose, 124 P.2d 757, 759 (Colo., 1942); "Ex-Lynn Legislator, Wife Accused of Enslaving Maid for 27 Years," *Boston Globe,* Feb. 26, 1947, 1, file 50–12–3, RG 60, National Archives.

22. Edward S. Corwin, *The Constitution and What It Means Today,* 9th ed. (Princeton, N.J., 1947), 169.

23. William M. Leiserson, *Right and Wrong in Labor Relations* (Berkeley, Calif., 1938), 27, quoted in Jerold S. Auerbach, *Labor and Liberty: The La Follette Committee and the New Deal* (Indianapolis, Ind., 1966), 7. See generally William E. Forbath, "The Ambiguities of Free Labor: Labor and the Law in the Gilded Age," *Wisconsin Law Review,* 1985:767–817; James Gray Pope, "Labor's Constitution of Freedom," *Yale Law Journal* 106 (1997): 941–1031; Julie Greene, *Pure and Simple Politics: The American Federation of Labor, 1881 to 1917* (New York, 1998); Joseph A. Mc-Cartin, *Labor's Great War: The Struggle for Industrial Democracy and the Origins of Modern American Labor Relations, 1912–1921* (Chapel Hill, N.C., 1997). See, for example, *Lochner,* 198 U.S. 45; Charles Wolff Packing Co. v. Court of Indus. Relations, 267 U.S. 552 (1925). *Adair,* 208 U.S. 161; *Coppage,* 236 U.S. at 1; Hitchman Coal & Coke Co. v. Mitchell, 245 U.S. 229 (1917). Courts occasionally supported organized labor. Arguably, *Wolff Packing Co.* recognized the right to strike as a constitutional right (262 U.S. at 540). That is how Felix Frankfurter understood the case (Editorial, "Exit the Kansas Court," *New Republic,* June 27, 1923, 112–113, reprinted in Philip Kurland, ed., *Felix Frankfurter on the Supreme Court* [Cambridge, Mass., 1970], 140–143). In 1926, the Court also suggested protection for labor's rights when it upheld the rights of one group of workers to organize—railway workers (Tex. & New Orleans R.R. Co. v. Bhd. of Ry. & S.S. Clerks, 281 U.S. 548 [1930]). The Court also occasionally sustained protective legislation (Cushman, *Rethinking,* 56–105).

24. Franklin D. Roosevelt, " 'New Conditions Impose New Requirements upon Government and Those Who Conduct Government' " (address,

Commonwealth Club, San Francisco, Calif., Sept. 23, 1932), in *The Public Papers and Addresses of Franklin D. Roosevelt*, ed. Samuel I. Rosenman (New York, 1938–1950), 1:742–756, 752; "Democratic Platform of 1936," in *National Party Platforms, 1840–1972*, 5th ed., comp. Donald Bruce Johnson and Kirk H. Porter (Urbana, Ill., 1973), 360–363, 360; Robert H. Jackson, "The Call for a Liberal Bar," *National Lawyers Guild Quarterly* 1 (1938): 88–91, 88, reprinted in Ann Fagan Ginger and Eugene M. Tobin, eds., *The National Lawyers Guild: From Roosevelt through Reagan* (Philadelphia, 1988), 23–24. See generally, Sidney M. Milkis, "Franklin D. Roosevelt, the Economic Constitutional Order, and the New Politics of Presidential Leadership," in *The New Deal and the Triumph of Liberalism*, ed. Sidney M. Milkis and Jerome M. Mileur (Amherst, Mass., 2002), 31–72; Jennifer Klein, *For All These Rights: Business, Labor, and the Shaping of America's Public-Private Welfare State* (Princeton, N.J., 2003), 6–7; Meg Jacobs, *Pocketbook Politics: Economic Citizenship in Twentieth-Century America* (Princeton, N.J., 2005).

25. Franklin D. Roosevelt, " 'We Are Fighting to Save a Great and Precious Form of Government for Ourselves and the World' " (address accepting renomination for the presidency, Democratic National Convention, Philadelphia, Pa., June 27, 1936), in *Public Papers of Roosevelt*, 234; Jackson, "Call for a Liberal Bar," 23–24.

26. "New Attacks upon Liberties," *Social Action*, Jan. 10, 1936, 18–24, 19, quoted in Auerbach, *Labor and Liberty*, 75; American Civil Liberties Union, foreword to *A Year's Fight for Free Speech: The Work of the American Civil Liberties Union from Sept. 1921, to Jan. 1923* (New York, 1923), 3; National Civil Liberties Bureau, memorandum, "Proposed Reorganization of the Work for Civil Liberty," Dec. 31, 1919, quoted in David Kairys, "Freedom of Speech," in *The Politics of Law: A Progressive Critique*, ed. David Kairys, rev. ed. (New York, 1990), 237–272, 255; Roger N. Baldwin, "Organized Labor and Political Democracy," in Roger N. Baldwin and Clarence B. Randall, *Civil Liberties and Industrial Conflict* (Cambridge, Mass., 1938), 3–45, 17; Edwin S. Smith, "The Current Attack on Our Civil Liberties," *Lawyers Guild Review* 1, no. 4 (June 1941): 5–10, 5. See generally Robert C. Cottrell, *Roger Nash Baldwin and the American Civil Liberties Union* (New York, 2000), 199–236; Samuel Walker, *In Defense of American Liberties: A History of the ACLU* (New York, 1990).

27. "It Happened in Steel," *Fortune*, May 1937, 91–94, 176, 179–180, 91 (internal quotation marks omitted); Norris-LaGuardia Anti-Injunction Act of 1932, ch. 90, §2, 47 Stat. 70, 70 (codified as amended at 29 U.S.C. §102 [2000]); Lauf v. E. G. Shinner & Co., 303 U.S. 323 (1938); S.

1482, 70th Cong. §2 (as amended by ad hoc subcommittee of Senate Committee on the Judiciary, May 26, 1928), *Congressional Record* 69, pt. 10:10,050–10,051, 10,050, reprinted in Felix Frankfurter and Nathan Greene, *The Labor Injunction* (New York, 1930), 279–288, 280–281.

28. National Industrial Recovery Act, ch. 90, §7(a), 48 Stat. 195, 196–197 (1933); Senator Robert F. Wagner of New York, "N.R.A. Codes" (address, Conference of Code Authorities, Washington, D.C., Mar. 5, 1934), in *Congressional Record* 78, pt. 4:3678–3679, 3679, quoted in James Gray Pope, "The Thirteenth Amendment versus the Commerce Clause: Labor and the Shaping of American Constitutional Law, 1921–1957," *Columbia Law Review* 102 (2002): 1–122, 48; Franklin D. Roosevelt, "Presidential Statement on N.I.R.A.—'To Put People Back to Work'" (Washington, D.C., June 16, 1933), in *Public Papers of Roosevelt,* 253, quoted in Irving Bernstein, *Turbulent Years: A History of the American Worker, 1933–1941* (Boston, 1970), 172.

29. Bureau of the Census, "Labor Union Membership: 1931 to 1949," in *Statistical Abstract of the United States: 1950,* 71st ed. (Washington, D.C.: US GPO 1950), table 249; Representative Carpenter of Nebraska, "Welfare of the Laboring Class" (extension of remarks, May 17, 1934), in *Congressional Record* 78, pt. 8:9060–9061, 9061, quoted in Pope, "Thirteenth Amendment," 48 n. 227;. U.S. Senate Committee on Education and Labor, *National Labor Relations Act and Proposed Amendments: Hearings,* 76th Cong., 1st sess., 1939, pt.1:17 (statement of Sen. Robert F. Wagner), quoted in Louis G. Silverberg, ed., *The Wagner Act: After Ten Years* (Washington, D.C., 1945), 31. See generally National Labor Relations Act, ch. 372, 49 Stat. 449 (1935); William E. Forbath, "Caste, Class, and Equal Citizenship," *Michigan Law Review* 98 (1999): 1–91.

30. On farmworker exclusions, see Marc Linder, "Farm Workers and the Fair Labor Standards Act: Racial Discrimination in the New Deal," *Texas Law Review* 65 (1987): 1335–1393. On the "family wage" and the image of the male breadwinner, see Linda Gordon, *Pitied but Not Entitled: Single Mothers and the History of Welfare, 1890–1935* (Cambridge, Mass., 1994), 209–306; Theda Skocpol, "Political Response to Capitalist Crisis: Neo-Marxist Theories of the State and the Case of the New Deal," *Politics and Society* 10 (1980): 155–201; Suzanne Mettler, *Dividing Citizens: Gender and Federalism in New Deal Public Policy* (Ithaca, N.Y., 1998); Eileen Boris, "'The Right to Work Is the Right to Live!': Fair Employment and the Quest for Social Citizenship," in *Two Cultures of Rights: The Quest for Inclusion and Participation in Modern America and Germany,* ed. Marfred Berg and Martin H. Geyer (Cambridge, Mass., 2002), 121–142; Gwendolyn Mink, *The Wages of Motherhood: Inequality in*

the Welfare State, 1917–1942 (Ithaca, N.Y., 1995); Alice Kessler-Harris, *Out to Work: A History of Wage-Earning Women in the United States* (New York, 1982).

31. Auerbach, *Labor and Liberty.*

32. NLRB v. Jones & Laughlin Steel Co., 301 U.S. at 33. Such language echoed statements the Supreme Court had made in earlier cases, such as American Steel Foundries v. Tri-City Central Trades Council, 257 U.S. 184 (1921), and especially *Texas & New Orleans Railroad*, upholding the Railway Labor Act (281 U.S. at 548). *Jones & Laughlin* differed from those cases, however, in upholding legislation that created substantial federal protection for the collective bargaining rights of most industrial employees.

33. "Judgment Day: Supreme Court Gives Its Blessing to Labor Relations Act and Hands Roosevelt a Victorious Defeat," *News-Week*, Apr. 17, 1937, 7; Robert Morss Lovett, "A G.M. Stockholder Visits Flint," *Nation* 144 (1937): 123–124; NLRB, Press Release no. R-2549, n.d., quoted in D. O. Bowman, *Public Control of Labor Relations: A Study of the National Labor Relations Board* (New York, 1942), 445 n. 39; Baldwin, "Organized Labor," in Baldwin and Randall, *Civil Liberties*, 23. See generally Drew D. Hansen, "The Sit-Down Strikes and the Switch in Time," *Wayne Law Review* 46 (2000): 49–133.

34. Senator La Follette of Wisconsin, speaking to the Senate on Apr. 3, 1942 in support of S. 2435, 77th Cong., 2nd sess., *Congressional Record* 88, pt. 3:3311; Roger Baldwin, interview by David Kairys, May 5, 1981, quoted in Kairys, "Freedom of Speech" in *Politics of Law*, 255. See generally Paul L. Murphy, *The Meaning of Freedom of Speech: First Amendment Freedoms from Wilson to FDR* (Westport, Conn., 1972), 122–132, 275–286; Walker, *In Defense*, 51–55, 106–112, 153–160; Jerold S. Auerbach, "The La Follette Committee: Labor and Civil Liberties in the New Deal," *Journal of American History* 51 (1964): 435–459; Jerold S. Auerbach, "The Depression Decade," in *The Pulse of Freedom: American Liberties: 1920–1970s*, ed. Alan Reitman (New York, 1975): 65–104.

35. C. Gordon Post, "The Subversive Party," *Bill of Rights Review* 2 (1941): 23–30, 24; De Jonge v. Oregon, 299 U.S. 353, 358–359 (1937); Herndon v. Lowry, 301 U.S. 242, 249 (1937) (quoting the Georgia Supreme Court); Senn v. Tile Layers Protective Union, 301 U.S. 468, 482 (1937). See Geoffrey D. Berman, "Notes: A New Deal for Free Speech; Free Speech and the Labor Movement in the 1930s," *Virginia Law Review* 80 (1994): 291–322. This is not to say that all of the justices who signed onto such opinions uniformly supported labor's rights. For example, Justice Owen J. Roberts simultaneously supported the First

Amendment cases and opposed labor's rights in other contexts
(Cushman, *Rethinking*, 31). The opinions themselves, however, did
seem to make labor's rights central.

36. New Negro Alliance v. Sanitary Grocery Co., 303 U.S. 552, 560, 561
(1938). See Paul D. Moreno, *From Direct Action to Affirmative Action: Fair
Employment Law and Policy in America, 1933–1972* (Baton Rouge, La.,
1997), 41–54.

37. Hague v. CIO, 307 U.S. 496, 512, 513, 525 (1939) (Stone, J., concurring). See Michael J. Klarman, "Rethinking the Civil Rights and Civil
Liberties Revolutions," *Virginia Law Review* 82 (1996): 1–67.

38. Thornhill v. Alabama, 310 U.S. 88, 102, 102–103 (1940); see also
Carlson v. California, 310 U.S. 106, 113 (1940). Eugene Gressman, "Mr.
Justice Murphy—A Preliminary Appraisal," *Columbia Law Review* 50
(1950): 29–47, 45; C. Herman Pritchett, *The Roosevelt Court: A Study in
Judicial Politics and Values, 1937–1947* (New York, 1948), 229; Corwin,
Constitution and What It Means, 9th ed., 195–196. See also Edward S.
Corwin, *The Constitution and What It Means Today*, 7th ed. (Princeton,
N.J., 1941), 197–198. The Court did not uniformly find in favor of the
unions in the late 1930s and 1940s. See Sidney Fine, "Frank Murphy,
the *Thornhill* Decision, and Picketing as Free Speech," *Labor History* 6
[1965]: 99–120, 108).

39. Grenville Clark, "Perversions of Civil Liberty," *Bill of Rights Review* 1
(1941): 262–264, 263–264; William B. Hale, "Principles of Free Enterprise," *Bill of Rights Review* 1 (1941): 186–195; T. V. Smith, "Political Liberty Today: Is It Being Restricted or Enlarged by Economic Regulation?" *American Political Science Review* 31 (1937): 243–252, 249. See also
Ernest O. Kooser, letter to the editor, "The Unfinished Bill of Rights:
Economic Freedom," *Bill of Rights Review* 2 (1942): 153; S & W Fine
Foods, Inc. v. Retail Delivery Drivers & Salesmen's Union, 118 P.2d 962,
968 (Wash. 1941) (Robinson, C.J., concurring).

40. Corwin, *Constitution and What It Means*, 7th ed., vii–viii, 200; Corwin,
Constitution and What It Means, 9th ed., 169.

41. Nelson Lichtenstein, *Labor's War at Home: The CIO in World War II* (New
York, 1982), 44–62, 82–109.

42. Alan Brinkley, *The End of Reform: New Deal Liberalism in Recession and
War* (New York, 1995), 137–174; Lichtenstein, *Labor's War at Home*, 46–
81, 110–111, 113, 121–122, 167–168; Richard Polenberg, *War and Society: The United States, 1941–1945* (Philadelphia, 1972), 159–161, 167.

43. Franklin D. Roosevelt, "The Annual Message to the Congress" (Washington, D.C., Jan. 6, 1941), in *Public Papers of Roosevelt*, 672; Franklin D.
Roosevelt, "Message to the Congress on the State of the Union" (Wash-

ington, D.C., Jan. 11, 1944), in *Public Papers of Roosevelt*, 41–42. For the continuing emphasis on economic rights, see, for example, Charles E. Merriam, "The National Resources Planning Board; A Chapter in American Planning Experience," *American Political Science Review* 38 (1944): 1075–1088; Charles E. Merriam, *On the Agenda of Democracy* (Cambridge, Mass., 1941), 98–99; Robert L. Hale, "Bargaining, Duress, and Economic Liberty," *Columbia Law Review* 43 (1943): 603–628. For the relation of these developments to the international scene, see Declaration of Principles, Known as the Atlantic Charter, Aug. 14, 1941, 55 Stat. 1603, 204 L.N.T.S. 384; United Kingdom, Inter-departmental Committee on Social Insurance and Allied Services, *Social Insurance and Allied Services: Report,* Cmd. 6404 (London, 1942); Elizabeth Borgwardt, *A New Deal for the World: America's Vision for Human Rights* (Cambridge, Mass., 2005), 46–86, 285–300.

44. American Law Institute, Committee of Advisors, Representing the Principal Cultures of the World, *Report to the Council of the Institute and Statement of Essential Human Rights* (St. Paul, Minn., 1944), 20; Charter of the United Nations, art. 55, §a, June 26, 1945, 59 Stat. 1031, 1045, *American Journal of International Law* 39, supp. (1945): 190–215. See generally Borgwardt, *New Deal for the World.*

45. Serviceman's Readjustment Act of 1944, ch. 286, 58 Stat. 284; Full Employment Act of 1945, S. 380, 79th Cong. §2(b) (as introduced Jan. 22, 1945), *Congressional Record* 91, pt. 1:377–378, 377.

46. Fair Employment Practice Bill, Sec. 4, H.R. 2232 (1945). See, for example, *Buchanan,* 245 U.S. at 81.

47. Harvard Sitkoff, *A New Deal for Blacks: The Emergence of Civil Rights as a National Issue* (New York, 1978), 1. Brinkley, *End of Reform,* 165–166.

48. "The Courier's Double 'V' for a Double Victory Campaign Gets Country–Wide Support," *Pittsburgh Courier,* Feb. 14, 1942, 1. On black newspapers, see Lee Finkle, *Forum for Protest: The Black Press during World War II* (Rutherford, N.J., 1975). On rising black rights consciousness, see Patricia Sullivan, *Days of Hope: Race and Democracy in the New Deal Era* (Chapel Hill, N.C., 1996); Robert W. Mullen, *Blacks in America's Wars: The Shift in Attitudes from the Revolutionary War to Vietnam* (New York, 1973), 54–55; Richard M. Dalfiume, "The 'Forgotten Years' of the Negro Revolution," *Journal of American History* 55 (1968): 90–106; Harvard Sitkoff, "Racial Militancy and Interracial Violence in the Second World War," *Journal of American History* 58 (1971): 661–681; John Modell, Marc Goulden, and Sigurdur Magnusson, "World War II in the Lives of Black Americans: Some Findings and an Interpretation," *Journal of American History* 76 (1989): 838–848; Robin D. G. Kelley,

"Congested Terrain: Resistance on Public Transportation," in *Race Rebels: Culture, Politics, and the Black Working Class* (New York, 1994), 55–75. On increasing black radicalism, see Wilson Record, *Race and Radicalism: The NAACP and the Communist Party in Conflict* (Ithaca, N.Y., 1964), 84–131; Penny M. Von Eschen, *Race against Empire: Black Americans and Anticolonialism, 1937–1957* (Ithaca, N.Y., 1997); Carol Anderson, *Eyes Off the Prize: The United Nations and the African American Struggle for Human Rights, 1944–1955* (New York, 2003). On blacks in unions and working-class activism, see Kimberley L. Phillips, *Alabama-North: African-American Migrants, Community, and Working-Class Activism in Cleveland, 1915–45* (Urbana, Ill., 1999); Megan Taylor Shockley, *We, Too, Are Americans: African-American Women in Detroit and Richmond, 1940–54* (Urbana, Ill., 2003); Shirley Ann Wilson Moore, *To Place Our Deeds: The African American Community in Richmond, California, 1910–1963* (Berkeley, Calif., 2000); Eric Arnesen, *Brotherhoods of Color: Black Railroad Workers and the Struggle for Equality* (Cambridge, Mass., 2001); August Meier and Elliott Rudwick, *Black Detroit and the Rise of the UAW* (New York, 1979), 120; Robert R. Korstad, *Civil Rights Unionism: Tobacco Workers and the Struggle for Democracy in the Mid-Twentieth-Century South* (Chapel Hill, N.C., 2003); Robert Korstad and Nelson Lichtenstein, "Opportunities Found and Lost: Labor, Radicals, and the Early Civil Rights Movement," *Journal of American History* 75 (1988): 786–811. See generally Nancy J. Weiss, *Farewell to the Party of Lincoln: Black Politics in the Age of FDR* (Princeton, N.J., 1983); Neil A. Wynn, *The Afro-American and the Second World War*, rev. ed. (New York, 1993).

49. H.R. 2232, 79th Cong., §4 (1945); Steele v. Louisville & Nashville R.R. Co., 323 U.S. 192, 208–209 (1944) (Murphy, J., concurring); *America on Guard*, KSFO (radio), Nov. 27, 1943, transcript, 6, 8, in *Papers of the NAACP*, ed. August Meier (Frederick, Md., 1982), microfilm, pt. 13C, rl. 12:424–425; R. M. MacIver, *The More Perfect Union: A Program for the Control of Inter-group Discrimination in the United States* (New York, 1948), 113–144; In re Southport Petroleum Co., 8 War Lab. Rep. (BNA) 714, 715 (Nat'l War Labor Bd. 1943); Arnesen, *Brotherhoods of Color*, 214, 216. See generally Boris, " 'Right to Work,' " in *Two Cultures of Rights*, ed. Berg and Geyer. Some black lawyers and activists had long fought work-related discrimination, especially after the devastating consequences of the Depression for African Americans. Kenneth W. Mack, "Rethinking Civil Rights Lawyering and Politics in the Era Before *Brown*," *Yale Law Journal* 115 (2006): 256–354. It was not until World War II, however, that the issue gained a national profile.

50. See Sterling D. Spero and Abram L. Harris, *The Black Worker: The Negro*

and the Labor Movement (New York, 1931); Horace R. Cayton and
George S. Mitchell, *Black Workers and the New Unions* (College Park,
Md., 1939); William H. Harris, *The Harder We Run: Black Workers since the
Civil War* (New York, 1982).

51. See Peter H. Irons, *The New Deal Lawyers* (Princeton, N.J., 1982), 226;
Raymond Wolters, *Negroes and the Great Depression: The Problem of Eco-
nomic Recovery* (Westport, Conn., 1970), 183; Harris, *The Harder We Run;*
Kenneth Walter Mack, "Race Uplift, Professional Identity and the
Transformation of Civil Rights Lawyering and Politics, 1920–1940"
(Ph.D. diss., Princeton University, 2005), 255.

52. Editorial, "F.D.R.'s Executive Order," *New York Amsterdam Star-News,* July
5, 1941, 14, quoted in Louis Ruchames, *Race, Jobs, and Politics: The Story
of FEPC* (New York, 1953), 23; Exec. Order No. 8802, 6 Fed. Reg. 3109
(June 25, 1941). On labor-related activism, see Korstad, *Civil Rights
Unionism;* Arnesen, *Brotherhoods of Color;* Michael K. Honey, *Southern
Labor and Black Civil Rights: Organizing Memphis Workers* (Urbana, Ill.,
1993); Rick Halpern, "Solving the 'Labour Problem': Race, Work, and
the State in the Sugar Industries of Louisiana and Natal, 1870–1910,"
Journal of Southern African Studies 30 (2004): 19–40; Roger Horowitz,
*Negro and White, Unite and Fight! A Social History of Industrial Unionism in
Meatpacking, 1930–90* (Urbana, Ill., 1997); Michael Goldfield, "Race
and the CIO: The Possibilities for Racial Egalitarianism during the
1930s and 1940s," *International Labor and Working Class History,* no. 44
(Fall 1993): 1–32. On the March on Washington and the FEPC, see Ar-
nesen, *Brotherhoods of Color;* Herbert Garfinkel, *When Negroes March: The
March on Washington Movement in the Organizational Politics for FEPC*
(Glencoe, Ill., 1959); Paula F. Pfeffer, *A. Philip Randolph, Pioneer of the
Civil Rights Movement* (Baton Rouge, La., 1990); Polenberg, *War and So-
ciety,* 117–123; Merl E. Reed, *Seedtime for the Modern Civil Rights Move-
ment: The President's Committee on Fair Employment Practice, 1941–1946*
(Baton Rouge, La., 1991); Ruchames, *Race, Jobs, and Politics;* Andrew
Edmund Kersten, *Race, Jobs, and the War: The FEPC in the Midwest, 1941–
46* (Urbana, Ill., 2000); Daniel Kryder, *Divided Arsenal: Race and the
American State during World War II* (New York, 2000), 53–66; John H.
Bracey, Jr., and August Meier, "Allies or Adversaries? The NAACP, A.
Philip Randolph and the 1941 March on Washington," *Georgia Histor-
ical Quarterly* 75 (1991): 1–17; Dalfiume, "Forgotten Years," 98–99.

53. Franklin D. Roosevelt, "Message to the Congress on the State of the
Union" (Washington, D.C., Jan. 11, 1944), in *Public Papers of Roosevelt,*
41; Franklin D. Roosevelt, " 'We Are Not Going to Turn the Clock
Back' " (campaign address, Soldier's Field, Chicago, Ill., Oct. 28, 1944),

in *Public Papers of Roosevelt*, 374; *Southport Petroleum*, 8 War Lab. Rep.
(BNA) at 715; In re Miami Copper Co., 15 L.R.R.M. (BNA) 1538, 1539
(Nat'l War Labor Bd. 1944); In re Pittsburgh Plate Glass Co., 16
L.R.R.M. (BNA) 1529, 1531 (Nat'l War Labor Bd. 1945); In re Larus &
Brother Co., 62 N.L.R.B. 1075 (1945). See generally Gunnar Myrdal,
An American Dilemma: The Negro Problem and Modern Democracy (New
York, 1944), 417–418; Charles D. Chamberlain, *Victory at Home: Man-
power and Race in the American South during World War II* (Athens, Ga.,
2003); Kevin J. McMahon, *Reconsidering Roosevelt on Race: How the Presi-
dency Paved the Road to* Brown (Chicago, 2004).

54. See generally Benjamin L. Alpers, *Dictators, Democracy, and American
Public Culture: Envisioning the Totalitarian Enemy, 1920s–1950s* (Chapel
Hill, N.C., 2003); James R. Barrett, *William Z. Foster and the Tragedy of
American Radicalism* (Urbana, Ill., 1999), 226–251; Eleanor Bontecou,
The Federal Loyalty-Security Program (Ithaca, N.Y., 1953); Alan D. Harper,
*The Politics of Loyalty: The White House and the Communist Issue, 1946–
1952* (London, 1969); John Earl Haynes and Harvey Klehr, *Venona: De-
coding Soviet Espionage in the United States* (New Haven, Conn., 1999);
Irving Howe and Lewis Coser, *The American Communist Party: A Critical
History, 1919–1957* (Boston, 1957), 437–499; Earl Latham, *The Commu-
nist Controversy in Washington* (Cambridge, Mass., 1966); Mary Sperling
McAuliffe, *Crisis on the Left: Cold War Politics and American Liberals, 1947–
1954* (Amherst, Mass., 1978); Ellen Schrecker, *Many Are the Crimes: Mc-
Carthyism in America* (Boston, 1998).

55. Employment Act of 1946, ch. 33, §2, 60 Stat. 23 (codified as amended
at 15 U.S.C. §§1021–1024 [2000 & Supp. II 2002]); Portal-to-Portal Act
of 1947, ch. 52, 61 Stat. 84 (codified as amended at 29 U.S.C. §§216,
251–262 [2000 & Supp. II 2002]); Administrative Procedure Act, ch.
324, 60 Stat. 237 (1946) (codified as amended principally at 5 U.S.C.
§§551–559, 701–706 [2000 & Supp. II 2002]).

56. Labor Management Relations Act, 1947, ch. 120, sec. 101, §§8(b)(4),
(d), 9(h), 14(b), 61 Stat. 136, 141–143, 146, 151 (§8[b][4] and [d] are
codified as amended at 29 U.S.C. §§158[b][4], [d] 164[b] [2000];
§9[h] was repealed by Labor-Management Reporting and Disclosure
Act of 1959, Pub. L. No. 86–257, §201[d], 73 Stat. 519, 525). On the
political power of the South, see Ira Katznelson, Kim Geiger, and
Daniel Kryder, "Limiting Liberalism, The Southern Veto in Congress,
1933–1950," *Political Science Quarterly* 108 (1993): 283–306; Sean
Farhang and Ira Katznelson, "The Southern Imposition: Congress and
Labor in the New Deal and Fair Deal," *Studies in American Political Development* 19 (2005): 1–30. On the effects of Taft-Hartley, see Christopher

L. Tomlins, *The State and the Unions: Labor Relations, Law, and the Organized Labor Movement in America, 1880–1960* (New York, 1985), 247–328; Nelson Lichtenstein, *The Most Dangerous Man in Detroit: Walter Reuther and the Fate of American Labor* (New York, 1995), 310–318. On the racial egalitarianism of left-leaning unions, see, for example, Rick Halpern, *Down on the Killing Floor: Black and White Workers in Chicago's Packinghouses 1904–54* (Urbana, Ill., 1997); Honey, *Southern Labor;* Horowitz, *Negro and White.* Not all unions lost their radical edge, however. See Martha Biondi, *To Stand and Fight: The Struggle for Civil Rights in Postwar New York City* (Cambridge, Mass., 2003), 267, 277, 286; Steve Rosswurm, ed., *The CIO's Left-Led Unions* (New Brunswick, N.J., 1992). By 1958, nineteen states had passed "right to work" laws. See J. R. Dempsey, *The Operation of the Right-to-Work Laws: A Comparison between What the State Legislatures Say about the Meaning of the Laws and How State Court Judges Have Applied These Laws* (Milwaukee, Wis., 1961), 24–27; Gilbert J. Gall, *The Politics of Right to Work: The Labor Federations as Special Interests, 1943–1979* (New York, 1988), 230–231; Reuel E. Schiller, "From Group Rights to Individual Liberties: Post-war Labor Law, Liberation, and the Waning of Union Strength," *Berkeley Journal of Employment and Labor Law* 20 (1999): 1–73.

57. Ira Katznelson, *When Affirmative Action Was White: An Untold History of Racial Inequality in Twentieth-Century America* (New York, 2005), 55. See also Giboney v. Empire Storage & Ice Co., 336 U.S. 490, 495–498, 501–503 (1949); Bldg. Serv. Employees Int'l Union v. Gazzam, 339 U.S. 532, 537, 539–541 (1950); Hughes v. Superior Court, 339 U.S. 460, 464–465, 468 (1950); Int'l Bhd. of Teamsters v. Hanke, 339 U.S. 470, 474–479 (1950); Local Union No. 10, United Ass'n of Journeymen Plumbers v. Graham, 345 U.S. 192, 201 (1953). See generally, C. Herman Pritchett, *Civil Liberties and the Vinson Court* (Chicago, 1954), 52–56. Over time, the NLRB and the Court came to defer more to employer speech and curtail union and employee speech. See Karl E. Klare, "Judicial Deradicalization of the Wagner Act and the Origins of Modern Legal Consciousness," *Minnesota Law Review* 62 (1978): 265–339; James Gray Pope, "The First Amendment, the Thirteenth Amendment, and the Right to Organize in the Twenty-First Century," *Rutgers Law Review* 51 (1999): 941–969. However, Taft-Hartley did not affect NLRB decisions until after the 1952 election of Dwight Eisenhower and his nominations to the NLRB (Terry M. Moe, "Interests, Institutions, and Positive Theory: The Politics of the NLRB," *Studies in American Political Development* 2 [1987]: 236–299).

58. See, for example, R. M. MacIver, *The Web of Government* (New York,

1947), 331; Francis Biddle, *The World's Best Hope: A Discussion of the Role of the United States in the Modern World* (Chicago, 1949), 53–56, 84, 97–98; Harry K. Girvetz, *From Wealth to Welfare: The Evolution of Liberalism* (Stanford, Calif., 1950), 224; Alvin H. Hansen, *Economic Policy and Full Employment* (New York, 1947), 14–17; Clifton Brock, *Americans for Democratic Action: Its Role in National Politics* (Washington, D.C., 1962), 52; Americans for Democratic Action, "ADA Offers a Practical Program for Practical Liberals," ca. 1953–1961, reprinted in Brock, *Americans for Democratic Action*, 20. Universal Declaration of Human Rights arts. 22–26, Dec. 10, 1948, UN General Assembly Resolution 217 (III), A/810, 1948.

59. Harry S. Truman, "Annual Message to the Congress on the State of the Union" (Washington, D.C., Jan. 5, 1949), in Office of the Federal Register, *Public Papers of the Presidents of the United States: Harry S. Truman, 1949* (Washington, D.C., 1964), 1–7, 6; Seymour E. Harris, *Economic Planning: The Plans of Fourteen Countries with Analyses of the Plans* (New York, 1949).

60. Dwight D. Eisenhower to Edgar Eisenhower, May 5, 1960, Name Series, Ann Whitman File, Papers as President, 1953–61, Dwight D. Eisenhower Papers, Dwight D. Eisenhower Presidential Library, Abilene, Kan., quoted in Fred. I. Greenstein, *The Hidden-Hand Presidency: Eisenhower as Leader* (New York, 1982), 50, n. 74; Social Security Act Amendments of 1950, ch. 809, sec. 104(a), §§209(g)(2), 210(a)(1), (f), (k), 64 Stat. 477, 493, 494–495, 499, 500 (codified as amended at 42 U.S.C. §§409[a][6], [7], 410[f], [j] [2000]). See also Clayton Knowles, "House Passes Bill Adding 11,000,000 to Social Security," *New York Times*, Oct. 6, 1949, 1; Robert C. Lieberman, *Shifting the Color Line: Race and the American Welfare State* (Cambridge, Mass., 1998), 103–113. There was opposition, however, to even greater expansion. Social Security Amendments of 1954, ch. 1206, §101(a), 68 Stat. 1052, 1052–1053 (codified as amended primarily at 42 U.S.C. §§409[a][6], [7], 410[f], [j] [2000]); Lieberman, *Shifting the Color Line*, 113–117.

61. See Mary L. Dudziak, *Cold War Civil Rights: Race and the Image of American Democracy* (Princeton, N.J., 2002); Thomas Borstelmann, *The Cold War and the Color Line: American Race Relations in the Global Arena* (Cambridge, Mass., 2001).

62. See Biondi, *To Stand and Fight;* Korstad, *Civil Rights Unionism;* Timothy J. Minchin, *The Color of Work: The Struggle for Civil Rights in the Southern Paper Industry, 1945–1980* (Chapel Hill, N.C., 2001).

63. President's Committee on Civil Rights, *To Secure These Rights*, 53, 59 (compare 53–62 [discussing employment] with 62–79 [discussing edu-

cation, housing, and health care]); Charles S. Johnson and Associates, *Into the Main Stream: A Survey of Best Practices in Race Relations in the South* (Chapel Hill, N.C., 1947), 115, quoted in President's Committee on Civil Rights, *To Secure These Rights.*

64. Anthony S. Chen, "From Fair Employment to Equal Employment Opportunity and Beyond: Affirmative Action and the Politics of Civil Rights in the New Deal Order, 1941–1972" (Ph.D. diss., University of California, Berkeley, 2002); 153. Exec. Order No. 9981, 13 Fed. Reg. 4313 (July 26, 1948); Exec. Order No. 10,308, 16 Fed. Reg. 12,303 (Dec. 3, 1951); Exec. Order No. 10,479, 18 Fed. Reg. 4899 (Aug. 13, 1953); "President Asks Action on Discrimination," *Washington Post,* Aug. 20, 1953, 7. See Ruchames, *Race, Jobs, and Politics,* 199–213.

65. Ruchames, *Race, Jobs, and Politics,* 196.

66. For peonage cases, see Taylor v. Georgia, 315 U.S. 25, 31 (1942); United States v. Gaskin, 320 U.S. 527, 529 (1944); Pollock v. Williams, 322 U.S. 4, 25 (1944); for transportation, see Mitchell v. United States, 313 U.S. 80, 97 (1941); Morgan v. Virginia, 328 U.S. 373, 385–386 (1946); Henderson v. United States, 339 U.S. 816, 824–826 (1950); for voting, see Smith v. Allwright, 321 U.S. 649, 663–666 (1944); for police brutality, see Screws v. United States, 325 U.S. 91, 101–102, 107–113 (1945); for union discrimination, see *Steele,* 323 U.S. at 202–204, 208; Tunstall v. Bhd. of Locomotive Firemen, 323 U.S. 210, 213–214 (1944); for graduate education, see Sipuel v. Bd. of Regents, 332 U.S. 631, 632–633 (1948); McLaurin v. Okla. State Regents, 339 U.S. 637, 641–642 (1950); Sweatt v. Painter, 339 U.S. 629, 633–636 (1950); for residential segregation, see Shelley v. Kraemer, 334 U.S. 1, 18–21, 23 (1948), Barrows v. Jackson, 346 U.S. 249, 260 (1953). Peonage Act of 1867, ch. 187, §1, 14 Stat. 546 (codified as amended at 42 U.S.C. §1994 [2000]); Civil Rights Act of 1866, ch. 31, 14 Stat. 27 (codified as amended at 42 U.S.C. §§1981 [2000]); Interstate Commerce Act of 1887, ch. 104, 24 Stat. 379 (codified as amended in scattered sections of 49 U.S.C. [2000 & Supp. II 2002]); Railway Labor Act, ch. 347, 44 Stat. 577 (1926) (codified as amended at 45 U.S.C. §§151–188 [2000 & Supp. II 2002]).

67. *Smith,* 321 U.S. at 664–665. The Court had previously struck down white primary systems in United States v. Classic, 313 U.S. 299 (1941); *Condon,* 286 U.S. at 73; *Herndon,* 273 U.S. at 536, though it upheld one in *Grovey,* 295 U.S. at 45. The following year in *Screws,* the Court found that a police officer who beat an African American man in his custody in violation of state law nonetheless acted under color of state law for the purposes of federal criminal liability (325 U.S. at 108–109). Brief of the United States as Amicus Curiae, at 49 n. 28, *Shelley v. Kraemer* (No.

72); 334 U.S. at 20; Osmond K. Fraenkel, "The Federal Civil Rights Laws," *Minnesota Law Review* 31 (1947): 301–327, 320. See also George Brody, "Recent Decisions: Constitutional Law—Freedom of Speech and Religion—What Constitutes State Action," *Michigan Law Review* 44 (1946): 848–852; Clyde W. Summers, "The Right to Join a Union," *Columbia Law Review* 47 (1947): 33–74; John A. Huston, "Comments: Constitutional Law—State Court Enforcement of Race Restrictive Covenants as State Action within the Scope of Fourteenth Amendment," *Michigan Law Review* 45 (1947): 733–748.

68. United States v. Carolene Products Co., 304 U.S. 144, 152 n. 4 (1938).

69. Lewis F. Powell, Jr., "*Carolene Products* Revisited," *Columbia Law Review* 82 (1982): 1087–1092; *Carolene Products,* 304 U.S. at 152 n. 4.

70. See Louis H. Pollak, "Racial Discrimination and Judicial Integrity: A Reply to Professor Wechsler," *University of Pennsylvania Law Review* 108 (1959): 1–34; Bruce Ackerman, "Beyond *Carolene Products,*" *Harvard Law Review* 98 (1985): 713–746; Robert M. Cover, "The Origins of Judicial Activism in the Protection of Minorities," *Yale Law Journal* 91 (1982): 1287–1316; William E. Nelson, *The Legalist Reformation: Law, Politics, and Ideology in New York, 1920–1980* (Chapel Hill, N.C., 2001).

71. Missouri ex rel. Gaines v. Canada, 305 U.S. 337 (1938). During these years the Court began to apply the footnote outside the race context, in the context of the Dormant Commerce Clause and the First Amendment. See Michael Klarman, "An Interpretive History of Modern Equal Protection," *Michigan Law Review* 90 (1991): 213–318.

72. Korematsu v. United States, 323 U.S. 214, 216 (1944); Hirabayashi v. United States, 320 U.S. 81, 100 (1943). See Klarman, "Interpretive History," 220.

73. Louis Lusky, "Footnote Redux: A *Carolene Products* Reminiscence," *Columbia Law Review* 82 (1982): 1093–1109 (internal quotation marks omitted).

74. Takahashi v. Fish & Game Comm'n, 30 Cal. 2d 719, 728, 731, 743 (Carter, J., dissenting) (1947), rev'd, 334 U.S. 410 (1948). See Klarman, "Interpretive History," 226–246.

75. Mendez v. Westminster Sch. Dist., 64 F. Supp. 544, 548 (S.D. Cal. 1946); Kemp v. Rubin, 69 N.Y.S.2d 680, 683 (Sup. Ct. 1947); Inland Steel Co. v. NLRB, 170 F.2d 247, 265 (7th Cir. 1948) (Kerner, J., concurring) (considering Communist Party affiliation, rather than race, as the relevant characteristic); Lapides v. Clark, 176 F.2d 619, 620 (D.C. Cir. 1949); Perez v. Sharp, 32 Cal. 2d 711, 731–732 (1948).

76. *Takahashi,* 334 U.S. at 420; Oyama v. California 332 U.S. 633, 640, 646, 663 (1948) (Murphy, J., concurring).

77. The National Bar Association was founded in 1925, in response to the ex-
    clusion of African Americans from the American Bar Association (J. Clay
    Smith, *Emancipation: The Making of the Black Lawyer, 1844–1944* [Philadel-
    phia, 1993], 556–572). For articles mentioning *Carolene Products,* see Basil
    O'Connor, "Constitutional Protection of the Alien's Right to Work," *New
    York University Law Quarterly Review* 18 (1941): 483–497, 492; Charles P.
    Curtis, Jr., "Due, and Democratic, Process of Law," *Wisconsin Law Review,*
    1944:39–52, 44–45. See also Lusky, "Footnote Redux," 1099. "It should
    not be forgotten," Lusky wrote, "that, in the entire four years between
    the Footnote's appearance and the *Gobitis* decision, not one legal scholar
    had accepted the invitation it extended for further analysis and discus-
    sion." On *Korematsu* and *Hirabayashi* see, for example, Bartholomew B.
    Coyne, "Recent Decisions: Constitutional Law—An Exclusion Order Di-
    rected against an Entire Class of Civilians, Is Not an Unreasonable Dis-
    crimination Offending Due Process of Law, if Deemed Necessary by the
    Military," *Georgetown Law Journal* 33 (1945): 224–237; Margaret M. Quill,
    "Notes and Comments: Constitutional Law—War Power—Due Process,
    Kiyoshi Hirabayashi v. United States," *Boston University Law Review* 23 (1943):
    503–509; Eleanor C. Flynn, "War Law Notes: The War Relocation Au-
    thority and Japanese-Americans; Constitutional Aspects," *George Wash-
    ington Law Review* 11 (1943): 482–520.
78. *Gaines,* 305 U.S. 337; "Recent Cases: Constitutional Law—'Equal Pro-
    tection' under the Fourteenth Amendment—Exclusion of Negro from
    State Law School," *Temple Law Quarterly* 13 (1939): 255–256, 256;
    Cushman, "Constitutional Law in 1938–1939," 276. Bernard S. Jef-
    ferson, "Race Discrimination in Jury Service," *Boston University Law Re-
    view* 19 (1939): 413–447, 416.
79. On the Japanese specifically, see Edwin E. Ferguson, "The California
    Alien Land Law and the Fourteenth Amendment," *California Law Re-
    view* 35 (1947): 61–90; Ida Gobelet Turner, "Recent Decisions: Consti-
    tutional Law—Miscegenation Statutes Questioned," *University of Kansas
    City Law Review* 17 (1948): 146–152; J. R. Mackenzie, "Constitutional
    Law—Equal Protection—California Alien Land Law," *Michigan Law Re-
    view* 46 (1948): 830–832; "Notes: Is Racial Segregation Consistent with
    Equal Protection of the Laws? *Plessy v. Ferguson* Reexamined," *Columbia
    Law Review* 49 (1949): 629–639. On race cases, see Clifford R. Moore,
    "Notes: Anti-Negro Restrictive Covenants and Judicial Enforcement
    Constituting State Action under the Fourteenth Amendment," *Temple
    Law Quarterly* 21 (1947): 139–148; "Cases Noted: Validity of Electoral
    Qualifications under 14th and 15th Amendments," *Columbia Law Re-
    view* 49 (1949): 1144–1160. See also Turner, "Recent Decisions: Misce-

genation Statutes," 152; Joseph Tussman and Jacobus tenBroek, "The Equal Protection of the Laws," *California Law Review* 37 (1949): 341–381. The delayed awareness of the potential importance of *Carolene Products* is also suggested by the fact that one constitutional law case-book did not include *Carolene Products* in its 1941 edition but did include it in its 1949 edition. Compare Dodd, *Cases and Materials* 3rd ed. (1941), xxviii, with Dodd, *Cases and Materials,* 4th ed. (1949), xxvi.

80. Tussman and tenBroek, "Equal Protection," 357, 380.

2. Claiming Rights in the Agricultural South

1. Col. Elton D. Wright VI to U.S. Dept. of Justice, Nov. 1943, file 50–72–5, RG 60, National Archives (hereafter cited as DOJ Files); Snell to Luther M. Swygert, Sept. 11, 1947, in *Papers of the NAACP,* ed. August Meier (Frederick, Md., 1982), microfilm, pt. 13C, rl. 12:424–425 (hereafter cited as *NAACP Papers*).

2. See Risa L. Goluboff, " 'Won't You Please Help Me Get My Son Home': Peonage, Patronage, and Protest in the World War II Urban South," *Law and Social Inquiry* 24 (1999): 777–806.

3. Homer C. Hawkins, "Trends in Black Migration from 1863 to 1960," *Phylon* 34 (1973): 140–152; U.S. Bureau of the Census, "Series A 172–194: Population of Regions, by Sex, Race, Residence, Age, and Nativity; 1790 to 1970," in *Historical Statistics of the United States: Colonial Times to 1970,* Bicentennial ed. (Washington, D.C., 1975), pt. 1:22–23. In 1940, one-third of all white men worked in agriculture and more than one-half of African American men did. Marc Linder, "Farm Workers and the Fair Labor Standards Act: Racial Discrimination in the New Deal," *Texas Law Review* 65 (1987): 1335–1393. It was not until 1954 that production work overtook farming in the South. Jack Temple Kirby, *Rural Worlds Lost: The American South, 1920–1960* (Baton Rouge, La., 1987), 306, fig. 12. See generally Bruce J. Schulman, *From Cotton Belt to Sunbelt: Federal Policy, Economic Development, and the Transformation of the South, 1938–1980* (New York, 1991).

4. See generally James R. Grossman, *Land of Hope: Chicago, Black Southerners, and the Great Migration* (Chicago, 1989); Nicholas Lemann, *The Promised Land: The Great Black Migration and How It Changed America* (New York, 1991); Joe William Trotter, Jr., ed., *The Great Migration in Historical Perspective: New Dimensions of Race, Class, and Gender* (Bloomington, Ind., 1991); Joe William Trotter, Jr., *Black Milwaukee: The Making of an Industrial Proletariat 1915–45* (Urbana, Ill., 1985); Greta de Jong, *A Different Day: African American Struggles for Justice in Rural*

Louisiana, 1900–1970 (Chapel Hill, N.C., 2002), 65–84. On the debate about whether mechanization displaced African American farmworkers or whether the migration of those workers led farmers to turn to mechanization as a replacement, see Pete Daniel, *Breaking the Land: The Transformation of Cotton, Tobacco, and Rice Cultures since 1880* (Urbana, Ill., 1985); Gilbert C. Fite, *Cotton Fields No More: Southern Agriculture, 1865–1980* (Lexington, Ky., 1984); Kirby, *Rural Worlds Lost;* James H. Street, *The New Revolution in the Cotton Economy* (Chapel Hill, N.C., 1957); Gavin Wright, *Old South, New South: Revolutions in the Southern Economy since the Civil War* (New York, 1986); Richard H. Day, "The Economics of Technological Change and the Demise of the Sharecropper," *American Economic Review* 57 (1967): 427–449; Moses S. Musoke, "Mechanizing Cotton Production in the American South: The Tractor, 1915–1960," *Explorations in Economic History* 18 (1981): 347–375; Willis Peterson and Yoav Kislev, "The Cotton Harvester in Retrospect: Labor Displacement or Replacement?" *Journal of Economic History* 46 (1986): 199–216; Warren C. Whatley, "A History of Mechanization in the Cotton South: The Institutional Hypothesis," *Quarterly Journal of Economics* 100 (1985): 1191–1215; Warren C. Whatley, "Labor for the Picking: The New Deal in the South," *Journal of Economic History* 45 (1983): 905–929. On the effect of the Depression and New Deal on African Americans, see Jacqueline Jones, *Labor of Love, Labor of Sorrow: Black Women, Work, and the Family from Slavery to the Present* (New York, 1985), 196–231; Harvard Sitkoff, *A New Deal for Blacks: The Emergence of Civil Rights as a National Issue* (New York, 1978), 1:34–57; Nancy J. Weiss, *Farewell to the Party of Lincoln: Black Politics in the Age of FDR* (Princeton, N.J., 1983), 163, 167–168.

5. Department of Agriculture, Bureau of Agricultural Economics, Division of Program Surveys, "Plans and Attitudes of Winter Vegetable Growers in Palm Beach and Broward Counties, Florida," July 21, 1943, box 8, Project Files 1940–45, Division of Program Surveys, entry 207, RG 83, National Archives (hereafter cited as BAE DPS PF 1940–45). See Kirby, *Rural Worlds Lost;* de Jong, *Different Day,* 116–143; Nan Elizabeth Woodruff, *American Congo: The African American Freedom Struggle in the Delta* (Cambridge, Mass., 2003), 193–197.

6. "Plans Attitudes Winter Growers," BAE DPS PF 1940–45, box 8. See also [Mr.] Zellers, interview by Bureau of Agricultural Economics, Division of Program Surveys, near Rome, Ga., Sept. 20, 1944, transcript, in "Scouting on Migration near Rome, Ga.," 1944, BAE DPS PF 1940–45, box 4. See generally Woodruff, *American Congo,* 193–197; de Jong, *Different Day,* 116–143.

7. "Plans Attitudes Winter Growers," BAE DPS PF 1940–45, box 8. See generally Daniel Kryder, *Divided Arsenal: Race and the American State during World War II* (New York, 2000), 217–222.

8. Oscar F. Bledsoe III, "Agriculture and the Federal Government," Apr. 1943, box 29, Walter Sillers, Jr., Papers, Roberts Memorial Library, Delta State University, Cleveland, Miss., quoted in Nan Elizabeth Woodruff, "Mississippi Delta Planters and Debates over Mechanization, Labor, and Civil Rights in the 1940s," *Journal of Southern History* 60 (1994): 263–284, 271; Woodruff, "Mississippi Delta Planters," 265. For the "all the Negro papers" quote and the "farmers used to" quote, see "Plans Attitudes Winter Growers," BAE DPS PF 1940–45, box 8. For the BAE investigator's quotes, see U.S. Department of Agriculture, Bureau of Agricultural Economics, Division of Program Surveys, "The Problem of Increasing Race Tension in Augusta and Richmond County Georgia," Aug. 18, 1942, 3, BAE DPS PF 1940–45, box 4.

9. Kryder, *Divided Arsenal*, 211–212; Kitty Calavita, *Inside the State: The Bracero Program, Immigration, and the I.N.S.* (New York, 1992); Robert D. Billinger, *Hitler's Soldiers in the Sunshine State: German POWs in Florida* (Gainesville, Fla., 2000); Joseph T. Butler, Jr., "Prisoner of War Labor in the Sugar Cane Fields of Lafourche Parish, Louisiana, 1943–1944," *Louisiana History* 14 (1973): 283–296; Pete Daniel, "Going among Strangers: Southern Reactions to World War II," *Journal of American History* 77 (1990): 886–911.

10. For the planter's quotes and the FSA home supervisor's quotes, see "Plans Attitudes Winter Growers," BAE DPS PF 1940–45, box 8. Howard Devon Hamilton, "The Legislative and Judicial History of the Thirteenth Amendment," pt. 2, *National Bar Journal* 10 (1952): 7–85, 34. See generally Woodruff, *American Congo*, 193–197; de Jong, *Different Day*, 116–143.

11. Peyton Norville, FBI Report, Dec. 30, 1942, DOJ Files, 50–1–7; Workers' Defense League, statement to the United Nations, received Dec. 20, 1947, in *NAACP Papers*, pt. 13C, rl. 12:694–696; William Henry Huff to Roosevelt, Nov. 25, 1944, DOJ Files, 50–40–9; Eleanor Bontecou, oral history interview by Richard D. McKinzie, Washington, D.C., June 5, 1973, 9, transcript, Harry S. Truman Library, Independence, Mo. See also A. Philip Randolph to Homer Cummings, Mar. 5, 1937, DOJ Files, 50–18–12; Frank McAllister, "Confidential Memorandum on Alleged Peonage in Milledgeville," July 9, [1941?], in *NAACP Papers*, pt. 13C, rl. 12:794–797.

12. "Peonage in the South," clipping ca. 1939, in *Schomburg Center Clipping File, 1925–1974* (New York, comp. 1975–81), FSN Sc. 003, 902–2 (here-

after cited as *Schomburg Center Clipping File*); Leslie S. Perry to Victor
Rotnem, May 27, 1943, in *NAACP Papers,* pt. 13C, rl. 12:586–587, 586;
U.S. Department of Agriculture, Bureau of Agricultural Economics, Division of Program Surveys, "Impressions (Regarding Negroes)," Sept.
27, 1941, 2, BAE DPS PF 1940–45, box 8. The Guide to the relevant
NAACP Papers collection gives a good sense of how widespread and geographically diverse the complaints were. It lists complaints from
Georgia, New York, Texas, Arkansas, Virginia, and Florida, among
other states. See Randolph Boehm, comp., *A Guide to the Microfilm Edition of Papers of the NAACP: Part 13, NAACP and Labor, 1940–1955; Series
C, Legal Department Files on Labor, 1940–1955* (Bethesda, Md., 1991), 19–
20 (describing *NAACP Papers,* pt. 13C, rl. 12:440–896). See also Knott
to L. S. Perry, Nov. 18, 1947, in *NAACP Papers,* pt. 13C, rl. 12:691; file
on Millegeville, Ga., 1941, in *NAACP Papers,* pt. 13C, rl. 12:773–810;
Carolyn M. Davenport to Walter White, July 14, 1943, in *NAACP Papers,*
pt. 13C, rl. 12:612–617.

13. Willie May Washington to NAACP, May 12, 1941, in *NAACP Papers,* pt.
13C, rl. 12:469–471.

14. Editorial, "Slavery Seventy Years After," *Christian Century* 53 (Dec. 9,
1936): 1645, quoted in Pete Daniel, *The Shadow of Slavery: Peonage in the
South, 1901–1969* (Urbana, Ill., 1972), 174.

15. Strauder v. West Virginia, 100 U.S. 303 (1880); Editorial, "Textbooks in
Mississippi," *Opportunity* 18 (1940): 99–100. On African American activism in this period despite these developments, see Steven Hahn, *A
Nation under Our Feet: Black Political Struggles in the Rural South from
Slavery to the Great Migration* (Cambridge, Mass., 2003); de Jong,
Different Day; Woodruff, *American Congo.* In 1940, around 2 percent of
the eligible black population was registered to vote. After Smith v. Allwright eliminated the white primary in 1944, southern blacks registered in greater numbers. Eighty to 85 percent of these black voters,
however, lived in cities. David R. Goldfield, *Black, White, and Southern:
Race Relations and Southern Culture 1940 to the Present* (Baton Rouge, La.,
1990), 45–47; Steven F. Lawson, *Black Ballots: Voting Rights in the South,
1944–1969* (New York, 1976).

16. President's Committee on Civil Rights, *To Secure These Rights: The Report
of the President's Committee on Civil Rights* (Washington, D.C., 1947), 24.
See Sitkoff, *New Deal for Blacks;* Daniel, "Going among Strangers;"
Screws v. United States, 325 U.S. 91 (1945).

17. On the real possibility of black land ownership, see, for example,
Robert Higgs, *Competition and Coercion: Blacks in the American Economy,
1865–1914,* Phoenix ed. (Chicago, 1980); Stephen J. DeCanio, "Accu-

mulation and Discrimination in the Postbellum South," in *Market Institutions and Economic Progress in the New South, 1865–1900: Essays Stimulated by "One Kind of Freedom: The Economic Consequences of Emancipation,"* ed. Gary M. Walton and James F. Shepherd (New York, 1981), 103–125. "Cropper farming is a Negro institution," wrote Arthur F. Raper in 1936. *Preface to Peasantry: A Tale of Two Black-Belt Counties* (Chapel Hill, N.C., 1936), 148–149.

18. Frank J. Welch gives a detailed description of both the terms by which black farmworkers labored and the system as a whole in "The Plantation Land Tenure System in Mississippi," *Bulletin of the Mississippi Agricultural Experiment Station* 385 (1943): 5–54. On the accumulation of debt and the effects thereof, see Jacqueline Jones, *The Dispossessed: America's Underclasses from the Civil War to the Present* (New York, 1992), 13–205; de Jong, *Different Day,* 10–40. See also United States v. Gaskin, 320 U.S. 527 (1944); Taylor v. Georgia, 315 U.S. 25 (1942); United States v. Reynolds, 235 U.S. 133 (1914); Bailey v. Alabama, 219 U.S. 219 (1911). Historians have debated the extent of African American mobility following the Civil War and into the twentieth century. For the argument that the combination of law and custom succeeded in curtailing almost all African American movement, see Daniel, *Shadow of Slavery;* Gerald David Jaynes, *Branches without Roots: Genesis of the Black Working Class, 1862–1882* (New York, 1986); Jay R. Mandle, *Not Slave, Not Free: The African American Economic Experience since the Civil War* (Durham, N.C., 1992); Daniel A. Novak, *The Wheel of Servitude: Black Forced Labor after Slavery* (Lexington, Ky., 1978); Pete Daniel, "The Metamorphosis of Slavery, 1865–1900," *Journal of American History* 66 (1979): 88–99; Jonathan M. Wiener, "Class Structure and Economic Development in the American South, 1865–1955," *American Historical Review* 84 (1979): 970–992. For assessments that despite the law, African Americans moved freely throughout the South, see Higgs, *Competition and Coercion;* DeCanio, "Accumulation and Discrimination," in *Market Institutions and Progress,* ed. Walton and Shepherd, 103–125; Joseph D. Reid, Jr., "White Land, Black Labor, and Agricultural Stagnation: The Causes and Effects of Sharecropping in the Postbellum South," in *Market Institutions and Progress,* ed. Walton and Shepherd, 33–55. For integrative views, see Roger Ransom and Richard Sutch, *One Kind of Freedom: The Economic Consequences of Emancipation* (New York, 1977); William Cohen, *At Freedom's Edge: Black Mobility and the Southern White Quest for Racial Control, 1861–1915* (Baton Rouge, La., 1991); William Cohen, "Negro Involuntary Servitude in the South: 1865–1940; A Preliminary Analysis," *Journal of Southern History* 42 (1976): 31–60. See generally Jen-

nifer Roback, "Southern Labor Law in the Jim Crow Era: Exploitative or Competitive?" *University of Chicago Law Review* 51 (1984): 1161–1192.

19. Welch, "Plantation Land Tenure System," 37. See Pete Daniel, "The Legal Basis of Agrarian Capitalism: The South since 1933," in *Race and Class in the American South since 1890,* ed. Melvyn Stokes and Rich Halpern (Providence, R.I., 1994), 79–102; Clarence Mitchell to Thurgood Marshall, memorandum, June 17, 1947, in *NAACP Papers,* pt. 13C, rl. 2:720; Kirby, *Rural Worlds Lost,* 144–148; Brewer to Marshall, Nov. 22, 1948, in *NAACP Papers,* pt. 13C, rl. 2:464–468; Gudrun G. Rom to W. White, Jan. 10, 1946, in *NAACP Papers,* pt. 13C, rl. 2:658–659; Jane E. McAllister and Dorothy M. McAllister, "Adult Education for Negroes in Rural Areas: The Work of the Jeanes Teachers and Home and Farm Demonstration Agents," *Journal of Negro Education* 14 (1945): 331–340; George N. Redd, "The Educational and Cultural Level of the American Negro," *Journal of Negro Education* 19 (1950): 244–252.

20. Chas. G. Irving to Edward R. Dudley, Nov. 2, 1944, in *NAACP Papers,* pt. 13C, rl. 2:395–396; Bright to W. White, Jan. 20, 1945, in *NAACP Papers,* pt. 13C, rl. 2:401. See also Mary Hollys to Roosevelt, July 3, 1939, DOJ Files, 50–0.

21. Rom to W. White, Jan. 10, 1946, in *NAACP Papers,* pt. 13C, rl. 2:658–659; Willie Dixon to attorney general, Apr. 24, 1939, DOJ Files, 50–0. See Beth Biderman, "The Condition of Farm Workers in 1949: Report to the Board of Directors of National Sharecroppers' Fund, Inc.," [1950?], 4, in *NAACP Papers,* pt. 13C, rl. 2:586–589.

22. Franklin H. Williams, "Re: Wyatt Trueblood," news release, Jan. 29, 1947, in *NAACP Papers,* pt. 13C, rl. 9:88. See Robert L. Zangrando, *The NAACP Crusade against Lynching, 1909–1950* (Philadelphia, 1980); J. T. Smith to NAACP, Nov. 20, 1946, in *NAACP Papers,* pt. 13C, rl. 9:77–79; NAACP Legal Department, *Semi-Annual Report,* Jan. 1–June 30, 1944, 12–14, in *NAACP Papers,* pt. 18A, rl. 4:788–790; NAACP Legal Department, *The Legal Front: Some Highlights of the Past Year* (New York, 1940), in *NAACP Papers,* pt. 18A, rl. 4:574–584; See also Charles H. Martin, "Race, Gender, and Southern Justice: The Rosa Lee Ingram Case," *American Journal of Legal History* 29 (1985): 251–268; Lela Bond Phillips, *The Lena Baker Story* (Atlanta, 2001).

23. Rev. Valco R. Harris to George S. Schuyler, Oct. 9, 1944, in *NAACP Papers,* pt. 13C, rl. 2:391–392, 392; Gene S. Norris, FBI Report, Feb. 3, 1944, DOJ Files, 50–9–14.

24. Franklin to Sir, Oct, 25, 1945, in *NAACP Papers,* pt. 13C, rl. 2:407–408; Tinnie Mary Rodgers to Unicle [*sic*] Sam, Oct. 17, 1939, DOJ Files, 50–

0; see also Rom to W. White, Jan. 10, 1946, in *NAACP Papers*, pt. 13C, rl. 2:658–659.

25. "Impressions (Regarding Negroes)," BAE DPS PF 1940–45, box 8; Joel D. Hankins to Department of Justice, May 1, 1937, DOJ Files, 50–0.

26. James K. Gordon, FBI Report, Sept. 1, 1943 (statement of Walter "Pete" Tarver), DOJ Files, 50–1–12; Stetson Kennedy and Kay Kennedy, "The Charge Is Slavery: Company Housing Spells Pionage [*sic*]," *(New York) Daily Compass*, Sept. 23, 1952, 12. On the plight of other sawmill workers, see, for example, Norville, FBI Report, Dec. 30, 1942, DOJ Files, 50–1–7; Oscar Lee Golden, FBI Report, Apr. 3, 1943, DOJ Files, 50–74–0.

27. Henry David McDonald to judge, Dec. 25, 1942, DOJ Files, 50–74–9; Norville, FBI Report, Jan. 18, 1944, DOJ Files, 50–1–13; Edwin Paul Murphy, FBI Report, Aug. 2, 1944, DOJ Files, 50–2–5. See also DOJ Files, 50–18–31; Wendell Berge to Day, June 18, 1943, DOJ Files, 50–810. Norris, FBI Report, Dec. 8, 1943, DOJ Files, 50–9–14.

28. Bernice Wims to Attorney General Murphy, Oct. 25, 1939, DOJ Files, 50–0.

29. Kryder, *Divided Arsenal*, 215; Daniel, *Shadow of Slavery*, 177.

30. Norris, FBI Report, Feb. 3, 1944, DOJ Files, 50–9–14. See also Joseph T. Hill, FBI Report, June 11, 1945, DOJ Files, 50–40–10. See generally George S. Mitchell and Anna Holden, "Money Income of Negroes in the United States," *Journal of Negro Education* 22 (1953): 333–342.

31. NAACP, "Department of Justice," news release, Nov. 4, 1942, in *NAACP Papers*, pt. 13C, rl. 12:544; John E. Keane, FBI Report, Memphis, Tenn., March 11, 1942 (statement of Vernon Lawhorn), DOJ Files, 50–18–15, 10; C. B. McCullar to Roger Baldwin, May 19, 1941, in *NAACP Papers*, pt. 13C, rl. 12:775–776. See generally Risa L. Goluboff, "Vernon Lawhorn, Thomas James Buchner, and the Green Brothers: Reverse Migration in World War II," in *The Human Tradition in American Labor History*, ed. Eric Arnesen (Wilmington, Del., 2004), 193–209.

32. Letter from William Lucas, Mar. 21, 1943, in *NAACP Papers*, pt. 13C, rl. 12:582; FBI Report, Corwin Johnson, July 27, 1942 (statement of Vernon Lawhorn), DOJ Files, 50–18–15, 8–9. See also Edward L. Nixon to Steven B. McCord, Oct. 29, 1946, in *NAACP Papers*, pt. 13C, rl. 12:812. On employers making little effort to hide the practice, see, for example, *Gaskin*, 320 U.S. at 529; *Reynolds*, 235 U.S. at 144.

33. Huff to Frank Murphy, Sept. 26, 1939, DOJ Files, 50–0; Letter from J. D. Bowser, A. V. Bowser, and Richard Johnnie Young, May 8, 1943, DOJ Files, 50–74–11. For the "ax handles" quote and the "plantation Negroes" quote, see Wims to Attorney General Murphy, Oct. 25, 1939,

DOJ Files, 50–0. George Tailor to "Gentlemen," Aug. 29, 1941, in *NAACP Papers*, pt. 13C, rl. 12:494–499; Indictment, United States v. Castle, DOJ Files, 50–41–20; McAllister, "Report on Peonage at Sealy Springs," Jan. 15, 1942, 2, in *NAACP Papers*, pt. 13C, rl. 12:844–845. See also Henry A. Onsgard, Jr., FBI Report, Apr. 13, 1943, DOJ Files, 50–19M–6; H. A. Childs, FBI Report, June 16, 1942, DOJ Files, 50–18–18.

34. Stephen A. Smith, FBI Report, July 10, 1946, DOJ Files, 50–79–2. For the "some white folks" quote and the "worse than she can explain" quote, see Mattie Lomax to NAACP, Mar. 10, 1946, in *NAACP Papers*, pt. 13C, rl. 12:752. Affidavit of Polly Johnson, 1946, 1, in *NAACP Papers*, pt. 13C, rl. 12:764–766. See also Graves to Marshall, Aug. 9, 1940, in *NAACP Papers*, pt. 13C, rl. 12:463–464; Walter Pate, FBI Report, Feb. 24, 1945, DOJ Files, 50–67–9.

35. LeRoy White to Marshall, Oct. 14, 1947, in *NAACP Papers*, pt. 13C, rl. 12:416–417, 417; Affidavit of Elizabeth Coker, Jan. 30, 1947, in *NAACP Papers*, pt. 13C, rl. 12:390–391.

36. Sproull Colbert to Arthur W. Mitchell, Apr. 21, 1941, DOJ Files, 50–19–6.

37. Welch, "Plantation Land Tenure System," 32. See Novak, *Wheel of Servitude*, 1–8; Fla. Stat. chs. 83.10, 85.22 (1943); Ga. Code Ann. §§61–201 to 61–203 and annotations (1937); Daniel, "Legal Basis," in *Race in American South*, ed. Stokes and Halpern, 79–102. See also Ga. Code Ann. §§67–110, 67–1105 (1937). The following state laws gave first priority to landlords and second to tenants: S.C. Code Ann. §8773 (Law. Co-op. 1942); N.C. Gen. Stat. §2355 (1935); Tex. Code Ann. §5222 (Vernon 1947); Miss. Code Ann. §336 (1942).

38. N.C. Gen. Stat. §2621(99e) (1935); Ark. Stat. Ann. §75–630 (1947); Va. Code Ann. app. (Tax Code) §183 (Michie 1942); 51 Ala. Code §513 (1940). See also S.C. Code Ann. §1378 (1942); Fla. Stat. §205.39 (1943); N.C. Gen. Stat. §7880(85) (1935); Novak, *Wheel of Servitude*; Roback, "Southern Labor Law," 1169; David E. Bernstein, *Only One Place of Redress: African Americans, Labor Regulations, and the Courts from Reconstruction to the New Deal* (Durham, N.C., 2001), 27 n. 111.

39. United Cannery, Agricultural, Packing and Allied Workers of America (UCAPAWA), "UCAPAWA Asks Slavery Investigation," news release, ca. 1939, in *Schomburg Center Clipping File*, FSN Sc. 003, 902–2. See N.C. Gen. Stat. §§4469, 4470 (1935); Ga. Code Ann. §§66–9904 to 66–9905 (1937); Tenn. Code Ann. §8559 (1938); S.C. Code Ann. §7030–10 (Law Co-op. 1942); Fla. Stat. ch. 448.02 (1943); Ark. Code Ann. §81–210 (Michie 1947); 26 Ala. Code §332 (1940); Roback, "Southern Labor Law"; Novak, *Wheel of Servitude*, 39.

40. John E. Wyndham to Jim C. Smith, Jan. 10, 1944, reprinted in Joseph Donald Auel, FBI Report, Feb. 4, 1944, DOJ Files, 50–1–15; DOJ Files, 50–794; Marcus B. Calhoun, FBI Report, Dec. 21, 1943, 4 (statement of Joe Armstead, quoting Sheriff McCart), DOJ Files, 50–19–18; Frank Coleman to Rotnem, Jan. 8, 1943, DOJ Files, 50–40–5. See also "The Slave Market Is Still Doing Business in the South," Aug. 26, 1951, in *Schomburg Center Clipping File,* FSN 003, 902–2; Roy Porter, FBI Report, June 11, 1943, DOJ Files, 50–18–25.

41. Robert Reece Rogers, FBI Report, Apr. 3, 1944 (statement of T. J. Lord), DOJ Files, 50–20–19; Noel H. Malone to assistant attorney general, Mar. 30, 1953, DOJ Files, 50–40–30. See, for example, "Report of Disposition of Criminal Case," Dec. 31, 1943, DOJ Files, 50–1–10; Charles W. Mauze, FBI Report, May 17, 1943, DOJ Files, 50–41–19; George R. Bixler, FBI Report, May 4, 1944, DOJ Files, 50–41–24; R. Bert Carter, FBI Report, May 1, 1942, DOJ Files, 50–74–4; William Frankling Gigray, Jr., FBI Report, Oct. 15, 1943, DOJ Files, 50–74–14; Julian B. Brown, FBI Report, Oct. 5, 1943, DOJ Files, 50–18–21.

42. Berge to J. Edgar Hoover, memorandum, June 12, 1942, DOJ Files, 50–19–10; Stetson Kennedy and Kay Kennedy, "The Charge Is Slavery," *(New York) Daily Compass,* Oct. 13–22, 1952 (article series); Harrison H. Southworth, FBI Report, May 16, 1946, DOJ Files, 50–1–21. See also Mrs. Frank Ballard to Steve King, Dec. 19, 1941, reprinted in David M. Harris, FBI Report, Mar. 21, 1942, DOJ Files, 50–74–2.

43. Tom C. Clark to solicitor general, memorandum, Jan. 20, 1944, DOJ Files, 50–18–29. See 14 Ala. Code §226 (1940); Tex. Code Ann. §1416 note 3 (Vernon 1926); Fla. Stat. ch. 817.09 (1941); N.C. Gen. Stat. §4281 (1935); S.C. Code Ann. §7030–2 (Law. Co-op. 1942); Va. Code Ann. §4454a (Michie 1942); Ark. Stat. Ann. §51–508 (1947); Pollock v. Williams, 322 U.S. 4 (1944); *Taylor,* 315 U.S. 25; John P. Cowart to attorney general, Dec. 28, 1949, DOJ Files, 50–19–37; Alexander M. Campbell to director, FBI, Oct. 26, 1948, DOJ Files, 50–19–31; Herbert S. Phillips to Hon. Warren Olney, III, Apr. 16, 1953, DOJ Files, 50–18–63; Cowart to attorney general, Apr. 13, 1950, DOJ Files, 50–19–37; J. Sewell Elliott to William M. Sneed and Sheriff J. R. Nix, DOJ Files, 50–19M–48; Fla. Stat. ch. 817.09 (repealed 1951).

44. Va. Code Ann. §2808 (Michie 1942); Tenn. Code Ann. §5248 (Vernon 1938); Ark. Stat. Ann. §41–4301 (Michie 1947). See also, for example, Tex. Code Ann. §607 (Vernon 1938); Tex. Code Ann. §607 (Vernon Supp. 1952); Ga. Code Ann. §26–7001 (1936); Fla. Stat. ch. 856.02 (1944); 14 Ala. Code §437 (1940). For a discussion of the history of vagrancy laws in the post–Civil War era, see Amy Dru Stanley, *From*

Bondage to Contract: Wage Labor, Marriage, and the Market in the Age of Slave Emancipation (New York, 1998), 98–137.

45. Berge to Phillips, Nov. 17, 1942, DOJ Files, 50–18–16; Clare Franklin Carter, FBI Report, Oct. 1, 1942 (statement of B. F. King), DOJ Files, 50–18–16; Phillips to Berge, July 7, 1943, DOJ Files, 50–18–16. See also Childs, FBI Report, June 16, 1942, DOJ Files, 50–18–18.

46. E. O. Gilleylen to Roosevelt, Oct. 31, 1943, DOJ Files, 50–41–23; William E. Oglesby, FBI Report, Oct. 14, 1941 (statement of Mrs. Ola Aultman), DOJ Files, 50–816. See Rev. Aron S. Gilmartin to W. White, June 22, 1944, in *NAACP Papers*, pt. 13A, rl. 19:192; *Reynolds*, 235 U.S. 133; Joe B. Klay to Frances [*sic*] Biddle, Nov. 19, 1942, DOJ Files, 50–18–22. See also John L. Madala, FBI Report, Dec. 9, 1944, DOJ Files, 50–18–32.

47. Arthur D. Shores to Marshall, Feb. 24, 1943, in *NAACP Papers*, pt. 13C, rl. 12:560–561; W. J. Lacy to Huff, n.d., in *NAACP Papers*, pt. 13C, rl. 12:625; E. F. James to Dept. of Justice, June 6, 1944, DOJ Files, 50–19M–8.

48. Milton R. Konvitz to L. S. Perry, July 8, 1943, in *NAACP Papers*, pt. 13C, rl. 12:608–609.

49. Gordon, FBI Report, Sept. 1, 1943 (statement of Walter "Pete" Tarver), DOJ Files, 50–1–12. See, for example, Joel D. Colglazier, FBI Report, July 11, 1945, DOJ Files, 50–1–20.

50. Clarence J. Stokes, Sr., to U.S. district attorney, May 18, 1943, DOJ Files, 50–18–23.

51. Fred W. Gooding, FBI Report, July 24, 1942, DOJ Files, 50–19M–7. See generally Peter W. Bardaglio, *Reconstructing the Household: Families, Sex, and the Law in the Nineteenth-Century South* (Chapel Hill, N.C., 1995), 161–163; Laura F. Edwards, *Gendered Strife and Confusion: The Political Culture of Reconstruction* (Urbana, Ill., 1997), 40–44.

52. A. Maceo Smith to Marshall, Nov. 7, 1945, in *NAACP Papers*, pt. 13C, rl. 2:624; NAACP, "NAACP Urges Justice Dept. to Investigate Peonage," news release, May 28, 1943, in *NAACP Papers*, pt. 13C, rl. 12:588; Edwin B. Poorman, FBI Report, Feb. 6, 1945, DOJ Files, 50–1–14. See also "Maryland 'Peonage' Studied," *New York Herald Tribune*, Sept. 27, 1943, 21, in *NAACP Papers*, pt. 13A, rl. 19:209; Kryder, *Divided Arsenal*, 213–214.

53. Hoover to attorney general, memorandum, Oct. 25, 1945, DOJ Files, 50–3–3.

54. Felix Tate to Frank Murphy, Aug. 29, 1939, DOJ Files, 50–0; Lulu B. White to Marshall, Dec. 4, 1944, in *NAACP Papers*, pt. 13C, rl. 2:398. See Agricultural Adjustment Act of 1938, ch. 30, secs. 101, 102, §8(b), (e),

52 Stat. 31, 31–32, 34 (§8[b] is codified as amended at 16 U.S.C. §590h[b] [2000 & Supp. II 2002]; §8[e] was repealed by Pub. L. No. 104–127, §336[a][1][A][ii], 110 Stat. 1004 [1996]); see also J. C. Faulk to attorney general, Jan. 1, 1940, DOJ Files, 50–0; Marshall to secretary of agriculture, Feb. 14, 1940, in *NAACP Papers,* pt. 13A, rl. 1:308–309; Kirby, *Rural Worlds Lost,* 61–68; John Calvin Rice, FBI Report, July 29, 1943, DOJ Files, 50–74–14; F. H. Green, FBI Report, Oct. 1, 1940, DOJ Files, 50–804; Colbert to A. W. Mitchell, Apr. 21, 1941, DOJ Files, 50–19–6; Daniel, "Legal Basis," in *Race in American South,* ed. Stokes and Halpern, 79–102.

55. Cecil C. Humphreys, FBI Report, Dec. 19, 1946, DOJ Files, 50–9–23. See L. S. Perry to Dudley, Hastie, and W. White, memorandum, Oct. 11, 1945, in *NAACP Papers,* pt. 13C, rl. 2:599–600; Norville, FBI Report, Jan. 18, 1944, DOJ Files, 50–1–13; Hugh C. Norton, FBI Report, Jan. 10, 1944, DOJ Files, 50–9–14.

56. Rogers, FBI Report, Apr. 3, 1944, DOJ Files, 50–20–19. See, for example, Marshall to Rotnem, Oct. 18, 1943, DOJ Files, 50–40–7. See also James C. Cobb, " 'Somebody Done Nailed Us on the Cross': Federal Farm and Welfare Policy and the Civil Rights Movement in the Mississippi Delta," *Journal of American History* 77 (1990): 912–936; Kryder, *Divided Arsenal,* 215.

57. Interview 69, Coahoma County, Miss., Aug. 25, 1944, transcript, Low Income Farmer Survey, Division of Program Surveys, RG 83, National Archives (hereafter cited as BAE DPS LIFS), quoted in Daniel, "Going among Strangers," 891.

58. Act of April 29, 1943, ch. 82, §§2–3, 4(a), 57 Stat. 70, 70–71. See Woodruff, *American Congo,* 201–213; de Jong, *Different Day,* 116–143; Kryder, *Divided Arsenal,* 215.

59. Petition for Injunction, 3, Shackelford v. U.S. Dep't of Agric., No. H-257 (E.D. Ark. 1945) (citing Exec. Order No. 9599, 10 Fed. Reg. 10,155 [Aug. 18, 1945]), in *NAACP Papers,* pt. 13C, rl. 2:595–598. See Emergency Price Control Act of 1942, ch. 26, 56 Stat. 23 (terminated 1947, per Price Control Extension Act of 1946, ch. 671, §1, 60 Stat. 664); Petition for Injunction, 1, *Shackelford,* No. H-257, in *NAACP Papers,* pt. 13C, rl. 2:595–598; H. L. Mitchell, "A Ceiling on Cotton Pickers' Wages," statement submitted to the secretary of agriculture, Sept. 10, 1945, 1, in *NAACP Papers,* pt. 13C, rl. 2:591–594 (hereafter cited as Mitchell statement). In Missouri, where the STFU was able to organize opposition to the ceilings, the wage board decided not to impose them. H. L. Mitchell to L. S. Perry, Dec. 7, 1945, in *NAACP Papers,* pt. 13C, rl. 2:629–630. See generally Woodruff, *American Congo,* 201–213.

60. Mitchell statement, 2, in *NAACP Papers,* pt. 13C, rl. 2:591–594, 592. See generally Mitchell and Holden, "Money Income," 335.

61. L. S. Perry to Clinton P. Anderson, Feb. 27, 1946, in *NAACP Papers,* pt. 13C, rl. 2:661–662; NFLU, news release, n.d., in *NAACP Papers,* pt. 13C, rl. 2:666–667; L. S. Perry to Dudley, Hastie, and W. White, memorandum, Oct. 11, 1945, in *NAACP Papers,* pt. 13C, rl. 2:599–600.

62. W. C. Holley to L. S. Perry, Mar. 13, 1946 (internal quotation marks omitted), in *NAACP Papers,* pt. 13C, rl. 2:673–674.

63. Mitchell statement, 1, in *NAACP Papers,* pt. 13C, rl. 2:591–594. See also Lewis to W. White, Oct. 15, 1945, in *NAACP Papers,* pt. 13C, rl. 2:604.

64. Mitchell statement, in *NAACP Papers,* pt. 13C, rl. 2:591; L. S. Perry to Anderson, Feb. 27, 1946, in *NAACP Papers,* pt. 13C, rl. 2:661–662, 662. See also Claude A. Barnett to L. S. Perry, May 20, 1946, in *NAACP Papers,* pt. 13C, rl. 2:683–684; Lewis to W. White, Oct. 15, 1945, in *NAACP Papers,* pt. 13C, rl. 2:604.

65. Poorman, FBI Report, Sept. 9, 1944, 3, DOJ Files, 50–1–14. David M. Bixby noted that almost all federal anti-peonage prosecutions were brought on behalf of black farm tenants against white farmers. "The Roosevelt Court, Democratic Ideology, and Minority Rights: Another Look at United States v. Classic," *Yale Law Journal* 90 (1981): 741–815.

66. Henry Calhoun Weathers, oral history interview by Bernice Kelly Harris, Mar. 1, 1939, transcript, Federal Workers' Project Life Histories Files, Southern Historical Collection, University of North Carolina, quoted in Kirby, *Rural Worlds Lost,* 237; Theodore Rosengarten, comp., *All God's Dangers: The Life of Nate Shaw* (New York, 1975), 488.

67. Interview 70, Coahoma County, Miss., Aug. 25, 1944, transcript, BAE DPS LIFS, quoted in Daniel, "Going among Strangers," 895.

68. Welch, "Plantation Land Tenure System," 52.

69. U.S. Department of Agriculture, Bureau of Agricultural Economics, Division of Program Surveys, "Preliminary Study of Negro Youth," Nov. 26, 1941, 2, BAE DPS PF 1940–45, box 5.

70. Hamilton, "Legislative and Judicial History," pt. 2, 36; Welch, "Plantation Land Tenure System," 54; "Slavery in the United States, Peonage," n.d., in *Schomburg Center Clipping File,* FSN Sc. 003, 902–2.

71. Kennedy and Kennedy, "The Charge Is Slavery"; Huff to W. White, Nov. 24, 1941, in *NAACP Papers,* pt. 13C, rl. 12:727–729; Huff to Marshall, Dec. 21, 1941, in *NAACP Papers,* pt. 13C, rl. 12:737–740; "Abolish Peonage Committee Hails U.S. Indictment of Georgia Peonage Landlord," news release, n.d. (quoting Huff), in *NAACP Papers,* pt. 13C, rl. 12:723.

72. Lewis to W. White, Oct. 15, 1945, in *NAACP Papers,* pt. 13C, rl. 2:604;

Lewis to W. White, Nov. 1, 1945, in *NAACP Papers*, pt. 13C, rl. 2:615; Lewis to Marian Perry, Jan. 15, 1945, in *NAACP Papers*, pt. 13C, rl. 2:653.

73. Robert Hammond to Sir [NAACP], Apr. 26, 1947, in *NAACP Papers*, pt. 13C, rl. 12:679–680.

3. Claiming Rights in the Industrial Economy

1. Affidavit of John J. Allen, n.d., in *Papers of the NAACP*, ed. August Meier (Frederick, Md., 1982), microfilm, pt. 13A, rl. 4:295 (hereafter cited as *NAACP Papers*).

2. Anonymous to Walter White, May 30, 1942, in *NAACP Papers*, pt. 13A, rl. 4:421; Theodore Johnson to NAACP, Aug. 31, 1944, in *NAACP Papers*, pt. 13C, rl. 5:91.

3. Daniel Kryder, *Divided Arsenal: Race and the American State during World War II* (New York, 2000), 112.

4. William C. Crump to Whom It May Concern, n.d., in *NAACP Papers*, pt. 13A, rl. 1:519; Mrs. J. P. Byrd to NAACP, Jan. 19, 1940, in *NAACP Papers*, pt. 13C, rl. 7:688. See Neil A. Wynn, *The Afro-American and the Second World War* (New York, 1975), 40; Wendell E. Pritchett, "World War II and Black Labor," chap. 4 in "Working along the Color Line: The Life and Times of Robert Weaver" (manuscript, University of Pennsylvania Law School, n.d.), 45; Lee Finkle, "The Conservative Aims of Militant Rhetoric: Black Protest during World War II," *Journal of American History* 60 (1973): 692–713.

5. Wynn, *Afro-American Second World War*, 55.

6. Eileen Boris, "Black Workers, Trade Unions, and Labor Standards: The Wartime FEPC" in *Historical Roots of the Urban Crisis: African Americans in the Industrial City, 1900–1950*, ed. Henry Louis Taylor, Jr., and Walter Hill (New York, 2000), 251–273, 265.

7. Merl E. Reed, *Seedtime for the Modern Civil Rights Movement: The President's Committee on Fair Employment Practice, 1941–1946* (Baton Rouge, La., 1991), 16; Hugh Davis Graham, *The Civil Rights Era: Origins and Development of National Policy, 1960–1972* (New York, 1990), 10.

8. Bessie W. Armstrong to NAACP, July 31, 1942, in *NAACP Papers*, pt. 13A, rl. 2:196.

9. See, for example, President's Committee on Civil Rights, *To Secure These Rights: The Report of the President's Committee on Civil Rights* (Washington, D.C., 1947), 58.

10. Gunnar Myrdal, *An American Dilemma: The Negro Problem and Modern Democracy* (New York, 1944), 417–418; U.S. Employment Service, U.S.E.S.

Operations Bulletin, no. C-45, n.d., 2–3. See generally Charles D. Chamberlain, *Victory at Home: Manpower and Race in the American South during World War II* (Athens, Ga., 2003).

11. Robert C. Weaver, *Negro Labor: A National Problem* (New York, 1946), 146; Fair Employment Practice Committee, *Final Report* (Washington, D.C., 1947), 34–35; Reed, *Seedtime*, 156, 199, 222–225; Louis Ruchames, *Race, Jobs, and Politics: The Story of FEPC* (New York, 1953), 188, 191.

12. Weaver, *Negro Labor*, 147; Affidavit of Arthur St. Cyr, Oct. 30, 1940, in *NAACP Papers*, pt. 13A, rl. 3:17. See also Freddie Peale to NAACP, March 2, 1941, in *NAACP Papers*, pt. 13A, rl. 1:423.

13. Ruchames, *Race, Jobs, and Politics*, 11–16.

14. Weaver, *Negro Labor*, 53, 54, 59. See Reed, *Seedtime*, 176–177; Wynn, *Afro-American Second World War*, 77. By April 1941, for example, the United States Office of Education had provided $230,000 for training equipment in Tennessee, of which $2,000 had been allocated to courses for African Americans. Weaver, *Negro Labor*, 53–54.

15. Letter from Hamilton, Feb. 10, 1943, in *NAACP Papers*, pt. 13A, rl. 10:57; Ferdinand M. Barry to White, Aug. 19, 1941, in *NAACP Papers*, pt. 13A, rl. 4:348. See also Lester Hall to NAACP, Feb. 22, 1943, in *NAACP Papers*, pt. 13C, rl. 10:347.

16. *Pittsburgh Courier*, Dec. 13, 1941, 3, quoted in Reed, *Seedtime*, 179–180; Affidavit of John Joseph Woods, July 1941, in *NAACP Papers*, pt. 13A, rl. 2:169.

17. Administrative assistant to Ralph A. Bard, Feb. 15, 1943, in *NAACP Papers*, pt. 13A, rl. 7:103–104.

18. Harvard Sitkoff, "The New Deal and Race Relations," in *Fifty Years Later: The New Deal Evaluated*, ed. Harvard Sitkoff (Philadelphia, 1985), 93–112, 100; Harvard Sitkoff, *A New Deal for Blacks: The Emergence of Civil Rights as a National Issue* (New York, 1978), 1:67.

19. Robert L. Carter to Roy Wilkins, memorandum, Mar. 22, 1945, in *NAACP Papers*, pt. 13C, rl. 4:207; Ernestine Welch to NAACP, Mar. 25, 1945, in *NAACP Papers*, pt. 13C, rl. 9:470.

20. Grace Morton to Clarence Mitchell, Sept. 27, 1948, in *NAACP Papers*, pt. 13C, rl. 4:516–517.

21. Affidavit of Lela P. Leverette, Sept. 4, 1941, in *NAACP Papers*, pt. 13A, rl. 3:82; Affidavit of Annie E. Powell Campbell, Nov. 10, 1941, in *NAACP Papers*, pt. 13A, rl. 3:145.

22. Melba Sunday to White, Sept. 2, 1941, in *NAACP Papers*, pt. 13C, rl. 8:543; Affidavit of P. M. Sunday, Sept. 20, 1941, in *NAACP Papers*, pt. 13C, rl. 8:549.

23. James K. McClendon to Mr. McNutt, Aug. 7, 1942, in *NAACP Papers*, pt.

13A, rl. 3:751. See John Wallace to NAACP, July 21, 1941, in *NAACP Papers,* pt. 13A, rl. 17:568; Ernest Poree to NAACP, Aug. 14, 1943, in *NAACP Papers,* pt. 13C, rl. 7:399; Glenn C. Adair to NAACP, Apr. 12, 1944, in *NAACP Papers,* pt. 13C, rl. 2:236.

24. National Labor Relations Act, ch. 372, §8(3), 49 Stat. 449, 452 (1935) (codified as amended at 29 U.S.C. §158[a][3] [2000]); Weaver, *Negro Labor,* 143; Charles H. Graham to editor, *New York Age,* July 9, 1941, in *NAACP Papers,* pt. 13C, rl. 4:21.

25. Wynn, *Afro-American Second World War,* 41.

26. Samuel G. Whitney to NAACP, June 1, 1941, in *NAACP Papers,* pt. 13C, rl. 9:284. See Affidavit of William Kennedy, Jr., Sept. 15, 1941, in *NAACP Papers,* pt. 13A, rl. 3:94; Letter from Larry Watts, July 24, 1942, in *NAACP Papers,* pt. 123A, rl. 7:067; Affidavit of St. Cyr, Oct. 30, 1940, in *NAACP Papers,* pt. 13A, rl. 3:17.

27. Direct Examination of J. O. Murray at 30, In re Kaiser Co. (F.E.P.C. Portland, Ore., Oct. 18–19, 1944), in *Selected Documents from Records of the Committee on Fair Employment Practice: RG 228, National Archives,* ed. Bruce I. Friend (Glen Rock, N.J., 1971), microfilm, rl. 13 (hereafter cited as *FEPC Documents*); Direct Examination of Virginia Lemire at 157, In re Kaiser Co., in *FEPC Documents,* rl. 13. See also Johnson to NAACP, Aug. 31, 1944, in *NAACP Papers,* pt. 13C, rl. 5:91.

28. Miss Beulah Newton to NAACP, Feb. 9, 1945, in *NAACP Papers,* pt. 13C, rl. 6:781. See McClendon to McNutt, Aug. 7, 1942, in *NAACP Papers,* pt. 13A, rl. 3:751; Herbert W. Francois to White, Apr. 22, 1942, in *NAACP Papers,* pt. 13A, rl. 7:43.

29. Elizabeth P. Scott to NAACP, Oct. 24, 1942, in *NAACP Papers,* pt. 13C, rl. 5:65. See Letter from Hamilton, Feb. 10, 1943, in *NAACP Papers,* pt. 13A, rl. 10:57; Henry E. DuPort to White, Oct. 22, 1940, in *NAACP Papers,* pt. 13A, rl. 4:265.

30. See Affidavit of Frank Smith, Aug. 29, 1941, in *NAACP Papers,* pt. 13A, rl. 3:76; Francois to White, Apr. 22, 1942, in *NAACP Papers,* pt. 13A, rl. 7:43; Affidavit of Catherine Coleman, n.d., in *NAACP Papers,* pt. 13C, rl. 3:70.

31. Affidavit of P. M. Sunday, Sept. 20, 1941, in *NAACP Papers,* pt. 13C, rl. 8:549; Samuel A. Brown to White, Feb. 25, 1941, in *NAACP Papers,* pt. 13A, rl. 1:505.

32. Affidavit of Edmond Van Osten, July 31, 1941, in *NAACP Papers,* pt. 13A, rl. 2:171.

33. Affidavit of Esterline Davis, March 4, 1942, in *NAACP Papers,* pt. 13C, rl. 3:404; Affidavit of Thomas Allen Trayler, July 18, 1941, in *NAACP Papers,* pt. 13A, rl. 3:83; Joseph Gordon to White, Oct. 30, 1941, in

NAACP Papers, pt. 13A, rl. 3:436; Anonymous to NAACP, Oct. 4, 1940, in *NAACP Papers,* pt. 13A, rl. 17:748. See also Laurona F. Hunter to NAACP, May 1, 1943, in *NAACP Papers,* pt. 13C, rl. 10:363; Frances Young to White, May 24, 1943, in *NAACP Papers,* pt. 13C, rl. 4:38; Affidavit of Rev. J. O. Clark, n.d., in *NAACP Papers,* pt. 13C, rl. 4:27; Affidavit of Scott Harper, Oct. 24, 1941, in *NAACP Papers,* pt. 13A, rl. 3:143.

34. Gordon to White, Oct. 30, 1941, in *NAACP Papers,* pt. 13A, rl. 3:436; Cecil V. Garcia to NAACP, Sept. 5, 1944, in *NAACP Papers,* pt. 13C, rl. 4:50. See also Letter to NAACP, Jan. 27, 1943, in *NAACP Papers,* pt. 13A, rl. 11:298; J. H. Pollitt to NAACP, Nov. 6, 1943, in *NAACP Papers,* pt. 13C, rl. 4:42.

35. William D. Radford to NAACP, Sept. 24, 1942, in *NAACP Papers,* pt. 13A, rl. 4:465; J. B. Harren and Reddick Strickland to White, Nov. 15, 1941, in *NAACP Papers,* pt. 13C, rl. 6:731.

36. Direct Examination of Sidney Wolf at 200–201, In re Or. Shipbuilding Corp. (F.E.P.C. Portland, Ore., Nov. 15–16, 1943), in *FEPC Documents,* rl. 13; Complaint of Joyce Ray Washington, n.d. [1943?], in *FEPC Documents,* rl. 14.

37. Gordon to White, Oct. 30, 1941, in *NAACP Papers,* pt. 13A, rl. 3:436; Affidavit of Thomas Harrison, n.d., in *NAACP Papers,* pt. 13C, rl. 11:479; Affidavit of William Brinson, n.d., in *NAACP Papers,* pt. 13C, rl. 11:478; Radford to NAACP, Sept. 24, 1942, in *NAACP Papers,* pt. 13A, rl. 4:465. See also T. H. Allen to White, Feb. 16, 1941, in *NAACP Papers,* pt. 13A, rl. 1:12.

38. Ruchames, *Race, Jobs, and Politics,* 60–61. White railroad unions and the railroads colluded after World War I to exclude African American railroaders from many positions they had held since the end of the Civil War. Eric Arnesen, *Brotherhoods of Color: Black Railroad Workers and the Struggle for Equality* (Cambridge, Mass., 2001), 70–83. See, for example, Brian Paxton to Thurgood Marshall, June 9, 1944, in *NAACP Papers,* pt. 13C, rl. 7:476.

39. A friend to White, Sept. 10, 1942, in *NAACP Papers,* pt. 13A, rl. 4:453; Bruce Nelson, "Organized Labor and the Struggle for Black Equality in Mobile during World War II," *Journal of American History* 80 (1993), 952–988; Harvard Sitkoff, "Racial Militancy and Interracial Violence in the Second World War," *Journal of American History* 58 (1971): 661–681.

40. National Labor Relations Act, ch. 372, §9(a), 49 Stat. 449, 453 (1935) (codified as amended at 29 U.S.C. §159[a] [2000]).

41. Ruchames, *Race, Jobs, and Politics,* 11–12. See generally, Herbert Hill, "The Importance of Race in American Labor History," *International Journal of Politics, Culture and Society* 9 (1995): 317–343; Timothy J.

Minchin, *The Color of Work: The Struggle for Civil Rights in the Southern Paper Industry, 1945–1980* (Chapel Hill, N.C., 2001), 73–98; Eric Arnesen, "Following the Color Line of Labor: Black Workers and the Labor Movement before 1930," *Radical History Review* 55 (1993): 53–87. Unions were not uniformly hostile to black workers. See, for example, Eric Arnesen, *Waterfront Workers of New Orleans: Race, Class, and Politics, 1863–1923* (New York, 1991); Robert R. Korstad, *Civil Rights Unionism: Tobacco Workers and the Struggle for Democracy in the Mid-Twentieth-Century South* (Chapel Hill, N.C., 2003); Robert Korstad and Nelson Lichtenstein, "Opportunities Found and Lost: Labor, Radicals, and the Early Civil Rights Movement," *Journal of American History* 75 (1988): 786–811; Michael Goldfield, "Race and the CIO: The Possibilities for Racial Egalitarianism during the 1930s and 1940s," *International Labor and Working Class History* 44 (1993): 1–32; Judith Stein, "Southern Workers in National Unions: Birmingham Steelworkers, 1936–1951," in *Organized Labor in the Twentieth-Century South*, ed. Robert H. Zieger (Knoxville, Tenn., 1991), 183–222. On the debate generally, see Eric Arnesen, "Up from Exclusion: Black and White Workers, Race, and the State of Labor History," *Reviews in American History* 26 (1998): 146–174; Rick Halpern, "Organized Labor, Black Workers and the Twentieth-Century South: The Emerging Revision," *Social History* 19 (1994): 359–383.

42. D. N. Unthank to Mark Ethridge, Aug. 19, 1941, in *NAACP Papers*, pt. 13A, rl. 2:77.

43. Thomas A. Webster to Sidney Hillman, Mar. 8, 1941, in *NAACP Papers*, pt. 13A, rl. 3:395.

44. Unemployed women pressers of Local 60 to NAACP, May 28, 1941, in *NAACP Papers*, pt. 13A, rl. 17:634. See Weaver, *Negro Labor*, 217.

45. Affidavit of Eddie Kemp, Sept. 13, 1941, in *NAACP Papers*, pt. 13A, rl. 3:93; Affidavit of James Phelps, Sept. 13, 1941, in *NAACP Papers*, pt. 13A, rl. 3:95.

46. Alphonso Morris to NAACP, Apr. 9, 1940, in *NAACP Papers*, pt. 13A, rl. 7:006; Adolphus Braithwaite to NAACP, Apr. 15, 1940, in *NAACP Papers*, pt. 13A, rl. 7:012.

47. Wilkins to A. Philip Randolph, Oct. 7, 1941, in *NAACP Papers*, pt. 13A, rl. 17:581.

48. Ruchames, *Race, Jobs, and Politics*, 159–160; Wynn, *Afro-American Second World War*, 55–57; William H. Harris, *The Harder We Run: Black Workers since the Civil War* (New York, 1982), 122.

49. Weaver, *Negro Labor*, 78, 81, 97; Wynn, *Afro-American Second World War*, 59.

50. Editorial, "Postwar Reconversion and the Negro," *Norfolk Journal and*

Guide, Aug. 19, 1944, 10, in box 516, Newspaper Clippings, RG 228, National Archives, quoted in Reed, *Seedtime,* 323. See Ruchames, *Race, Jobs, and Politics,* 165; Servicemen's Readjustment Act of 1944, ch. 268, §§800(d)(1), 901(a), 1100(a), (c), (d), (f), 58 Stat. 284, 297–299 (repealed by Pub. L. No. 85–857, §14[87], 72 Stat. 1105, 1273 [1958]).

51. Reed, *Seedtime,* 328.

52. Marian Wynn Perry to Wilkins, memorandum, Dec. 13, 1945, in *NAACP Papers,* pt. 13C, rl. 5:137. See Reed, *Seedtime,* 327.

53. Wynn, *Afro-American Second World War,* 56; Boris, "Black Workers, Trade Unions, Labor Standards," ed. Taylor and Hill, 265; Nelson, "Organized Labor," 987–988. See generally Reed, *Seedtime,* 330.

54. Complaint of Rothana Serrano to N.Y. State Commission Against Discrimination (SCAD), June 1948, in *NAACP Papers,* pt. 13C, rl. 11:554; Complaint of Walter Tannis to SCAD, Oct. 6, 1948, in *NAACP Papers,* pt. 13C, rl. 11:629 (internal quotation marks omitted); "A group of nurses who want justice" to NAACP, Nov. 14, 1947, in *NAACP Papers,* pt. 13C, rl. 12:317. See also Israel Gillard to NAACP, Apr. 7, 1946, in *NAACP Papers,* pt. 13C, rl. 4:160.

55. Complaint of Caroline Dominguez to SCAD, Nov. 17, 1947, in *NAACP Papers,* pt. 13C, rl. 10:217; Complaint of Lloyd Joseph to SCAD, Jan. 1949, in *NAACP Papers,* pt. 13A, rl. 10:103; Complaint of Max H. Jacobs to SCAD, Aug. 12, 1947, in *NAACP Papers,* pt. 13C, rl. 10:542.

56. M. W. Perry to James E. Rossell, Apr. 30, 1946, in *NAACP Papers,* pt. 13C, rl. 4:69; Shirley May Codrington to Sir, May 26, 1947, in *NAACP Papers,* pt. 13C, rl. 3:245.

57. Weaver, *Negro Labor,* 4.

58. Ibid., 238; Ruchames, *Race, Jobs, and Politics,* 188, 190, 191; Fair Employment Practice Committee, *Final Report,* 36.

59. Radford to NAACP, Sept. 24, 1942, in *NAACP Papers,* pt. 13A, rl. 4:465.

60. Armstrong to NAACP, July 31, 1942, in *NAACP Papers,* pt. 13A, rl. 2:196; John Grantham to White, Nov. 3, 1943, in *NAACP Papers,* pt. 13A, rl. 11:135.

61. "Your friend" to White, Jan. 15, 1941, in *NAACP Papers,* pt. 13C, rl. 7:16.

62. Wm. R. Henderson, Jr., to John P. Davis, Apr. 17, 1940, in *NAACP Papers,* pt. 13A, rl. 4:99.

63. Josephine Geary to NAACP, Nov. 5, 1946, in *NAACP Papers,* pt. 13C, rl. 4:125; M. Sunday to White, Sept. 2, 1941, in *NAACP Papers,* pt. 13C, rl. 8:543. See also Whitney to NAACP, June 1, 1941, in *NAACP Papers,* pt. 13C, rl. 9:284.

64. Testimony of James Olow at 93–109 and Robert Rhone at 130–131 (for quote), In re Or. Shipbuilding Corp., in *FEPC Documents,* rl. 13.

65. Direct Examination of William Johnson at 220 and Lee Anderson at 249, In re Or. Shipbuilding Corp. (F.E.P.C. Portland, Ore., Nov. 15–16, 1943), in *FEPC Documents,* rl. 13; Complaint of Shipyard Negro Org. for Victory at 1, In re Kaiser Co. (F.E.P.C. Portland, Ore., n.d. [1943?]), in *NAACP Papers,* pt. 13C, rl. 2:129–137.

66. Grantham to White, Nov. 3, 1943, in *NAACP Papers,* pt. 13A, rl. 11:135.

67. Morris to NAACP, Apr. 9, 1940, in *NAACP Papers,* pt. 13A, rl. 7:6–9; Braithwaite to NAACP, Apr. 15, 1940, in *NAACP Papers,* pt. 13A, rl. 7:12–14.

68. As Chapter 7 elaborates, these black workers were not advocating purely *Lochner*ian rights to contract. Rather, they were reworking such rights for the post–New Deal era. For a different argument that *Lochner* rights pure and simple would have benefited black workers, see David E. Bernstein, *Only One Place of Redress: African Americans, Labor Regulations, and the Courts from Reconstruction to the New Deal* (Durham, N.C., 2001).

69. Rayford W. Logan, ed., *What the Negro Wants* (Chapel Hill, N.C., 1944).

70. Frederick D. Patterson, "The Negro Wants Full Participation in the American Democracy," in ibid., 259–280, 260; Willard S. Townsend, "One American Problem and a Possible Solution," in ibid., 163–192, 165–166.

71. Rayford W. Logan, "The Negro Wants First-Class Citizenship," in ibid., 1–30, 14, 21; W. E. Burghardt Du Bois, "My Evolving Program for Negro Freedom," in ibid., 31–70, 65; Charles H. Wesley, "The Negro Has Always Wanted the Four Freedoms," in ibid., 90–112, 91, 111. See Franklin D. Roosevelt, "The Annual Message to the Congress" (Washington, D.C., Jan. 6, 1941), in *The Public Papers and Addresses of Franklin D. Roosevelt,* ed. Samuel I. Rosenman (New York, 1938–50), 9:663–672.

72. A. Philip Randolph, "March on Washington Movement Presents Program for the Negro," in *What the Negro Wants,* ed. Logan, 133–162, 140, 141, 143–144, 145; Townsend, "One American Problem," in ibid., 185–187.

73. Pauli Murray, "The Right to Equal Opportunity in Employment," *California Law Review* 33 (1945): 388–433, 432; Weaver, *Negro Labor,* 100, 254.

74. Ruchames, *Race, Jobs, and Politics,* 194.

75. Affidavit of M. C. Howard, et al., n.d., in *NAACP Papers,* pt. 13A, rl. 3:409; Newton to NAACP, Feb. 9, 1945, in *NAACP Papers,* pt. 13C, rl. 6:781; Byrd to NAACP, Jan. 19, 1940, in *NAACP Papers,* pt. 13C, rl. 7:688; Young to White, May 24, 1943, in *NAACP Papers,* pt. 13A, rl. 4:38.

76. Codrington to Sir, May 26, 1947, in *NAACP Papers,* pt. 13C, rl. 3:245.

4. The Work of Civil Rights in the Department of Justice

1. Att'y Gen. Order No. 3204 (Feb. 3, 1939), reprinted in *Justice Department Civil Rights Policies prior to 1960: Crucial Documents from the Files of Arthur Brann Caldwell*, ed. Michael R. Belknap (New York, 1991), 3, quoted in Robert K. Carr, *Federal Protection of Civil Rights: Quest for a Sword* (Ithaca, N.Y., 1947), 1. The creation of a unit within the Criminal Division required only the authority of the attorney general, whereas the unit's expansion into its own division in 1957 required congressional action. Civil Rights Act of 1957, Pub. L. No. 85–315, §101, 71 Stat. 634, 634 (codified as amended in scattered sections of 28 U.S.C. and 42 U.S.C. [2000 & Supp. II 2002]).

2. See, for example, Twining v. New Jersey, 211 U.S. 78 (1908). " 'Civil Rights' Unit Set Up by Murphy," *New York Times,* Feb. 4, 1939, 2.

3. Carr, *Federal Protection,* 24 n. 35.

4. Two DOJ cases that emerged from the committee's investigations were particularly significant precedents for labor-related prosecutions. The first concerned violent and deadly battles over the organizing of black and white coal miners in "Bloody Harlan" County, Kentucky. The department indicted twenty-two coal companies, twenty-four mine officials, and the county sheriff and twenty-two deputies. The second concerned labor repression in Jersey City, New Jersey. Sidney Fine, *Frank Murphy: The Washington Years* (Ann Arbor, Mich., 1984), 77–78.

5. Ibid., 76–98. See Jerold S. Auerbach, *Labor and Liberty: The La Follette Committee and the New Deal* (Indianapolis, Ind., 1966), 205–209. Carr, *Federal Protection,* 74–86; Lee Pressman, interview by Sidney Fine, Nov. 12, 1964, quoted in Fine, *Washington Years,* 78–79; Ann Fagan Ginger, "The 1946 Convention," in *The National Lawyers Guild: From Roosevelt through Reagan,* ed. Ann Fagan Ginger and Eugene M. Tobin (Philadelphia, 1988), 67; Sidney Fine, *Frank Murphy: The New Deal Years* (Chicago, 1979), 293–352; Carr, *Federal Protection,* 25, 25–26 n. 37; Mark V. Tushnet, *Making Civil Rights Law: Thurgood Marshall and the Supreme Court, 1936–1961* (New York, 1994), 49; Frank Murphy to Morris L. Ernst, Jan. 9, 1939, and Henry Morgenthau to Frank Murphy, Jan. 27, 1939, both in Frank Murphy Papers, Michigan Historical Collections, Bentley Historical Library, University of Michigan, and both quoted in Fine, *Washington Years,* 79; John T. Elliff, *The United States Department of Justice and Individual Rights, 1937–1962* (New York, 1987), 94–95.

6. Brien McMahon to attorney general, memorandum, Mar. 4, 1939, rl. 114, box 59, Murphy Papers (hereafter cited as McMahon memo).

"Curry to Aid Fund for Gov. Roosevelt," *New York Times,* Sept. 23, 1932, 2; Morgan Baker, "The Federal Diary," *Washington Post,* Jan. 9, 1936, 7.

7. McMahon memo; 18 U.S.C. §52 (1934).

8. McMahon memo; 18 U.S.C. §51 (1934).

9. McMahon memo. The only other agency mentioned was the Federal Communications Commission.

10. "Personnel Changes Announced by SEC," *Washington Post,* Aug. 14, 1938, R7. See Elliff, *United States Department of Justice,* 66–67; Fine, *Washington Years,* 82, 90–98; "O. J. Rogge Is Named to M'Mahon Post," *New York Times,* May 20, 1939, 7; "Rogge Is Named U.S. Prosecutor in Sedition Case," *Chicago Daily Tribune,* Feb. 7, 1943, 12. Indeed, Rogge's career path in private practice after 1946 points up his leftward stance. Rogge traveled to a number of peace conferences held in Communist countries; served as counsel for the Joint Anti-Fascist Refugee Committee, vice president of the National Lawyers Guild, chairman of the New York State Wallace for President committee; and was a member of the executive board of the Progressive Party and the African Aid committee. He and his law firm represented the government of Yugoslavia to the United Nations, and he publicly supported the country's attempts to build a socialist nation independent from the Soviet Union. "Justice Dept. Fires Rogge," *Chicago Daily Tribune,* Oct. 26, 1946, 1. "Rogge Is Signed as Yugoslavian Aid before U.N.," *Chicago Daily Tribune,* Mar. 26, 1950, 15. "Rogge Raps Red Aggression at Warsaw Parley," *Chicago Daily Tribune,* Nov. 20, 1950, 17.

11. Lewis Wood, "Attacks Bar Group for Fight on Hague," *New York Times,* July 14, 1939, 3; O. John Rogge, "Justice and Civil Liberties," *American Bar Association Journal* 25 (1939): 1030–1031; Auerbach, *Labor and Liberty,* 184.

12. Job evaluation by Wendell Berge, personnel file for Henry Schweinhaut, RG 60, National Archives (hereafter cited as DOJ Files); Henry A. Schweinhaut, "The Civil Liberties Section of the Department of Justice," *Bill of Rights Review* 1 (1941): 206–216, 210–211.

13. See Auerbach, *Labor and Liberty,* 120–121; Elliff, *United States Department of Justice,* 74–86; Kenneth O'Reilly, "The Roosevelt Administration and Black America: Federal Surveillance Policy and Civil Rights during the New Deal and World War II," *Phylon* 48 (1987): 12–25; Fine, *Washington Years,* 83–85.

14. Fine, *Washington Years,* 86–88; McMahon to attorney general, memorandum, Mar. 12, 1939, rl. 114, box 59, Murphy Papers. The department worried that filing the brief would create a precedent that would lead to pressure to file amicus briefs in many other cases. It also did not

think a brief in *Hague* would change the outcome of the case, as it seemed likely to be well argued by counsel. See Gordon Dean to attorney general, memorandum, Feb. 8, 1939, rl. 114, box 59, Murphy Papers.

15. Elliff, *United States Department of Justice,* 72; Peonage Act of 1867, ch. 187, 14 Stat. 546 (codified in the late 1930s at 18 U.S.C. §444 [1934]); Arvarh E. Strickland, "The Plight of the People in the Sharecroppers' Demonstration in Southeast Missouri," *Missouri Historical Review* 81 (1987): 403–416; Louis Cantor, "A Prologue to the Protest Movement: The Missouri Sharecropper Roadside Demonstration of 1939," *Journal of American History* 55 (1969): 804–822.

16. Fine, *Washington Years,* 89.

17. Pollock v. Williams, 322 U.S. 4, 25 (1944); West Virginia State Board of Education v. Barnette, 319 U.S. 624 (1943); Edwards v. California, 314 U.S. 160 (1941). But see Screws v. United States, 325 U.S. 91, 138–161 (1945).

18. Robert H. Jackson, "Message on the Launching of the 'Bill of Rights Review,'" *Bill of Rights Review* 1 (1940): 34–36; Peter Irons, "Politics and Principle: An Assessment of the Roosevelt Record on Civil Rights and Liberties," *Washington Law Review* 59 (1984): 693–722, 708 n. 69 (quoting Arent). See also John T. Elliff, "Aspects of Federal Civil Rights Enforcement: The Justice Department and the FBI, 1939–1964," in *Law in American History,* ed. Donald Fleming and Bernard Bailyn (Boston, 1971), 605–673; Elliff, *United States Department of Justice,* 98, 115–116, 119; Eugene C. Gerhart, *America's Advocate: Robert H. Jackson* (Indianapolis, Ind., 1958).

19. Francis Biddle, *A Casual Past* (Garden City, N.Y., 1961), 291.

20. Ibid., 360, 368–369.

21. See Peter H. Irons, *The New Deal Lawyers* (Princeton, N.J., 1982), 225.

22. Ibid., 221–225; Francis Biddle, *In Brief Authority* (Garden City, N.Y., 1962), 152–153; Elliff, *United States Department of Justice,* 136; Fair Labor Standards Act, ch. 676, 52 Stat. 1060 (1938) (codified as amended at 29 U.S.C. §§201–219 [2000 & Supp. II 2002]); United States v. Darby, 312 U.S. 100 (1941); Mitchell v. United States, 313 U.S. 80 (1941).

23. Cabell Phillips, "No Witch Hunts," *New York Times,* Sept. 21, 1941, SM8; Elizabeth Zoe Vicary, "Biddle, Francis Beverley," Vol. 2, *American National Biography,* ed. John A. Garraty and Mark C. Carnes (New York 1999), 729–731.

24. H. Graham Morison, oral history interview by Jerry N. Hess, Washington, D.C., Aug. 4, 1972, 133, transcript, Harry S. Truman Library, Independence, Mo.; "Biographical Sketch," *Weekly Bulletin,* Mar. 4, 1943,

DOJ Files, personnel file for Victor Rotnem; "Other Officials Likely to Sever AAA Relations," *Washington Post*, Feb. 7, 1935, 2; Eleanor Bontecou, interview by John T. Elliff, Arlington, Va., Feb. 22, 1967, quoted in Elliff, *United States Department of Justice*, 137. See Elliff, "Aspects," in *Law in American History*, ed. Fleming and Bailyn, 615; Irons, *New Deal Lawyers*, 175; "Notes of Society," *Washington Post*, Feb. 9, 1941, SA1; Elizabeth Henney, "Friends View the Biddles' New Home," *Washington Post*, Mar. 6, 1941, 14; "The Wendell Berges Give Buffet Supper," *Washington Post*, Mar. 27, 1942, 18.

25. Frank Coleman to Ralph S. Fuchs, May 13, 1943, DOJ Files, personnel file for Frank Coleman; Fred Folsom, interview by the author, July 10, 2002, transcript on file with the author (hereafter cited as Folsom Interview). Hector Gutierrez, "Franklin Folsom, Chronicler of the Underdog," *Rocky Mountain News*, May 20, 1995, 69A; Franklin Folsom, *Impatient Armies of the Poor: The Story of Collective Action of the Unemployed, 1808–1942* (Niwot, Colo., 1991); "Wins Pollock Medal for Criticism of Play," *New York Times*, Dec. 24, 1931, 22; Albert Arent, telephone interview by author, Oct. 24, 2006 (hereafter cited as Arent Interview).

26. Henry Putzel, Jr., interview by the author, May 2001, transcript on file with the author (hereafter cited as Putzel Interview); "Application for Federal Employment," May 22, 1946, DOJ Files, personnel file for Maceo Hubbard; Eleanor Bontecou, oral history interview by Richard D. McKinzie, Washington, D.C., June 5, 1973, 39, transcript, Truman Library (hereafter cited as Bontecou Interview); Arent Interview.

27. Folsom Interview; Bontecou Interview, 30–31, 35–36.

28. Bontecou Interview, 31, 35; Albert Arent, letter to author, Oct. 4, 2005.

29. Franklin D. Roosevelt, "The Annual Message to the Congress" (Washington, D.C., Jan. 6, 1941), in *The Public Papers and Addresses of Franklin D. Roosevelt*, ed. Samuel I. Rosenman (New York, 1938–50), 9:663–672, 672; Franklin D. Roosevelt, "Message to the Congress on the State of the Union" (Washington, D.C., Jan. 11, 1944), in ibid., 13:32–44, 41–42. See also, for example, Charles E. Merriam, "The National Resources Planning Board; A Chapter in American Planning Experience," *American Political Science Review* 38 (1944): 1075–1088; Bontecou Interview, 5–6.

30. Francis Biddle, "Civil Rights and the Federal Law," in *Safeguarding Civil Liberty Today: The Edward L. Bernays Lectures of 1944 Given at Cornell University* (Ithaca, N.Y., 1945), 109–144, 132–133.

31. Ibid., 144; Victor W. Rotnem, "Civil Rights during the War: The Role of the Federal Government," *Iowa Law Review* 29 (1944): 409–414, 411; U.S. Senate Committee on Education and Labor, *National Labor Rela-*

tions Board: Hearings on S. 1958, 74th Cong., 1st sess., 1935, pt. 1:47
(statement of Sen. Robert F. Wagner); Victor W. Rotnem, "Federal
Criminal Jurisdiction of Labor's Civil Rights," *Lawyers Guild Review* 2,
no. 5 (Sept. 1942): 21–24, 21.

32. O'Reilly, "Roosevelt Administration," 17.

33. Francis Biddle, "Democracy and Racial Minorities" (address, Institute
for Religious Studies, New York, Nov. 11, 1943); see Frank Coleman,
"Freedom from Fear on the Home Front," *Iowa Law Review* 29 (1944):
415–429; O'Reilly, "Roosevelt Administration," 17.

34. Kevin J. McMahon, *Reconsidering Roosevelt on Race: How the Presidency
Paved the Road to* Brown (Chicago, 2004), 121–124; Sidney M. Milkis,
*The President and the Parties: The Transformation of the American Party
System since the New Deal* (New York, 1993), 75–97.

35. "Memorandum on Negro Situation," 1943, DOJ Files, 144–012, quoted
in Elliff, *United States Department of Justice,* 156. See generally Daniel
Kryder, *Divided Arsenal: Race and the American State during World War II*
(New York, 2000).

36. R. M. MacIver, *The More Perfect Union: A Program for the Control of Inter-
group Discrimination in the United States* (New York, 1948), 86; Gunnar
Myrdal, *An American Dilemma: The Negro Problem and Modern Democracy*
(New York, 1944), 61 (italics omitted); *The Color Line in Industry,* Public
Opinion Index for Industry (Princeton, N.J., Apr. 1944), quoted in
MacIver, *More Perfect Union,* 124. See also Wendell E. Pritchett, "World
War II and Black Labor," chap. 4 in "Working along the Color Line:
The Life and Times of Robert Weaver" (manuscript, University of
Pennsylvania Law School, n.d.), 19; Harvard Sitkoff, *A New Deal for
Blacks: The Emergence of Civil Rights as a National Issue* (New York, 1978),
1:310–312. Though white southerners were less recalcitrant on eco-
nomic issues, they often invoked the bogey of miscegenation to deflect
black claims for economic progress. Eileen Boris, " 'The Right to Work
Is the Right to Live!': Fair Employment and the Quest for Social Citi-
zenship," in *Two Cultures of Rights: The Quest for Inclusion and Participation in Modern America and Germany,* ed. Marfred Berg and Martin H.
Geyer (Cambridge, Mass., 2002), 121–142; Merl E. Reed, *Seedtime for the
Modern Civil Rights Movement: The President's Committee on Fair Employment
Practice, 1941–1946* (Baton Rouge, La., 1991), 159–160.

37. Fair Employment Practice Committee, *Final Report:* June 28, 1946
(Washington, 1947), viii, x.

38. Victor Rotnem, memorandum, "Fair Employment Practices Committee," n.d., 5, 6–7, file 5, box 124, Francis Haas Papers, Catholic University of America Archives, Washington, D.C. See also Reed, *Seedtime,*

77–143; Andrew Edmund Kersten, *Race, Jobs, and the War: The FEPC in the Midwest, 1941–46* (Urbana, Ill., 2000), 37–46. The unit believed it could find jurisdiction to intervene on behalf of black industrial workers, and very occasionally did so. See Rotnem, "Civil Rights during the War," 411–412; Bontecou Interview, 5–6. For more on the relationship of the CRS and the FEPC, see "Memorandum on Negro Situation," quoted in Elliff, *United States Department of Justice*, 156; Bontecou Interview, 3; Reed, *Seedtime*, 111–112.

39. Bontecou Interview, 3. See generally William Cohen, *At Freedom's Edge: Black Mobility and the Southern White Quest for Racial Control* (Baton Rouge, La., 1991), 274–298.

40. Rep. John E. Rankin of Mississippi, remarks on Mar. 24, 1943, in the House, *Congressional Record* 89, pt. 9:A 1396.

41. Snell to Luther M. Swygert, Sept. 11, 1947, in *Papers of the NAACP,* ed. August Meier (Frederick, Md., 1982), microfilm, pt. 13C, rl. 12:424–425 (hereafter cited as *NAACP Papers*); Civil Rights Cases, 109 U.S. 3 (1883); Plessy v. Ferguson, 163 U.S. 537, 540–552 (1896). For Thirteenth Amendment cases, see, for example, United States v. Reynolds, 235 U.S. 133, 150 (1914); Bailey v. Alabama, 219 U.S. 219, 227–231 (1911). For separate-but-not-equal claims, see Sweatt v. Painter, 339 U.S. 629 (1950); McLaurin v. Okla. State Regents for Higher Educ., 339 U.S. 637 (1950). In *Mitchell*, 313 U.S. at 80, and Henderson v. United States, 339 U.S. 816 (1950), plaintiffs did have some success challenging segregation on federal statutory grounds. See also Carr, *Federal Protection*, 3.

42. Sydney Brodie, "The Federally-Secured Right to Be Free from Bondage," *Georgetown Law Journal* 40 (1952): 367–398, 374 n. 35. See U.S. Const. amends. XIV, §1, XIII; Peonage Act of 1867, ch. 187, 14 Stat. 546 (codified during the 1940s at 18 U.S.C. §444 [1940] and 18 U.S.C. §444 [1946]). The report of the President's Committee on Civil Rights in 1947, which contained several sections on peonage, also contributed to interest in such cases. President's Committee on Civil Rights, *To Secure These Rights: The Report of the President's Committee on Civil Rights* (Washington, D.C., 1947), 29–30, 107–108, 128, 158.

43. J. C. McMurphy and Edward Jones to Richard McLemoore, Nov. 22, 1947, in *NAACP Papers,* pt. 13C, rl. 12:687; Booker T. Fossett to Franklin D. Roosevelt, Mar. 16, 1942, 2, DOJ Files, 50–41–8.

44. Bob Wirtz, memorandum, "Policy Statement of Abolish Peonage Committee," n.d. [1941?], in *NAACP Papers,* pt. 13C, rl. 12:478–480; International Labor Defense, unsigned petition letter to Francis Biddle, n.d., in *NAACP Papers,* pt. 13C, rl. 12:519; Howard Devon Hamilton, "The

Legislative and Judicial History of the Thirteenth Amendment," pt. 2, *National Bar Journal* 10 (1952): 7–85, 77. See also Thurgood Marshall to Hon. Vito Marcantonio, Mar. 9, 1942, in *NAACP Papers*, pt. 13C, rl. 12:526; NAACP, ACLU, Southern Committee for People's Rights, and Workers' Defense League, news release, [1941–42?], in *NAACP Papers*, pt. 13A, rl. 19:206.

45. William Henry Huff to Walter White, Nov. 24, 1941, in *NAACP Papers*, pt. 13C, rl. 12:727–729.

46. Bontecou Interview, 28. See also Folsom Interview; Putzel Interview.

47. Berge to Clinton H. Barry, memorandum, Aug. 8, 1942, DOJ Files, 50–9–5. See also Berge to Toxey Hall, Aug. 10, 1942, DOJ Files, 50–41–11; Berge to Steve M. King, Aug. 8, 1942, DOJ Files, 50–74–4.

48. Editorial, "A Significant Trial," *Corpus Christi (Tex.) Times*, Mar. 23, 1943, cited in Douglas W. McGregor to attorney general, attn. Berge, Mar. 29, 1943, DOJ Files, 50–74–6; Victor W. Rotnem, "Clarifications of the Civil Rights' [*sic*] Statutes," *Bill of Rights Review* 2 (1942): 252–261, 260. As part of its agenda of taking peonage cases in order to publicize federal protection of African Americans, the Office of War Information issued many press releases during the war informing the public about the Justice Department's anti-peonage activities. See, for example, U.S. Office of War Information, news release, Nov. 12, 1942, in *NAACP Papers*, pt. 13C, rl. 12:548; U.S. Office of War Information, news release, Nov. 4, 1942, in *NAACP Papers*, pt. 13C, rl. 12:543–544; U.S. Office of War Information, news release, Aug. 7, 1942, in *NAACP Papers*, pt. 13C, rl. 12:538.

49. "Memorandum on Negro Situation," 1943, DOJ Files, 144–012, quoted in Elliff, *United States Department of Justice*, 156.

50. Biddle, "Civil Rights," in *Safeguarding Civil Liberty Today*, 132–133.

51. Howard Devon Hamilton, "The Legislative and Judicial History of the Thirteenth Amendment," pt. 1, *National Bar Journal* 9 (1951): 26–134; Description of Rotnem position, Oct. 16, 1943, DOJ Files, personnel file for Victor Rotnem.

52. Carr, *Federal Protection*, 23, 33; Biddle, "Civil Rights," in *Safeguarding Civil Liberty Today*, 112 ("resentment . . ."), 120 ("constituting . . ."); Victor W. Rotnem, "Enforcement of Civil Rights," *National Bar Journal* 3 (1945): 1–9. See also Slaughter-House Cases, 83 U.S. 36, 89–102 (1873). The statutes Congress enacted included the Civil Rights Act of 1866, ch. 31, 14 Stat. 27; the Peonage Act of 1867, ch. 187, 14 Stat. 546; the Enforcement Act of 1870, ch. 114, 16 Stat. 140; the Ku Klux Klan Act of 1871, ch. 22, 17 Stat. 13; and the Civil Rights Act of 1875, ch. 114, 18 Stat. 335. Today, the remains of the Reconstruction statutes are codi-

fied at 42 U.S.C. §§1981, 1982, 1983, 1985 (3), 1986, and 1988 (2000 & Supp. II 2002), and the civil rights procedural statutes at 28 U.S.C. §§1343, 1443 (2000). This chapter focuses on the criminal sanctions for both peonage, codified at 18 U.S.C. §1584 (2000 & Supp. II 2002), and the other civil rights laws, codified at 18 U.S.C. §241 (2000), which prohibits conspiracies against civil rights by two or more persons, and 18 U.S.C. §242 (2000), which prohibits the deprivation of rights under color of law. During the 1940s, the peonage statute was codified at 18 U.S.C. §444 (1940), section 241 was codified at 18 U.S.C. §51 (1940), and section 242 was codified at 18 U.S.C. §52 (1940).

53. Biddle, "Civil Rights," in *Safeguarding Civil Liberty Today,* 120, 134; Rotnem, "Enforcement of Civil Rights," 5; Coleman, "Freedom from Fear," 417–418. See also Carr, *Federal Protection,* 27–29; Brodie, "Federally-Secured Right," 374 n. 33.

54. See Michael Vorenberg. *Final Freedom: The Civil War, the Abolition of Slavery, and the Thirteenth Amendment* (New York, 2001); *Slaugher-House Cases,* 83 U.S. at 36; *Civil Right Cases,* 109 U.S. at 3; Hodges v. United States 203 U.S. 1 (1906).

55. Peonage Act of 1867, ch. 187, §1, 14 Stat. 546 (codified as amended at 42 U.S.C. §1994 [2000 & Supp. II 2002]); *Bailey,* 219 U.S. at 227–231, 242. See also *Reynolds,* 235 U.S. at 133, 150; Clyatt v. United States, 197 U.S. 207 (1905); Pete Daniel, *The Shadow of Slavery: Peonage in the South, 1901–1969* (Urbana, Ill., 1972); Daniel Novak, *The Wheel of Servitude: Black Forced Labor after Slavery* (Lexington, Ky., 1978).

56. Carr, *Federal Protection,* 49.

57. Rogge to all United States attorneys, memorandum, "Federal Criminal Jurisdiction over Violations of Civil Liberties," May 21, 1940, Department of Justice Circular no. 3356, supp. no. 1, 1, reprinted in *Justice Civil Rights Policies,* 12–51, 21, quoted in Elliff, *United States Department of Justice,* 99. In the *Slaughter-House Cases,* the Court determined that only the "privileges and immunities" of national, as opposed to state, citizenship found protection in the Fourteenth Amendment. National privileges and immunities included only such rights as access to government, assembling and petitioning the government for redress of grievances, and the use of navigable waters. *Slaughter-House Cases,* 83 U.S. at 74–80.

58. Coleman, "Freedom from Fear," 418; Sydney Brodie to McGohey, March 28, 1948, DOJ Files 144–51–0. See generally Elliff, *United States Department of Justice,* 259–264.

59. Brodie to Kenneth Macrorie, Jan. 16, 1948, DOJ Files 144–80–0, quoted in Elliff, *United States Department of Justice,* 260. See also, for example, T.

Vincent Quinn to J. Saxton Daniel, Feb. 13, 1948, DOJ Files, 144–20–27. The Fourteenth Amendment commands, "No State shall make or enforce any law." U.S. Const. amend. XIV, §1. The Fifteenth Amendment states, "The right of citizens of the United States to vote shall not be denied or abridged by the United States or by any State." U.S. Const. amend. XV, §1.

60. Victor W. Rotnem, "Criminal Enforcement of Federal Civil Rights," *Lawyers Guild Review* 2, no. 3 (May 1942): 18–23; Biddle, "Civil Rights," in *Safeguarding Civil Liberty Today*, 130–131.

61. See Biddle, "Civil Rights," in *Safeguarding Civil Liberty Today*, 136–137, 139–142; Rotnem, "Clarifications of the Civil Rights' [*sic*] Statutes," 255, 260; Coleman, "Freedom from Fear"; Carr, *Federal Protection*, 163–176; Sitkoff, *New Deal for Blacks*, 1:268–297; Dominic J. Capeci, Jr., "The Lynching of Cleo Wright: Federal Protection of Constitutional Rights during World War II," *Journal of American History* 72 (1986): 859–887; Christopher Waldrep, "War of Words: The Controversy over the Definition of Lynching, 1899–1940," *Journal of Southern History* 66 (2000): 75–100; Robert L. Zangrando, *The NAACP Crusade against Lynching, 1909–1950* (Philadelphia, 1980), The Department of Justice succeeded in an election frauds case in United States v. Classic, 313 U.S. 299 (1941).

62. Rotnem, "Civil Rights during the War," 409; *Screws*, 325 U.S. at 103–105, 113. The section did nonetheless occasionally succeed in using section 52, as in the police brutality case of Crews v. United States, 160 F.2d 746 (5th Cir. 1947). On the section's efforts in these other areas of civil rights see Elliff, *United States Department of Justice*; Carr, *Federal Protection*; President's Committee on Civil Rights, *To Secure These Rights*; McMahon, *Reconsidering Roosevelt*, 144–176.

63. *Pollock*, 322 U.S. at 25; United States v. Gaskin, 320 U.S. 527, 529 (1944); Taylor v. Georgia, 315 U.S. 25, 31 (1942).

64. John Thomas Murphy, FBI Report, Savannah, Ga., Mar. 10, 1943, DOJ Files, 50–18–15; Robert Edward Lee, FBI Report, Atlanta, Mar. 9, 1943, 4 (statement of Ernest Cochran), DOJ Files, 50–18–15; Assistant Attorney General Warren Olney to Vernon Lawhorn, Feb. 17, 1955, DOJ Files, 50–18–15.

65. Rotnem, "Criminal Enforcement," 21; Fred G. Folsom, Jr., "A Slave Trade Law in a Contemporary Setting," *Cornell Law Quarterly* 29 (1943): 203–216, 203; U.S. House Committee on the Judiciary, Subcommittee No. 4, "H.R. 2118: Peonage and Slavery[; Hearing]," 82nd Cong., 1st sess., 1951, 3 (statement of George Triedman), in *Unpublished U.S. House of Representatives Committee Hearings, 1947–1954* (Bethesda, Md.,

1992), microfiche, 82 HJ-T.15A8. See also Schweinhaut, "Civil Liberties Section," 209.

5. A New Deal for Civil Rights

1. Robert K. Carr, *Federal Protection of Civil Rights: Quest for a Sword* (Ithaca, N.Y., 1947), vii, 5; Pollock v. Williams, 322 U.S. 4, 8 (1944).
2. Carr, *Federal Protection,* vii, 193, 210.
3. Sydney Brodie, "The Federally-Secured Right to Be Free from Bondage," *Georgetown Law Journal* 40 (1952): 367–398; President's Committee on Civil Rights, *To Secure These Rights: The Report of the President's Committee on Civil Rights* (Washington, D.C., 1947), 20.
4. Clyatt v. United States, 197 U.S. 207 (1905); United States v. Reynolds, 235 U.S. 133 (1914); Bailey v. Alabama, 219 U.S. 219, 241 (1911).
5. *Bailey,* 219 U.S. 219.
6. Taylor v. Georgia, 315 U.S. 25, 26–30 (1942); United States v. Gaskin, 320 U.S. 527, 527–528 (1944); *Pollock,* 322 U.S. at 5–13.
7. Francis Biddle, "Civil Rights and the Federal Law," in *Safeguarding Civil Liberty Today: The Edward L. Bernays Lectures of 1944 Given at Cornell University* (Ithaca, N.Y., 1945), 109–144.
8. Pierce v. United States, 146 F.2d 84, 86 (5th Cir. 1944).
9. *Pierce,* 146 F.2d at 87–88 (Hutcheson, J., concurring in part, dissenting in part) (emphasis added).
10. Department of Justice Circular no. 3591, Dec. 12, 1941, 1–3, in *Justice Department Civil Rights Policies prior to 1960: Crucial Documents from the Files of Arthur Brann Caldwell* (New York, 1991), 61–63. See also O. John Rogge to all United States attorneys, memorandum, "Federal Criminal Jurisdiction over Violations of Civil Liberties," May 21, 1940, Department of Justice Circular no. 3356, supp. no. 1, 1–31, reprinted in ibid., 12–51; John T. Elliff, "Aspects of Federal Civil Rights Enforcement: The Justice Department and the FBI, 1939–1964," in *Law in American History,* ed. Donald Fleming and Bernard Bailyn (Boston, 1971), 608–609.
11. Lindbergh Kidnaping Act, ch. 271, 47 Stat. 326 (1932) (current version at 18 U.S.C. §§1201–1202 [2000]), codified during the 1940s at 18 U.S.C. §408(a), (c) (1940); United States v. Gantt, No. 10,031n (N.D. Ala. Nov. 5, 1949), cited in Brodie, "Federally-Secured Right," 374 n. 34; John T. Elliff, *The United States Department of Justice and Individual Rights, 1937–1962* (New York, 1987), 301–302.
12. Pete Daniel, *The Shadow of Slavery: Peonage in the South, 1901–1969* (Urbana, Ill., 1972), 172 (internal quotation marks omitted); Fred G. Folsom, Jr., "A Slave Trade Law in a Contemporary Setting," *Cornell*

Law Quarterly 29 (1943): 203–216, 203, 203–204, 206. See An Act to Prevent and Punish Kidnapping, ch. 86, 14 Stat. 50 (1866), subsequently codified at ch. 321, §268, 35 Stat. 1141–1142 (1909), and 18 U.S.C. §443 (1940) (current version at 18 U.S.C. §1583 [2000]); United States v. Sabbia (C.C.S.D.N.Y. 1907) (unreported), quoted in Folsom, "Slave Trade Law," 209. See also Brodie, "Federally-Secured Right," 384–388; Howard Devon Hamilton, "The Legislative and Judicial History of the Thirteenth Amendment," pt. 2, *National Bar Journal* 10 (1952): 7–85, 26–28.

13. Brodie, "Federally-Secured Right," 367. See, for example, Ben Scott Whaley to attorney general, Jan. 8, 1948, file 50–67–11, RG 60, National Archives (hereafter cited as DOJ Files).

14. "Federal Prosecution of a Georgia Planter for Peonage," *The Daily Worker,* Nov. 20, 1939, 1; Daniel, *Shadow of Slavery,* 175; Memorandum, May 1941, DOJ Files, 50–708.

15. Biddle, "Civil Rights," in *Safeguarding Civil Liberty Today,* 138.

16. DOJ files, 50–18–15.

17. Harry S. Truman, *Memoirs: Year of Decisions* (Garden City, N.Y., 1955), 325–326, quoted in Elliff, *United States Department of Justice,* 210.

18. Fred Folsom, interview by the author, July 10, 2002, transcript on file with the author; Elliff, *United States Department of Justice,* 211–212; Henry Putzel, Jr., interview by the author, May 2001, transcript on file with the author.

19. Elliff, *United States Department of Justice,* 283; "Triedman to Head Civil Rights Unit at Justice Dept.," *Washington Post,* Jan. 6, 1950, 1.

20. Brodie, "Federally-Secured Right," 372; Henry Putzel, Jr., "Federal Civil Rights Enforcement: A Current Appraisal," *University of Pennsylvania Law Review* 99 (1951): 439–454, 445. See 18 U.S.C. §§1581–1588 (1952). They did continue to use that combination into the 1950s, however, often in conjunction with the slavery statute. See, for example, DOJ Files, 50–19M–36.

21. Francis Biddle, *Democratic Thinking and the War: The William H. White Lectures at the University of Virginia, 1942–1943* (New York, 1944), 19.

22. Harry S. Truman, "Statement on Executive Order 9808 Establishing the President's Committee on Civil Rights," Dec. 5, 1946, quoted in President's Committee on Civil Rights, *To Secure These Rights,* vii; Harry S. Truman, "Address before the National Association for the Advancement of Colored People" (Lincoln Memorial, Washington, D.C., June 29, 1947), in *Public Papers of the Presidents of the United States: Harry S. Truman, 1947* (Washington, D.C., 1963), 311–313.

23. President's Committee on Civil Rights, *To Secure These Rights,* 106, 103.

24. Truman, "Statement Executive Order 9808," quoted in President's Committee on Civil Rights, *To Secure These Rights,* vii; see also Frank Coleman, "Freedom from Fear on the Home Front," *Iowa Law Review* 29 (1944): 415–429.

25. William Blackstone, *Commentaries on the Laws of England* (Oxford, 1765), 1:125; Civil Rights Act of 1866, ch. 31, §1, 14 Stat. 27. Freedman's Bureau Bill, ch. 200, §14, 14 Stat. 173, 176 (1866). See President's Committee on Civil Rights, *To Secure These Rights,* 20; Thomas I. Emerson and David Haber, *Political and Civil Rights in the United States: A Collection of Legal and Related Materials* (Buffalo, N.Y., 1952), 1. Language about the "security of the person" also occasionally resurfaced in some of the signal civil rights dissents of the late nineteenth century, such as the *Slaughter-House Cases* (83 U.S. 36, 115–119 [1873] [Bradley, J., dissenting]) and *Plessy v. Ferguson* (163 U.S. 537, 555–556, 560 [1896] [Harlan, J., dissenting]).

26. Brodie, "Federally-Secured Right," 367, 376.

27. National Labor Relations Act, ch. 372, §2(3), 49 Stat. 449, 450 (1935) (current version at 29 U.S.C. §§151–169 [2000]). Fair Labor Standards Act, ch. 676, §13(a)(6), 52 Stat. 1060, 1067 (1938) (current version at 29 U.S.C. §§201–219 [2000 & Supp. II 2002]). Social Security Act, ch. 531, §§210(b)(1), (2), 811(b)(1), (2), 907(c)(1), (2), 49 Stat. 620, 625, 639, 643 (1935) (current version at 42 U.S.C. §§301–1397jj [2000 & Supp. II 2002]). See also David Conrad, *The Forgotten Farmers: The Story of Sharecroppers in the New Deal* (Urbana, Ill., 1965); V. O. Key, Jr., *Southern Politics in State and Nation* (New York, 1949), 619–664; Harvard Sitkoff, *A New Deal for Blacks: The Depression Decade* (New York, 1978), 1:34–57; Nancy J. Weiss, *Farewell to the Party of Lincoln: Black Politics in the Age of FDR* (Princeton, N.J., 1983), 163–168; William E. Forbath, "Caste, Class, and Equal Citizenship," *Michigan Law Review* 98 (1999): 1–91; Ira Katznelson, Kim Geiger, and Daniel Kryder, "Limiting Liberalism: The Southern Veto in Congress, 1933–1950," *Political Science Quarterly* 108 (1993): 283–306; Marc Linder, "Farm Workers and the Fair Labor Standards Act: Racial Discrimination in the New Deal," *Texas Law Review* 65 (1987): 1335–1393. For discussions of the existence of a separate southern labor market until World War II, see Gavin Wright, *Old South, New South: Revolutions in the Southern Economy since the Civil War* (New York, 1986); Bruce J. Schulman, *From Cotton Belt to Sunbelt: Federal Policy, Economic Development, and the Transformation of the South, 1938–1980* (New York, 1991), 1–85.

28. Franklin D. Roosevelt, "A Message to the Conference on Economic Conditions of the South," July 4, 1938, in *The Public Papers and Addresses*

of Franklin D. Roosevelt, ed. Samuel I. Rosenman (New York, 1938–50), 7:421–422, quoted in Schulman, *From Cotton Belt to Sunbelt*, 3; Franklin D. Roosevelt, " 'The United States Is Rising and Is Rebuilding on Sounder Lines' " (address, Gainesville, Ga., Mar. 23, 1938), in *Public Papers of Roosevelt*, 7:164–169, 167–168, quoted in Kevin J. McMahon, *Reconsidering Roosevelt on Race: How the Presidency Paved the Road to Brown* (Chicago, 2004), 123; Franklin D. Roosevelt, "In These Past Six Years, the South Has Made Greater Economic and Social Progress up the Scale Than at Any Other Period in Her Long History" (address, University of Georgia, Athens, Ga., Aug. 11, 1938), in *Public Papers of Roosevelt*, 7:471–475, quoted in Schulman, *From Cotton Belt to Sunbelt*, 48; Franklin D. Roosevelt, " 'Nationwide Thinking, Nationwide Planning and Nationwide Action Are the Three Great Essentials to Prevent Nationwide Crises' " (address, Thomas Jefferson Dinner, New York, Apr. 25, 1936), in *Public Papers of Roosevelt*, 5:177–182, quoted in Schulman, *From Cotton Belt to Sunbelt*, 48. See also Sidney M. Milkis, *The President and the Parties: The Transformation of the American Party System since the New Deal* (New York, 1993), 87–92.

29. Edwards v. California, 314 U.S. 160, 171, 173–174, 177 (1941). See Cal. Welf. & Inst. Code §2615 (1937).

30. *Edwards*, 314 U.S. at 173–177 (quoting Justice Cardozo), 177–178, 181 (Douglas, J., concurring).

31. S. P. Meyers, "Federal Privileges and Immunities: Application to Ingress and Egress," *Cornell Law Quarterly* 29 (1944): 489–513; Hamilton, "Legislative and Judicial History," pt. 2, 62, 64; Herbert Roback, "Legal Barriers to Interstate Migration," pt. 1, *Cornell Law Quarterly* 28 (1943): 286–312. See Williams v. Fears, 179 U.S. 270 (1900); Ivan C. Rutledge, "Regulation of the Movement of Workers," *Washington University Law Quarterly* (1953): 150–181, 270–296.

32. Francis Biddle to Franklin D. Roosevelt, July 15, 1943, quoted in "Biddle's Report on Race Riots Asking FDR to Name Joint Board," *(New York) PM Daily*, Aug. 11, 1943, 12.

33. "Charge Biddle's Character Is Revealed through His Letter," *Michigan Chronicle*, Aug. 28, 1943, 4; "Along the N.A.A.C.P. Battlefront," *Crisis* 50 (1943): 280 (internal quotation marks omitted).

34. *Pollock*, 322 U.S. at 4.

35. *Bailey*, 219 U.S. at 241; *Taylor*, 315 U.S. at 26–30.

36. *Pollock*, 322 U.S. at 16, 18.

37. Brodie, "Federally-Secured Right," 398 (footnote omitted); Percy C. Fountain to attorney general, July 15, 1948, DOJ Files, 50–1–24.

38. Biddle, "Civil Rights," in *Safeguarding Civil Liberty Today*, 137–138.

39. Edwin B. Poorman, FBI Report, Feb. 6, 1945, DOJ Files, 50–1–14; Tom C. Clark to J. Edgar Hoover, memorandum, Nov. 3, 1943, DOJ Files, 50–3–3.

40. J. Sewell Elliott to William M. Sneed, Justice of the Peace, and Sheriff J. R. Nix, n.d., NARA, RG 60, No. 50–19M–48. See, for example, John P. Cowart to attorney general, Dec. 28, 1949, DOJ Files, 50–19–37; Alexander M. Campbell to director, FBI, Oct. 26, 1948, DOJ Files, 50–19–31; Herbert S. Phillips to Hon. Warren Olney, III, Apr. 16, 1953, DOJ Files, 50–18–63; Cowart to attorney general, Apr. 13, 1950, DOJ Files, 50–19–37.

41. Biddle, "Civil Rights," in *Safeguarding Civil Liberty Today*, 115. For discussions of the early delineations between free and unfree labor in England and the United States, see Robert J. Steinfeld, *Coercion, Contract, and Free Labor in the Nineteenth Century* (New York, 2001); Robert J. Steinfeld, *The Invention of Free Labor: The Employment Relation in English and American Law and Culture, 1350–1870* (Chapel Hill, N.C., 1991), 15–54; Christopher L. Tomlins, *Law, Labor, and Ideology in the Early American Republic* (New York, 1993), 232–292. For the classic treatment of antebellum free labor ideology, see Eric Foner, *Free Soil, Free Labor, Free Men: The Ideology of the Republican Party before the Civil War* (New York, 1970), 11–51. For an excellent discussion of laborers' changing conceptions of free labor in the postbellum period, see William E. Forbath, "The Ambiguities of Free Labor: Labor and the Law in the Gilded Age," *Wisconsin Law Review* (1985): 767–817. See also Amy Dru Stanley, *From Bondage to Contract: Wage Labor, Marriage, and the Market in the Age of Slave Emancipation* (New York, 1998); James Gray Pope, "Labor and the Constitution: From Abolition to Deindustrialization," *Texas Law Review* 65 (1987): 1071–1136; James Gray Pope, "Labor's Constitution of Freedom," *Yale Law Journal* 106 (1997): 941–1031; Lea S. VanderVelde, "The Labor Vision of the Thirteenth Amendment," *University of Pennsylvania Law Review* 138 (1989): 437–504; Risa L. Goluboff, "The Work of Civil Rights in the 1940s: The Department of Justice, the NAACP, and African American Agricultural Labor" (Ph.D. diss., Princeton University, 2003), 17–63.

42. Labor Disputes Act, S. 2926, 73rd Cong. §2 (1934), *Congressional Record* 78, pt. 4:3444.

43. Hamilton, "Legislative and Judicial History," pt. 2, 72.

44. National Labor Relations Act, ch. 372, §2(3), 49 Stat. 449, 450 (1935) (current version at 29 U.S.C. §§151–169 [2000]); Fair Labor Standards Act, ch. 676, §13(a)(6), 52 Stat. 1060, 1067 (1938) (current version at 29 U.S.C. §§201–219 [2000 & Supp. II 2002]); Social Security Act, ch.

531, §§210(b)(1), (2), 811(b)(1), (2), 907(c)(1), (2), 49 Stat. 620, 625, 639, 643 (1935) (current version at 42 U.S.C. §§301–1397jj [2000 & Supp. II 2002]); U.S. Senate Committee on Labor and Public Welfare, Special Subcommittee on Labor and Labor-Management Relations, *Labor Practices in Laurens County, Ga.: Hearing,* 82nd Cong., 1st sess., 1951, 74–75 (testimony of Charles H. Gilman), 93–94 (testimony of Curtis E. Johnson). See generally James Gray Pope, "The Thirteenth Amendment versus the Commerce Clause: Labor and the Shaping of American Constitutional Law, 1921–1957," *Columbia Law Review* 102 (2002): 1–122.

45. Hamilton, "Legislative and Judicial History," pt. 2, 15, 57–58; Howard Devon Hamilton, "The Legislative and Judicial History of the Thirteenth Amendment," pt. 1, *National Bar Journal* 9 (1951): 26–134, 69.

46. "Peonage," selections from *A Monthly Summary of Events and Trends in Race Relations,* Aug.–Oct. 1946, in *Papers of the NAACP,* ed. August Meier (Frederick, Md., 1982), pt. 13C, rl. 12:650–651 (hereafter cited as *NAACP Papers*); Allan Keller, "22 Brooklyn Boys Flee Slave Farm," *N.Y. World-Telegram and Sun,* Aug. 6, 1953, 1–2; NAACP, "FBI Asked to Probe New York State Farm," news release, Aug. 6, 1953, in *NAACP Papers,* pt. 13A, rl. 19:213. See also Marian Wynn Perry to Edward Knott, Jr., Dec. 1, 1947, in *NAACP Papers,* pt. 13C, rl. 12:690.

47. U.S. Senate Committee on Labor and Public Welfare, Special Subcommittee on Labor and Labor-Management Relations, *Labor Practices Laurens County,* 87–88 (testimony of Thomas W. Johnson), 94 (testimony of Curtis E. Johnson) (internal quotation marks omitted). See Frank Coleman to Victor Rotnem, Jan. 8, 1943, DOJ Files, 50–40–5.

48. See, for example, Clay A. William to Thurgood Marshall, Feb. 18, 1946, in *NAACP Papers,* pt. 13C, rl. 12:847–848.

49. Affidavit of Polly Johnson, 1946, 1, in *NAACP Papers,* pt. 13C, rl. 12:764–766; Affidavit of Elizabeth Coker, Jan. 30, 1947, in *NAACP Papers,* pt. 13C, rl. 12:390–391. See also Miss Mattie Lomax to NAACP, Mar. 10, 1946, in *NAACP Papers,* pt. 13C, rl. 12:752; Walter Pate, FBI Report, Feb. 24, 1945, DOJ Files, 50–67–9.

50. Folsom, "Slave Trade Law," 214. An Act to Prevent and Punish Kidnapping, ch. 86, 14 Stat. 50 (1866), subsequently codified at 18 U.S.C. §443 (1940), 18 U.S.C. §443 (1946) (current version at 18 U.S.C. §1583 [2000]).

51. United States v. Ingalls, 73 F. Supp. 76, 77 (S.D. Cal. 1947).

52. Ibid. at 77.

53. Ibid. at 78; "Daughter Tells More 'Slave' Case Details," *Los Angeles Times,* Feb., 27, 1947, pt. 2:1, DOJ Files, 50–12–3.

54. Brodie, "Federally-Secured Right," 388.

55. Leo Meltzer to file, memorandum, Oct. 22, 1946, DOJ Files, 50–79–2; FBI Report, Maurice D. duBois, Oct. 20, 1950, DOJ Files, 50–35–6. See, for example, Henry A. Donahoo, FBI Report, Jan. 5, 1948, DOJ Files, 50–1–23; Joseph A. Canale, FBI Report, Mar. 13, 1952, DOJ Files, 50–40–22; Special Agent George A. Gunter, FBI Report, July 1, 1948, DOJ Files, 50–350; T. Vincent Quinn to James M. Carter, Jan. 26, 1948, DOJ Files, 50–12–6; John B. Honeycutt, FBI Report, Apr. 3, 1948, DOJ Files, 50–41–51; Andrew M. Smith, FBI Report, Nov. 16, 1951, DOJ Files, 50–1–30.

56. LeRoy White to NAACP Legal Department, attn. Marshall, Oct. 14, 1947, 1–2, in *NAACP Papers,* pt. 13C, rl. 12:416–417.

57. James M. Carter to attorney general, Mar. 3, 1947, DOJ Files, 50–12–3; T. Howard Waldron, FBI Report, July 27, 1948, DOJ Files, 50–48–3; Isaiah Matlack to Campbell, Sept. 8, 1948, DOJ Files, 50–48–3.

58. Peyton Ford to Hon. Joseph P. O'Hara, June 10, 1949, DOJ Files, 50–39–2. See, for example, James M. Clayton, FBI Report, Sept. 28, 1949, DOJ Files, 50–35–4 (Pauline Anderson); "Couple Denies Enslavement of Ward, 41," *Washington Post,* Oct. 21, 1950, 9, DOJ Files, 50–35–6 (Elsie T. Jensen).

59. Chester L. Sumners to attorney general, June 23, 1950, DOJ Files, 50–40–18; T. Vincent Quinn to director, FBI, memorandum, Dec. 30, 1947, DOJ Files, 50–80–2; Hamilton, "Legislative and Judicial History," pt. 2, 57; Putzel, "Federal Civil Rights Enforcement," 445.

60. U.S. House Committee on the Judiciary, Subcommittee No. 4, "H.R. 2118: Peonage and Slavery[; Hearing]," 82nd Cong., 1st sess., 1951, 13–14, 18 (statement of George Triedman), 29, in *Unpublished U.S. House of Representatives Committee Hearings, 1947–1954* (Bethesda, Md., 1992), microfiche, 82 HJ-T.15, B4–B5, B9, C6. See H.R. 2118, 82nd Cong. (1951). A Bill to Strengthen the Laws Relating to Convict Labor, Peonage, Slavery, and Involuntary Servitude, S. 1739, 82nd Cong. (1951).

61. U.S. House Committee on the Judiciary, Subcommittee No. 4, "H.R. 2118 Hearing," 14–15, 21–25, in *Unpublished House Hearings 1947–1954,* 82 HJ-T.15, C5.

62. Ibid., 28. For a discussion of how the New Deal excluded women and minorities from the new liberal, national support system and left them to the semi-feudalism of the states, see Suzanne Mettler, *Dividing Citizens: Gender and Federalism in New Deal Public Policy* (Ithaca, N.Y., 1998), xi–xii.

63. Brodie, "Federally-Secured Right," 388.

64. Biddle, *Democratic Thinking,* 5–6. See Franklin D. Roosevelt, "The An-

nual Message to the Congress" (Washington, D.C., Jan. 6, 1941), in *Public Papers of Roosevelt,* 9:663–672, 672; Declaration of Principles, Known as the Atlantic Charter, Aug. 14, 1941, 55 Stat. 1603, 204 L.N.T.S. 384.

65. Biddle, *Democratic Thinking,* 8–10. See also "Our Common Catholic Interests: Inter-American Seminar on Social Studies Issues Statement Formulating Its Findings," *Catholic Action,* Oct. 1942, 3–5.

66. Biddle, *Democratic Thinking,* 16, 17.

67. By focusing on the origins of the Thirteenth Amendment as involving race and labor, I do not mean to suggest that it did not also involve other aspects of social life. Other possible understandings of the origins of the Thirteenth Amendment not addressed here include control over one's body and reproduction, intrusion into and revolution within hierarchies of the family, and self-ownership. See, for example, Laura F. Edwards, *Gendered Strife and Confusion: The Political Culture of Reconstruction* (Urbana, Ill., 1997), 24–65; Akhil Reed Amar and Daniel Widawsky, "Child Abuse as Slavery: A Thirteenth Amendment Response to *DeShaney,*" *Harvard Law Review* 105 (1992): 1359–1385; Patricia J. Williams, "On Being the Object of Property," in *The Alchemy of Race and Rights* (Cambridge, Mass., 1991), 216–236.

68. Universal Declaration of Human Rights, art. 2, Dec. 10, 1948, UN General Assembly Resolution 217 (III), A/810, 1948; UN Economic and Social Council, Ad Hoc Committee on Slavery, *Development of Article 4 of the Universal Declaration of Human Rights,* E/AC.33/5, 1950, 7. See Hamilton, "Legislative and Judicial History," pt. 2, 71; UN Economic and Social Council Resolution 238 (IX), E/1553, 1949, 31 (instructing the UN secretary general to appoint an ad hoc committee on slavery); UN Economic and Social Council, Ad Hoc Committee on Slavery, *Provisional Agenda,* E/AC.33/1, Nov. 30, 1949; UN Economic and Social Council, Tenth Session, Official Records, *Interim Report of the Ad Hoc Committee on Slavery,* E/1617, Feb. 21, 1950, 1 (stating that the committee "opened its first session" on Feb. 13, 1950); Elliff, *United States Department of Justice,* 267, 283.

69. Hamilton, "Legislative and Judicial History," pt. 2, 54, 71–73.

70. Robert L. Hale, "Some Basic Constitutional Rights of Economic Significance," *Columbia Law Review* 51 (1951): 271–326. See also, for example, Brodie, "Federally-Secured Right"; Jacobus tenBroek, "Thirteenth Amendment to the Constitution of the United States: Consummation to Abolition and Key to the Fourteenth Amendment," *California Law Review* 39 (1951): 171–203; "Notes: The Reach of the Thirteenth Amendment," *Columbia Law Review* 47 (1947): 299–307.

6. Work and Workers in the NAACP

1. *America on Guard*, KSFO (radio), Nov. 27, 1943, transcript, 9–10, in *Papers of the NAACP*, ed. August Meier (Frederick, Md., 1982), microfilm, pt. 13C, rl. 1:55–64, 63–64 (hereafter cited as *NAACP Papers*); Thurgood Marshall to Noah W. Griffin, May 9, 1946, in *NAACP Papers*, pt. 13C, rl. 1:492–493.

2. Marshall to W. F. Turner, Dec. 13, 1940, in *NAACP Papers*, pt. 13C, rl. 7:22. See also Motion for Leave to File Brief as Amicus Curiae, James v. Marinship Corp., 155 P.2d 329 (Cal. 1944) (S.F. No. 17015), in *NAACP Papers*, pt. 13C, rl. 1:259–260; Marian Wynn Perry, "Work of the National Office and Branches of the [NAACP] in the Field of Employment—New York," Apr. 16, 1946, in *NAACP Papers*, pt. 18A, rl. 7:762–765.

3. See Wilson Record, "Negro Intellectual Leadership in the National Association for the Advancement of Colored People: 1910–1940," *Phylon* 17 (1956): 375–389; Charles Flint Kellogg, *NAACP: A History of the National Association for the Advancement of Colored People* (Baltimore, Md., 1967), 1:9–45; Kevin Gaines, *Uplifting the Race: Black Leadership, Politics, and Culture in the Twentieth Century* (Chapel Hill, N.C., 1996), xiv–xv, 1–17. See also Glenda Elizabeth Gilmore, *Gender and Jim Crow: Women and the Politics of White Supremacy in North Carolina, 1896–1920* (Chapel Hill, N.C., 1996); Evelyn Brooks Higginbotham, *Righteous Discontent: The Women's Movement in the Black Baptist Church, 1880–1920* (Cambridge, Mass., 1993); Victoria W. Wolcott, *Remaking Respectability: African American Women in Interwar Detroit* (Chapel Hill, N.C., 2001); Kenneth Walter Mack, "Race Uplift, Professional Identity, and the Transformation of Civil Rights Lawyering and Politics, 1920–1940" (Ph.D. diss., Princeton University, 2005).

4. Mack, "Race Uplift."

5. Charles J. Bonaparte, "Legal and Economic Equality" (address at the 6th annual conference of the NAACP, Baltimore, Md., May 5, 1914), 1, in *NAACP Papers*, pt. 1, rl. 8:352–360, 353. See NAACP, Certificate of Incorporation, May 25, 1911, in *NAACP Papers*, pt. 18A, rl. 3:636–639; Kellogg, *NAACP*, 1:132; Mary White Ovington, *Black and White Sat Down Together: The Reminiscences of an NAACP Founder* (New York, 1995), 68. On the Urban League generally, see Jesse Thomas Moore, *A Search for Equality: The National Urban League, 1910–1961* (University Park, Pa., 1981).

6. James Weldon Johnson to Isadore Martin, Mar. 31, 1921, in *NAACP Papers*, pt. 10, rl. 17:36. See Bernard Eisenberg, "Only for the Bourgeois?

James Weldon Johnson and the NAACP, 1916–1930," *Phylon* 43 (1982): 110–124, 113; Beth Tompkins Bates, "A New Crowd Challenges the Agenda of the Old Guard in the NAACP, 1933–1941," *American Historical Review* 102 (1997): 340–377, 349–351, 358; Asst. sec. to Mr. J. A. G. LuValle, Sept. 7, 1933, in *NAACP Papers*, pt. 10, rl. 16:438; Raymond Wolters, *Negroes and the Great Depression: The Problem of Economic Recovery* (Westport, Conn., 1970), 337. See generally August Meier and John H. Bracey, Jr., "The NAACP as a Reform Movement, 1909–1965: 'To Reach the Conscience of America,'" *Journal of Southern History* 59 (1993): 3–30; Edwin D. Hoffman, "The Genesis of the Modern Movement for Equal Rights in South Carolina, 1930–1939," *Journal of Negro History* 44 (1959): 346–369; Dorothy Autrey, " 'Can These Bones Live?': The National Association for the Advancement of Colored People in Alabama, 1918–1930," *Journal of Negro History* 82 (1997): 1–12. Nan Elizabeth Woodruff points out that even though they were not always dues-paying members, rural African Americans became involved with the NAACP through more informal networks—receiving information from members, sharing copies of the *Crisis,* reading it aloud in groups. *American Congo: The African American Freedom Struggle in the Delta* (Cambridge, Mass., 2003), 116.

7. J. W. Johnson to J. D. Baker, June 5, 1922, in *NAACP Papers*, pt. 10, rl. 16:83; J. W. Johnson to Hugh M. Dorsey, telegram, Mar. 28, 1921, in *NAACP Papers*, pt. 10, rl. 17:8. See, for example, "Jasper County (Ga.) Peonage Cases," [1921?], in *NAACP Papers*, pt. 10, rl. 16:46; NAACP, "Peonage Atrocity Story Comes from South Carolina," news release, Apr. 27, 1923, in *NAACP Papers*, pt. 10, rl. 16:148–149; NAACP, "Peonage Widespread in South Declares Negro Poet and Leader," news release, Feb. 3, 1927, in *NAACP Papers*, pt. 10, rl. 16:303; "Peonage: Jasper County—Georgia," time line, [1921?], in *NAACP Papers*, pt. 10, rl. 16:44–46; "Peonage, 1921," case summaries, [1921?], in *NAACP Papers*, pt. 10, rl. 16:47–55; asst. sec. to Bert Aldrich, Apr. 11, 1921, in *NAACP Papers*, pt. 10, rl. 17:73; see generally Pete Daniel, *Deep'n as It Come: The 1927 Mississippi River Flood* (New York, 1977); Pete Daniel, *The Shadow of Slavery: Peonage in the South, 1901–1969* (Urbana, Ill., 1972), 154, 167–168. After a violent confrontation between Elaine, Arkansas, sharecroppers and their landlords over the sharecroppers' attempt to form a union, for example, seventy-nine black sharecroppers were convicted of conspiracy to murder whites, and twelve were sentenced to death. The NAACP pursued the case of *Moore v. Dempsey* all the way to the Supreme Court, which overturned the convictions. Robert C. Cortner, *A Mob Intent on Death: The NAACP and the Arkansas Riot Cases* (Middle-

town, Conn., 1988); Robert L. Zangrando, *The NAACP Crusade against Lynching, 1909–1950* (Philadelphia, 1980), 85–86. See also Kenneth Robert Janken, *White: The Biography of Walter White, Mr. NAACP* (New York, 2003), 49–54; Philip Dray, *At the Hands of Persons Unknown: The Lynching of Black America* (New York, 2002), 237–245. Kellogg, *NAACP,* 1:242–245; Woodruff, *American Congo,* 75–109.

8. Eric Arnesen, for example, recounts efforts to publicize killings of African American railroad workers. *Brotherhoods of Color: Black Railroad Workers and the Struggle for Equality* (Cambridge, Mass., 2001), 81–82.

9. Mack, "Race Uplift," 35–49. See, for example, Horace R. Cayton and George S. Mitchell, *Black Workers and the New Unions* (College Park, Md., 1939); William H. Harris, *The Harder We Run: Black Workers since the Civil War* (New York, 1982); Herbert R. Northrup, *Organized Labor and the Negro* (New York, 1944); Sterling D. Spero and Abram L. Harris, *The Black Worker: The Negro and the Labor Movement* (New York, 1931); Robert C. Weaver, *Negro Labor: A National Problem* (New York, 1946). On the class composition of the early NAACP, see Eisenberg, "Only for the Bourgeois?" 112; August Meier, "Some Observations on the Negro Middle Class," *Crisis* 64 (1957): 461–469, 517; E. Franklin Frazier, *Black Bourgeoisie* (Glencoe, Ill., 1957); Daniel Webster Wynn, *The NAACP versus Negro Revolutionary Protest* (New York, 1955), 34; Adam Fairclough, *Race and Democracy: The Civil Rights Struggle in Louisiana, 1915–1972* (Athens, Ga., 1995); Janken, *White;* Wolters, *Negroes and Great Depression;* Bates, "New Crowd;" Steven A. Reich, "Soldiers of Democracy: Black Texans and the Fight for Citizenship, 1917–1921," *Journal of American History* 82 (1996): 1478–1504; Judith Stein, *The World of Marcus Garvey: Race and Class in Modern Society* (Baton Rouge, La., 1986), 132; Robin D. G. Kelley, *Hammer and Hoe: Alabama Communists During the Great Depression* (Chapel Hill, N.C., 1990), 8–9; Robert Korstad and Nelson Lichtenstein, "Opportunities Found and Lost: Labor, Radicals, and the Early Civil Rights Movement," *Journal of American History* 75 (1988): 786–811; Robert C. Weaver, "The NAACP Today," *Journal of Negro Education* 29 (1960): 421–425.

10. Committee on Negro Work to directors of American Fund for Public Service (Garland Fund), memorandum, May 28, 1930, in *NAACP Papers,* pt. 3A, rl. 1:360–379, 376. Out of the three-person committee, one was the NAACP's executive secretary and one was a close legal advisor to the association. Mark V. Tushnet, *The NAACP's Legal Strategy against Segregated Education, 1925–1950* (Chapel Hill, N.C., 1987), 6–7.

11. See Nathan R. Margold, *Preliminary Report to the Joint Committee Supervising the Expenditure of the 1930 Appropriation by the American Fund for*

Public Service to the N.A.A.C.P. (New York, n.d. [1931?]), in *NAACP Papers,* pt. 3A, rl. 4:560–772. See also Tushnet, *NAACP's Legal Strategy,* 26–28; Mark V. Tushnet, *Making Civil Rights Law: Thurgood Marshall and the Supreme Court, 1936–1961* (New York, 1994), 12–13.

12. Meier and Bracey, "NAACP as Reform Movement," 15–18. See, for example, Marshall to Mr. W. A. Lynk, May 20, 1937, in *NAACP Papers,* pt. 10, rl. 16:452; "Peonage Cases Pending with the N.A.A.C.P.," Sept. 23, 1937, in *NAACP Papers,* pt. 10, rl. 16:460. Charles Hamilton Houston to Walter White, memorandum, Sept. 27, 1937, in *NAACP Papers,* pt. 10, rl. 16:478; "Suggestion from Mr. Houston," July 25, 1935, in *NAACP Papers,* pt. 10, rl. 16:445; Houston to Turner, memorandum, Sept. 27, 1937, in *NAACP Papers,* pt. 10, rl. 16:457. See also Janken, *White,* 233–259; Roy Wilkins, *Standing Fast: The Autobiography of Roy Wilkins* (New York, 1982), 146–164; Harvard Sitkoff, *A New Deal for Blacks: The Emergence of Civil Rights as a National Issue,* vol. 1 (New York, 1978); Houston to White, memorandum, Sept. 25, 1937, in *NAACP Papers,* pt. 10, rl. 16:479; Aron S. Gilmartin to Houston, Nov. 5, 1937, in *NAACP Papers,* pt. 10, rl. 16:539.

13. See James E. Goodman, *Stories of Scottsboro* (New York, 1994); Dan T. Carter, *Scottsboro: A Tragedy of the American South* (Baton Rouge, La., 1979); Kenneth W. Mack, "Law and Mass Politics in the Making of the Civil Rights Lawyer, 1931–1941," *Journal of American History* 93 (2006): 37–62. See also Charles H. Martin, "Communists and Blacks: The ILD and the Angelo Herndon Case," *Journal of Negro History* 64 (1979): 131–141. On the National Negro Congress, see John B. Kirby, *Black Americans in the Roosevelt Era: Liberalism and Race* (Knoxville, Tenn., 1980), 166–170; Wilson Record, *The Negro and the Communist Party* (Chapel Hill, N.C., 1951).

14. See NAACP, "Proposed Resolutions, 1936 Annual Conference," July 3, 1936, in *NAACP Papers,* pt. 1, rl. 9:939–943; NAACP, "Resolutions Adopted, 1938 Annual Conference," in *NAACP Papers,* pt. 1, rl. 10:48–53, 48–49. See generally Irving Bernstein, *Turbulent Years: A History of the American Worker, 1933–1941* (Boston, 1970); Robert H. Zieger, *The CIO: 1935–1955* (Chapel Hill, N.C., 1995); August Meier and Elliot Rudwick, *Black Detroit and the Rise of the UAW* (New York, 1979); Cayton and Mitchell, *Black Workers;* St. Clair Drake and Horace R. Cayton, *Black Metropolis: A Study of Negro Life in a Northern City* (New York, 1945), 312–341.

15. Ralphe J. Bunche, "The Programs of Organizations Devoted to the Improvement of the Status of the American Negro," *Journal of Negro Education* 8 (1939): 539–550, 546; Emmett E. Dorsey, "The Negro and So-

cial Planning," *Journal of Negro Education* 5 (1936): 105–109, 107. See also Ralph J. Bunche, "A Critical Analysis of the Tactics and Programs of Minority Groups," *Journal of Negro Education* 4 (July 1935): 308–320, 310; Jonathan Scott Holloway, *Confronting the Veil: Abram Harris, Jr., E. Franklin Frazier, and Ralph Bunche, 1919–1941* (Chapel Hill, N.C., 2002).

16. Roy Wilkins to Daisy E. Lampkin, Mar. 23, 1935, quoted in Bates, "New Crowd," 345; Charles Hamilton Houston, address at the 24th annual conference of the NAACP, Chicago, Ill., July 2, 1933, 8, in *NAACP Papers*, pt. 1, rl. 9:547–555, 554.

17. NAACP, "Address to the Country" (23rd annual conference of the NAACP, Washington, D.C., May 17–22, 1932), 1, in *NAACP Papers*, pt. 1, rl. 9:9–11; NAACP, "1933 Annual Conference," news release, June 25, 1933, in *NAACP Papers*, pt. 1, rl. 9:399–401; NAACP, "N.A.A.C.P. Resolutions Demand Jobs," news release, July 7, 1933, in *NAACP Papers*, pt. 1, rl. 9:408; Charles Hamilton Houston, "Proposed Legal Attacks on Educational Discrimination" (summary of address delivered to the National Bar Association, Aug. 1, 1935), quoted in Genna Rae McNeil, *Groundwork: Charles Hamilton Houston and the Struggle for Civil Rights* (Philadelphia, 1983), 134 (alteration in original; footnote omitted). See also "The Negro's Economic Status" (resolution adopted by the 24th annual conference of the NAACP, Chicago, Ill., June 29–July 2, 1933), 1–2, in *NAACP Papers*, pt. 1, rl. 9:423–427.

18. See Paul D. Moreno, *From Direct Action to Affirmative Action: Fair Employment Law and Policy in America, 1933–1972* (Baton Rouge, La., 1997), 30–54; Kimberley L. Phillips, *AlabamaNorth: African-American Migrants, Community, and Working-Class Activism in Cleveland, 1915–45* (Urbana, Ill., 1999); Holloway, *Confronting the Veil;* Anthony S. Chen, "From Fair Employment to Equal Opportunity and Beyond: Affirmative Action and the Politics of Civil Rights in the New Deal Order, 1941–1972" (Ph.D. diss., University of California, Berkeley, 2002). See, for example, NAACP, "Colored Women Forced off WPA to Pick Cotton," news release, in *NAACP Papers*, pt. 10, rl. 16:480; Alfred Edgar Smith to White, Oct. 5, 1937, in *NAACP Papers*, pt. 10, rl. 16:517–518; "WPA Workers Not Forced to Gather Cotton," *Memphis Press-Scimitar*, Sept. 27, 1937, in *NAACP Papers*, pt. 10, rl. 16:573; sec. to Harry L. Hopkins, Oct. 1, 1937, in *NAACP Papers*, pt. 10, rl. 16:481; Dona Cooper Hamilton and Charles V. Hamilton, *The Dual Agenda: Race and Social Welfare Policies of Civil Rights Organizations* (New York, 1997), 8–42; Robert L. Jack, *History of the National Association for the Advancement of Colored People* (Boston, 1943), 18–19. See also Arnesen, *Brotherhoods of Color*, 126–128.

19. NAACP, "Future Plan and Program of the NAACP," n.d., ca. Dec. 1941,

box 439, file "NAACP Programs: General, 1941–42," Records of the NAACP, Manuscript Division, Library of Congress, quoted in Carol Anderson, *Eyes Off the Prize: The United Nations and the African American Struggle for Human Rights, 1944–1955* (New York, 2003), 18. See Kenneth W. Mack, "Rethinking Civil Rights Lawyering and Politics in the Era Before *Brown*," *Yale Law Journal* 115 (2006): 256–354.

20. Houston to Secretary, Joint Committee, Sept. 25, 1937, in *NAACP Papers*, quoted in Tushnet, *NAACP's Legal Strategy*, 19. Only once in dozens of semimonthly, monthly, and annual reports did the NAACP's legal department describe the cases as involving "the right to a job." *Annual Report for Legal Department*, 1945, in *NAACP Papers*, pt. 18A, rl. 4:857–880, 859.

21. Tushnet, *NAACP's Legal Strategy*, 37, 160. See generally Richard Kluger, *Simple Justice: The History of* Brown v. Board of Education *and Black America's Struggle for Equality* (New York, 1977).

22. NAACP, *Procedure for Legal Defense and Voting Cases* (New York, 1939), in *NAACP Papers*, pt. 1, rl. 10:622–634; Thurgood Marshall, *Procedure to Equalize Educational Opportunities* (New York, 1939), in *NAACP Papers*, pt. 1, rl. 10:635–638.

23. McNeil, *Groundwork*, 131–132.

24. See ibid.

25. The education, economic circumstances, and professional lives of the black middle class differed significantly from the white middle class. See, for example, Charles Pete T. Banner-Haley, *To Do Good and to Do Well: Middle-Class Blacks and the Depression, Philadelphia, 1929–1941* (New York, 1993); Kevin Boyle, *Arc of Justice: A Saga of Race, Civil Rights, and Murder in the Jazz Age* (New York, 2004); Lynne B. Feldman, *A Sense of Place: Birmingham's Black Middle-Class Community, 1890–1930* (Tuscaloosa, Ala., 1999); Vincent P. Franklin, *The Education of Black Philadelphia: The Social and Educational History of a Minority Community, 1900–1950* (Philadelphia, 1979); Frazier, *Black Bourgeoisie*; Gaines, *Uplifting the Race*; Higginbotham, *Righteous Discontent*; Darlene Clark Hine, *Speak Truth to Power: Black Professional Class in United States History* (Brooklyn, N.Y., 1996); David Levering Lewis and Deborah Willis, *A Small Nation of People: W. E. B. Du Bois and African American Portraits of Progress* (New York, 2003); H. Viscount Nelson, *The Philadelphia N.A.A.C.P.: Epitome of Middle Class Consciousness* (Los Angeles, 1972); Larry Tye, *Rising from the Rails: Pullman Porters and the Making of the Black Middle Class* (New York, 2004); Burton Bledstein and Robert Johnston, eds., *The Middling Sorts: Explorations in the History of the American Middle Class* (New York, 2001).

26. Prentice Thomas to Marshall, May 28, 1942, in *NAACP Papers*, pt. 13C, rl. 12:1015. See "Prentice Thomas," n.d., in *NAACP Papers*, pt. 13C, rl. 12:1026; "Re: Prentice Thomas," Nov. 7, 1942, in *NAACP Papers*, pt. 13C, rl. 12:1030; "Re Biography of Prentice Thomas," Dec. 7, 1942, in *NAACP Papers*, pt. 13C, rl. 12:1037; Diane McWhorter, *Carry Me Home: Birmingham, Alabama: The Climactic Battle of the Civil Rights Revolution* (New York, 2001), 237. See John M. Glen, *Highlander: No Ordinary School, 1932–1962* (Lexington, Ky., 1988).

27. Thomas to Howard Kester, May 12, 1943, in *NAACP Papers*, pt. 13C, rl. 12:905; Thomas to White, memorandum, May 5, 1943, in *NAACP Papers*, pt. 13A, rl. 6:568–572, 568; White to Thomas, memorandum, July 20, 1943, in *NAACP Papers*, pt. 13C, rl. 12:1067. See Thomas to H. L. Mitchell, May 4, 1943, in *NAACP Papers*, pt. 13C, rl. 12:904; Juan Williams, *Thurgood Marshall: American Revolutionary* (New York, 1998), 105; Houston to Thomas, May 12, 1943, in *NAACP Papers*, pt. 13C, rl. 12:1055; Thomas to George Weaver, Aug. 5, 1943, in *NAACP Papers*, pt. 13C, rl. 12:1072.

28. Wilkins to Ellis Byrd, May 25, 1946, in *NAACP Papers*, pt. 18C, rl. 7:58. See Marian Wynn Perry to Marshall, Oct. 10, 1945, in *NAACP Papers*, pt. 18A, rl. 7:755; Denton L. Watson, *Lion in the Lobby: Clarence Mitchell, Jr.'s Struggle for the Passage of Civil Rights Laws*, rev. ed. (Lanham, Md., 2002), 145–178. See also NAACP Labor Department, "Objectives," July 26, 1946, in *NAACP Papers*, pt. 13C, rl. 6:525–527.

29. Thomas to White, memorandum, May 5, 1943, 4, in *NAACP Papers*, pt. 13A, rl. 6:568–572, 572.

30. NAACP Legal Defense and Educational Fund, Inc., "By-laws," adopted Oct. 13, 1941, 1, in *NAACP Papers*, pt. 18A, rl. 3:384–389, 385. See Marshall to John Crawford, July 2, 1942, in *NAACP Papers*, pt. 13C, rl. 3:50.

31. Milton R. Konvitz to William Carter, Nov. 26, 1943, in *NAACP Papers*, pt. 13C, rl. 3:125. See also Edward R. Dudley to Glenn C. Adair, May 4, 1944, in *NAACP Papers*, pt. 13C, rl. 2:228.

32. Tushnet, *NAACP's Legal Strategy*, 46–47; Perry, "Work of National Office," in *NAACP Papers*, pt. 18A, rl. 7:762–765, 762.

33. Marshall to James Hoy, Oct. 27, 1941, in *NAACP Papers*, pt. 13C, rl. 12:500. See also NAACP Legal Department, *Report . . . for the Month of July 1946*, in *NAACP Papers*, pt. 18A, rl. 4:928–931; M. W. Perry to Hon. Joseph H. Rainey, July 10, 1946, in *NAACP Papers*, pt. 13C, rl. 2:689; Frank D. Reeves to Henry Flowers, Jr., Aug. 13, 1941, in *NAACP Papers*, pt. 13C, rl. 12:474; M. W. Perry to Ogan, Jan. 19, 1946, in *NAACP Papers*, pt. 13C, rl. 7:305–306.

34. See Houston, memorandum, "In re Steele and Tunstall Cases," Dec. 20,

1944, 5, in *NAACP Papers,* pt. 13C, rl. 8:90–95, 94; Tushnet, *Making Civil Rights Law,* 47; A. W. Clemon and Bryan K. Fair, "Making Bricks without Straw: The NAACP Legal Defense Fund and the Development of Civil Rights Law in Alabama 1940–1980," *Alabama Law Review* 52 (2001): 1121–1152, 1132; Marshall to Rev. M. M. Flynn, Feb. 3, 1940, in *NAACP Papers,* pt. 13C, rl. 7:830. See generally, J. Clay Smith, Jr., *Emancipation: The Making of the Black Lawyer, 1844–1944* (Philadelphia, 1993), 190–320.

35. See Clement E. Vose, *Caucasians Only: The Supreme Court, the NAACP, and the Restrictive Covenant Cases* (Berkeley, Calif., 1959); Darlene Clark Hine, "Blacks and the Destruction of the Democratic White Primary 1935–1944," *Journal of Negro History* 62 (1977): 43–59; Tushnet, *Making Civil Rights Law,* 88.

36. Clarence Mitchell to M. W. Perry, Oct. 7, 1946, in *NAACP Papers,* pt. 13C, rl. 2:432. The fight against the white primary was southern in location, though largely urban, not rural. See, for example, Darlene Clark Hine, *Black Victory: The Rise and Fall of the White Primary in Texas* (Millwood, N.Y., 1979); Steven F. Lawson, *Black Ballots: Voting Rights in the South, 1944–1969* (New York, 1976); Tushnet, *Making Civil Rights Law,* 99–115. Lynching, the NAACP's only other long-term interest in the rural South, also lost some of the association's attention in the 1940s. Zangrando, *NAACP Crusade,* 166–186. The NAACP still also represented black criminal defendants in the South, but the threshold for taking such cases was higher than in the North. See *NAACP Papers,* pt. 8B.

37. See Tushnet, *Making Civil Rights Law,* 45; Earl B. Dickerson to Marshall, Jan. 14, 1941, in *NAACP Papers,* pt. 13C, rl. 12:467; Marshall to Dickerson, Jan. 21, 1941, in *NAACP Papers,* pt. 13C, rl. 12:466; William Henry Huff to Marshall, Aug. 29, 1941, in *NAACP Papers,* pt. 13C, rl. 12:725–726; Huff to White, Nov. 24, 1941, in *NAACP Papers,* pt. 13C, rl. 12:727–729; Donald Harrington to Wilkins, Dec. 18, 1947, in *NAACP Papers,* pt. 13C, rl. 12:692–696.

38. See Meier and Rudwick, *Black Detroit;* NAACP, "Resolutions Adopted by the Thirty-first Annual Conference" (June 22, 1940), 5, in *NAACP Papers,* pt. 1, rl. 10:740–747, 744; Horace R. Cayton, "A Strategy for Negro Labor" (address at the 32nd annual conference of the NAACP, Houston, Tex., June 24, 1941), 6, in *NAACP Papers,* pt. 1, rl. 10:1191–1204, 1196; John L. Lewis, address at the 31st annual conference of the NAACP, Philadelphia, June 18, 1940, 5, in *NAACP Papers,* pt. 1, rl. 10:807–814, 811. Historians disagree about the extent to which the CIO, or the AFL for that matter, supported interracial unions and suc-

cessfully supported civil rights efforts. Compare Korstad and Lichtenstein, "Opportunities Found," with Judith Stein, "Southern Workers in
National Unions: Birmingham Steelworkers, 1936–1951," in *Organized
Labor in the Twentieth-Century South,* ed. Robert H. Zieger (Knoxville,
Tenn., 1991), 183–222. On the debate, see Eric Arnesen, "Up from Exclusion: Black and White Workers, Race, and the State of Labor History," *Reviews in American History* 26 (1998): 146–174; Michael Goldfield, "Race and the CIO: The Possibilities for Racial Egalitarianism
during the 1930s and 1940s," *International Labor and Working-Class History* 44 (1993): 1–32; Rick Halpern, "Organised Labour, Black Workers,
and the Twentieth-Century South: The Emerging Revision," *Social History* 19 (1994): 359–383.

39. Alfred Baker Lewis to M. W. Perry, Jan. 15, 1945, in *NAACP Papers,* pt.
13C, rl. 2:653.

40. See Patricia Sullivan, *Days of Hope: Race and Democracy in the New Deal Era*
(Chapel Hill, N.C., 1996), 141–143; Meier and Bracey, "NAACP as Re-
form Movement," 19, 21; Gunnar Myrdal, *An American Dilemma: The
Negro Problem and Modern Democracy* (New York, 1944), 703; Richard M.
Dalfiume, "The 'Forgotten Years' of the Negro Revolution," *Journal of
American History* 55 (1968): 90–106; Tushnet, *NAACP's Legal Strategy,* 135.
For speculations on the extent of working-class membership, see, for ex-
ample, "Motion to File Brief as Amicus," in *NAACP Papers,* pt. 13C, rl.
1:259–260; Wilkins to Cy W. Record, Dec. 21, 1949, in *NAACP Papers,* pt.
18B, rl. 7:900–903; August Meier, "Negro Protest Movements and Orga-
nizations," *Journal of Negro Education* 32 (1963): 437–450; Berky Nelson,
"Before the Revolution: Crisis within the Philadelphia and Chicago
NAACP, 1940–1960," *Negro History Bulletin* 61 (1998): 20–27.

41. Tushnet, *Making Civil Rights Law,* 34.

42. Janken, *White;* NAACP, "Future Plan and Program," box 439, file
"NAACP Programs: General, 1941–42," Records of the NAACP, quoted
in Anderson, *Eyes Off the Prize,* 18; White to Wilkins, memorandum, May
19, 1942, in *NAACP Papers,* pt. 13C, rl. 12:1006. See generally Bruce
Nelson, "Organized Labor and the Struggle for Black Equality in Mobile During World War II," *Journal of American History* 80 (1993): 952–
988.

43. Marshall to Joseph James, Jan. 5, 1945, in *NAACP Papers,* pt. 13C, rl.
1:219–220. See Marshall to Griffin, May 9, 1946, in *NAACP Papers,* pt.
13C, rl. 1:492–493.

44. Capt. E. Frederick Morrow, "Employment Problems of Negro Veterans"
(address at the 37th annual conference of the NAACP, Cincinnati,
Ohio, June–July, 1946), 8, in *NAACP Papers,* pt. 1, rl. 11:705–713, 712; J.

LeRoy Baxter to Thomas, Oct. 9, 1942, in *NAACP Papers*, pt. 13C, rl. 7:384–385. See Henry Lee Moon to Wilkins, memorandum, Nov. 1, 1948, in *NAACP Papers*, pt. 13C, rl. 5:871; Bessie W. Armstrong to NAACP, July 31, 1942, in *NAACP Papers*, pt. 13C, rl. 2:196–197; Frances Young to White, May 24, 1943, in *NAACP Papers*, pt. 13C, rl. 4:38–39; LeRoy Hayden to NAACP, Jan. 30, 1945, in *NAACP Papers*, pt. 13C, rl. 4:792–795; Brian Paxton to Marshall, June 9, 1944, in *NAACP Papers*, pt. 13C, rl. 7:476–477; Adair to White, Apr. 12, 1944, in *NAACP Papers*, pt. 13C, rl. 2:236–239; Theodore Johnson to NAACP, Aug. 31, 1944, in *NAACP Papers*, pt. 13C, rl. 5:91–93; NAACP, "Resolutions Adopted by the Fortieth Annual Convention" (Los Angeles, July 16, 1949), in *NAACP Papers*, pt. 1, rl. 12:646–657; Marshall to C. Brown, Oct. 25, 1949, in *NAACP Papers*, pt. 13C, rl. 3:560–561. See generally Moreno, *From Direct Action*, 84–106.

45. McK. Nicholson to Konvitz, Sept. 14, 1943, in *NAACP Papers*, pt. 13C, rl. 2:209; Robert Hammond to NAACP, Apr. 26, 1947, in *NAACP Papers*, pt. 13C, rl. 12:679–680. See also Risa L. Goluboff, " 'Won't You Please Help Me Get My Son Home': Peonage, Patronage, and Protest in the World War II Urban South," *Law and Social Inquiry* 24 (1999): 777–806; McCord to Williams, Dec. 30, 1941, in *NAACP Papers*, pt. 13C, rl. 12:819; Julia E. Baxter to Marshall, memorandum, June 11, 1947, in *NAACP Papers*, pt. 13C, rl. 2:711.

46. Marshall to Charley Bright, Jan. 26, 1945, in *NAACP Papers*, pt. 13C, rl. 2:400. See NAACP Legal Department, *Semi-Annual Report*, Jan. 1–June 30, 1944, 12–14, in *NAACP Papers*, pt. 18A, rl. 4:788–790. See also, for example, Marshall to Tommie Knox, Feb. 24, 1941, in *NAACP Papers*, pt. 13A, rl. 19:341; Franklin H. Williams, "re: Wyatt Trueblood," news release, Jan. 29, 1947, in *NAACP Papers*, pt. 13C, rl. 9:88. See generally NAACP Legal Department, *The Legal Front: Some Highlights of the Past Year* (New York, 1940), in *NAACP Papers*, pt. 18A, rl. 4:574–584; Zangrando, *NAACP Crusade;* Janken, *White;* Dray, *Hands of Persons Unknown.*

47. See, for example, Marshall to Mrs. Texanne Thornton, Sept. 6, 1945, in *NAACP Papers*, pt. 13C, rl. 2:402; Rev. Valco R. Harris to George S. Schulyer, Oct. 9, 1944, in *NAACP Papers*, pt. 13C, rl. 2:391–392; Dudley to E. R. Avant, Nov. 2, 1944, in *NAACP Papers*, pt. 13C, rl. 2:394; Reeves to Flowers, Jr., Aug. 13, 1941, in *NAACP Papers*, pt. 13C, rl. 12:474; Marshall to Miss Lucy Graves, Aug. 12, 1940, in *NAACP Papers*, pt. 13C, rl. 12:462; Graves to Marshall, Aug. 9, 1940, in *NAACP Papers*, pt. 13C, rl. 12:463–464. Mrs. Julius White to Marshall, May 25, 1943, in *NAACP Papers*, pt. 13C, rl. 12:577–578; M. W. Perry to Mrs. Augustus Evans, July 23, 1947, in *NAACP Papers*, pt. 13C, rl. 2:721.

48. Lewis to White, Nov. 1, 1945, in *NAACP Papers,* pt. 13C, rl. 2:615. See Minutes of the NAACP Board of Directors, Oct. 17, 1945, in *NAACP Papers,* pt. 13C, rl. 2:606–607.

49. Dudley to H. L. Mitchell, Oct. 30, 1945, in *NAACP Papers,* pt. 13C, rl. 2:632; M. W. Perry to Joseph Freeland, Jan. 2, 1945, in *NAACP Papers,* pt. 13C, rl. 2:672; Lewis to L. Perry, May 28, 1946, in *NAACP Papers,* pt. 13C, rl. 2:655. See M. W. Perry to Lewis, Nov. 30, 1945, in *NAACP Papers,* pt. 13C, rl. 2:627; Lewis to Marshall, Jan. 2, 1946, in *NAACP Papers,* pt. 13C, rl. 2:647. See also Lewis to White, Dec. 27, 1945, in *NAACP Papers,* pt. 13C, rl. 2:640–641; Lewis to White, Nov. 1, 1945, in *NAACP Papers,* pt. 13C, rl. 2:615; Leslie Perry to Clinton P. Anderson, Feb. 27, 1946, in *NAACP Papers,* pt. 13C, rl. 2:661–662.

50. See, for example, Marshall to Henry A. Wallace, Feb. 14, 1940, in *NAACP Papers,* pt. 13A, rl. 1:308–309; M. W. Perry to Anderson, July 2, 1947, in *NAACP Papers,* pt. 13C, rl. 2:710; J. E. Baxter to Marshall, memorandum, June 11, 1947, in *NAACP Papers,* pt. 13C, rl. 2:711; Marshall to Thomas H. Browne, Aug. 11, 1941, in *NAACP Papers,* pt. 13C, rl. 12:472; Marshall to Arthur Shores, Mar. 3, 1943, in *NAACP Papers,* pt. 13C, rl. 12:566.

51. M. W. Perry to Wilkins, May 12, 1947, in *NAACP Papers,* pt. 13C, rl. 12:676; Taylor v. Georgia, 315 U.S. 25 (1942). See Pollock v. Williams, 322 U.S. 4 (1944); Bailey v. Alabama, 219 U.S. 219 (1911); Frank McAllister, "Confidential Memorandum on Alleged Peonage in Milledgeville," July 9, [1941?], in *NAACP Papers,* pt. 13C, rl. 12:794–797; McAllister to Marshall, Jan. 15, 1942, in *NAACP Papers,* pt. 13C, rl. 12:842; Williams to White, Feb. 27, 1947, in *NAACP Papers,* pt. 13C, rl. 12:406. For the occasional intervention, see M. W. Perry to Herman L. Taylor, Sept. 17, 1946, in *NAACP Papers,* pt. 13C, rl. 12:643–644.

52. See Carolyn Hoecker Luedtke, "On the Frontier of Change: A Legal History of the San Francisco Civil Rights Movement, 1944–1970," *Temple Political and Civil Rights Law Review* 10 (2000): 1–47, 8; Merl E. Reed, *Seedtime for the Modern Civil Rights Movement: The President's Committee on Fair Employment Practice, 1941–1946* (Baton Rouge, La., 1991), 267–317; Draft Brief as Amicus Curiae at pt. 1:1–17, James v. Marinship Corp., 155 P.2d 329 (Cal. 1944) (S.F. No. 17015), in *NAACP Papers,* pt. 13C, rl. 1:376–428, 376–392; NAACP, "NAACP Aids Coast Shipyard Workers," news release, Dec. 3, 1943, in *NAACP Papers,* pt. 13C, rl. 1:42; NAACP, "War Production Board: Labor Division," news release, Jan. 24, 1942, in *NAACP Papers,* pt. 13C, rl. 1:27; James v. Marinship Corp., 155 P.2d 329 (Cal. 1944); Williams v. Int'l Bhd. of Boilermakers, 165 P.2d 903 (Cal. 1946). See generally Herbert Hill, *Black Labor and the Amer-*

ican Legal System (Washington, D.C., 1977), 1:185–206; Charles Wollenberg, "*James v. Marinship:* Trouble on the New Black Frontier," in *Working People of California*, ed. Daniel Cornford (Berkeley, Calif., 1995), 159–179; William H. Harris, "Federal Intervention in Union Discrimination: FEPC and West Coast Shipyards during World War II," *Labor History* 22 (1981): 325–347; Marilynn S. Johnson, *The Second Gold Rush: Oakland and the East Bay in World War II* (Berkeley, Calif., 1993); Lester Rubin, *The Negro in the Shipbuilding Industry* (Philadelphia, 1970).

53. See Dudley to Marshall, memorandum, Mar. 29, 1944, in *NAACP Papers,* pt. 13C, rl. 1:532–533; Marshall to White and Wilkins, memorandum, Dec. 22, 1943, in *NAACP Papers,* pt. 13C, rl. 1:872; Wilkins to White, Nov. 1, 1942, in *NAACP Papers,* pt. 13C, rl. 1:574–576; W. H. Warren, "Negro Leader Scores Union Racial Discrimination Here," *Oregon Journal,* Oct. 14, 1943, 16.

54. N.Y. Civ. Rights Law §43 (McKinney 2005) (original version enacted in 1940 and amended in 1945); Railway Mail Ass'n v. Corsi, 326 U.S. 88 (1945). See Martha Biondi, *To Stand and Fight: The Struggle for Civil Rights in Postwar New York City* (Cambridge, Mass., 2003), 17–37; Morroe Berger, "The New York State Law against Discrimination: Operation and Administration," *Cornell Law Quarterly* 35 (1950): 747–796; Elmer A. Carter, "The New York Commission Succeeds," *Interracial Review* 20 (1947): 166–167; Michael E. Phenner, "Legislation and Administration: Labor Law—Discrimination—State Fair Employment Practice Acts and Multi-state Employers," *Notre Dame Lawyer* 36 (1961): 189–201; "The New York State Commission Against Discrimination: A New Technique for an Old Problem," *Yale Law Journal* 56 (1947): 837–863; Chen, "From Fair Employment."

55. See Tushnet, *Making Civil Rights Law,* 46; Anne Mather, "Report on the Experience of the Urban League, NAACP, and American Jewish Congress with the State Commission Against Discrimination," draft, Feb. 26, 1948, in *NAACP Papers,* pt. 13C, rl. 11:888–894. See also, for example, NAACP Legal Department, *Annual Report of Legal Department,* 1946, in *NAACP Papers,* pt. 18A, rl. 4:958–963; *Legal Department Annual Report,* 1947, in *NAACP Papers,* pt. 18A, rl. 4:1066–1085, 1084.

56. See Arnesen, *Brotherhoods of Color,* 203–210; Tushnet, *Making Civil Rights Law,* 78; Steele v. Louisville & Nashville R.R. Co., 323 U.S. 192 (1944); Tunstall v. Bhd. of Locomotive Firemen, 323 U.S. 210 (1944). The NLRB interpreted *Steele* and *Tunstall* as also applying to unions regulated by the NLRA. See In re Sw. Portland Cement Co., 61 N.L.R.B. 1217 (1945); In re Carter Mfg. Co., 59 N.L.R.B. 804 (1944). Without citing *Tunstall* or *Steele,* in Wallace Corp. v. NLRB, 323 U.S. 248 (1944),

the Court also found a duty of fair representation under the National Labor Relations Act. Four justices dissented, finding the RLA and the NLRA significantly different on the point. Ibid. at 270–271. See also Clyde W. Summers, "The Right to Join a Union," *Columbia Law Review* 47 (1947): 33–74, 44–51. See generally Reuel E. Schiller, "From Group Rights to Individual Liberties: Post-war Labor Law, Liberation, and the Waning of Union Strength," *Berkeley Journal of Employment and Labor Law* 20 (1999): 1–73, 23–29.

57. Marshall to Griffin, May 9, 1946, in *NAACP Papers,* pt. 13C, rl. 1:492–493. See *America on Guard,* 9–10, in *NAACP Papers,* pt. 13C, rl. 1:55–64, 63–64.

7. Litigating Labor in the Wartime NAACP

1. See, for example, Herbert Resner to Thurgood Marshall, Feb. 10, 1944, in *Papers of the NAACP,* ed. August Meier (Frederick, Md., 1982), microfilm, pt. 13C, rl. 1:88 (hereafter cited as *NAACP Papers*); Marshall to Resner, Feb. 15, 1944, in *NAACP Papers,* pt. 13C, rl. 1:89.

2. Smith v. Allwright, 321 U.S. 649 (1944); Screws v. United States 325 U.S. 91 (1945); Marsh v. Alabama, 326 U.S. 501 (1946); Osmond K. Fraenkel, "The Federal Civil Rights Laws," *Minnesota Law Review* 31 (1947): 301–327, 320. See also George Brody, "Recent Decisions: Constitutional Law—Freedom of Speech and Religion—What Constitutes State Action," *Michigan Law Review* 44 (1946): 848–852; Clyde W. Summers, "The Right to Join a Union," *Columbia Law Review* 47 (1947): 33–74, 56–58; John A. Huston, "Comments: Constitutional Law—State Court Enforcement of Race Restrictive Covenants as State Action within the Scope of Fourteenth Amendment," *Michigan Law Review* 45 (1947): 733–748.

3. See generally Mark V. Tushnet, *Making Civil Rights Law: Thurgood Marshall and the Supreme Court, 1936–1961* (New York, 1994), 76–80. Around one-quarter of the complaints the FEPC received in one war year were brought against the federal government. President's Committee on Civil Rights, *To Secure These Rights: The Report of the President's Committee on Civil Rights* (Washington, D.C., 1947), 58.

4. Pauli Murray, "The Right to Equal Opportunity in Employment," *California Law Review* 33 (1945): 388–433, 392. See D. O. McGovney, "Racial Residential Segregation by State Court Enforcement of Restrictive Agreements, Covenants or Conditions in Deeds Is Unconstitutional," *California Law Review* 33 (1945): 5–39, 22–24.

5. I refer largely to the theoretical writings of progressive and realist legal

scholars. See, for example, Barbara H. Fried, *The Progressive Assault on Laissez Faire: Robert Hale and the First Law and Economics Movement* (Cambridge, Mass., 1998); Robert L. Hale, "Coercion and Distribution in a Supposedly Non-coercive State," *Political Science Quarterly* 38 (1923): 470–478; Robert L. Hale, "Force and the State: A Comparison of 'Political' and 'Economic' Compulsion," *Columbia Law Review* 35 (1935): 149–201.

6. Nebbia v. New York, 291 U.S. 502 (1934); National Labor Relations Act, ch. 372, §7(3), (4), 49 Stat. 449–457, 452–453 (1935) (codified as amended at 29 U.S.C. §158[a][3], [4] [2000]). See Barry Cushman, *Rethinking the New Deal Court: The Structure of a Constitutional Revolution* (New York, 1998), 78–83; Murray, "Right to Equal Opportunity," 433. The Supreme Court began to undermine the employer's prerogative when it upheld the Railway Labor Act in Tex. & New Orleans R.R. Co. v. Bhd. of Ry. & S.S. Clerks, 281 U.S. 548 (1930). But that case, as the statute it upheld, was limited to railroads.

7. Murray, "Right to Equal Opportunity," 389; Louis C. Kesselman, "The Fair Employment Practice Commission Movement in Perspective," *Journal of Negro History* 31 (1946): 30–46.

8. Motion and Brief for the National Association for the Advancement of Colored People as Amicus Curiae at 5–6, Ry. Mail Ass'n v. Corsi, 326 U.S. 88 (1945) (No. 691), in *U.S. Supreme Court Records and Briefs* (Bethesda, Md., n.d.); *Corsi*, 326 U.S. at 95; E. Merrick Dodd, "The Supreme Court and Organized Labor, 1941–1945," *Harvard Law Review* 58 (1945): 1018–1071; Summers, "Right to Join," 57.

9. See Dodd, "Supreme Court and Labor," 1061; Charles W. Cobb, Jr., "The Outlook Regarding State FEPC Legislation," *Journal of Negro History* 31 (1946): 247–253; Kesselman, "Fair Employment Practice Commission," 34 n. 6, 42–43. See also G. James Fleming, "Educational Aspects of FEPC Laws," *Journal of Negro Education* 19 (1950): 7–15.

10. Steele v. Louisville & N. R. Co., 323 U.S. 192 (1944); Tunstall v. Brotherhood of Locomotive Firemen, 323 U.S. 210 (1944).

11. Murray, "Right to Equal Opportunity," 405. See *Steele*, 323 U.S. at 201–203; *Tunstall*, 323 U.S. at 213.

12. Kesselman, "Fair Employment Practice Commission," 33. See Exec. Order No. 8802, 6 Fed. Reg. 3109 (June 25, 1941).

13. Marshall to W. F. Turner, Dec. 13, 1940, in *NAACP Papers*, pt. 13C, rl. 7:22.

14. George R. Andersen and Resner to Hon. Michael J. Roche, Dec. 22, 1943, in *NAACP Papers*, pt. 13C, rl. 1:247–248; James v. Marinship

Corp., 155 P.2d 329 (Cal. 1945). See Marshall to Andersen and Resner, Jan. 8, 1945, in *NAACP Papers*, pt. 13C, rl. 1:225–226.

15. *James*, 155 P.2d at 339 (citing Smith v. Allwright, 321 U.S. 649; *Steele*, 323 U.S. 192), 335. See Mayer v. Journeymen Stone-Cutters' Ass'n, 20 A. 492 (N.J. Ch. 1890); Summers, "Right to Join," 37.

16. *James*, 155 P.2d at 339–340; Williams v. Int'l Brotherhood of Boiler-makers, 165 P.2d 903, 905 (Cal. 1946). See also Murray, "Right to Equal Opportunity," 433.

17. Betts v. Easley, 169 P.2d 831, 838 (Kan. 1946).

18. John A. C. Hetherington, "State Economic Regulation and Substantive Due Process of Law," *Northwestern University Law Review* 53 (1958): 226–251; Slaughter-House Cases, 83 U.S. 36 (1873); Allgeyer v. Louisiana, 165 U.S. 578 (1897). See, for example, Noble v. Davis, 161 S.W.2d 189 (Ark. 1942); Kirtley v. State, 84 N.E.2d 712 (Ind. 1949); Moore v. Grillis, 39 So. 2d 505 (Miss. 1949); State v. Ballance, 51 S.E.2d 731 (N.C. 1949); State v. Greeson, 124 S.W.2d 253 (Tenn. 1939); State v. Harris, 6 S.E.2d 854, 865 (N.C. 1940); Takahashi v. Fish & Game Comm'n, 185 P.2d 805, 809–812 (Cal. 1947). See also Valle v. Stengel, 176 F.2d 697 (3d Cir. 1949). See generally, Risa L. Goluboff, "The Work of Civil Rights in the 1940s: The Department of Justice, the NAACP, and African American Agricultural Workers" (Ph.D. diss. Princeton University, 2003), 35–45.

19. Prentice Thomas to Clayborne George, Dec. 8, 1942, in *NAACP Papers*, pt. 13C, rl. 3:700. See also Thomas to Walter White, memorandum, May 5, 1943, 2, in *NAACP Papers*, pt. 13A, rl. 6:568–572.

20. Marian Wynn Perry to Marshall (copies to Carter and Peyser), memorandum, "Discriminatory Practices by State Employment Services," June 20, 1949, 4, 2, in *NAACP Papers*, pt. 13C, rl. 8:789–795 (emphasis added). For the efforts of African Americans to make *Lochner*-type arguments work for them, see David E. Bernstein, *Only One Place of Redress: African Americans, Labor Regulations, and the Courts from Reconstruction to the New Deal* (Durham, N.C., 2001).

21. Memorandum Brief for Complainants at pt. 2:1, Hill v. Int'l Bhd. of Boilermakers, Equity No. 17760 (R.I. Super. Ct. filed Dec. 16, 1943) (quoting "Labor," §33, in *American Jurisprudence*, vol. 31 [San Francisco, 1940], 851), in *NAACP Papers*, pt. 13C, rl. 1:1191–1222, 1193 (internal quotation marks and footnote omitted); Draft Brief as Amicus Curiae at pt. 2:5, 2:7, 11, James v. Marinship Corp., 155 P.2d 329 (Cal. 1945) (S.F. No. 17015), in *NAACP Papers*, pt. 13C, rl. 1:376–428, 399 (quoting Wilson v. Newspaper & Mail Deliverers' Union, 197 A. 720, 722 [N.J. Ch. 1938]) (internal quotation marks omitted), 400 (paraphrasing Car-

roll v. Local No. 269 Int'l Bhd. of Elec. Workers, 31 A.2d 223, 224–225 [N.J. Ch. 1943]), 404 (paraphrasing Cameron v. Int'l Alliance of Theatrical Stage Employees, 176 A. 692, 697 [N.J. 1935]). Motion and Brief for the National Association for the Advancement of Colored People as Amicus Curiae at 9, Takahashi v. Fish and Game Commission, 334 U.S. 410 (1948) (No. 533), in *NAACP Papers,* pt. 15A, rl 8:188–273. The NAACP's was the only major brief on behalf of the workers to cite *Allgeyer.*

22. Draft Brief as Amicus, *James,* 155 P.2d 329 (S.F. No. 17,015), in *NAACP Papers,* pt. 13C, rl. 1:376–428, 401–402; see also Memorandum Brief for Complainants at pt. 2:1, *Hill,* Equity No. 17760, in *NAACP Papers,* pt. 13C, rl. 1:1191–1222, 1193. For a different view of the relationship between these rights, see Ken I. Kersch, *Constructing Civil Liberties: Discontinuities in the Development of American Constitutional Law* (New York, 2004), 188–225.

23. Summers, "Right to Join," 66. See Bernstein, *Only One Place,* 6, 85, 94–99; Herbert Hill, *Black Labor and the American Legal System* (Washington, D.C., 1977), 1:93–136; Raymond Wolters, *Negroes and the Great Depression: The Problem of Economic Recovery* (Westport, Conn., 1970), 182–187; Paul Frymer, "Race, Labor, and the Twentieth-Century American State," *Politics and Society* 32 (2004): 475–509, 480–82; NAACP, "JimCro [*sic*] Policies Aimed at in Action against Boilermakers," news release, Sept. 7, 1944, in *NAACP Papers,* pt. 13C, rl. 1:194–195. See also Eric Arnesen, *Brotherhoods of Color: Black Railroad Workers and the Struggle for Equality* (Cambridge, Mass., 2001), 86–87, 145, 168.

24. *James,* 155 P.2d at 335, 336 (quoting *Carroll,* 31 A.2d at 225), 335 (quoting *Wilson,* 197 A. at 722) (internal quotation marks omitted); *Williams,* 165 P.2d at 905–906; *Betts,* 169 P.2d at 839, 843 (citation omitted).

25. Murray, "Right to Equal Opportunity," 388, 388 nn. 3, 5, 431; Summers, "Right to Join," 73. See generally Eileen Boris, " 'The Right to Work Is the Right to Live!': Fair Employment and the Quest for Social Citizenship," in *Two Cultures of Rights: The Quest for Inclusion and Participation in Modern America and Germany,* ed. Marfred Berg and Martin H. Geyer (Cambridge, Mass., 2002), 121–142, 128–129.

26. John Grantham to White, Nov. 3, 1943, in *NAACP Papers,* pt. 13A, rl. 11:135. See, for example, Bruce Nelson, "Organized Labor and the Struggle for Black Equality in Mobile during World War II," *Journal of American History* 80 (1993): 952–988, 982; Charles D. Chamberlain, *Victory at Home: Manpower and Race in the American South during World War II* (Athens, Ga., 2003), 141.

27. Herman Laws to White, June 16, 1942, in *NAACP Papers,* quoted in John M. McLarnon, "Pie in the Sky vs. Meat and Potatoes: The Case of Sun Ship's Yard No. 4," *Journal of American Studies* 34 (2000): 67–88, 73.

28. NAACP to John G. Pew, [1942?], quoted in "Along the N.A.A.C.P. Battlefront," *Crisis* 49 (1942): 227–230, 228; White to Laws, June 30, 1942, in *NAACP Papers,* quoted in McLarnon, "Pie in the Sky," 74.

29. Marshall to Jospeh P. Ryan, Apr. 10, 1940, in *NAACP Papers,* pt. 13A, rl. 7:002.

30. Roy Wilkins to White, Nov. 1, 1942, in *NAACP Papers,* pt. 13C, rl. 1:574–576, 576. See also Rev. J. J. Clow to White, Dec. 22, 1942, in *NAACP Papers,* pt. 13C, rl. 1:618.

31. *James,* 155 P.2d at 342; *Williams,* 165 P.2d at 906.

32. In re Bethlehem-Alameda Shipyard, Inc., 53 N.L.R.B. 999, 1016 (1943); In re Larus & Brother Co., 62 N.L.R.B. 1075, 1081, 1082 (1945); *Williams,* 165 P.2d at 906. See also In re Carter Mfg. Co., 59 N.L.R.B. 804, 806 (1944); In re Sw. Portland Cement Co., 61 N.L.R.B. 1217, 1219 (1945).

33. Marshall to Andersen and Resner, Jan. 8, 1945, in *NAACP Papers,* pt. 13C, rl. 1:225–226; Marshall to Resner, Feb. 13, 1946, in *NAACP Papers,* pt. 13C, rl. 1:486. See NAACP, "California Supreme Court Outlaws Jim Crow Auxiliary Unions," news release, Jan. 4, 1945, in *NAACP Papers,* pt. 13C, rl. 1:218.

34. Clarence Mitchell to Robert Carter, Apr. 27, 1949, in *NAACP Papers,* pt. 13C, rl. 8:785; Clarence Mitchell to Guy Moffett, Nov. 12, 1948, in *NAACP Papers,* pt. 13C, rl. 4:520–521; Perry to Will Maslow (copied to Mitchell), memorandum, May 12, 1947, in *NAACP Papers,* pt. 13C, rl. 8:776; Perry to Clarence Mitchell, memorandum, Feb. 25, 1948, in *NAACP Papers,* pt. 13C, rl. 6:617. See Department of Labor Appropriation Act, 1947, ch. 672, 60 Stat. 679, 684 (1946).

35. See "Excerpts from Resolutions Adopted by NAACP 42nd Annual Convention," June 30, 1951, in *NAACP Papers,* pt. 18C, rl. 7:395. See also NAACP, "Resolutions Adopted at the 41st Annual Convention," June 23, 1950, in *NAACP Papers,* pt. 1, rl. 12:942–955, 947; NAACP, "Resolutions Adopted at the 40th Annual Convention," July 16, 1949, in *NAACP Papers,* pt. 1, rl. 12:646–657, 655; NAACP, "Resolutions Adopted at the 39th Annual Conference," June 26, 1948, in *NAACP Papers,* pt. 1, rl. 12:354–366, 356; NAACP, "Resolutions Adopted at the 38th Annual Conference," June 28, 1947, in *NAACP Papers,* pt. 1, rl. 12:119–125, 119. See generally Mark V. Tushnet, *The NAACP's Legal Strategy against Segregated Education, 1925–1950* (Chapel Hill, N.C., 1987), 103–137.

36. Charles Hamilton Houston to Association of Colored Railway

Trainmen and Locomotive Firemen et al., memorandum, Dec. 20, 1944, folder 14, box 163–23, Charles Hamilton Houston Papers, Moorland-Spingarn Research Center, Howard University, Washington, D.C., quoted in Genna Rae McNeil, *Groundwork: Charles Hamilton Houston and the Struggle for Civil Rights* (Philadelphia, 1983), 170 (internal quotation marks omitted); Walter White, "Closing Session Remarks" (NAACP 41st annual conference, June 25, 1950), in *NAACP Papers,* pt. 1, rl. 12:1070–1077, 1074. See Sweatt v. Painter, 339 U.S. 629 (1950); McLaurin v. Okla. State Regents for Higher Educ., 339 U.S. 637 (1950); Henderson v. United States, 339 U.S. 816 (1950).

37. Resner to Marshall, May 31, 1946, in *NAACP Papers,* pt. 13C, rl. 2:1048–1049; Murray, "Right to Equal Opportunity," 433. See NAACP Labor Secretary, *Monthly Report,* Aug. 31, 1946, 1, in *NAACP Papers,* pt. 13A, rl. 9:429–431, 429; Denton L. Watson, *Lion in the Lobby: Clarence Mitchell, Jr.'s Struggle for the Passage of Civil Rights Laws,* rev. ed. (Lanham, Md., 2002), 152–156; Dona Cooper Hamilton and Charles V. Hamilton, *The Dual Agenda: Race and Social Welfare Policies of Civil Rights Organizations* (New York, 1997), 63; Tushnet, *Making Civil Rights Law,* 79.

38. See Perry to Marshall, memorandum, Sept. 17, 1948, in *NAACP Papers,* pt. 13A, rl. 14:476; NLRB, *Annual Report* 10 (1945): 18, quoted in NAACP Labor Secretary, *Monthly Report,* Aug. 31, 1946, 2, in *NAACP Papers,* pt. 13A, rl. 9: 429–431, 430; Herbert Hill to White, memorandum, Sept. 11, 1952, in *NAACP Papers,* pt. 13A, rl. 20:304; Sophia Z. Lee, "Hotspots in a Cold War: The NAACP's Postwar Labor Constitutionalism, 1948–1964" (working paper, Social Science Research Network, 2005), http://papers.ssrn.com/sol3/papers.cfm?abstract_id=814067 (accessed Jan. 23, 2006); In re Veneer Prods., Inc., 81 N.L.R.B. 492, 493 (1949); Bhd. of R.R. Trainmen v. Howard, 343 U.S. 768 (1952), aff'g Howard v. St. Louis-S.F. Ry. Co., 191 F.2d 442 (8th Cir. 1951), aff'g in part, rev'g in part Howard v. Thomas, 72 F. Supp. 695 (E.D. Mo. 1947); Arnesen, *Brotherhoods of Color,* 203–229. See also Pac. Mar. Ass'n, 110 N.L.R.B. 1647, 1648 (1954); Hughes Tool Co., 104 N.L.R.B. 318, 321 (1953).

39. Charles H. Houston, "The Legal Struggle for Protection of Minority Workers' Rights on American Railroads" (address at the 40th annual conference of the NAACP, Los Angeles, July 14, 1949), 12, in *NAACP Papers,* pt. 1, rl. 12:694–707, 705. See Arnesen, *Brotherhoods of Color,* 209.

40. Charles H. Houston, "The Highway," *Afro-American* (Washington, D.C.), April 19, 1947, 4. See McNeil, *Groundwork,* 195.

41. Summers, "Right to Join," 56; Editorial, "Post-war Prospects for the Negro," *Chicago Defender,* Dec. 30, 1944, 10, quoted in Arnesen, *Brotherhoods of Color,* 208.

8. Eliminating Work from the NAACP's Legal Strategy

1. NAACP Legal Department, "First Draft Statement Program Legal Department Action for 1945 and Contemplated Legal Action for 1946," Dec. 20, 1945, in *Papers of the NAACP*, ed. August Meier (Frederick, Md., 1982), microfilm, pt. 18A, rl. 4:853–856 (hereafter cited as *NAACP Papers*).

2. See Nelson Lichtenstein, *Labor's War at Home: The CIO in World War II* (New York, 1982), 221–222; George Lipsitz, *Rainbow at Midnight: Labor and Culture in the 1940s* (Urbana, Ill., 1994), 99–100; James T. Patterson, *Grand Expectations: The United States 1945–1974* (New York, 1996), 61–64. Eventually, the postwar job market stabilized, as machinery was retooled to produce consumer goods. In the meantime, inflation far outstripped wage increases, and the dislocations associated with the transition to a peacetime economy especially affected African American workers.

3. See Martha Biondi, *To Stand and Fight: The Struggle for Civil Rights in Postwar New York City* (Cambridge, Mass., 2003); Gerald Horne, *Black and Red: W.E.B. Du Bois and the Afro-American Response to the Cold War: 1944–1963* (Albany, N.Y., 1986); Gerald Horne, *Black Liberation/Red Scare: Ben Davis and the Communist Party* (Newark, Del., 1994), 172–191; Wilson Record, *Race and Radicalism: The NAACP and the Communist Party in Conflict* (Ithaca, N.Y., 1964), 135–168; Penny M. Von Eschen, *Race against Empire: Black Americans and Anticolonialism, 1937–1957* (Ithaca, N.Y., 1997); John T. Elliff, *The United States Department of Justice and Individual Rights, 1937–1962* (New York, 1987), 280–282.

4. NAACP, "Resolutions Adopted at the 41st Annual Convention," June 23, 1950, in *NAACP Papers*, pt. 1, rl. 12:939–941. See James L. Roark, "American Black Leaders: The Response to Colonialism and the Cold War, 1943–1953," *African Historical Studies* 4 (1971): 253–270; Carol Anderson, *Eyes Off the Prize: The United Nations and the African American Struggle for Human Rights, 1944–1955* (New York, 2003), 20–25, 113–165; Roy Wilkins to Milton Murray, Apr. 2, 1947, in *NAACP Papers*, pt. 18B, rl. 6:814; NAACP, "Congress Committee Warned about Loose 'Red' Label," news release, Oct. 16, 1947, in *NAACP Papers*, pt. 18B, rl. 7:70; NAACP, "Walter White: A Real Program to Combat Communism," news release, Jan. 2, 1947, in *NAACP Papers*, pt. 18B, rl. 6:772; Wilkins to Dr. Carlton B. Goodlet, telegram, Apr. 20, 1949, in *NAACP Papers*, pt. 18C, rl. 7:208; "The Patterson-Wilkins Correspondence," Nov. 23, 1949, in *NAACP Papers*, pt. 18C, rl. 7:227–228; Juan Williams, *Thurgood Marshall: American Revolutionary* (New York, 1998), 169; NAACP, "Compila-

tion of Anti-Communist Resolutions," in *NAACP Papers*, pt. 18B, rl. 7:263; Gloster B. Current to NAACP branches and youth councils, July 18, 1951, in *NAACP Papers*, pt. 18C, rl. 7:394. See also Michael L. Krenn, *Black Diplomacy: African Americans and the State Department, 1945– 1969* (Armonk, N.Y., 1999), 67; Martin Bauml Duberman, *Paul Robeson* (New York, 1988), 316–445; Horne, *Black and Red*, 97–124, 183–191; Von Eschen, *Race against Empire*; Record, *Race and Radicalism*, 162–163; Mark V. Tushnet, *Making Civil Rights Law: Thurgood Marshall and the Supreme Court, 1936–1961* (New York, 1994), 295. See generally Brenda Gayle Plummer, *Rising Wind: Black Americans and U.S. Foreign Affairs, 1935–1960* (Chapel Hill, N.C., 1996); Gerald Horne, *Communist Front? The Civil Rights Congress, 1946–1956* (Rutherford, N.J., 1988).

5. Madison S. Jones, Jr., to Wood, July 12, 1949, Records of the NAACP, Manuscript Division, Library of Congress, quoted in Duberman, *Paul Robeson*, 359. See Gunnar Myrdal, *An American Dilemma: The Negro Problem and Modern Democracy* (New York, 1944); "Kremlin Gremlins," unsigned review of *Communism versus the Negro*, by William A. Nolan, *Crisis* 59 (1952): 59–60; Eric Arnesen, "No 'Graver Danger': Black Anti-communism, the Communist Party, and the Race Question," *Labor: Studies in Working-Class History of the Americas* 3, no. 4 (2006). Historical evidence suggests that Communists did obtain some black support. See, for example, Robin D. G. Kelley, *Race Rebels: Culture, Politics, and the Black Working Class* (New York, 1996); Von Eschen, *Race against Empire*.

6. See Mary L. Dudziak, *Cold War Civil Rights: Race and the Image of American Democracy* (Princeton, N.J., 2000); Thomas Borstelmann, *The Cold War and the Color Line: American Race Relations in the Global Arena* (Cambridge, Mass., 2001); Anderson, *Eyes Off the Prize*.

7. Walter White to William Green, Oct. 6, 1947, in *NAACP Papers*, pt. 13C, rl. 2:350. See, for example, Dona Cooper Hamilton and Charles V. Hamilton, *The Dual Agenda: Race and Social Welfare Policies of Civil Rights Organizations* (New York, 1997); August Meier and John H. Bracey, Jr., "The NAACP as a Reform Movement, 1909–1965: 'To Reach the Conscience of America,'" *Journal of Southern History* 59 (1993): 3–30, 23.

8. Wilkins to Cy W. Record, Dec. 21, 1949, 3, in *NAACP Papers*, pt. 18B, rl. 7:900–903, 902. See also Herbert Hill to Wilkins, memorandum, Mar. 3, 1949, in *NAACP Papers*, pt. 13A, rl. 20:346. See generally Kevin M. Schultz, "The Strange Career of the FEPC and the Legacy of the Labor-Based Civil Rights Movement of the 1940s," *Labor History* (forthcoming, Nov. 2007).

9. See Anderson, *Eyes Off the Prize*, 80; NAACP, *Annual Report*, 1950, in

NAACP Papers, pt. 1, rl. 14:943–969, 947, 948; August Meier, "Negro Protest Movements and Organizations," *Journal of Negro Education* 32 (1963): 437–450, 438; Ellen Schrecker, *Many Are the Crimes: McCarthyism in America* (Boston, 1998), 393.

10. Denton L. Watson, *Lion in the Lobby: Clarence Mitchell, Jr.'s Struggle for the Passage of Civil Rights Laws,* rev. ed. (Lanham, Md., 2002), 145–178. Mitchell's successor, Herbert Hill, more vociferously attacked union discrimination in the late 1940s and the succeeding decades. See Herbert Hill, *Black Labor and the American Legal System* (Washington, D.C., 1977); Paul Frymer, "Race, Labor, and the Twentieth-Century American State," *Politics and Society* 32 (2004): 475–509.

11. Marian Wynn Perry to Thurgood Marshall, memorandum, Sept. 17, 1948, in *NAACP Papers,* pt. 13A, rl. 14:476. See Brief of NAACP as Amicus Curiae at 8, In re Bethlehem-Alameda Shipyard, Inc., 53 N.L.R.B. 999 (1943) (Nos. R-5693, R-5694), in *NAACP Papers,* pt. 13C, rl. 1:850–862, 859.

12. Clarence Mitchell, "Statement . . . on the Repeal of the Taft-Hartley Law," submitted to the Senate Committee on Labor and Public Welfare, Feb. 10, 1949, 1–2, in *NAACP Papers,* pt. 13A, rl. 6:754–757, 754–755.

13. Perry to Mitchell, Jan. 27, 1947, in *NAACP Papers,* pt. 13A, rl. 6:639.

14. Mitchell, "Statement on Taft-Hartley," in *NAACP Papers,* pt. 13A, rl. 6:754–757, 756. See also Charles H. Houston, "The Legal Struggle for Protection of Minority Workers' Rights on American Railroads" (address at the 40th annual conference of the NAACP, Los Angeles, July 14, 1949), 5, in *NAACP Papers,* pt. 1, rl. 12:694–707, 698.

15. Marshall to Noah W. Griffin, May 9, 1946, in *NAACP Papers,* pt. 13C, rl. 1:492–493; Thurgood Marshall, address at the 37th annual meeting of the NAACP, Cincinnati, Ohio, June 28, 1946, 7, in *NAACP Papers,* pt. 1, rl. 11:768–775, 774.

16. Sophia Z. Lee, "Hotspots in a Cold War: The NAACP's Postwar Labor Constitutionalism, 1948–1964" (working paper, Social Science Research Network, 2005), 1–24, http://papers.ssrn.com/sol3/papers.cfm ?abstract_id=814067 (accessed Jan. 23, 2006). See, for example, Perry to NLRB, Jan. 30, 1948, in *NAACP Papers,* pt. 13A, rl. 7:93.

17. Jack Greenberg, *Crusaders in the Courts: How a Dedicated Band of Lawyers Fought for the Civil Rights Revolution* (New York, 1994), 152–155.

18. Plessy v. Ferguson, 163 U.S. 537 (1896); Civil Rights Cases, 109 U.S. 3 (1883); Buck v. Bell, 274 U.S. 200, 208 (1927). See Richard Primus, "The Civil War in Constitutional Interpretation: Race, Regime Change, and the Civil Rights Cases" (manuscript, University of Michigan Law School, n.d.).

19. Conference of NAACP Lawyers, "Report to 40th Annual Conference of [NAACP]," June 23–25, 1949, 1, in *NAACP Papers,* pt. 1, rl. 12:575–577.

20. Sweatt v. Painter, 339 U.S. 629 (1950); McLaurin v. Oklahoma, 339 U.S. 637 (1950); Marshall to Charles Bunn, June 12, 1950, in *NAACP Papers,* quoted in Mark V. Tushnet, *The NAACP's Legal Strategy against Segregated Education, 1925–1950* (Chapel Hill, N.C., 1987), 135. See Henderson v. United States, 339 U.S. 816 (1950); Tushnet, *NAACP's Legal Strategy,* 88–99, 106–117.

21. Shelley v. Kraemer, 334 U.S. 1, 23 (1948); Pauli Murray, "The Right to Equal Opportunity in Employment," *California Law Review* 33 (1945): 388–433.

22. Tushnet, *Making Civil Rights Law,* 81–98; Clement E. Vose, *Caucasians Only: The Supreme Court, the NAACP, and the Restrictive Covenant Cases* (Berkeley, Calif., 1959), 50–73. Moreover, although the legal department had made creative state action arguments in the white primary case of *Smith v. Allwright* in 1944, by 1953, it left the follow-up case to NAACP advisor and Howard Law School professor James Nabrit. See "Decision Ends Vote Bias, Thurgood Marshall Holds," news release, May 7, 1953, in *NAACP Papers,* pt. 18A, rl. 6:405.

23. Committee on Negro Work to directors of American Fund for Public Service (Garland Fund), memorandum, May 28, 1930, 17, in *NAACP Papers,* pt. 3A, rl. 1:360–379, 376.

24. Railway Mail Ass'n v. Corsi, 326 U.S. 88, 93 (1945).

25. Ibid. at 93–94 (citing Steele v. Louisville & N.R. Co., 323 U.S. 192 [1944]) (emphasis added), 98 (Frankfurter, J., concurring).

26. Lincoln Federal Labor Union v. Northwestern Iron & Metal Co., 335 U.S. 525, 537 (1949). See State v. Whitaker, 45 S.E.2d 860, 874 (N.C. 1947); Nelson Lichtenstein, *State of the Union: A Century of American Labor* (Princeton, N.J., 2002), 117–118.

27. "Excerpts from Resolutions Adopted by NAACP 42nd Annual Convention," June 30, 1951, in *NAACP Papers,* pt. 18C, rl. 7:395; Current to NAACP branches and youth councils, July 18, 1951, in *NAACP Papers,* pt. 18C, rl. 7:394.

28. See, for example, David Levering Lewis, *W.E.B. Du Bois: The Fight for Equality and the American Century, 1919–1963* (New York, 2000), 335–348; Tushnet, *NAACP's Legal Strategy,* 8–10, 113–116; Elliot M. Rudwick, "W.E.B. Du Bois in the Role of *Crisis* Editor," *Journal of Negro History* 43 (1958): 214–240; Mark Tushnet, "The Politics of Equality in Constitutional Law: The Equal Protection Clause, Dr. Du Bois, and Charles Hamilton Houston," *Journal of American History* 74 (1987): 884–903.

29. Current to NAACP branches and youth councils, July 18, 1951, in

NAACP Papers, pt. 18C, rl. 7:394. See "Excerpts from Resolutions Adopted by NAACP 42nd Annual Convention," June 30, 1951, in *NAACP Papers,* pt. 18C, rl. 7:395.

30. Mitchell, "Statement on Taft-Hartley," in *NAACP Papers,* pt. 13A, rl. 6:754–757, 755. See In re Larus & Brother Co., 62 N.L.R.B. 1075, 1080–1081, 1084 (1945). Mitchell also cited as problematic In re Atlanta Oak Flooring Co., 62 N.L.R.B. 973 (1945), and In re Texas & Pacific Motor Transport Co., 77 N.L.R.B. 87 (1948).

31. See generally Kenneth Walter Mack, "Race Uplift, Professional Identity and the Transformation of Civil Rights Lawyering and Politics, 1920–1940" (Ph.D. diss., Princeton University, 2005).

32. Tushnet, *NAACP's Legal Strategy,* 114.

33. Clarence Mitchell, address at the 40th annual conference of the NAACP, Los Angeles, July 14, 1949, 9, in *NAACP Papers,* pt. 1, rl. 12:684–693, 692.

34. Conference of NAACP Lawyers, "Report to 40th Annual Conference of [NAACP]," June 23–25, 1949, in *NAACP Papers,* pt. 1, rl. 12:575–577. See Walter White, "Excerpts from Remarks" (39th annual meeting of the NAACP, New York, Jan. 5, 1948), in *NAACP Papers,* pt. 1, rl. 14:819–824.

35. Mitchell to Marshall, June 9, 1950, in *NAACP Papers,* pt. 15A, rl. 9:107.

36. Marshall to Mitchell, June 13, 1950, in *NAACP Papers,* pt. 15A, rl. 9:106. See *Sweatt,* 339 U.S. 629; *McLaurin,* 339 U.S. 637.

37. Notes of Lawyers Session of the 42nd Annual Convention of the NAACP, June 26, 1951, in *NAACP Papers,* pt. 1, supp. 1951–1955, rl. 3:880–882.

9. *Brown* and the Remaking of Civil Rights

1. Robert M. Hutchins, foreword to *Political and Civil Rights in the United States: A Collection of Legal and Related Materials,* by Thomas I. Emerson and David Haber (Buffalo, 1952), iii–iv. Jack Greenberg, *Race Relations and American Law* (New York, 1959), vii.

2. Brown v. Board of Education, 347 U.S. 483 (1954).

3. For a recent discussion of the contestation over *Brown,* see Tomiko Brown Nagin, "Black Ambivalence about Legal Liberalism: A Pragmatically Conservative Path to Civil Rights, Atlanta, 1895–1979" (manuscript, University of Virginia Law School, n.d.); see also Derrick Bell, "Serving Two Masters: Integration Ideals and Client Interests in School Desegregation Litigation," *Yale Law Journal* 85 (1976): 470–516; Lani Guinier, "From Racial Liberalism to Racial Literacy: *Brown v. Board of Education* and the Interest-Divergence Dilemma," *Journal of American History* 91 (2004): 92–118; Reva B. Siegel, "Equality Talk: Antisubordi-

nation and Anticlassification Values in Constitutional Struggles over Brown," *Harvard Law Review* 117 (2004): 1470–1547.

4. *Brown*, 347 U.S. 483, 494–495. See Sweatt v. Painter, 339 U.S. 629 (1950); McLaurin v. Oklahoma, 339 U.S. 637 (1950).

5. Brief for Appellants[, 1952,] at 5, Brown v. Bd. of Educ., 347 U.S. 483 (1954) (No. 8), reprinted in *Landmark Briefs and Arguments of the Supreme Court of the United States: Constitutional Law,* ed. Philip B. Kurland and Gerhard Casper (Arlington, Va., 1975–), 49:23–42; Brief for the United States as Amicus Curiae[, 1952,] at 25–26, Brown v. Bd. of Educ., 347 U.S. 483 (1954) (Nos. 8, 101, 191, 413, 448), in ibid., 49:113–147, 140–141.

6. *Brown*, 347 U.S. at 495.

7. U.S. Const. amend. XIV, §1; 347 U.S. at 499. See David E. Bernstein, "*Bolling*, Equal Protection, Due Process, and *Lochner*phobia," *Georgetown Law Journal* 93 (2005): 1253–1285, for an alternative argument about the relationship between the due process and equal protection clauses in *Bolling*. See generally Richard Primus, "*Bolling* Alone," *Columbia Law Review* 104 (2004): 975–1041.

8. Col. Elton D. Wright VI to U.S. Dept. of Justice, Nov. 1943, file 50–72–5, RG 60, National Archives (hereafter cited as DOJ Files).

9. Alphonso Morris to NAACP, Apr. 9, 1940, in *Papers of the NAACP,* ed. August Meier (Frederick, Md., 1982), microfilm, pt. 13A, rl. 7:006 (hereafter cited as *NAACP Papers*).

10. Plessy v. Ferguson, 163 U.S. 537, 551 (1896). See Brief for Appellants at 5, 1952, *Brown*, 347 U.S. 483 (No. 8), in *Landmark Briefs*, ed. Kurland and Casper, 49:23–42, 31.

11. See Daryl Michael Scott, *Contempt and Pity: Social Policy and the Image of the Damaged Black Psyche, 1880–1996* (Chapel Hill, N.C., 1997), 71–91, 119–136; Rebecca Lyn de Schweinitz, " 'If They Could Change the World': Children, Childhood, and African-American Civil Rights Politics" (Ph.D. diss., University of Virginia, 2004), 130–194; Ellen Herman, *The Romance of American Psychology: Political Culture in the Age of Experts* (Berkeley, Calif., 1995), 174–207.

12. Brief for Appellants at 5, 1952, *Brown*, 347 U.S. 483 (No. 8), in *Landmark Briefs*, ed. Kurland and Casper, 49:23–42; Appendix to Appellants' Briefs[, 1952,] at [i], 4, Brown v. Bd. of Educ., 347 U.S. 483 (1954) (Nos. 8, 101, 191), in *Landmark Briefs*, ed. Kurland and Casper, 49:41–66. See Richard Kluger, *Simple Justice: The History of* Brown v. Board of Education *and Black America's Struggle for Equality,* rev. ed. (New York, 2004), 315–319; Scott, *Contempt and Pity,* 32, 82–83, 95–96, 123–130.

13. *Brown*, 347 U.S. at 492, 494, 495 n. 11.

14. Affidavit of Elizabeth Coker, Jan. 30, 1947, in *NAACP Papers*, pt. 13C, rl. 12:390–391; C. B. McCullar to Roger Baldwin, May 19, 1941, in *NAACP Papers*, pt. 13C, rl. 12:775–776.

15. *Plessy*, 163 U.S. at 544.

16. Brief for Appellants at 9, 1952, *Brown*, 347 U.S. 483 (No. 8), in *Landmark Briefs*, ed. Kurland and Casper, 49:23–42, 35; Appendix to Appellants' Briefs at 2, 8, 9, 1952, *Brown*, 347 U.S. 483 (Nos. 8, 101, 191), in ibid., 49: 41–66, 44, 50, 51; Brief for United States at 3, 1952, *Brown*, 347 U.S. 483 (Nos. 8, 101, 191, 413, 448), in ibid., 49:113–147, 118.

17. *Brown*, 347 U.S. at 494 (quoting the lower court) (internal quotation marks omitted).

18. Harry S. Truman, "Address before the National Association for the Advancement of Colored People" (Lincoln Memorial, Washington, D.C., June 29, 1947), in Office of the Federal Register, *Public Papers of the Presidents of the United States: Harry S. Truman, 1947* (Washington, D.C., 1963), 311–313, quoted in President's Committee on Civil Rights, *To Secure These Rights: The Report of the President's Committee on Civil Rights* (Washington, D.C., 1947), 99.

19. *Sweatt*, 339 U.S. at 633.

20. Supplemental Brief for the United States on Reargument[, 1952,] at 143, Brown v. Bd. of Educ., 347 U.S. 483 (1954) (Nos. 1, 2, 4, 8, 10), in *Landmark Briefs*, ed. Kurland and Casper, 49:853–1054, 1009. See also Brief for Appellants in Nos. 1, 2, and 4 and for Respondents in No. 10 on Reargument[, 1953,] at 120–125, Brown v. Bd. of Educ., 347 U.S. 483 (1954) (Nos. 1, 2, 4, 10), in ibid., 49:481–748, 633–638. For a related discussion of the elevation of education in *Brown*, see Michael Klarman, "An Interpretive History of Modern Equal Protection," *Michigan Law Review* 90 (1991): 213–318, 235–239.

21. Brief for Appellants at 27, 28 1953, *Brown*, 347 U.S. 483 (Nos. 1, 2, 4, 10), in *Landmark Briefs*, ed. Kurland and Casper, 49:481–748, 540, 541; Brief for Appellants at 9, 1952, *Brown*, 347 U.S. 483 (No. 8), in ibid., 49:23–42, 35. See also Brief for United States at 8, 1952, *Brown*, 347 U.S. 483 (Nos. 8, 101, 191, 413, 448), in ibid., 49:113–147, 123. See de Schweinitz, " 'If They Could Change,' " 130–194; Scott, *Contempt and Pity*, 85–86, 125.

22. *Brown*, 347 U.S. at 492–493, 495.

23. Ibid. at 494; Editorial, "The Court Has Made an Historic Decision," *New Republic*, May 24, 1954, 3, quoted in Scott, *Contempt and Pity*, 136.

24. See Gunnar Myrdal, *An American Dilemma: The Negro Problem and Modern Democracy* (New York, 1944), 61. See also R. M. MacIver, *The More Perfect Union: A Program for the Control of Inter-group Discrimination in the United*

States (New York, 1948); Wendell E. Pritchett, "World War II and Black Labor," chap. 4 in "Working along the Color Line: The Life and Times of Robert Weaver" (manuscript, University of Pennsylvania Law School, n.d.), 19; Harvard Sitkoff, *A New Deal for Blacks: The Emergence of Civil Rights as a National Issue* (New York, 1978), 1:309–312.

25. Robert K. Carr, *Federal Protection of Civil Rights: Quest for a Sword* (Ithaca, N.Y., 1947), 19, 20, 123, 133–134. See also, for example, Francis Biddle, "Democracy and Racial Minorities" (speech before the Jewish Theological Seminary of America, New York, Nov. 11, 1943), in *Representative American Speeches; 1943–1944,* ed. A. Craig Baird (New York, 1944–), 172–187; Joseph Tussman and Jacobus tenBroek, "The Equal Protection of the Laws," *California Law Review* 37 (1949): 341–381, 356.

26. Robert Hammond to Sir [NAACP], Apr. 26, 1947, in *NAACP Papers,* pt. 13C, rl. 12:679–680.

27. See, for example, Editorial, "Equal Education for All," *Washington Post,* May 19, 1954, 14. See also Michael J. Klarman, *From Jim Crow to Civil Rights: The Supreme Court and the Struggle for Racial Equality* (Oxford, 2004), 344–363.

28. See John T. Elliff, *The United States Department of Justice and Individual Rights, 1937–1962* (New York, 1987), 171–174, 254–259; Kevin J. McMahon, *Reconsidering Roosevelt on Race: How the Presidency Paved the Road to Brown* (Chicago, 2004), 153–154; Sidney Fine, *Frank Murphy: The Washington Years* (Ann Arbor, Mich., 1984), 86; Gordon Dean to attorney general, memorandum, Feb. 8, 1939, box 59, reel 114, Frank Murphy Papers, Michigan Historical Collections, Bentley Historical Library, University of Michigan.

29. See President's Committee on Civil Rights, *To Secure These Rights,* 151–173, 114–120; Norman I. Silber, *With All Deliberate Speed: The Life of Philip Elman; An Oral History Memoir* (Ann Arbor, Mich., 2004), 191.

30. See Elliff, *United States Department of Justice,* 254–255; President's Committee on Civil Rights, *To Secure These Rights,* 169. Silber, *With All Deliberate Speed,* 190–191; McMahon, *Reconsidering Roosevelt,* 188.

31. Silber, *With All Deliberate Speed,* 191, 194–196.

32. Elliff, *United States Department of Justice,* 323, 325–326, 391–392; Silber, *With All Deliberate Speed,* 195, 202–206, 214. See, for example, Graham v. Bhd. of Locomotive Firemen, 338 U.S. 232 (1949).

33. Elliff, *United States Department of Justice,* 268.

34. Silber, *With All Deliberate Speed,* 205–207, 209–212.

35. United States v. Bailes, 120 F. Supp. 614 (S.D.W. Va. 1954); Elman to solicitor general, memorandum, May 5, 1954, DOJ Files, 144–84–14, quoted in Elliff, *United States Department of Justice,* 386; Leo Meltzer to Caldwell, memorandum, May 26, 1954, DOJ Files, 144–84–14, quoted

in ibid., 388. Voluminous records on the *Bailes* case can be found in the Department of Justice Records at the National Archives, RG 60, no. 144–84–14. Unlike most of the CRS's NLRA cases, *Bailes* aimed to vindicate the right to work without joining a union (the United Mine Workers), rather than the right to join a union. Some Eisenhower administration officials took interest in the case because of its antiunion implications and its potential to undermine West Virginia Democrats reliant on the UMW. Such politics were largely beside the point for the CRS lawyers, however, who saw their interest in the case as defending their traditional jurisdiction over labor rights writ large. The only political motivation they even implied was the possibility that *Bailes* might disabuse observers of the belief that the CRS was systematically biased in favor of liberal groups and causes. Ibid., 387–388.

36. Elliff, *United States Department of Justice*, 409–419.
37. Pub. L. No. 85–315, §§121, 131, 71 Stat. 634–638, 637–638 (1957). See Hugh Davis Graham, *The Civil Rights Era: Origins and Development of National Policy, 1960–1972* (New York, 1990), 23.
38. See Civil Rights Act of 1957, §111, 637; Elliff, *United States Department of Justice*, 535–536.
39. Bill Penix to Robert F. Kennedy, Feb. 13, 1961, DOJ Files, Personnel Files. See Elliff, *United States Department of Justice*, 547.
40. John T. Elliff, "Aspects of Federal Civil Rights Enforcement: The Justice Department and the FBI, 1939–1964," in *Law in American History*, ed. Donald Fleming and Bernard Bailyn (Boston, 1971), 605–673, 641–73; Elliff, *United States Department of Justice*, 406–738.
41. Pub. L. No. 88–352, tit. VII, §§705(g)(6), 707, 78 Stat. 241–268, 253–266, 259, 261–262 (1964). Graham, *Civil Rights Era*, 146.
42. Mark V. Tushnet, *Making Civil Rights Law: Thurgood Marshall and the Supreme Court, 1936–1961* (New York, 1994), 272–300; Klarman, *From Jim Crow*, 310–311, 335–340, 352–353, 382–384.
43. Thurgood Marshall, oral history interview by Ed Edwin, June 7, 1977, transcript, 178, Oral History Project, Columbia University, quoted in Jack Greenberg, *Crusaders in the Courts: How a Dedicated Band of Lawyers Fought for the Civil Rights Revolution* (New York, 1994), 224.
44. Tushnet, *Making Civil Rights Law*, 311. See Sophia Z. Lee, "Hotspots in a Cold War: The NAACP's Postwar Labor Constitutionalism, 1948–1964" (working paper, Social Science Research Network, 2005), http://papers.ssrn.com/sol3/papers.cfm?abstract_id=814067 (accessed Jan. 23, 2006).
45. Brown v. Bd. of Educ. II, 349 U.S. 294, 301 (1955). See Tushnet, *Making Civil Rights Law*, 234–235.
46. Greenberg, *Crusaders*, 263.

47. Dawson v. Mayor of Baltimore, 220 F.2d 386 (4th Cir. 1955), aff'd, 350 U.S. 877 (1955) (mem.); Holmes v. City of Atlanta, 223 F.2d 93 (5th Cir. 1955), vacated, 350 U.S. 879 (1955) (mem.); Browder v. Gayle, 142 F. Supp. 707 (M.D. Ala. 1956), aff'd, 352 U.S. 903 (1956) (mem.).

48. Muir v. Louisville Park Theatrical Ass'n, 347 U.S. 971, 971 (1954) (mem.). See Burton v. Wilmington Parking Auth., 365 U.S. 715 (1961); Greenberg, *Crusaders,* 199.

49. Greenberg, *Race Relations,* 58.

50. Greenberg, *Crusaders,* 270–279.

51. Brief for Appellants[, 1964], McLaughlin v. Florida, 379 U.S. 184 (1964) (No. 11); McLaughlin v. Florida, 379 U.S. 184, 191–192 (1964) (internal citations omitted); Korematsu v. United States, 323 U.S. at 216 (1944), quoted in ibid. at 192. See, for example, Burton v. Wilmington Parking Authority, 365 U.S. 715 (1961); Simkins v. Moses H. Cone Memorial Hosp., 323 F.2d 959 (4th Cir. 1963), cert. denied, 376 U.S. 938 (1964). See also Greenberg, *Crusaders,* 304–305.

52. Loving v. Virginia, 388 U.S. 1, 11 (1967) (quoting Hirabayashi v. United States, 320 U.S. at 100 [1943] and *Korematsu,* 323 U.S. at 216). Compare ibid. with *McLaughlin,* 379 U.S. at 191–192.

53. Greenberg, *Crusaders,* 366.

54. Herbert Wechsler, "Toward Neutral Principles of Constitutional Law," *Harvard Law Review* 73 (1959): 1–35.

55. See Louis H. Pollak, "Racial Discrimination and Judicial Integrity: A Reply to Professor Wechsler," *University of Pennsylvania Law Review* 108 (1959): 1–34. United States v. Carolene Products Co., 304 U.S. 144, 152 n. 4 (1938). See also Charles L. Black, Jr., "The Lawfulness of the Segregation Decisions," *Yale Law Journal* 69 (1960): 421–430. See generally Morton J. Horwitz, *The Warren Court and the Pursuit of Justice* (New York, 1998), 78–82; Barry Friedman, "Neutral Principles: A Retrospective," *Vanderbilt Law Review* 50 (1997): 503–536; Gary Peller, "'Neutral Principles' in the 1950's," *University of Michigan Journal of Law Reform* 21 (1988): 561–622.

56. Martin Luther King, Jr., "I Have a Dream" (speech, Lincoln Memorial, Washington, D.C., August 28, 1963); Civil Rights Act of 1964, tit. VII, §703(b). See Sidney M. Milkis, "Lyndon Johnson, the Great Society, and the 'Twilight' of the Modern Presidency," in *The Great Society and the High Tide of Liberalism,* ed. Sidney M. Milkis and Jerome M. Mileur (Boston, 2005), 1–50. On Title VII as transformative of American society, see Nancy MacLean, *Freedom Is Not Enough: The Opening of the American Workplace* (Cambridge, Mass., 2006). See generally Jacquelyn Dowd Hall, "The Long Civil Rights Movement and the Political Uses of the Past," *Journal of American History* 91 (2005): 1233–1263.

57. Emerson and Haber, *Political and Civil Rights*, xx, 1–102 ("Chapter I: The Right to Security of the Person"), 993–1172 ("Chapter IX: Discrimination"). See also Edwin S. Newman, *The Freedom Reader: A Collection of Materials on Civil Rights and Civil Liberties in America* (New York, 1955); Noel T. Dowling, *Cases on Constitutional Law*, 5th ed. (Brooklyn, 1954), xxiii; Noel T. Dowling, *Cases on Constitutional Law*, 6th ed. (Brooklyn, 1959), xxiii.

58. Thomas I. Emerson and David Haber, *Political and Civil Rights in the United States: A Collection of Legal and Related Materials*, 2nd ed. (Buffalo, N.Y., 1958), 1:xiv, 2:vi; Thomas I. Emerson, David Haber, and Norman Dorsen, *Political and Civil Rights in the United States: A Collection of Legal and Related Materials*, 3rd ed. (Boston, 1967), 2:v–vi. See also Noel T. Dowling, *Cases on Constitutional Law*, 3rd ed. (Chicago, 1946), xx; Noel T. Dowling and Gerald Gunther, *Cases and Materials on Constitutional Law*, 7th ed. (Brooklyn, N.Y., 1965), xxxiii–xxxiv, xxxvii, xl–xli.

59. Milton R. Konvitz, ed., *Bill of Rights Reader: Leading Constitutional Cases* (Ithaca, N.Y., 1954), xiv–xv; Milton R. Konvitz, ed., *Bill of Rights Reader: Leading Constitutional Cases*, 2nd ed. (Ithaca, N.Y., 1960), xv–xvi; Milton R. Konvitz, ed., *Bill of Rights Reader: Leading Constitutional Cases*, 3rd ed. (Ithaca, N.Y., 1965), xix–xx. See, for example, Alison Reppy, *Civil Rights in the United States* (New York, 1951), 187–207.

60. Paul G. Kauper, *Constitutional Law: Cases and Materials* (New York, 1954), xiv–xvi, Paul G. Kauper, *Constitutional Law: Cases and Materials*, 2nd ed. (Boston, 1960), xxi–xxiii.

61. Paul G. Kauper, *Constitutional Law: Cases and Materials*, 3rd ed. (Boston, 1966), xx, 869–871; Paul G. Kauper, *Constitutional Law: Cases and Materials*, 4th ed. (Boston, 1972), xviii–xxiii, 530–532, 778.

62. Greenberg, *Race Relations*, 157–158; Dowling, *Cases on Constitutional Law*, 6th ed. (1959), xxi, xxi–xxiii. See Kauper, *Constitutional Law*, 4th ed. (1972), xviii–xxiii, 530–531; Konvitz, *Bill of Rights Reader*, 3rd ed. (1965), xv–xx, xxiii; Milton R. Konvitz, ed., *Bill of Rights Reader: Leading Constitutional Cases*, 4th ed. (Ithaca, N.Y., 1968), xv–xx, xxiii.

63. See, for example, Kenneth F. McLaughlin, comp., *Color Me Justice* (Orford, N.H., 1969), 1:v; William B. Lockhart, Yale Kamisar, and Jesse H. Choper, *Cases and Materials on Constitutional Rights and Liberties*, 2nd ed. (St. Paul, Minn., 1967), xxx–xxxi ("Equality under the Law" divided into "Racial Discrimination," "Discrimination against Aliens," "Discrimination by Racial Segregation," and "Other Racial Classifications"); M. Glenn Abernathy, *Civil Liberties under the Constitution* (New York, 1968), xii ("Equal Protection of the Law").

Acknowledgments

As with any long-term project, this book has evolved much over the years. Early versions appeared in "The Thirteenth Amendment and the Lost Origins of Civil Rights," *Duke Law Journal* 50 (2001): 1609–1685; " 'We Live's in a Free House Such as It Is': Class and the Creation of Modern Civil Rights," *University of Pennsylvania Law Review* 151 (2003): 1977–2018; and " 'Let Economic Equality Take Care of Itself': The NAACP, Labor Litigation, and the Making of Civil Rights in the 1940s," *UCLA Law Review* 52 (2005): 1393–1486.

The Lost Promise of Civil Rights would not look remotely like it does today without the help of many wonderful people along the way. Albert Arent, Fred Folsom, and Henry Putzel—all former Civil Rights Section lawyers—graciously shared their memories of the section and personal stories with me. Eric Arnesen, Eileen Boris, Mike Klarman, Richard Primus, Mark Tushnet, and Linda Goluboff each read the entire manuscript at various stages with a critical eye and a generous spirit. David Bernstein, Sheila Blackford, Tomiko Brown-Nagin, Anthony Chen, Brenda Coughlin, Ariela Dubler, Mary Dudziak, Dan Ernst, Willie Forbath, Paul Frymer, Jesse Furman, Myriam Gilles, Bryan Goluboff, Erik Goluboff, Nicole Belsen Goluboff, Sally Gordon, Lani Guinier, Ira Katznelson, Sophia Lee, Nelson Lichtenstein, Ken Mack, Guian McKee, Christian McMillen, James Gray Pope, Wendell Pritchett, Rob Reich, Gil Seinfeld, Todd Stevens, Kathy Stone, Tom Sugrue, Chris Tomlins, Jay Turner, John Witt, and Noah Zatz all offered insight and encouragement on various parts of the manuscript. The students

361

in my seminars on civil rights history challenged me to rethink many of my ideas. So too did participants in Princeton University's Modern America Workshop; the University of Pennsylvania's "Conference on Law and the Disappearance of Class in the Twentieth-Century United States"; Columbia University's Historical Dynamics Workshop; the May Gathering; annual meetings of the American Society for Legal History, the Law and Society Association, and the American Studies Association; and workshops at Yale, Harvard, Stanford, and UCLA law schools.

I have been especially lucky to find folks who shared my excitement for this project at the various institutions I have called home for the last decade. Without the personal and financial support of Deans Bob Scott and John Jeffries at the University of Virginia Law School, the completion of this book would still be years away. The same goes for the amazing staff of the University of Virginia Law Library. The entire staff, but especially Ben Doherty, Michelle Morris, Kent Olson, Robert Richards, and Alison White, went above and beyond in service of this book. My colleagues, most notably Barry Cushman, George Rutherglen, Mike Klarman, Chuck McCurdy, Ted White, and Rip Verkerke, welcomed me to the fold and immeasurably improved my work. I also profited enormously from the input of my colleagues when I presented parts of the book at various workshops at UVA—the Faculty Retreat, Legal History Workshop, Faculty Workshop, and the Center for the Study of Race and the Law. Andrew Genz, Clayton Holland, Leslie Kendrick, Mitchell Mosvick, Laurie Ripper, Allein Sabel, and especially Paul Crane, Deborah Carlton Milner, Jamie McDonald, Maia Ridberg, Sheri Shepherd, Marcy Smirnoff, Sarah Teich, and Justin Zelikovitz provided excellent research assistance. Brian Balogh, Sid Milkis, and the American Political Development program and colloquium at the Miller Center for Public Affairs contributed immensely to my intellectual development at UVA.

Archivists and librarians at Alderman Library at the University of Virginia, the National Archives and Records Administration, the Library of Congress, the Schomburg Center for Research in Black Culture, the Lauringer Library at Georgetown University, the Bentley Historical Library at the University of Michigan, and the American Catholic History Research Center and University Archives at Catholic University also offered essential assistance. I received financial support at various points from the Princeton University history and African

American studies departments and the William Nelson Cromwell Foundation.

This book's intellectual roots go back to my undergraduate years. In my first serious engagements with American history, Jim Goodman introduced me to the South and Eric Arnesen to the relationships between racial and economic equality. That this book is in fair part about the intersection of racial and economic inequality in the rural South attests to the lasting impact their guidance has had.

My good fortune in finding mentors who expanded my horizons continued throughout law school and graduate school. Justice Stephen Breyer, Judge Guido Calabresi, Brett Dignam, Owen Fiss, Liz Lunbeck, Nell Painter, and Colin Palmer offered support and inspiration. Bob Gordon shepherded this project from its inception, always with critical insights and suggestions for new ways of thinking. Reva Siegel encouraged more theoretical directions and historical analogies. Bruce Ackerman pushed me to think bigger at a crucial juncture. Dan Rodgers was a vital part of this project from my first semester at Princeton. He consistently probed my implicit assumptions, asked hard questions, and gave me both the encouragement and the tools to expand my intellectual ambitions.

Most important, Dirk Hartog surpassed any expectations I might have had for an advisor. An incisive reader and a challenging critic, he shaped and improved this book in countless ways. His imprint is on every page. He also provided (sometimes to his embarrassment) much-needed and always sage advice on matters great and small, academic and intellectual, personal and professional. His responsiveness, his support, and his caring are unmatched. I am so glad that even after our official advising relationship came to a close, the friendship that grew out of it has continued.

Finally, I thank my children, Solly and Ellie, and my husband, Rich. Solly's main contribution to this book was his timing: he waited patiently until I completed the manuscript to come into the world. Ellie's contributions have largely been in the joy she offers during breaks. Her equanimity about my going back to work, and her insistence that I put on my glasses, allow her to push my chair in, and get busy at my computer before she leaves my office have me writing, even in the hard times, with a smile on my face. I look forward to answering her frequent question, Is Mommy still working? with a happy no for a little while. As for Rich, he has given almost as much to this book (minus any mistakes; those are mine alone) as I have. He has read drafts, debated conclusions, and always provided support, sanity, and tough love in the perfect proportions. His personal and intellectual contributions to me and to this book are immeasurable. I can imagine no better partner in all things. This project brought us together, and, happily, its completion will allow us to enjoy more of each other and the adventures to come.

Index

Abolish Peonage Committee, 132
Administrative Procedure Act, 39
African Americans: auxiliary unions for, 106; complaints of, 3, 5–6, 51–110, 112–113, 174, 186; discrimination by unions and, 3, 7, 43, 55, 84, 96–99, 106, 129, 174, 211–215; disfranchisement of, 53; domestic workers, 29, 41, 64–66, 143, 160–162, 172–173, 244–247; "Double V" campaign of, 36; elite, 11, 175–177, 190–191, 198, 234, 252; family income of, 100; full employment as goal for, 109; hate strikes against, 96; hiring of, as unskilled workers, 94–95; labor-based civil rights movement and, 4; lawyers, 11, 79, 132, 175–177, 179, 183, 187–188, 234, 257; *Lochner* era and, 9; longshoremen in New York City, 98–99; middle-class, 11, 174–177, 179, 181, 183, 190–192, 235, 237, 252, 261; migration of, 36, 53, 153, 182; NAACP representation of, 174–238; National Urban League pursuit of rights for, 35–36; New Deal and, 36, 53–54, 57, 72, 107, 142, 152–153, 169, 172, 178, 180; peonage and involuntary servitude complaints by, 51, 56, 62–64, 68, 129–133, 139, 143, 161, 182, 187; protest activity of, 9, 37–38, 54–55; racial barriers for, 60, 79–80, 84, 124, 126–127, 170, 172, 199, 218, 230, 235, 252; skilled or semiskilled labor by, 94, 97, 100; slavery complaints by, 51, 56, 64, 65, 103, 112–113, 160, 165; Thirteenth Amendment claims and, 51, 56, 129–131, 167, 242; underrepresentation in government, 57; union membership of, 3, 37, 97–98, 106, 189–190; and uplift ideology, 175–176; voting rights and, 18, 20; white terrorization of, 53; white worker resistance to advancement, 96–99; women discriminated against, 91–93; workers during World War II, 1, 11, 36, 42, 52, 53–54, 81–82, 83, 90–91, 99–102, 130, 181, 219, 221–223, 250; working conditions suffered by, similar to slavery, 1–2, 6–7, 52, 55–56, 71, 102, 131, 146, 160, 172

Agricultural Adjustment Act (1938), 72–74, 125, 153

Agricultural labor: complaint letters from African American, 51–53, 59–60, 82, 84–85, 112–113, 186; and debt, 59–61, 63–64; mechanization of, 53; NAACP and, 192–193; racialized political economy of, 7, 76–80; sharecroppers, 55–56, 58–61, 66, 72–77, 118–119, 153; tenant farming, 7, 27, 58–61, 66–68, 72, 74–76, 118, 153; wage labor, 53, 55, 58–59, 61–64, 74–76